WAR
TRADE AND
PHILANTHROPY

JUAN PÉREZ
AGIRREGOIKOA

The Museo Centro de Arte Dos de Mayo, attached to the Regional Ministry of Culture, Tourism and Sport of the Community of Madrid, is a leading institution in the realm of contemporary art. Its mission is to support artistic creation today through the production of new works and the generation of critical thinking. Ever since the museum opened, it has championed a programme that promotes dialogue between artists, audiences and institutions.

In this context, CA2M is pleased to present the exhibition *War, Trade and Philanthropy*, a proposal by the artist Juan Pérez Agirregoikoa curated by Chus Martínez. This is not a retrospective show but a foray into the concept of painting as a critical tool, an aspect keenly explored by the artist. In an era dominated by the digital sphere, Agirregoikoa emphasises the density of the pictorial gesture and symbolic complexity.

The exhibition is organised into five themed ambits, each of the which generates metaphors of action and builds paradoxical scenes that straddle the tragic and the absurd, and features a group of works in which narrative, concept and visuality are all intertwined.

Through the conscious use of the materiality of the image, Agirregoikoa constructs a discourse shot through with sarcasm and conceptual acuity aimed directly at the spectator. Moreover, his work does not ignore the pleasure of form or the intelligence of the symbolic. As a consequence, *War, Trade and Philanthropy* is also a reflection on the art system itself.

Juan Pérez Agirregoikoa is one of the most distinctive voices in contemporary art at home and abroad. Over the course of his career, he has developed a critical body of work based on the use of various supports that combines humour, irony and aesthetics. Through painting, drawing, video and installation art, he has formulated an idiom of his own capable of questioning the social structures that shape contemporaneity. The artist employs acerbity in articulating a language that does not provide answers but suggests questions and reflections. The selection of works in this exhibition, which includes iconic as well as newly produced pieces, proposes a reading of recent history based on estrangement and irony.

We would like to express our sincere thanks to Juan Pérez Agirregoikoa for his involvement in every stage of the project, as well as to Chus Martinez for her painstaking work in this exhibition, which is accompanied by a publication consisting of an interview between the artist and curator, as well as essays by the theorists Ingo Niermann and Svetlana Slapšak, to whom we also wish to extend our gratitude. We are also grateful to the public and private collections that have generously loaned works from their holdings, and to all the people who have helped to make this proposal a reality. We are certain that this is an exhibition that will leave a lasting impression on visitors.

Mariano de Paco Serrano
Regional Minister of Culture, Tourism and Sport of the Community of Madrid

FOREWORD

CHUS MARTÍNEZ

The book you've just opened is not your regular exhibition catalogue, conceived instead as an instrument to help understand Juan Pérez Agirregoikoa's working method and as a guide of sorts for interpreting the themes and ideas behind his work. It focuses above all on his painting and on some of the videos he has made to date. The texts include an interview with the artist discussing the contents and changing motifs of his work and his way of addressing issues and arguments through image-making. Following this opening salvo with the artist's own voice, we continue with texts by Ingo Niermann and Svetlana Slapšak.

Ingo Niermann is a German writer with an interest in philosophy dating back to his early academic studies in Berlin. He develops his work at the crossroads between literature, essays and contemporary art, paying special attention to the speculative nature of contemporary social and political processes. His text here focuses on 'harlequinism', leveraging the metaphor of the harlequin to examine different historical and current forms of identity, power and transgression. Originated in the *commedia dell'arte* as a comic, self-serving character, in modernity the harlequin evolved into the archetype of the seductive and autonomous avant-garde artist who turns himself into a work of art in his own right. Later on, harlequinism was embodied by extravagant dictators in satellite countries during the Cold War and, more recently, in figures like Donald Trump, the perfect combination of spectacle, personality cult and political power.

Svetlana Slapšak was born in Belgrade. After taking classical studies and linguistics at the University of Belgrade, she soon made a name for herself as a researcher and teacher. Her academic career took her to Slovenia, serving at the Institute of Human Sciences in Ljubljana as professor and dean until her retirement. She is an expert in ancient world anthropology, gender studies and Balkan analysis. Slapšak's narrative outlines a path in which art becomes a catalyst for memory, historical reflection and social critique. Here she investigates the ways in which the personal and the political are intertwined: she links the memory of dictatorships and repression in Belgrade and in Athens to the artist's images; and she unmasks traditional symbols of power, like the eagle and the phoenix, as caricatures of violence and nationalism.

After these essays, the book continues with the section of images, in which the artist briefly overviews each body of work in his own words.

Juan Pérez Agirregoikoa's work cannot be properly understood without his deepfelt and genuine love for irreverence. The use of irreverence in his overall body of work reveals his profound respect for the possibility of a horizontal voice, of a world that can live up to the expectations of many different individuals and very diverse groups.

This is an exhibition of paintings. Here, in this exhibition, painting is viewed as the most fitting language for a motion of confidence. Confidence in the ability to subvert villains and villainy. Which is where the harlequins come in. Confidence in our ability to create shared meanings for the ideas, values and parameters that define a society at a given moment in history. Which is where the big diagrams on the wall come in. Confidence in the myths of heroes that foster a sense of collective superiority, moral or otherwise. Which is where the hands and tigers come in. And, finally, the exhibition advances the possibility that we will not do away with everything, that suicide is an imaginary exercise but not an option, at least we hope not. Which is where the scenes of hangings on horseback come in.

For some decades now, Juan Pérez Agirregoikoa's video works have been a core part of his practice and thinking. The common denominator of his video and animation works is a reflection on the performative nature of politics and public life. And there is no better time than now to understand what that means. Inquiring into the state of health of our public space, of our public life, is a way of connecting his interest in social justice with the features that define global debates and ways of communicating intellectual life. His videos dissect a form of politics focused on representation, theatricality and hyperbole, turning the aesthetic of the grotesque and the extreme into a critical device: by presenting the strange and freakish, his video works create a sense of dissonance that asks us to question the apparent normalcy of power and the cultural conventions that underpin it. Not only do painting and video coexist as languages – they actively support and complete each other. In his work Juan Pérez Agirregoikoa uses the moving image as a means to investigate the dynamics of power, culture and identity in the public sphere.

ART IS A MORE SINCERE INSTRUMENT THAN TRUTH

A CONVERSATION BETWEEN JUAN PÉREZ AGIRREGOIKOA AND CHUS MARTÍNEZ

Juan Pérez Agirregoikoa

There's great respect in your work for the Marxist view of society. An understanding based on grasping the material conditions that define the relationship between ideas and social institutions; the way in which wealth is generated; the exploitation and alienation of those who work or produce; the class conflict; and the possibility of establishing a communist society, or at last one oriented towards equal opportunities and returns.

How do you think the spectator perceives these ideas in your work? How would you like your work to be perceived or discussed? And how would you like this perception and debate to unfold?

I've always been interested in the theme of social ties and much of what I do addresses how we humans relate to each other and the different ways in which we understand the world. To a large extent, we are the outcome of the psychological state of our parents and of the psychological state of the place where we happen to live. What we commonly call 'my culture'. In my case, I suppose being born in a country that still has feudal structures, on the losing side during a dictatorship, and educated in a religious institution are conditioning factors, so that anyone trying to engage with what I do has some points of reference for what might be going on. As that unmentionable minimalist one said, culture is what is done to us, the cards we're dealt, the good ones and the bad ones. Culture is a vast prison but, at once, it is also the tool that will help us escape from it. The way I see it, this context means that my thinking is bound more to the communal than to Hobbes' artificial construct without free will or to individual freedom.

The issue of perception is complex and I don't have a straight answer. I don't usually think about the spectator when I'm working. I'm interested in communication, connection, which is a very strange thing and when it occurs it needs to be celebrated. We work with language, and language is signs and signs cannot be relied on because they are variable, associative and ambiguous. Moreover, each person has their own set of signifiers, which is why more often than not communication is like a deep abyss into which words sometimes disappear.

I remember that at an exhibition I'd hung a banner imitating cut-out letters from a newspaper, like in an anonymous letter, a ridiculous gesture seeing as you know who wrote it. The banner read: 'Ramón, we know where you live!' On the day of the opening, someone I knew came up to me and asked how I dared to put that up, knowing what a difficult time Ramón was going through, that he was being threatened. I was a bit astonished because I had no idea which Ramón he was talking about. I'd been out of the country for more than a decade and at no point had I thought about the context of the Basque Country when I was creating the letter. The Ramón I was thinking about in it was the character from a film I'd really liked, *Mutant Action*. That fine line we walk, which is not without its own charms.

Have these core ideas evolved into others? Or have your views about them changed?

Yes, of course my views have undergone an evolution and many changes. This is a continuous learning process, though my feeling or impression is that I keep addressing the same themes. This process began with intuitions in my teenage years, when you begin to realise there is something strange about the conventions you've been told and you recognise that you have to ditch all that idiocy and re-educate yourself.

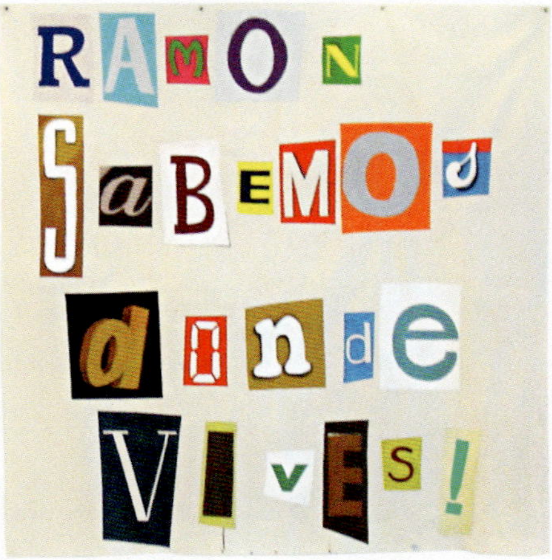

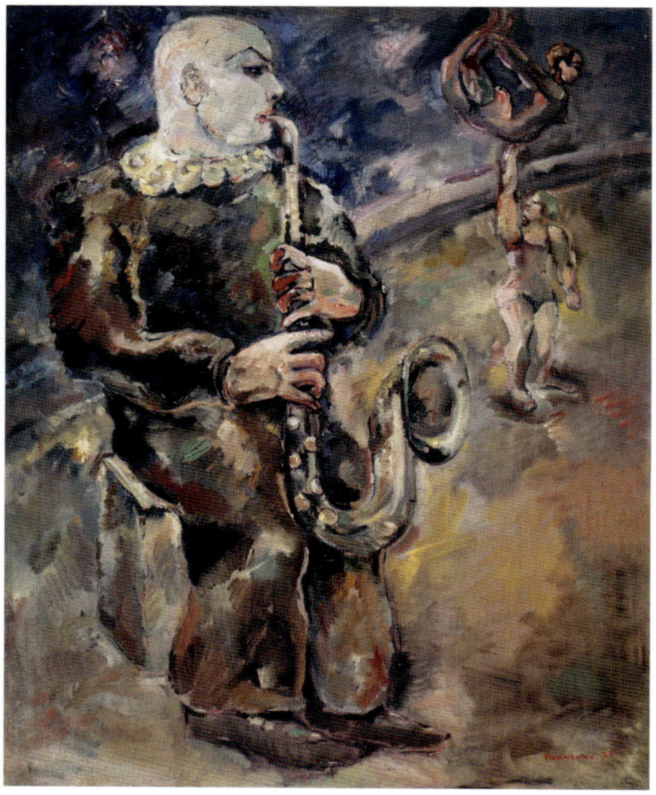

Sabemos dónde vives, 2002
Acrylic on canvas
220 x 220 cm

Aleksandr Rodchenko
Clown with Saxophone, 1938
Oil on canvas
100 x 80 cm

In general, I work on things I don't quite understand, that elude me, like the impossibility of social bonds, the failure of revolutions, how human energy is channelled, why the master signifiers have the power to make us work for free, the industrialisation of desire, or culture, which I am especially interested in.

As you know, I see culture as contingency, a matter of luck – good or bad – and that's why I find it so difficult to understand those who defend it. And I'm not referring to languages or intelligence, to the techniques developed in different places to improve people's lives. I'm talking about that part of culture steeped in stupidity foisted on us, fantasy stories, heroes, fatherlands, flags, morals, oceanic feelings of superstructures and other nonsense that we pass on and perpetuate, consciously or otherwise, from one generation to the next.

What remains constant in my way of thinking is the certainty that one of the many functions of art is precisely to destroy culture, particularly the culture of 'normal' people who believe in the existence of natural law.

The series that opens the exhibition portrays harlequins. Many will have forgotten or perhaps have never known about the historical roots of the harlequin, a central character in Italian *commedia dell'arte* who has become an iconic figure in European culture. His history contains a mixture of medieval and Renaissance roots, and he has evolved over the centuries to become a symbol both of comedy and social critique. When did he first appear in your work and why bring him up?

These drawings are from the late 1990s and were a side project to a series of large paintings of abstract harlequins I was doing at the time using wooden modules. I had spent years attempting to be contemporary with a medium as complex as painting, using quite a tedious methodology, and they were a form of escape from the formalism I had imposed on myself. Made on the side, they gave me a kind of licence I could not permit myself in the paintings, like using words and making the most of the immediacy of drawing with no constraints. They belong to a moment of abandon.

In Bilbao, we were educated in the idea of the project. Drawings of clowns and harlequins represented failure to me. I had seen a number of works with circus and clown scenes by Rodchenko that horrified me. How could someone who had been so modern end up producing such ugly things so different to his earlier work? I thought about the Russian avant-garde movements and interpreted it as the failure of the modern project, as disenchantment with a cultural revolution that turned into an ideological revolution. Practice as the matrix of semblance. It was in that mindset that I decided to do clowns and harlequins. It is curious, and coming back to communication, to see how these drawings, which hardly anyone was interested in back then, have come to be respected over time.

To follow on from this, references to Europe – with the exception of some Argentinian politicians – are important in your work. The continent's intellectual and political history, the birth and understanding of the European identity in art, the development of a shared aesthetic... Europe appears as both a reality and a nightmare. Should Europe be of interest to us?

When I think of Europe, I remember that comment by Goethe and what he regarded as the inseparable trinity of the West, war, trade and piracy, which, with a slight twist, is the source of the exhibition title.

For centuries, we have exported our values and our culture, bringing progress while seeing the rest of the world as inferior beings, forcing them to worship the one true god and stealing their resources

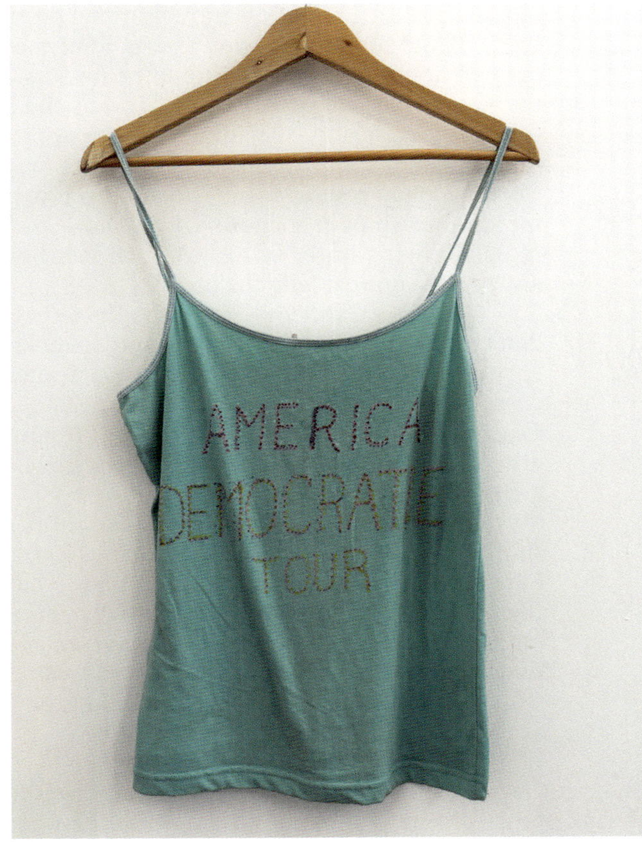

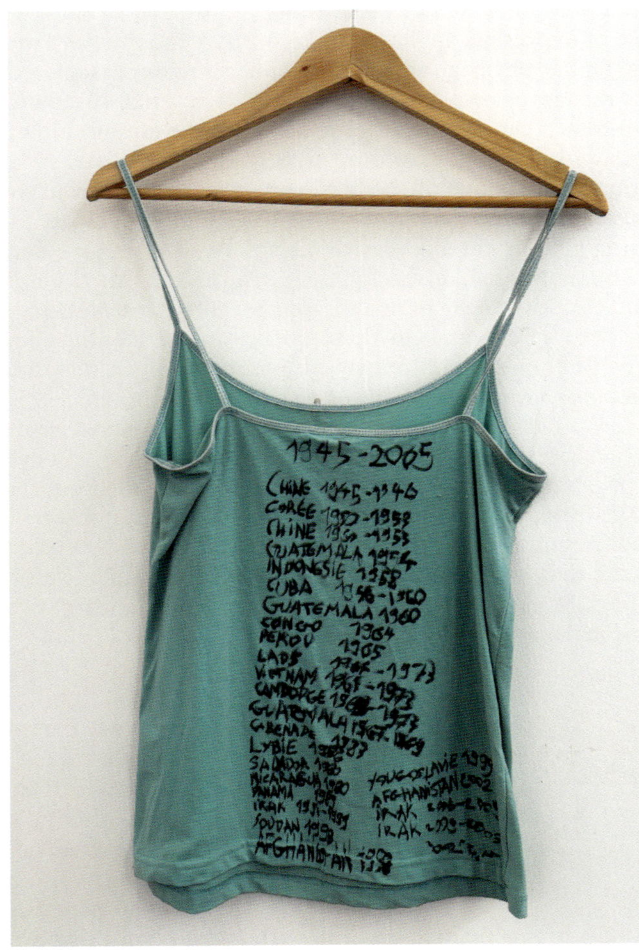

America Democratie Tour, 2005
Marker on fabric
Size S

in a process of simultaneous civilisation and epistemicide. In the final scene of the film *Apocalypto*, after a long chase in which two warriors pursue another from a different tribe, the characters emerge from the jungle and run onto a beach. Just as the two warriors are about to catch their quarry, the hunt suddenly stops. The camera focuses on the three men's astonishment as they look wide-eyed out to sea. The camera slowly rotates till it is behind the warriors, revealing, in the foreground, ships at anchor near the shore, their white sails with a red cross billowing in the wind. We then see rowing boats with soldiers and priests approaching the beach.

Now we feel threatened because they are invading us. They don't respect our culture, they're going to replace us, they have a different religion, they're criminals, they rape women, they steal and they've come to take advantage of our welfare state... They've even come to take our jobs that nobody wants to do. I'm sure people in many places around the world must have thought the same when they saw pale faces arrive in recent centuries.

When I think of Europe, I also think of quite the opposite. I think of Rousseau, of the French Revolution, social organisations, the Paris Commune, the fight for civil rights, secularism... In fact, I think that's what it's about: thinking about what it is you want to do with this real and symbolic legacy we've been given and making a decision on how you want to be and be present in this world. I'm still asking myself what kind of person I want to be when I grow up and how. All I know at the moment is what I don't want to be.

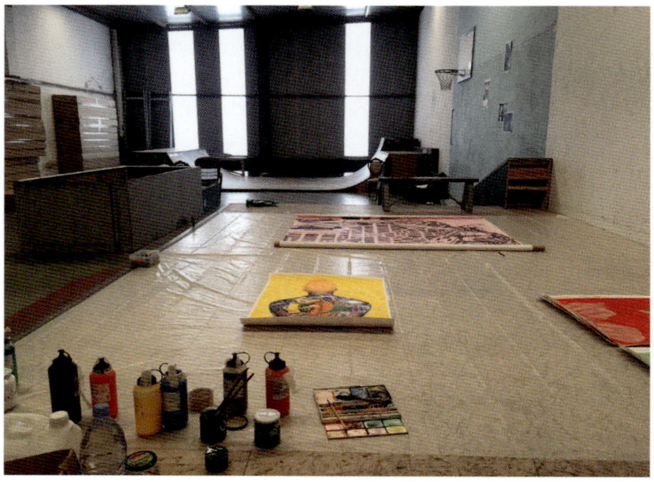

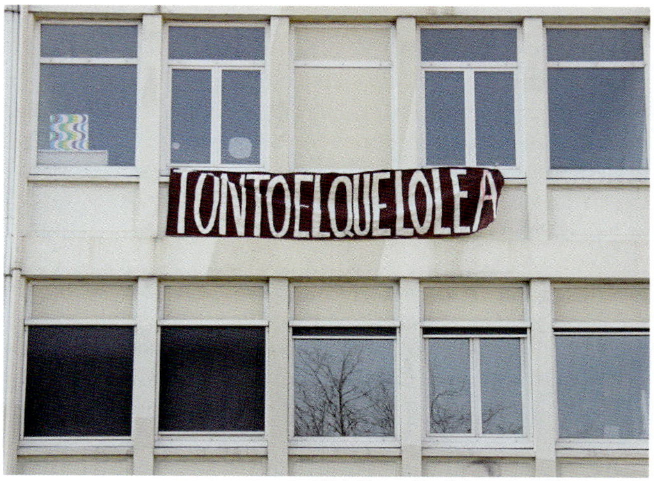

The jester is the direct ancestor of the clown. However, the modern clown originated with the modern circus. The first great clown we know of is Joseph Grimaldi, an Englishman who lived in the nineteenth century. It is to him that we owe the clown's white face, the use of expressive make-up to accentuate the eyes and mouth, and that particular physical, absurd and tender humour associated with clowns. As the circus became more popular, two types of clown emerged: the whiteface clown (the elegant one) and the clumsy clown (the chaotic one with a red nose, more brightly coloured make-up and big shoes. Your clown is one of the latter category. Why are you so interested in these archetypes (the clown, the harlequin), which are aimed at something similar yet are very different? A lot of people confuse them or think they are alike, though their origins and functions are very different. Horses appear in one of your recent series. Nothing in your work is there by chance. On these horses are harlequins about to commit suicide almost involuntarily, unintentionally yet inevitably if we complete in our mind's eye the course of action shown.

Before we focus on this suicide as absurd as it is funny, I'm struck by the horses. This is the first time they've appeared in your work, but they are a fundamental element throughout the long history of painting. The horse has symbolised power, nobility, war, freedom, movement and even spirituality. In Pablo Picasso's *Guernica*, it is the horse that is shown wounded and screaming, like History itself. Marc Chagall's are very different: they fly, float, dance or weep. They are magical animals. What do your horses do?

The signifier 'horse' can produce many significations, as Deleuze clearly explains in his seminar on Spinoza. For some, it will signify, for example, the droppings left by horses ridden by the mounted police in cities; for others, it will signify a make of car. What I can say is that when I created these works, I wasn't thinking about the long tradition of the depiction of horses going as far back as cave paintings. For me, the horse in this series signifies Westerns and colonisation.

If we look at the narratives surrounding colonisation, we have the Spanish version, with its argument that 'we gave them universities

Studio, Olatu, Oiartzun, 2016

Tonto el que lo lea, 2002
Acrylic on canvas
Studio, Arcueil

and churches, we mixed with them'; the English and the Dutch version, which is far more professional, with the invention of the concept of race and bureaucracy; then there is the 'benevolence' of the Belgian version. But I believe the United States and Hollywood are the propaganda champions, with all their cowboy films about conquering the Wild West. Pioneers risking their lives against savages with feathers in their hair, ululating as they ride around on their horses, drinking firewater and speaking poor English, to ensure these barbarians do not hinder the march of progress or the arrival of the railroad.

How different the version given by Lewis Henry Morgan or Engels, who demonstrate that the true civilised people were those deemed savages, and that the real savages were and still are the civilised. Though if you think about it, at least there was an account, a front, a cover-up, an attempt to simulate the true event. Now, seeing what is going on in Palestine, it's evident, it's brutal, and we are kept fully informed.

The figure of the hanged man – like the horse – has a long and complex history. It represents the martyr, but also the traitor, the victim and punishment. In the Middle Ages, when the hanged man appeared, it was a moral warning or a symbol of the power of the state or of God. Many people will recognise the figure, not so much from the history of painting but due to tarot, in which a man appears hanging from one foot, not his neck, the symbol of willing sacrifice. Are your suicidal figures on horseback willingly sacrificing themselves in the hope of a change in perspective?

I'm not very sure where my fixation with hanged men comes from. I recall a small painting I did when I was a student of a hanged man with a noose around his neck and the rope hanging from a tiny tree that needed to grow.

No, there is no sacrifice in these individuals, it's pure stupidity. I put the noose around my neck. I make the dreadful noise. I hang myself. I destroy myself.

In another room, we see hands and tigers, or tigers or hands. Once again archetypes or elements that can be interpreted without a context as symbols. It's difficult to see these hands and not be reminded of the hands, very different to yours, of the Golden Age (the sixteenth and seventeenth centuries). During the height of Spanish Baroque art, hands were the instruments of the soul. Given your affiliation with Marxism, I assume your hands play a different role. Yours are hands that rise up – after their labour – and work, that make gestures of peace or of power. What about the tigers?

With this, I continue to assert that we are living in a world of signs and we spend time interpreting them. When I began working on this series, I was trying to understand the return and rise of fascism. The whole time I was thinking about Sylvain Lazarus when he said that people think and that thought is a relation to the real. This got me wondering: if people thought that way, what then is that real? What is that real that makes them think like that and why don't I think the same?

Most of the hands are right hands giving the fascist salute, which is very similar to the gesture you make when you're on the point of drowning. They're hands that grow and which have fingers that multiply, growing independently in all directions, surrounded by butterflies, dragonflies, bees, all very rural idyll.

The tigers stemmed from a phrase by Mao, who said that American imperialism is a paper tiger, and the hands that appear on the tigers are those of the Great Helmsman in action, clapping, waving,

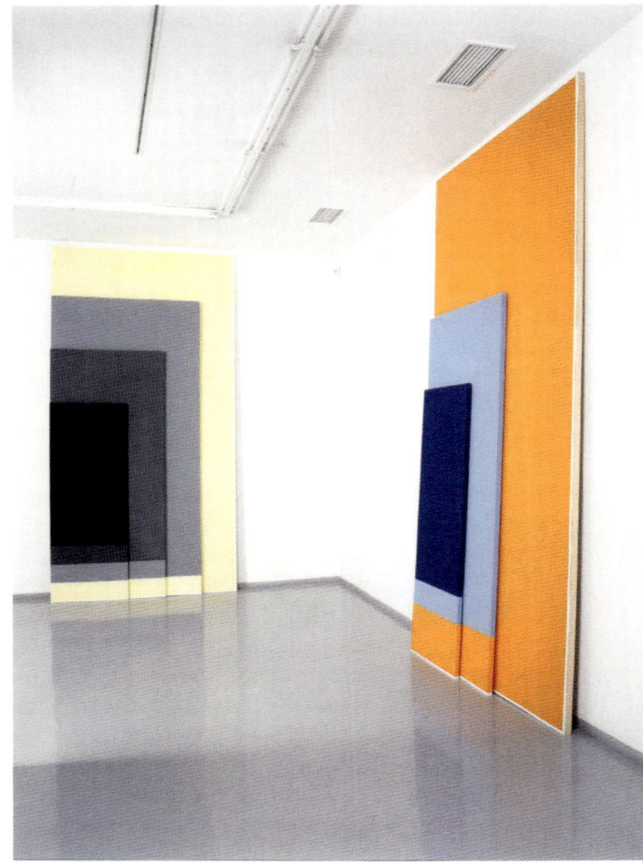

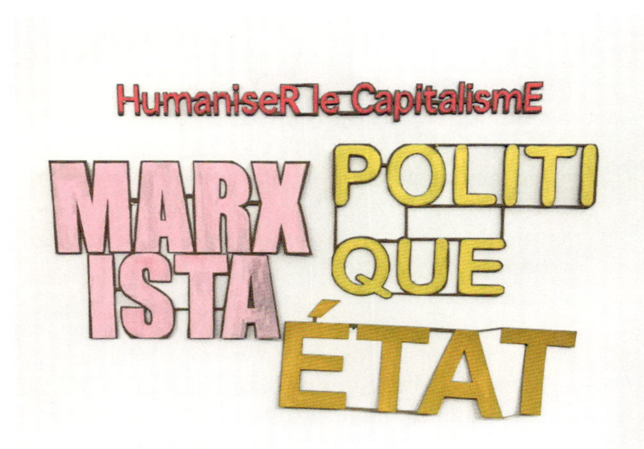

View of the exhibition: "Un Edipo correcto", 1996
Gingko Gallery, Madrid

Material from the filming of the video *Caveman*, 2017-25

high-fiving someone, opening something or frightening flies. I've always been interested in the propaganda of leaders doing things.

All these ideas are formalised as large collages made using painted pieces of tissue paper cut into small tesserae and glued onto canvas. In fact, it was about wasting time as an ethical and aesthetic stance. I remember when I finished the first tiger, I was surprised to have made something that looked so ugly to me.

We have decided to include only paintings and your work on video in this exhibition. The general public knows you for your banners on canvas and your extensive series of watercolours but is perhaps less familiar with your work as a painter. You yourself hesitate to talk of painting or to use the term 'painter'. Why should painting command more respect than any other artistic language?

I'm a fan of Paul McCarthy's video *The Painter*; I think that might suffice to explain what I think. Painting is all the same to me, it's just another tool, like video or drawing. I always decide on the medium in accordance with the project and what I believe will be the best way to express it.

Painting well – I'm not entirely sure what that means – is no easy matter. Personally, I like those artists that allow you to complete the work you're looking at, like Albers, Stella and Velázquez. I think the same about other disciplines. I had a long struggle with painting that served me as an apprenticeship for what I've done since, though at the time I wasn't aware how much its practice would contribute to the rest of my work, minimalism, narration, economy, light.

Humour and a certain sense of darker or more surreal satire have always been a feature, ever since Diego de Velázquez and Francisco de Goya and even in Salvador Dalí. Are you interested in or do you think it's important to be part of a tradition?

I'll answer by saying what I remarked at the beginning, that one of the functions of art is to destroy culture, and Goya, I think, is a good example of that, as are Cervantes, Góngora and Avellanada. In this respect, we have an astounding literary and pictorial tradition. I'm not much of a one for traditions, but it would be very foolish to waste something so valuable. With humour and hyperbole you can say things that couldn't be said otherwise, the kind of thing only a clown, a fool, a blabbermouth or an hysteric can get away with. There's the risk you won't be taken seriously, but that doesn't bother me personally.

But seeing as you've raised the subject of tradition, imagine if instead of the restoration of Ferdinand VII, the country had embraced the Enlightenment. This centre wouldn't be called Dos de Mayo. And just think how peaceful the world would be if neither the economy nor private property existed.

Video is another less widely known aspect of your work, though you've been making video animations and films for over twenty years. What does video offer you that you can't develop in other artistic languages?

I'm very interested in narration, the movement of images. I've always liked comics and cartoons. I've got works that are almost comic strips and which could function as storyboards. And I've done storyboards with a view to making a video, but which I eventually turned into animations for want of financing.

The problem is how difficult it is to bring audiovisual projects to fruition. I normally have half-written scripts or ideas and I make the most of the financing that exhibitions sometimes provide in order to produce them and to collaborate with friends. It's another completely different way of working.

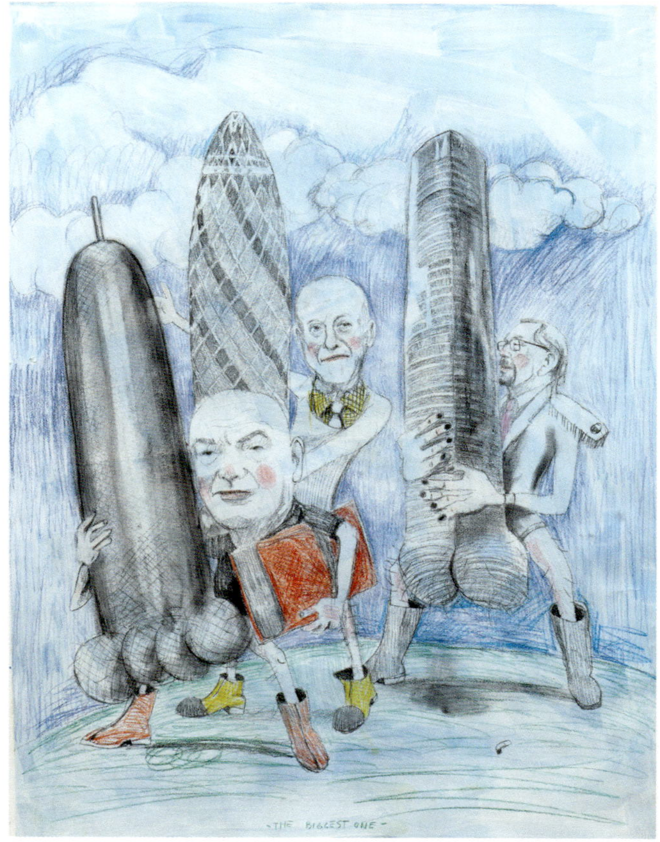

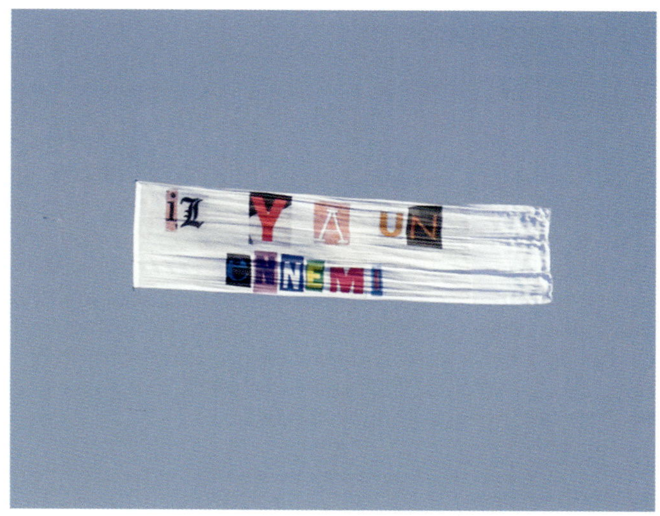

The Biggest One, 2016
Mixed media on paper
100 x 75 cm

Lalangue lavion, 2011
Banner dragged by aeroplane
Video
Anglet Biennial

War, Commerce and Philanthropy is the title of the exhibition and at the same time a way of naming the concepts – and forces – that underpin power. Philanthropy here is not a redeeming element of war, trade war or the ferocious trade of capitalism. Philanthropy appears in the title on an equal footing with two other evils – the 'mask' that contributes to the perpetuation of inequalities – present in this definition in the works of thinkers like Noam Chomsky, Michel Foucault and Karl Marx. Is there room for hope?

Yes. In the Communist Manifesto, philanthropy appears on the list that describes how *bourgeois society is desirous of redressing social grievances in order to secure the continued existence of bourgeois society* and that the bourgeois is a bourgeois for the benefit of the working class.

Some time ago, I was surprised to see a poster in the hall at Tate Britain indicating that the building had been constructed using money from the trade in humans from Africa. I'd never seen anything like it. I generally pay attention to the names of the generous patrons who fill museums. Of the pharmaceutical companies getting people hooked on opioids and then financing art and putting their names on galleries. Of those who finance a coup d'état and create a foundation where they put on attractive exhibitions and have a sculpture by Chillida in the gardens, for example the Fundación March. I'm aware of the many as yet unresolved contradictions that I have and mindful of where the money that finances some of my projects comes from.

Is there room for hope? I don't think hope is the right word. Hope, as Jacques Fradin says, is a mechanism of control. People are controlled by means of unfulfilled promises and a set-up that seeks to divert thanks to the hope for love. Human energy is captured by the religious text and the promise of the instrumentalisation of love. Love is the central tenet of political Christianity, the central tenet for channelling energy. I prefer to think like the materialists that the world is split in two and that there is an enemy.

Your work is a critical way of observing the relevance of contemporary social movements. The working-class struggle has been followed by movements not directly related to working conditions and class but of another nature: protest marches over the climate and the revolution in identities. Has this transformation in what we publicly demand changed anything in your work or is it doing so now?

Of course it drives some of my concerns, as does seeing how the various crises arising from capitalism are pushing some of the populace towards authoritarian and populist regimes that are destroying the pluralist concept of society. The climate, the destruction of the planet, identities, gender, migrations, defence, wars. It makes me deeply worried, thinking about what kind of world we are leaving to our children. How easily years of struggle are destroyed. While we worry that there are criminals of Maghrebi origin who steal phones and wallets. While the true criminals are working or lobbying in parliaments, on stock exchanges, in banks, in town halls, privatising public assets and so on and so forth.

Jacob Taubes pondered on the crisis in liberalism some time back. What is it that enables the right to survive when the left does not? I presume it is by being a scoundrel.

Is there anything you'd like to do but haven't?

No. Well, yes, but I'd rather not to talk about it.

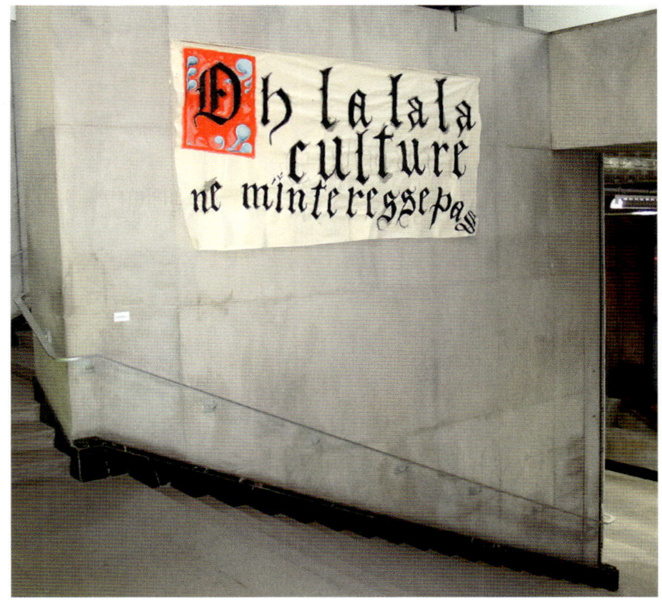

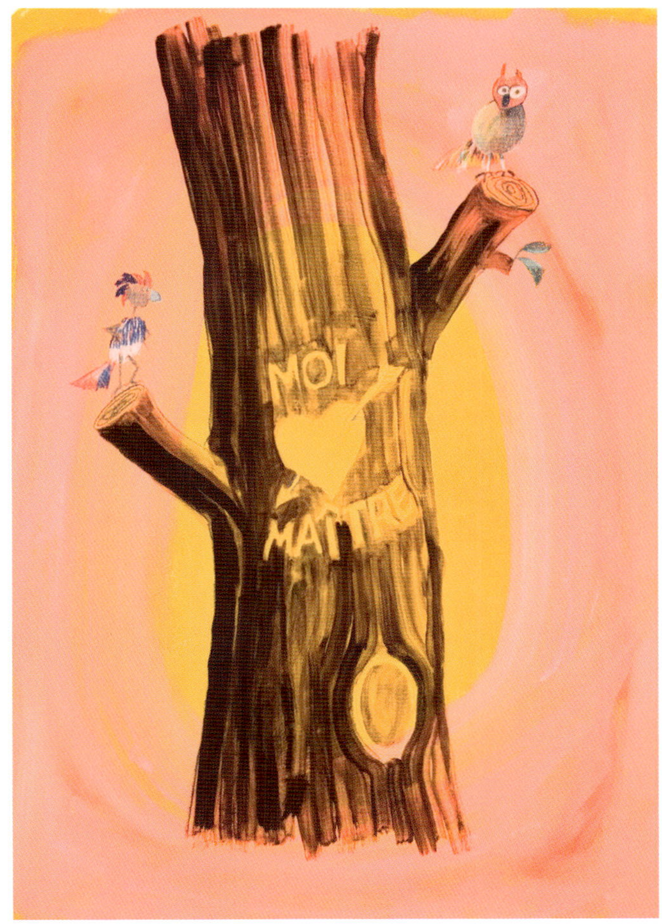

Oh là là la culture ne m' intéresse pas, 2004
160 x 230 cm
Altadis Prize, Palais de Tokyo, París

Moi maître, 2008
Acrylic on paper
71 x 52 cm

HARLEQUINISM (PAST, PRESENT AND FUTURE)

INGO NIERMANN

If you combine the colours at the two ends of the spectrum visible to the human eye, violet and red, you get magenta. Magenta is proof that a linear sequence of values can come full circle. Although not a primary colour, magenta is the RGB complement of green.

When it comes to the shades of masculinity – at one end of the spectrum complete domestication, marked by civility, cleanliness, and shaved hair, and at the other end complete wildness, marked by impulsiveness, unkemptness, and coarseness – the harlequin is the equivalent of magenta.

The more obvious – 50/50 – mix of male domestication and wildness is the bloke, chap, or dude. This is as if you were to mix violet and red in terms of wavelength – the shortest wavelength (violet) and the longest wavelength (red) adding up to a wavelength in the middle (green). But if you mix domestication and wildness the way you normally mix colours – adding up and not taking the mean – you end up with the harlequin.

You might ask: How is it possible to combine such contradictory features? Doesn't that sound more like quantum physics? No, because magenta and the harlequin do not oscillate between two states – red and violet, or domesticated and wild – but transcend both. Magenta marks a place on the spectrum (or places, if you think of it as a straight line) that would otherwise be invisible. In this sense, to be domesticated, to be wild beyond the recognizable spectrum, is to be completely "in you." When you are ultra-wild, your emotional outbursts are so powerful that no scream or act of violence promises instant gratification. To be ultra-domesticated is to consider so many harmful contingencies that in the end you are free to do whatever.

The harlequin is domesticated to a degree that frees him from any intuitive limitations, and he is wild to a degree that frees him from being a slave to his own emotions. This mental disposition allows the harlequin to serve and to rule, to be polite and to get what he wants, to be insatiable but not obese, to be mean and to get away with it.

The harlequin is so domesticated that his sword is a wooden dummy. He shaves not only his beard but also his scalp (making him the first secular skinhead) and, aware that this radical gesture might offend people, he wears a hat. The harlequin is so wild that, in addition to being a ruthless womanizer, he also fancies himself in his tight-fitting, colourful, diamond-patterned costume, his ballerina or elongated shoes and his constant acrobatic movements.

Suicide is the harlequin's favourite way to die, as it allows him to remain in control of his life until the very end. But actually killing himself is difficult, given his immense lust for life.

Harlequins are not happy about the existence of other harlequins. But rather than take the risk of fighting them, they pretend that they don't exist or ridicule them for not being fully initiated into the art of the harlequin.

***

The harlequin was brought to life by *commedia dell'arte* as a more sophisticated version of the fool and his many incarnations, such as the clown, the jester, or the prankster – again, secular trivializations of the sacred trickster that monotheistic societies came up with.

While the trickster subverts and inverts the normal, the fool's main purpose is to make fun of himself and others. The harlequin may do both, but his only commitment is to his own greed.

It's his ruthless selfishness that makes the harlequin a truly revolutionary force. The harlequin is the first manifestation of what a few hundred years later would be called *Eigner* (Max Stirner), *Übermensch* (Friedrich Nietzsche), *Anarch* (Ernst Jünger), or *freeman-on-the-land*. All these figures repeat the "magenta formula" of the harlequin: they are more than wild in that they owe themselves to nothing, and they are more than domesticated in that they meticulously follow their own momentary rules.

For Nietzsche, the Übermensch is created the moment an artist (obviously male) becomes his own work of art. Apparently, this is what

Me está saliendo bigote, 1997-99
Acrylic on paper
30 x 21 cm

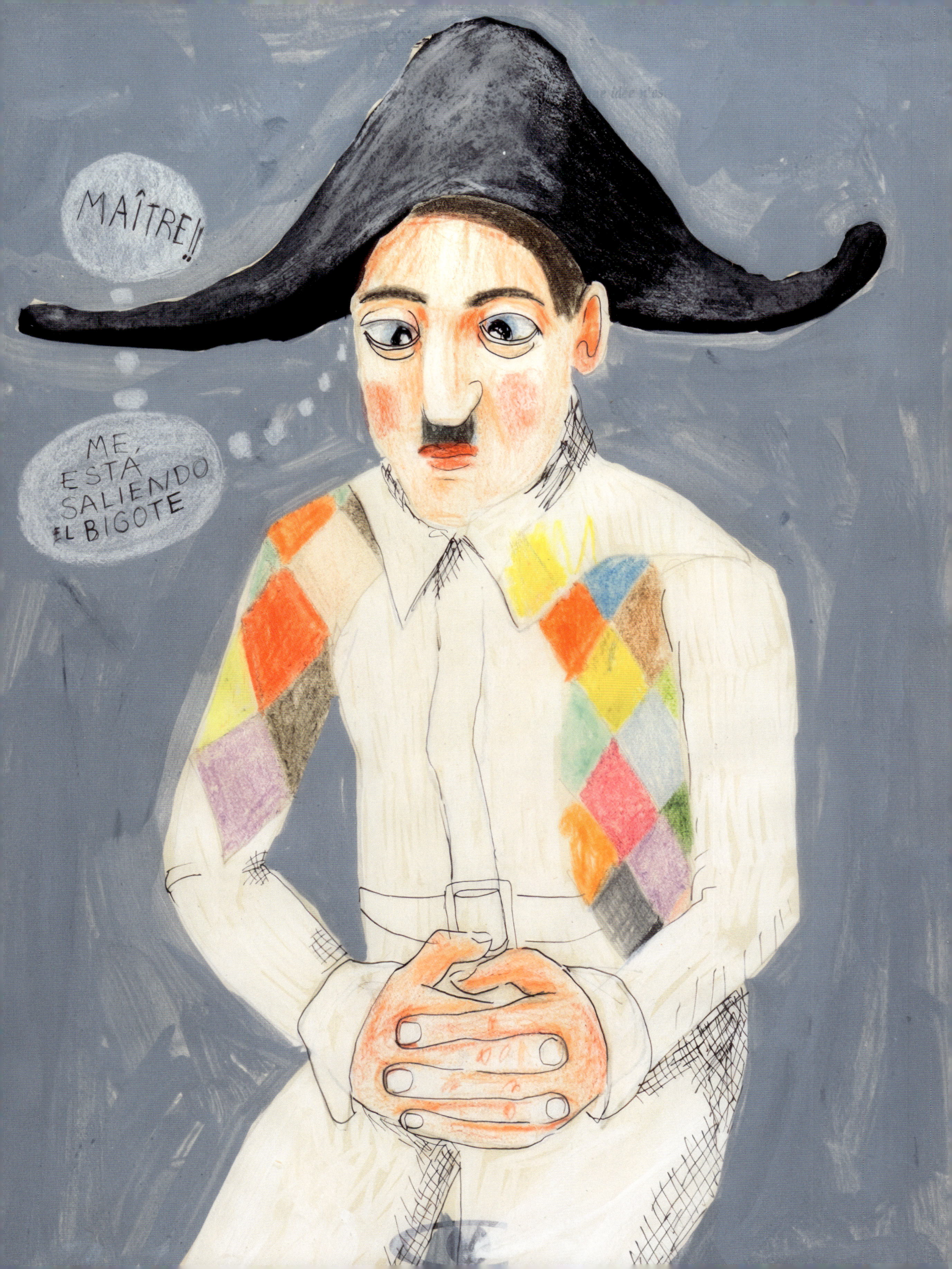
MAÎTRE!!
ME, ESTÁ SALIENDO EL BIGOTE

happened to the avant-garde artists of the twentieth century. Once the liberal era allows art to be potentially anything, there is no stopping artists from modeling themselves after their art, if not as its code.

While the bourgeoisie found inspiration in the monk – exchanging his radical, pleasure-denying devotion to God to money – the avant-garde artists took advantage of the declining role of religion to enthrone themselves as their own gods. Thus the harlequin went from being an artistic creation to becoming the archetype of the secular artist: seducing the rich (or, in the case of writers and singers, the masses) into buying his art, while at the same time playing with them; dressing up in an outlandish, instantly recognizable way (especially with peculiar hats and glasses); seemingly open to calls for female emancipation, if not male effeminacy, while actually clinging to an ultra-masculine identity; claiming his own, changing rules. Not surprisingly, one of the most famous artist harlequins, Pablo Picasso, became famous for painting harlequins.

Some artists declared the need to apply their personal rules to everyone – but this was merely a rhetorical gesture. The avant-garde artists weren't really interested in sharing their extravagance bonus with the masses.

And yet, this is what happened. Through pop and counter-culture, more and more people discovered the artist harlequin in themselves, contributing to a growing oversupply of artists and art. In order to protect its privileges, the established art world – including artists as well as exhibition organizers and museums – "professionalized" artistic practice and its evaluation with a variety of application, implementation and mediation processes. Furthermore, the art market (validated by an elite of rich collectors and galleries) and the pop market (validated by corporate distributors and the masses) selected hard workers willing to maintain their brand. Being a successful artist became more and more about creating the allure of a harlequin than actually acting like one. An increasing number of artists stopped pretending and gradually shifted their identity towards that of an activist, community worker or academic intellectual. Unfortunately, as society evolved into a post-industrial welfare state, all these identities also suffered from a massive oversupply.

Punk and street culture were attempts to exchange all the established processes of validation for a willingness to mess up one's life. With extreme poverty and homelessness on the decline, a lifestyle that rejected any insignia of affluence and involved the pretense or reality of living on the streets, begging for money to buy the next life-threatening fix, promised to make an impression. Elaborate hairstyles such as dreadlocks or mohawks would set them apart from ordinary street people and prove their claim to a harlequin identity. Clothes were elaborately torn or patched in a fashion similar to the original harlequin's peasant costume.

Nevertheless, the hard life of the street harlequin was easily accessible. All you had to do was become a drug addict, run out of money, and make the best of it by declaring it your own choice. Meanwhile, the danger of overdose and the roughness of street prostitution were very real.

***

When I began my career as a writer at the very end of the twentieth century, I was loosely associated with a clique of young men who made an impression by positioning themselves at the other end of the social spectrum: at the beginning of a precarious career, they cultivated an expensive lifestyle financed by dubious sources: rich parents?, secret side jobs? Far from being trust-fund or nepo babies, the group's dandyism resembled a cargo cult: pretend to be rich and the money will come. And for a few years it actually worked. In a German society that (delusively) saw itself as rather classless, this "new dandyism" would attract enough attention – awe, envy, and disgust – to provide them with advances high enough to support this lifestyle, at least in the still cheap, newly reunited Berlin. Even I, an associate with a rather monkish lifestyle, profited from the hype. But since most of us couldn't keep up with the sales expectations, the bubble burst all too soon.

Meanwhile, the harlequin virus had found a more powerful host than artists: rulers of developing countries. Monarchs had found legitimacy in gods, totalitarian dictators in ideology. This support came at a price: you could live with enormous pomp, but less so in public. Although deeply inspired by the persona of avant-garde artists, fascist rulers had to reduce their aesthetic extravagance to mere details (Mussolini sometimes wore feathered caps or carried a tiger cub, Hitler an unusually short moustache), while generally dressing in black or brown uniforms similar to those of their followers. As colonization was superseded by the Cold War and industrialization accelerated, a new breed of kleptocratic harlequin dictators took hold in the developing world. Instead of relying on any substantial legitimacy, they put all their faith in their armies, well-equipped by allies from the First or Second Worlds and paid for thanks to the latter's insatiable demand for natural resources. Harlequin dictators, dressed in outlandish, colourful interpretations of uniforms or traditional costumes, lived in multiple palaces, fed their opponents to crocodiles, wrote poetry, and partied in luxurious resorts and clubs around the world.

Compared to industrial and banking magnates, these dictators of so-called banana republics (because of their dependence on the export of natural resources) weren't particularly rich, and on the international stage they didn't rise above the status of servants. But the world powers protected their satellite dictators for fear they might change sides or be overthrown.

This constellation of co-dependence on a superior power provided a solid base for the harlequin dictatorship. All the more so as it often took place in countries where animistic beliefs – and therefore tricksters – were still present. But with the end of the Cold War came the end of the harlequin dictator. Following the killing of Muammar Gaddafi in 2011, the only one left (with some caveats) is Kim Jong-Un.

***

With artists and dictators no longer suitable hosts, the internet has brought a new wave of harlequinism, bigger than ever. Virtual games and personal avatars give fantasy and its application to yourself – 'autofantasy' – unprecedented evidence. At the same time, online trading leverages and democratizes capitalist speculation.

While the ideal self of the male internet geek tends towards exaggerated versions of the physically, socially, and sexually dominant alpha male, the constraints of his often nerdy appearance, his often timid character, and a largely emancipated society make the harlequin a more viable identity. The costuming focusses on baseball caps with a provocative image or wording, rare editions of motley sneakers, and shiny expensive cars. Everyday acrobatics are replaced by skilled video gaming until cyborg enhancements come into play. The masters of the internet harlequins are a few tech multi-billionaires who control the most seductive algorithms – soon to be replaced by AGI.

The emergence of the internet harlequin coincides with another new type of harlequin, which only fully manifests itself in the last third of a man's life expectancy. In a society that doesn't honor the elderly, but rather suffers from their abundance, old age brings with it the stigma of not having much to lose and the temptation to put all your eggs in one basket. Progressive senility only makes you more unpredictable and impatient. Accordingly, a new German movement of freemen on the land – *Reichsbürger* – consists mainly of pensioners. Some *Reichsbürger* have proclaimed their own kingdoms and dress up in voluminous robes. Yet the harlequin oldies were more potentiality than reality until Donald Trump became US president, not least with the support of the internet harlequins. But more importantly, he is riding on the decline of the West.

Since the US no longer dominates other banana republics, Trump has concluded that it is time for the US to become a banana republic itself

BLOC-NOTES
BLOC-NOTES

"On ne le dira jamais assez : une idée n'est bonne que lorsqu'elle est réalisée"

Christian Bourdon

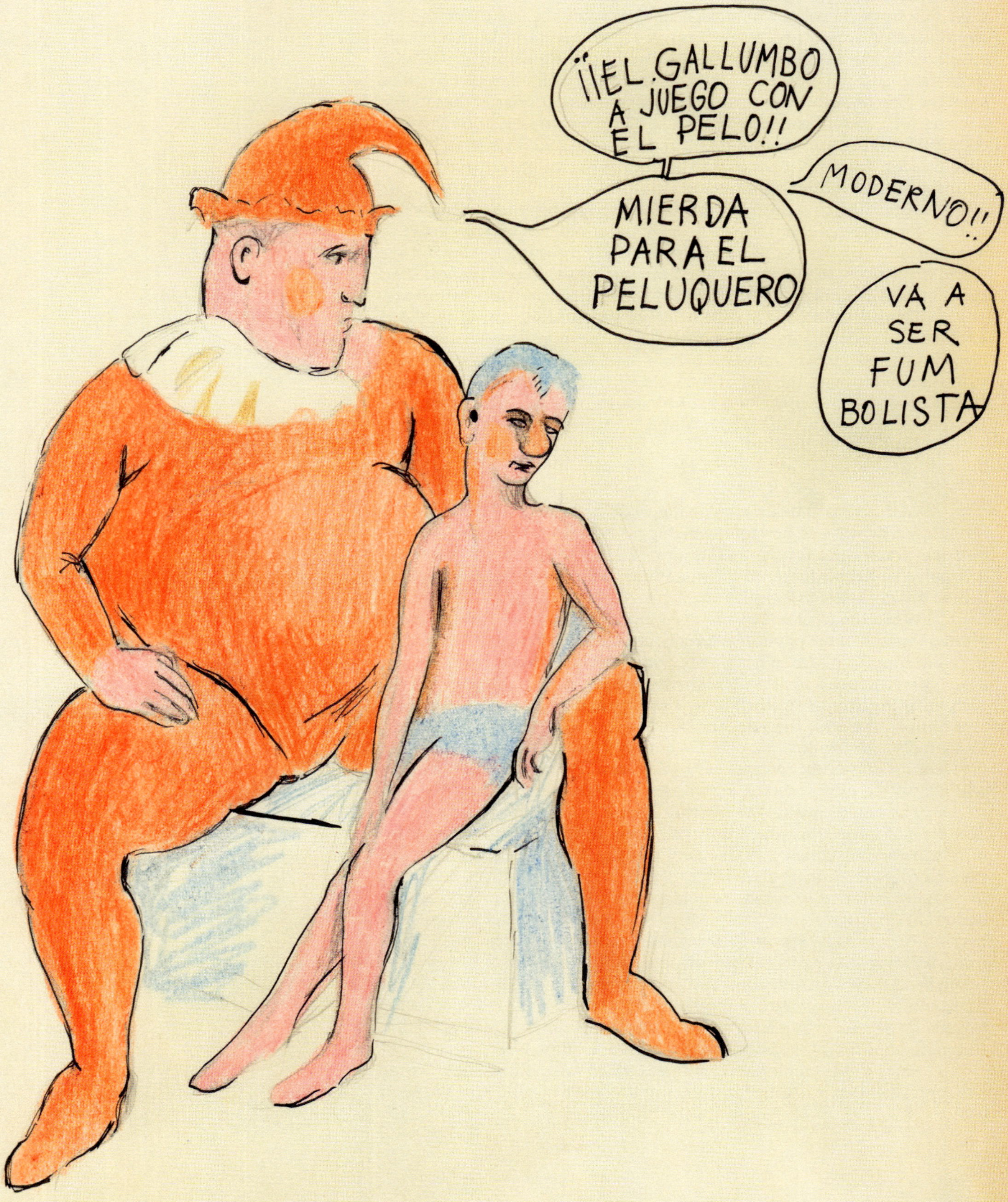

PIKATTU

– with him as its harlequin dictator. As the US wanes as a superpower, Trump's ambition is to at least make other countries pay for its decline – in particular to him personally. If it is no longer possible for the US to become greater in absolute terms, it can at least try to weaken its competitors and regain relative greatness.

This model of governance is a copy of what several European "populist" leaders had started earlier, not with the world but with the EU: to rail against the cow while trying to milk it like no one else. The first, the Italian Silvio Berlusconi, cultivated the appeal of a gangster. But Trump is the first to close the circle and become a harlequin dictator.

***

Originally a New York real estate mogul, several bankruptcies made Trump realize that he would have far more success if he focused on making himself a star. Inspired by the world-famous silver-wigged pop-art harlequin Andy Warhol, who had made admiration for capitalism part of his conceptual appeal, Trump turned making money into performance art, albeit more in the vein of arena rock. Trump's financial success was self-generating: with each landmark building that bore his name, the price of his name rose. The only problem with this business model was that there were only so many cities that could accommodate a Trump Tower. Furthermore, any economic crisis could put the branding process on hold or cast a shadow over Trump's fame as a real estate mascot. So Trump diversified his brand portfolio into luxury hotels and golf courses, even taking on the risk of running them.

Many pop, film, and sports stars have adopted Trump's strategy of being paid not just to appear in advertisements, but to brand a product from the outset with their name and supposed creative input (while avoiding the risk of any investment of their own). Sometimes with even greater success than Trump, as their broad appeal allows them to successfully sell to the masses: headphones, sneakers, alcohol, baby clothes, underwear, video games, you name it. In this way, a star whose fortune would otherwise have remained in the tens of millions could become a billionaire.

Trump made good as a mainstream celebrity by hosting a successful reality TV show in which he cast people to promote his real estate. Again, he had found a formula for self-generating success: casting people to promote his properties already did the promotion. Most importantly, the show promoted Trump himself and laid the groundwork for his election as US president.

For decades, Donald Trump had developed a peculiar harlequin appearance: a wavy hairdo (inspired by his mother's big hair, celebrating his ultra-femininity), a red tie down to his crotch (celebrating his ultra-masculinity, resembling less a penis than the devil's tongue), an orange face (celebrating his ultra-whiteness, because people of colour can whiten their skin, but they cannot make it orange), a subtle disco cha-cha (too lazy for acrobatics, but swinging enough to evade an otherwise lethal bullet), a winner's grin (usually without teeth, but as menacing as the Joker's), and a parlando full of catchphrases, hyperbole, and absurd babble. But it was only in his role as servant of the people that Trump could fully develop his potential as a harlequin: redefining the law day by day, mocking friends and enemies, and shaking up the whole world.

It is not surprising that Trump is very fond of Kim Jong-Un, the last remaining harlequin dictator of the developing world – and clearly in a junior position. Lacking any economic significance, North Korea nevertheless poses a certain threat to its neighbors. The US, on the other hand, has the capacity to plunge the entire world into catastrophic turmoil, even without starting a new war.

***

Moderno, 1997-99
Mixed media on paper
30 x 22 cm

Trump's power is based on his unbelievability. When we fall for impostors, we tend to sense that they are not for real. What they're telling us is too good to be true – and they'll punish us for falling for it anyway. With normal politicians, you can simply subtract x% (with some politicians its more like 30%, with others 80%) from their promises to get a realistic idea of what to expect. With Trump, you don't know. His claims are so irrational that the very audacity of making them turns them into a proof of power. Their exposure as a cynical hoax only reinforces that proof. And since all politicians lie, Trump's outrageous fabrications can even be perceived as a new honesty.

During his first term in office (2017–21), Trump effectively acted very much like a usual, usually corrupt neoliberal. But by calling his deselection a fraud, Trump took on one of the biggest stigmas of a trad man: being a sore loser. Sticking to the obvious lie, no matter what, turned him into a crooked Joan of Arc. Lying so badly for so long and getting away with it – how else can you be an enduring hero these days? Every ordinary hero is debunked sooner or later. So you have to go into fantasy mode and create your own gaga reality like a guru. Anyone who took Trump's side became a member of his cult.

The more absurd the claims of a cult, the more it becomes a dare to join, and the more it becomes a personal capitulation to leave. Saying the election was rigged is like a fraternity scar. In this way, Trump even manages to subordinate Elon Musk, the richest person in the world and main master of the internet harlequins. With Trump again as his master, Musk becomes a rival harlequin and raises the great question: which of the two is fooling whom?

The members of Trump's cult can only hope that he is hosing the others and not them. Trump treats reality like a boxing match in which only he can act as a wrestler, cheating and breaking the rules. Unlike trad dictators, he doesn't treat the world as a piece of clay in his hands, but as if it doesn't really exist beyond his own mind. So the only thing his cult really promises is to be as exciting and surprising as a piece of fantasy. Liberal presidents have tried to rewrite world history like a hopeful bildungsroman – with Trump, its greatness is a ghost ride full of gambles, hoaxes, hidden chambers, magical appearances, and a wide choice of more or less gruesome avatars.

***

While wokies celebrate Indigenous pagan knowledge, they tend to use rationalist rhetoric to condemn such new trickster practices within the post-industrial Western world. They even turn a blind eye to the harlequinism generated within their own ranks.

Woke rainbow harlequins focus mainly on overcoming the constraints of cisgender binarism by turning their own bodies into works of (fantasy) art. To legitimize gender transitions (also for minors), woke rhetoric commonly describes them as resulting from the realization of "being born in the wrong sex." But for good reason, the terms transgender and gender dysphoria have largely replaced the terms transsexuality and sex dysphoria.

Not identifying with the gender that traditionally aligns you with the sex you were born with opens up a wide range of possible gender identities and body appearances. What they all have in common is that they are at once ultra-domesticated and ultra-wild: ultra-wild in the sense of overcoming even the constraints of your own body, ultra-domesticated in the sense of not only disciplining your own body, but eliminating any naturalness you don't like.

To fully unfold its potential as a counter-identity to macho harlequinism, rainbow harlequinism needs to leave the safe harbor of the identity essentialism of the marginalized and celebrate itself as a luxury. Rich people don't defend and extend their privileges by pretending to be poor, but by claiming to be better. Rainbow harlequins need to develop a similar arrogance about being "more than cis" – and not just because they are treated worse than cis. When rich people self-victimize, it's not because they're treated worse than the poor, but because they're not treated better.

You might argue that the advantages of being rich seem far more obvious than those of being non-cis. But is being rich a natural state? No, it is based on technologies of storage, production, and exploitation that are at best a few thousand years old. Or is it unquestionable that being rich makes you happy? Not at all, and today's world religions haven't stopped insisting on personal wealth as an obstacle to divine salvation.

Once a society has reached a level of basic welfare (enough food and clothing, a home, health care for every citizen), rainbow harlequins can install themselves as the pinnacle of self-development. Heteronormativity has become lame because women are no longer dependent on men to support them, and men have lost the legal authority to dominate them. In contrast, non-cisism opens up a wide field of privileged pleasures: autoeroticism, sexual and other social encounters in which you can change gender at will, choosing a sex/gender identity that is currently in greatest demand, given your basic physique and age.

Since sexual fulfillment is the key to a steady supply of emotional highs, it's the rainbow harlequins who come closest to Nietzsche's Übermensch, not the bodybuilders or paleo dieters. In terms of individualization, non-cisism takes the top spot, while other forms of popular neurodiversity make up its middle class. In order to be fully validated for their paramount importance, rainbow harlequins need to cut ties with bourgeois humanism. The latter accepts non-cisism only insofar as it helps to intimidate conservatives as sexists (once women's emancipation is less of a concern). For bourgeois humanists, non-cis identities can at best be "just as good" as cis ones.

***

In the near future, profound modifications of body and mind will be less and less of a deal. The main challenge for the growing number of rainbow harlequins will be how to coexist without compromising their individual sovereignty. In a society where the harlequin is becoming a mass identity (not just for cis men), harlequins will have to find ways of coexisting that extend their ultra-domestication and ultra-wildness into the social, so as not to re-marginalize themselves.

On a social level, ultra-wild implies that any action is legitimate, while ultra-domesticated implies that any action must be done with the consent of all those significantly affected. Nothing is intrinsically good or bad, everything has to be adjusted in terms of supply and demand. A harlequin society is ultra-capitalist in the sense that it's all market, and ultra-communist in the sense that it pleases everyone in every possible way. It is ultra-anarchist in the sense that no state forces you to do anything, and ultra-authoritarian in the sense that it makes everyone a ruler. It's ultra-laissez-faire in the sense that there are no fixed rules, and ultra-planned in the sense that every demand is registered and processed.

A harlequin society is neither democratic nor oligarchic, but *egocratic*, guided by what each individual wants: If you want to trick someone in a certain way, you'll find someone who likes to be tricked in that way. If you want to help someone in a certain way, you'll find someone who likes to be helped in that way. If you want to kill someone in a certain way, you'll find someone who likes being killed in that way. If you want to love someone in a certain way, you'll find someone who likes to be loved in that way.

How is it possible for supply and demand to always meet? Capitalism promised an easy solution: money. Almost everything comes down to how much you are willing to pay. And the "invisible hand" of the market (Adam Smith) ensures that enough suppliers compete to meet a substantial demand with a good offer. What Smith meant, of course, is not

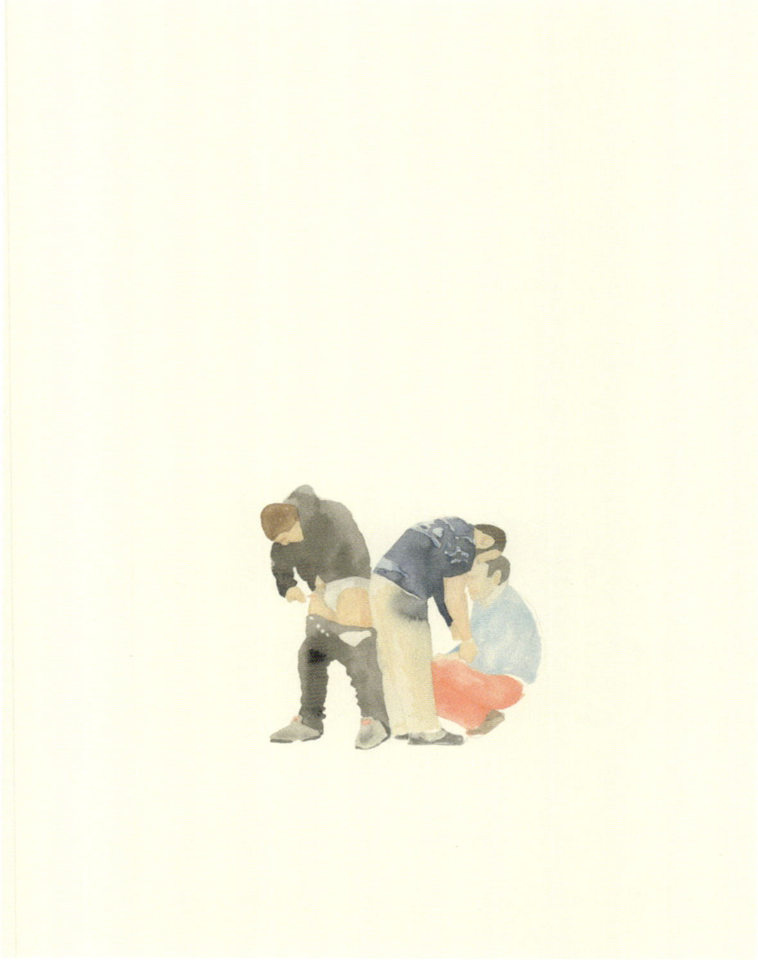

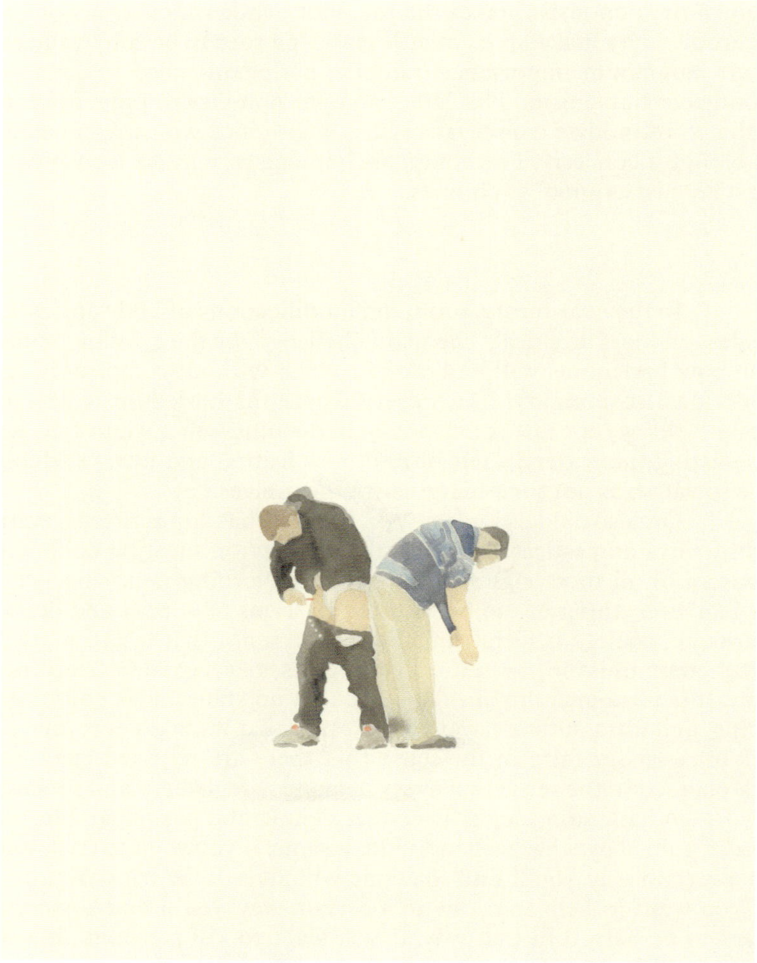

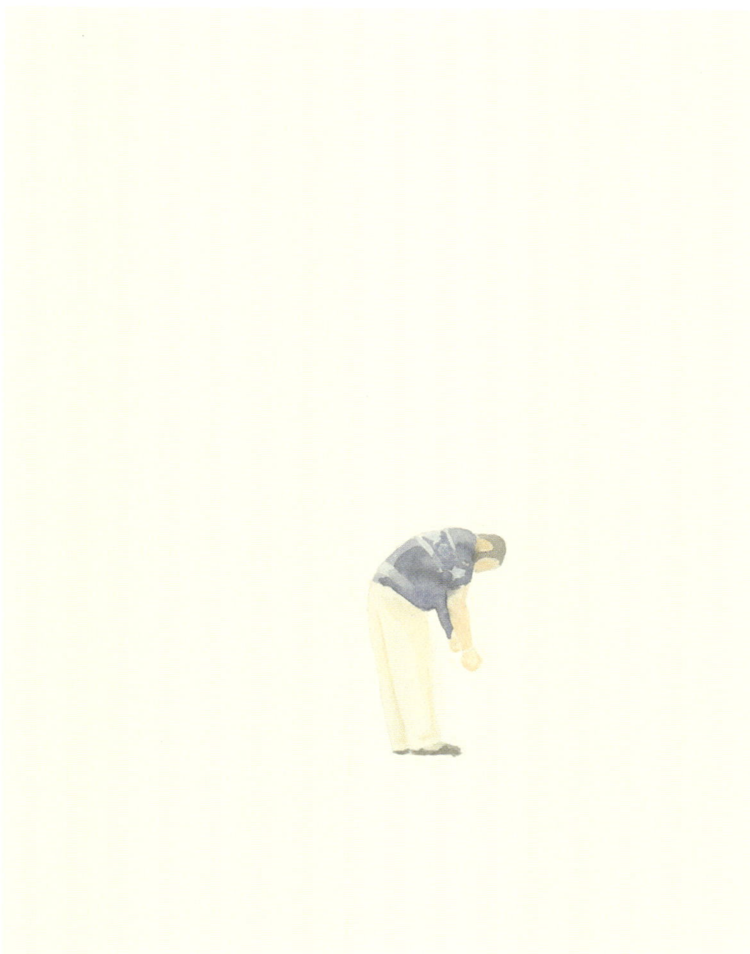

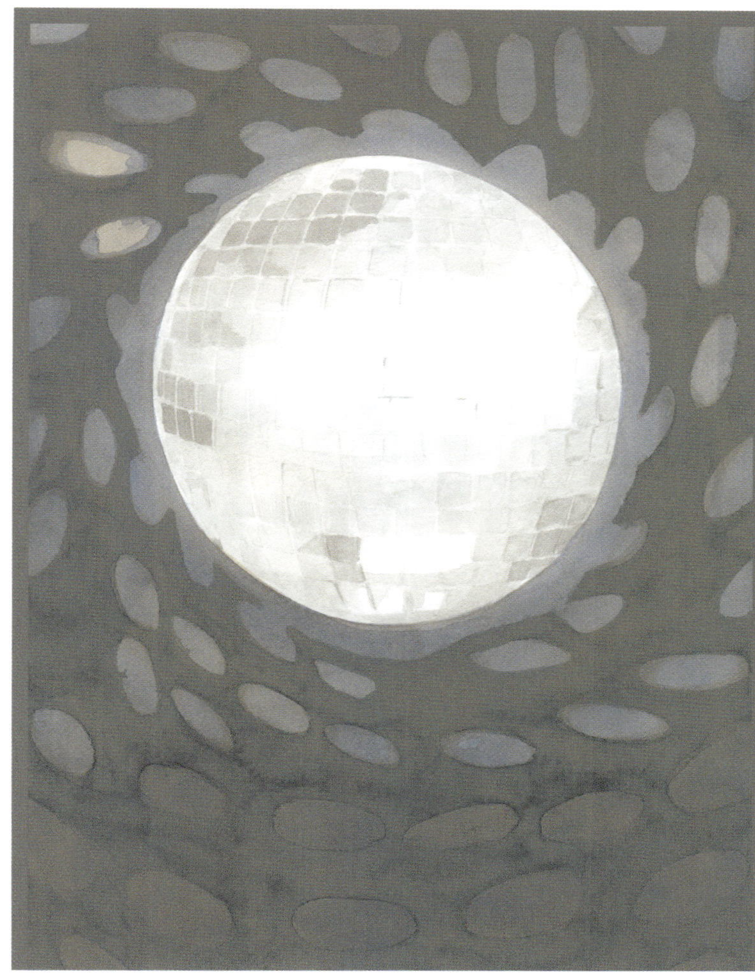

Junkies, 2008
Watercolour on paper
50 x 35 cm each

the invisible hand of the worker with the hammer or the accountant with the pen, but that of the master with the whip. The prospect of making or losing money is supposed to make people work like slaves for the common good. Nevertheless, under capitalism many things remain unaffordable for many, and some things still can't be bought at all.

Communism promised another simple solution: the state defines our most urgent needs and makes us work together to meet them; the rest is unimportant or free. Dull, repetitive work is given the beautiful aura of mutual aid. The hand of the worker is transformed into that of a caring and caressing friend. But in the end, working in a factory or an office for a defined collective good is just as alienating as working for money. And everything that is free, especially love, is also unequally distributed in communism.

Finally, rainbow harlequinism resolves the discrepancies between supply and demand. First, it can rely on robots and AI as ideal slaves: stronger and smarter than humans, but without consciousness and therefore without negative emotions. Second, rainbow harlequinism replaces the monkish self-discipline of the bourgeoisie with self-manipulation and self-drill. As your own work of art, your ambition is not only to enhance and transform your body according to your wants and needs, but also to transform your wants and needs themselves – to enhance both your ambitions and your success. You are (ultra-)opportunistic not only in the choice of your means but also in the definition of your ends. You are (ultra-)idealistic not only in your willingness to sacrifice yourself for a particular cause, but also in your definition of that cause. Rather than reshaping the outside world against all odds (as a right-wing harlequin), you set your hand to yourself. To validate your very personal transformation, you can initiate it with a public ritual in which you bury your former identity and dedicate yourself to your own cult. This process can be repeated whenever you are ready for a new identity.

POLYDACTYLISM: A CHANGE IN THE PRIMARY PATTERN

SVETLANA SLAPŠAK

My memory was merciful this time: after a while, the sound of the name brought back the images and I recollected that, over time, I saw works by Juan Pérez Agirregoikoa in Madrid, Frankfurt, and Ljubljana. In particular, there was this family tree consisting of pairs of eyes that return one's gaze. On closer examination, the dominant motif emerged: hands with many fingers, a real polydactylism. And more than anything else, this rich and diverse work of art offered many texts and demanded texts of interpretation in return. Ambitious, sharp, ironical and deeply engaged, the work of Agirregoikoa forced me to enter new spaces of radical thinking.

Polydactylism

Human hand with many fingers, different dimensions, often not orderly... Beyond the association with the forest of hands, which suggest life's brevity, cry for help and remind us of fear, polydactylism also brings about what we believe to be the first pictorial work of art: a human blowing coloured dust over his hand laid on the surface – of a cave wall, we presume – and thus leaving a trace of his existence. Maybe this was just a signature or a symbol in the codification of the artist and his public... But the thinkers of the pictorial rather like it to be something much simpler than the refined images of animals, and hence older than anything that developed. Maybe Agirregoikoa was offended or just bored by this evolutionist pretension, so he changed the course of the metaphor: multiple and different fingers symbolise the versatility, competence in work, artistic spirit and technology that enables humans to command work, creation, and all the differences they establish among humans – class, gender and more volatile aspects like beliefs, repression, exploitation. Handy hands with many fingers are ambivalent, symbolising creative passion and forced labour, freedom and chains, individual struggle and massive suffering. They also symbolise the defeat of nature, robotism, the merciless fight for profit. With this flood of meanings, we just have to ask ourselves about the sense of evolution, its dangers and its arbitrary directions, in order to help or prevent, and to measure wisely. As a unique visual imprint, they are alone in their innovative form, the sign, the hand of Agirregoikoa on the wall. The primary pattern has been changed by him: the past and the future can take new forms, the early human is no longer alone in the cave, the gaze is educated to turn to the different and away from stereotypes. The artist has given his view of evolution in another painting: the food chain goes from small animals devoured by bigger ones and then there is a rupture, when man just kills the animal and does not eat it. The fable ends with the snake that eats the elephant and the woman who wears the snake's skin (*Snakeskin jacket*). Evolution is neither logical nor sequential, man has introduced confusion, nonsense and injustice, he made food either scarce or overabundant. The arbitrary, mixed with class and fashion, has put an end to what we like to proclaim 'natural'. Can nature survive inadequate terminology, silly metaphors, incredible narratives?

Someone just put his/her hand with eleven fingers on my shoulder, and I am not afraid.

Black chickens

They are not chickens and they are not black. Agirregoikoa has drawn them brilliantly. But why? It is a series of highly symbolic birds of prey that decorate, *ad nauseam*, coats of arms, flags, shields, furniture and almost any object held by noble hands in the world of feudal power – mostly eagles and falcons and imaginary phoenixes. I just cannot help it – I immediately think of the words of a Slavic Macedonian folksong, in which a falcon is addressed as 'you, heroic chicken', and I burst into laughter. A much stronger association makes me shiver as I remember my coming to Greece on a grant in late 1973. The country was under military dictatorship, which was very much falling apart. Only a week after my arrival, the first clashes started in Athens and then developed as a movement, which led to the student occupation of the Polytechnic and the night of 17 November, when

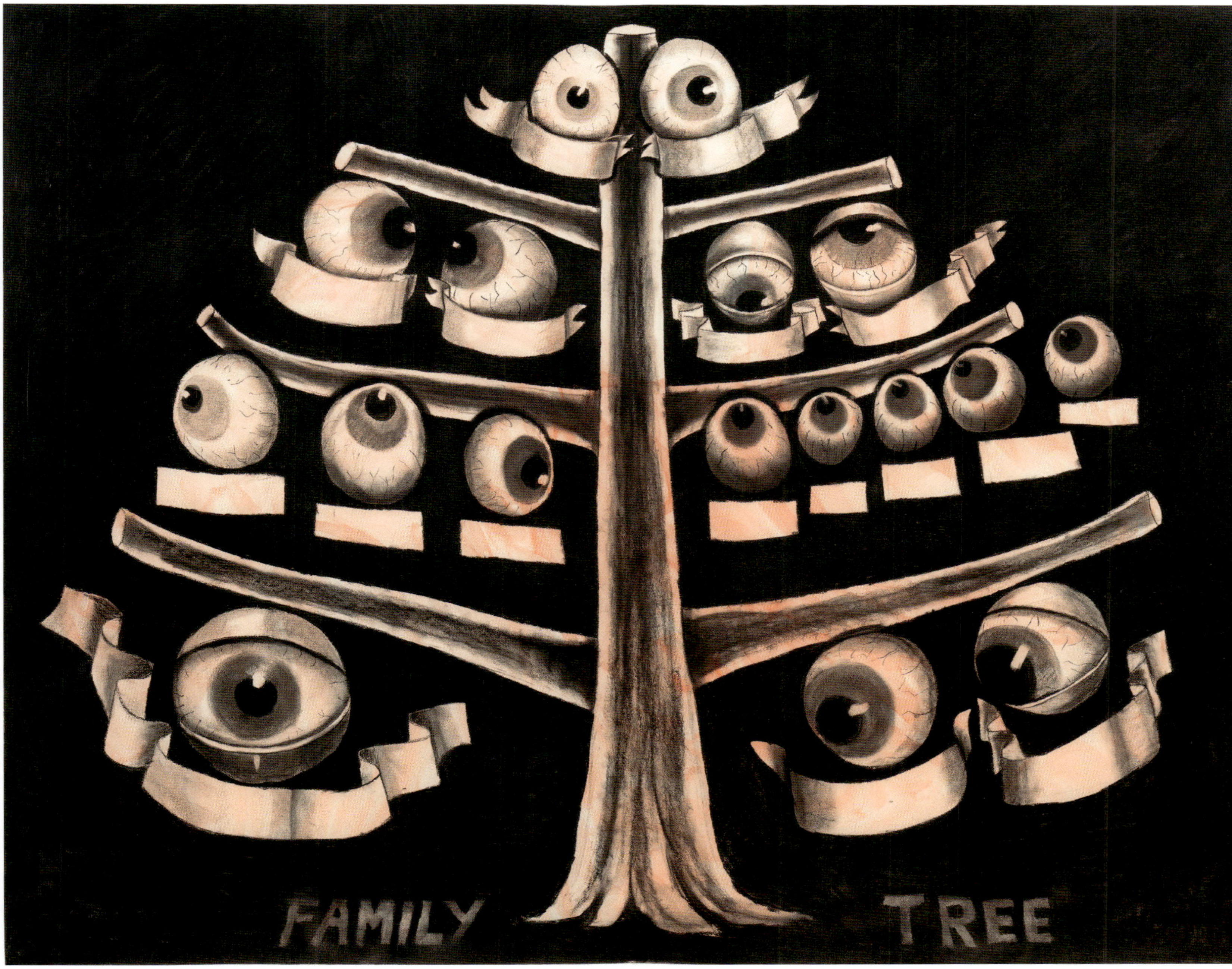

Family Tree, 2013
Mixed media on paper
160 x 200 cm

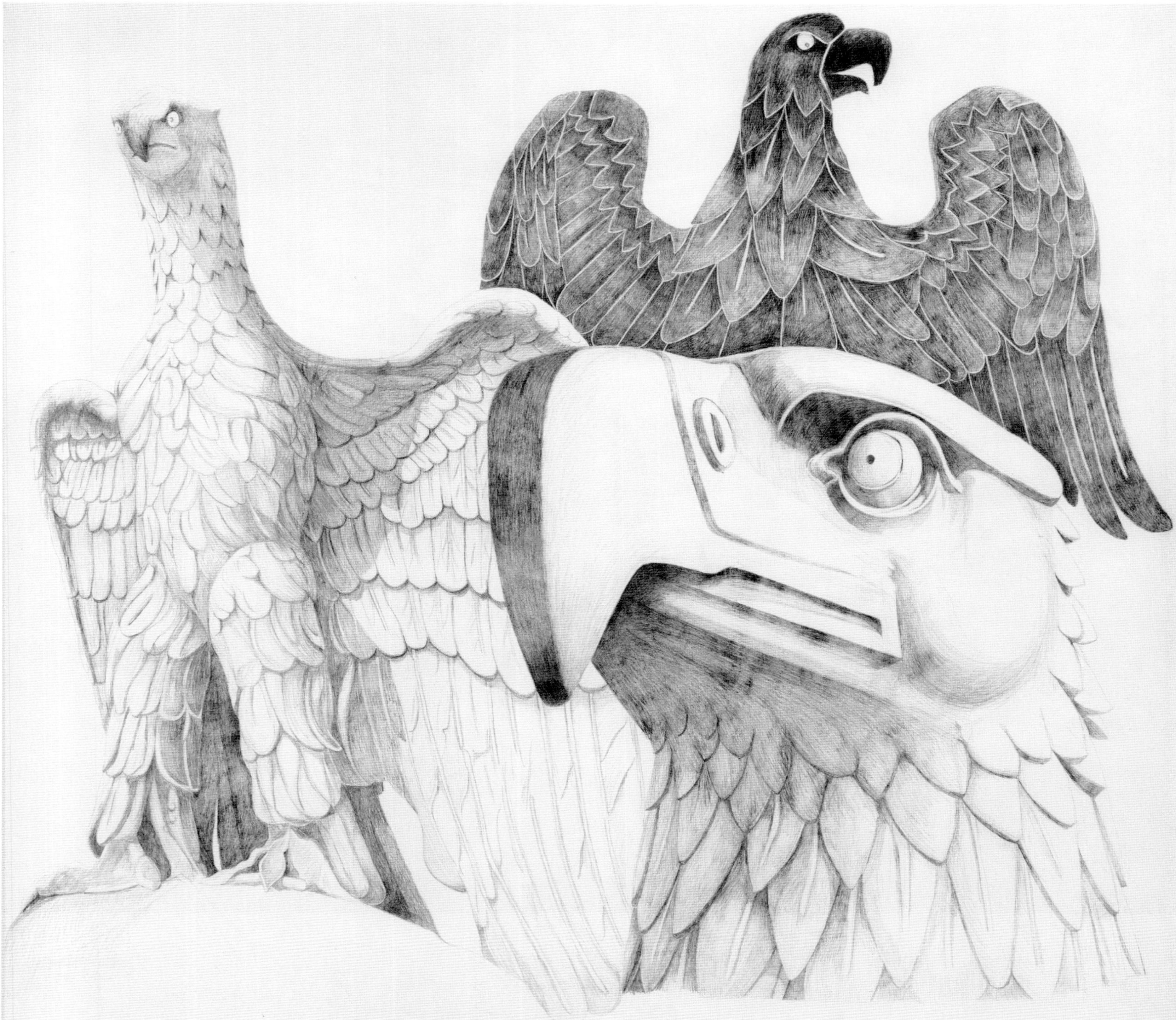

Black Chickens 3, 2021
Pencil on canvas
200 x 220 cm

tanks crashed through the campus gates and a still unknown number of protesters were killed. I went to the Polytechnic that afternoon. I had intended to visit the neighbouring Archaeological Museum but remained in the circle that reminded me of my own 1968 at the University of Belgrade. I was probably saved by a policeman who stopped me around midnight, asked for my passport and then forcibly threw me out. The next day I was driving through a street in a car with Yugoslav diplomat friends, and on both sides of the street sawdust was spread a metre wide to hide the blood. In that final year before the fall of the Colonels, all Greece was covered with huge panels, posters and billboards depicting a soldier in front of the phoenix rising from the flames. In everyday speech, but never in front of the police or in public, the phoenix was referred to as *pouli*, the bird or the chicken, and the notion was clearly ironical. You can only imagine the turn the performance of Aristophanes' *Birds* took that summer in Athens, just before the liberation...

I may be completely wrong in this interpretation of the work of Agirregoikoa, but black chickens are horrifying and at the same time laughable visions of dictators, with their stupid birdlike gaze, with their pompousness, aggressiveness and posturing. Some of them can be easily recognised. The monstrosity of these creatures points to the culpability of any group or nation that appropriated them as their symbols, because these symbols are just representations of violence, power, repression, patriarchy and nationalism. And still everybody wants the eagle! Forget the uniqueness of a specific nation, the eagle is claimed by everybody. The artist, therefore, accumulates eagles – in bunches, closely arranged, a real mess of eagles – in striking contrast with the solitary eagle who rules the skies and hovers above the frontiers of the sacred fatherland.

Some of the eagles are openly funny, and those that remain solemn are even funnier. This is a circus of confused megalomaniac birds. Still, in the face of them, everybody is supposed to feel like prey, even those culture-vultures who compare them with sketches and studies by the great masters of the past. There is a need for some artist's explanation here, and we find it in the painting of Hitler in a tutu, performing as a pink swan.

Silvae

The Roman poet Statius (first century BCE) organised his poetry in several books, each with an introduction in prose, and named everything *Silvae*, meaning 'forests, woods'. This clever poetic intervention was made by the poet to cover diverse poems, motifs, occasions, biographical sketches, events and moments of reflection. *Silvae* in Latin also means 'material': *Silvae* as poems are the raw material for poetry, to which the poet gives meaning and explains the form. The notion of truth is left lingering, and truth is important to Agirregoikoa. He is not afraid to talk about truth, unlike many other artists, and he wants meaning to be central to his work. I want to connect the artist and Statius, who gives meaning to rough material, to bits and pieces. *Silvae* is a basic concept of this self-organised chaos, in which animals, genitals, spirits and mysteries roam and provoke the gaze and the ear, and the artist then translates this chaos back to *silvae*.

The family tree with eyes that gaze in all directions is the most exciting visualisation of this process. His connection with Statius is also contextual – they both live in the world of crazy emperors, in which culture is overflowing but not sticking to people, who in their turn recognise a lot but understand very little.

Masks

All faces are masks in the artist's work, from blurred faces to brutally defined clowns' masks: humans, not individuals, are important for the artist because the narrative is what matters most. The caricature of Hitler or a blurred face of the drummer on horseback are both masks, offered to the viewer as a helping tool to direct him to society. In fact, there are no faces behind the masks, nor are they fused to one. There are no faces there at all.

Like George Grosz, Agirregoikoa depicts the ugliness of people, but blames the society from which they originate. The narrative goes further: their ugliness is not only the result, but also the reason for the deterioration of society. Grosz's bodies in movement, as if during an earthquake or just drunk, show that society is heading for a major catastrophe, and in Agirregoikoa's static clowns and other masks, society has already reached that point... beating the drum and ready to charge, with a rope around its neck.

Three humans in wheelchairs

Their power, coming from nowhere, meaning nothing, occupying undeserved places, looking down on others, not so lucky, and eventually, in their wheelchairs – bags of meat and bones in distress. Their power lies solely in the fact that we tolerate them and accept the rules they invented to protect their privileges. Why? The former king who shot an elephant should give the answer.

I have been in wheelchair for ten years now. When I look at these disfigured creatures on their last thrones, I see myself heading somewhere, holding a flag, in line with my friends.

Rats, dogs and tigers

The upper frieze, above the tender watercolours with wheelchairs, is in black and white and all about dogs. The dogs are pupils and teachers. They are taught to obey, which they do not always do. And they teach humans about the type of society that sustains a hierarchy of power. As power moves with circumstances, age and fate, hierarchy moves from one individual to the other next in line. No elections, no fuss, the criteria are clear. Humans have appropriated some of that, but they always were and still are possessed by things that can replace power, or give wrong information about power, or falsify power. Subordinated and well trained, the dogs serve humans, follow them and love them, but cannot quite deny their deeper feelings – so sometimes they resist. Black and white is ideal for representing this relationship...

Rats are different. In Agirregoikoa's work, they appear just like the rats in mediaeval bestiaries – they act like humans and provoke laughter. As performers, mimicking humans, they inhabit *silvae* and occasionally enter poetry and gladly hold the mirror up to humans, laughing and being laughed at.

Tigers are made of paper and thus they are colourful, surrounded by flowers and butterflies. Like many other verbal stereotypes, they have passed beyond the frontier of the imagination and sidestep stereotypical banality. Free from any sense and meaning, they roam in the world of eloquence lost. Even when they are used, their metaphorical strength cannot pair with the horrifying force of capitalism; they could never become signifiers. Utopian creatures, symbolic imaginary hippies of the Cold War, they are witness to the arbitrary poetical outbursts in the wooden language of ideology, to precious moments when signifiers run away from the signified and hide in *silvae*, waiting for a lonely poet to find them and love them just for their beauty.

Reject work!

Agirregoikoa's art is full of texts, often slogans, immediate reminders of reality. Detached from the context, these slogans open immense spaces of social constructivity and invention. The one that I mention in my subtitle is among my favourites. The ideology of work is dangerously related to religion and ethics in capitalism: humans should work because idleness is sin. In fact, work is the price to pay to be alive. The requirement to work remains firmly written in all existing political programmes today. The anomalies this belief generates are precarity, unemployment, poverty. Production, consumerism, class differences, all find some excuse in the ultimate obligation to work. Worst of all, human rights are being connected to work. And yet,

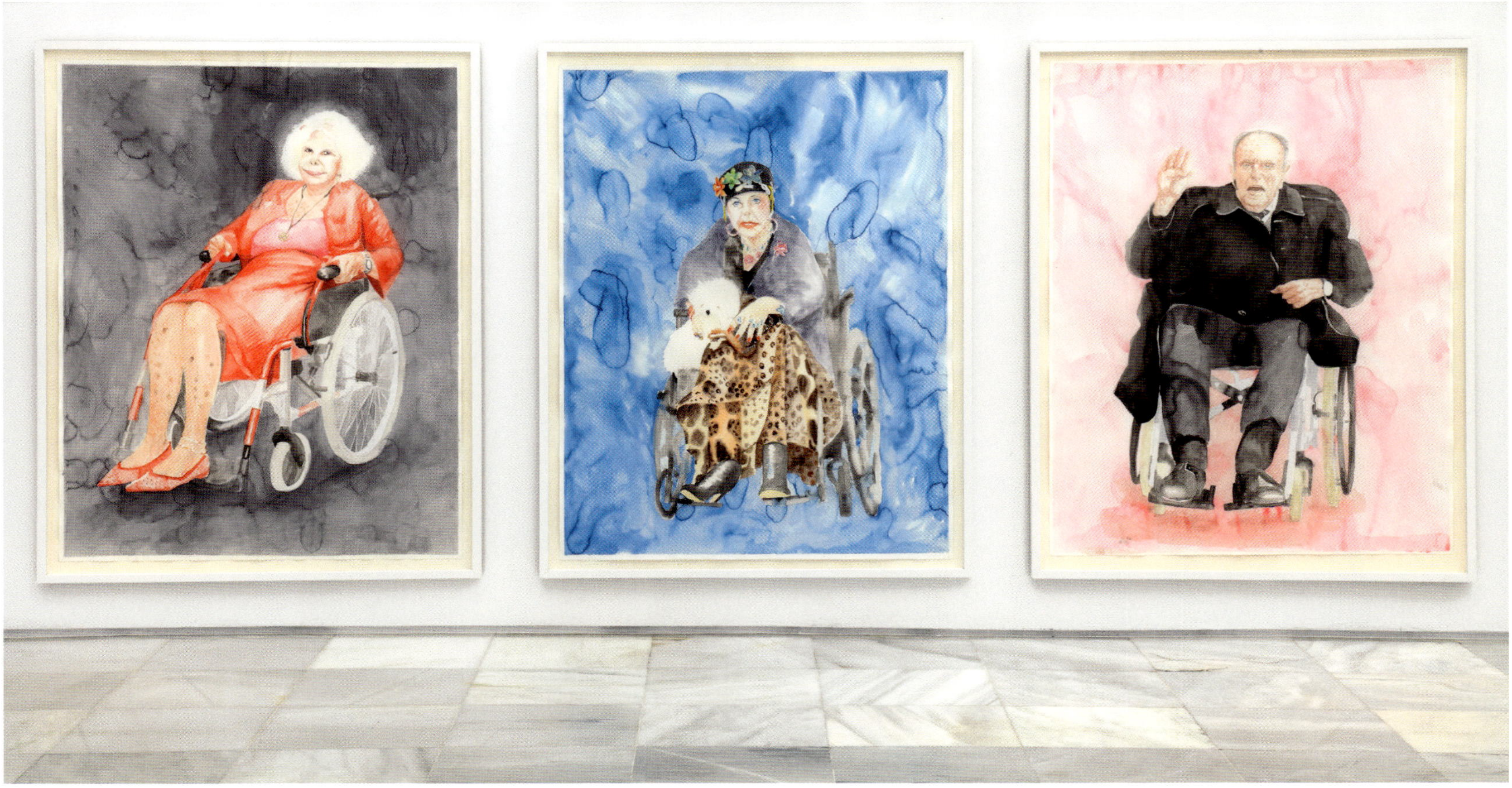

View of the exhibition "¿Queréis un amo? ¡Lo tendréis!",
Museo Nacional Centro de Arte Reina Sofía, Madrid, 2012

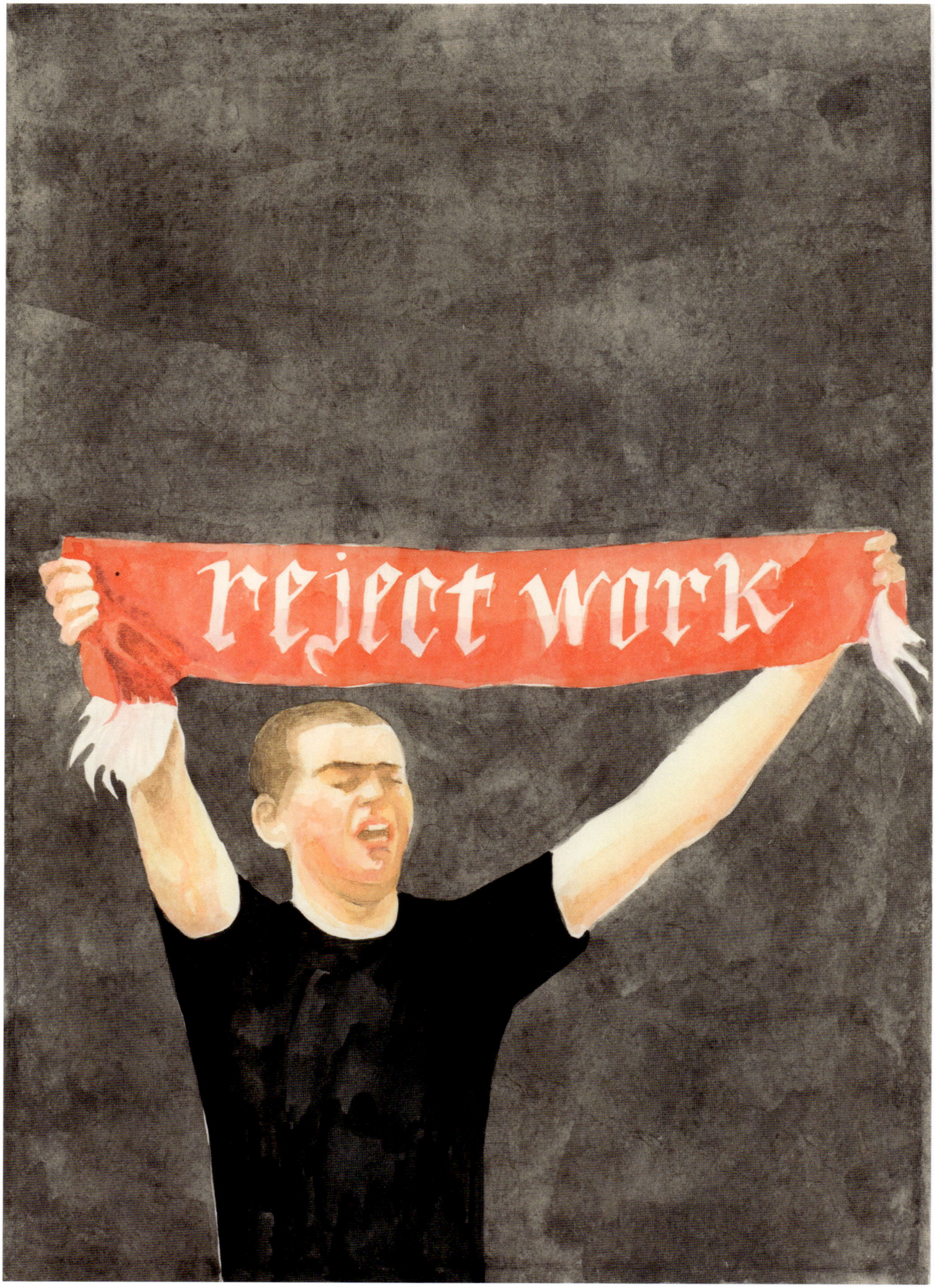

Reject Work, 2007
Watercolour on paper
50 x 35 cm

there are so many people who benefit humanity best if they do not work! And so many talents are destroyed by this obligation to work...

The necessity to work is questionable from both technological and historical points of view; it is one of the burdens of colonialism, a lie imposed upon the poor in order to subordinate them. Becoming rich through hard work is more a joke than a serious advice today. The need to demythologise work, not providing work but life for everybody, should be the aim of social movements. Work should be liberated and defined as a free choice, and the value of human life should be detached from work. The question of who is going to work should then be answered by changing needs and commodities, not just technology. The immanent problem, carefully hidden away by the rich, is the distribution of wealth, which could swiftly and simply cure most of the evil caused by exploitation.

The artist is not to be blamed for my daydreaming... But if his work (ha, work again!) has inspired such a reading, detached from the ruling schools of thought and re-attached to some less dominant thinking, then it has attained its goal, at least in my eyes. And I am thankful for that.

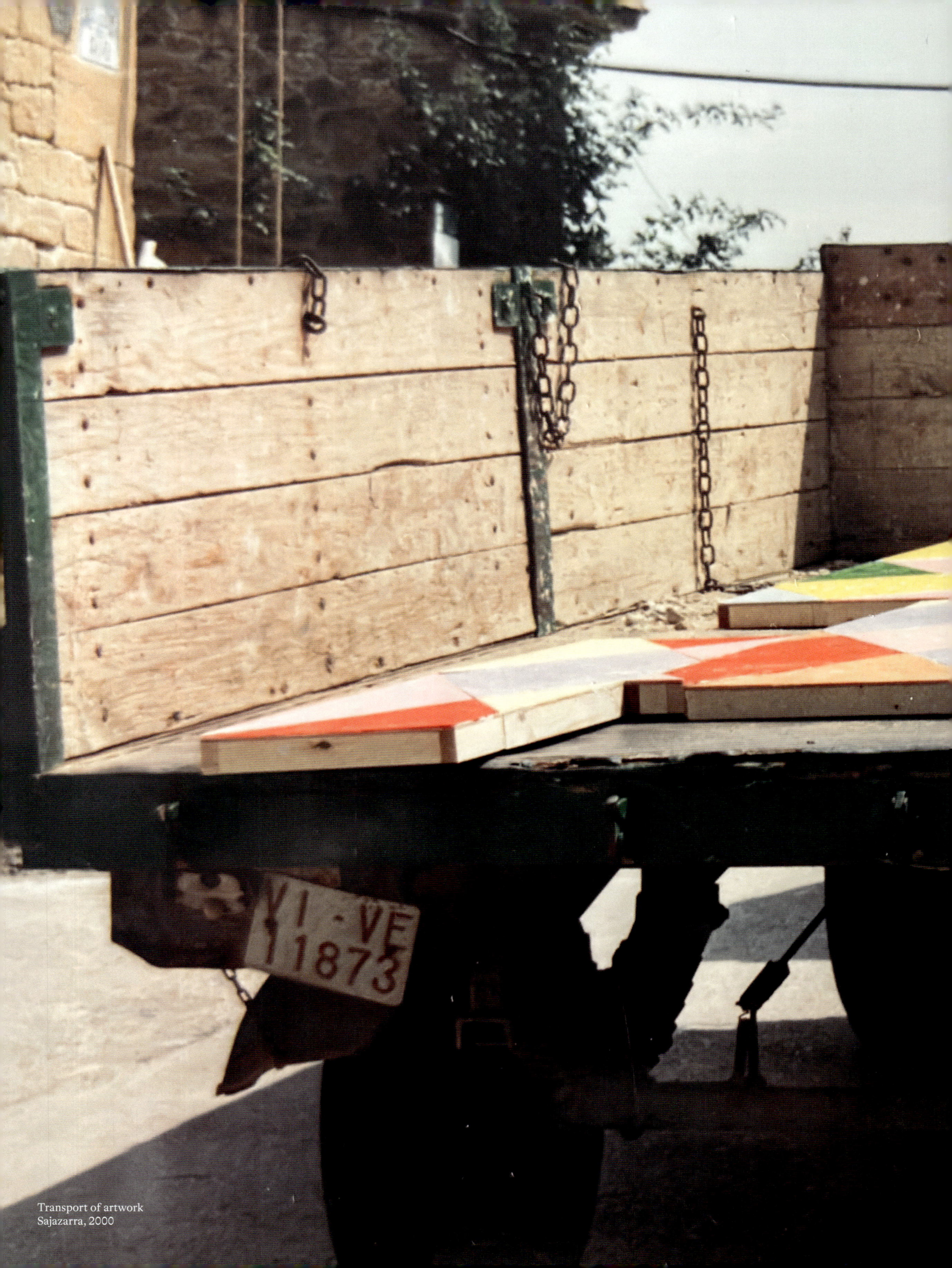

Transport of artwork
Sajazarra, 2000

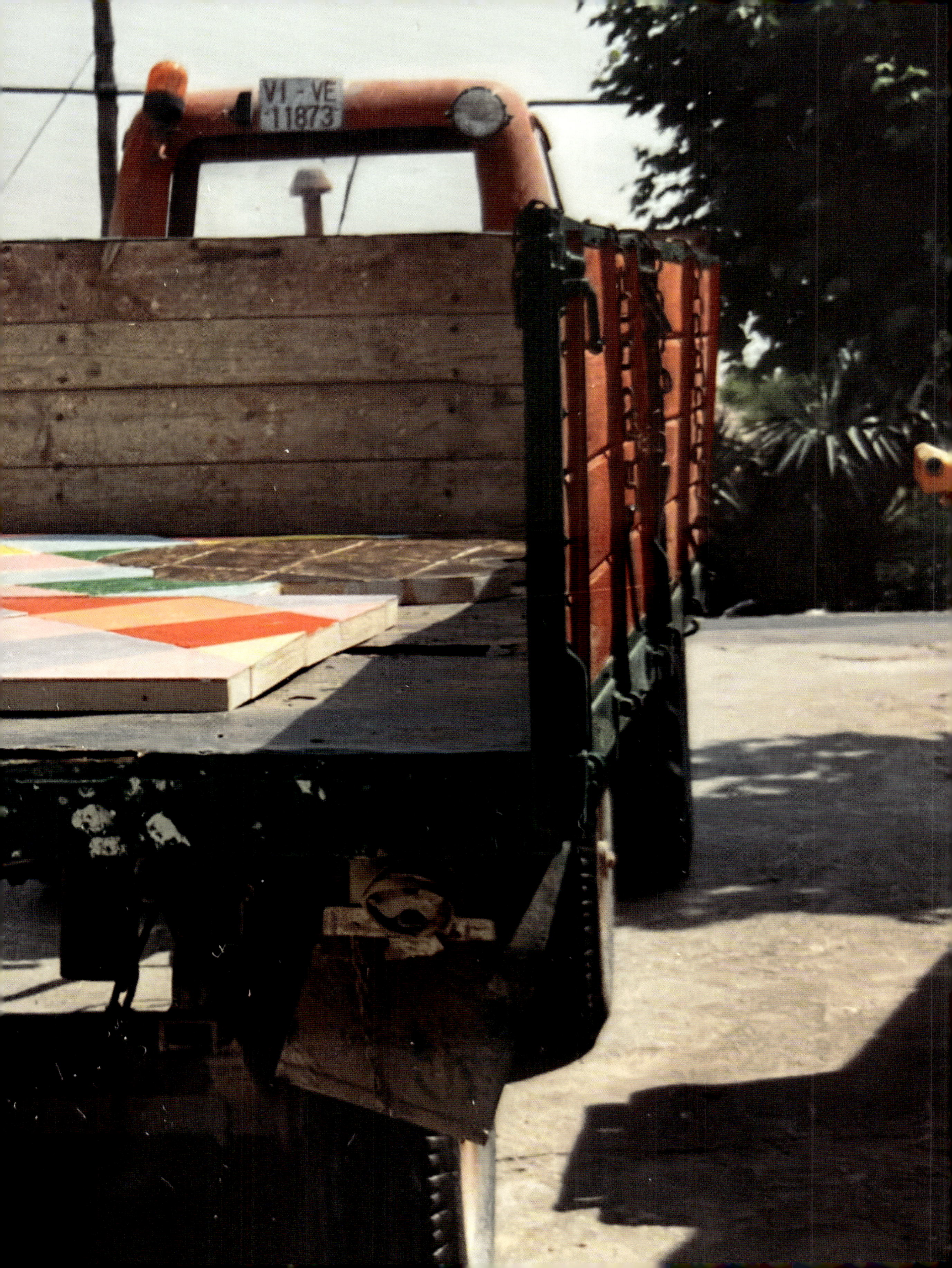
VI - VE
11873

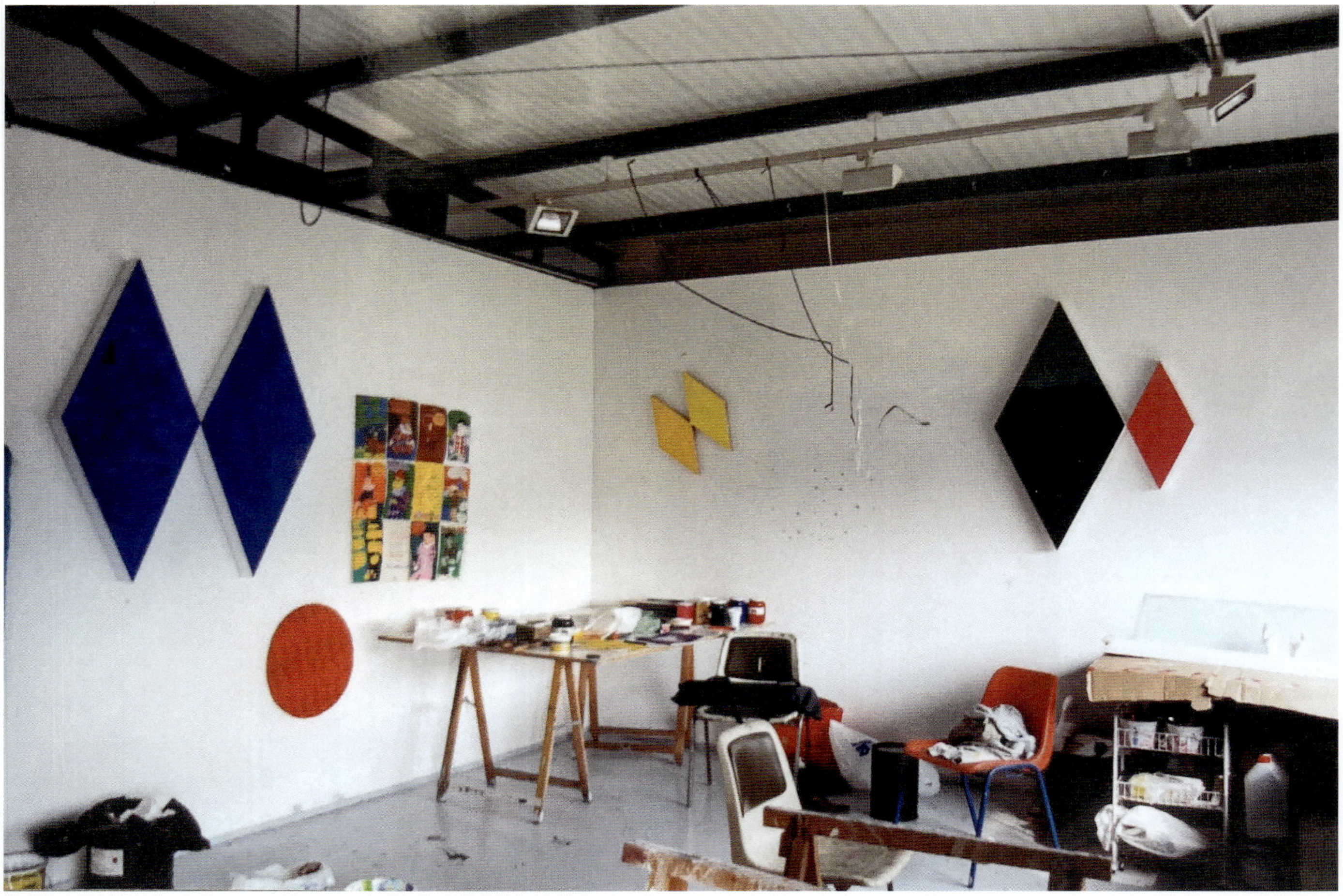

Studio, Arteleku, San Sebastian, 1999

I made this series of drawings during the late nineties at the same time as a series of abstract paintings with the same theme, but breaking with the formalism I had imposed on myself when making the latter.

At that time, I had already been trying for a number of years to be "modern" in such a complex medium as painting. But with pyrrhic results. For me, being modern meant leaving behind the romantic space of the One, with its depths, its searches for meaning, its horizons and its gods, where infinity was still represented as a horizon structure.

Shortly beforehand I had seen some circus paintings by Rodchenko from the late-1930s depicting clowns and harlequins, which struck me as terrible for an avant-garde artist. At the time I thought it was the very embodiment of failure. The proof that, once again, when bureaucracy prevails and becomes anti-revolutionary, there is nothing to be done because ideology wins out.

I've always felt an aversion to paintings of clowns and harlequins, those cynical buffoons in colourful geometric patterned costumes. The strange thing is that, at that moment, many people saw in them some of the basic characteristics of what, in terms of formal appearance, my work had been during that decade, namely, form and colour.

Nothing could have been further from my intention, but when it comes to communicating, if you don't explain yourself properly, the person who doesn't understand you is not to blame...

It was in that in-between period when you are no longer a young artist and enter into a kind of limbo because of your age when I decided to paint harlequins. I wanted to work from failure and feel what it was like to paint clowns.

No se juega, 1997-99
Mixed media on paper
30 x 22 cm

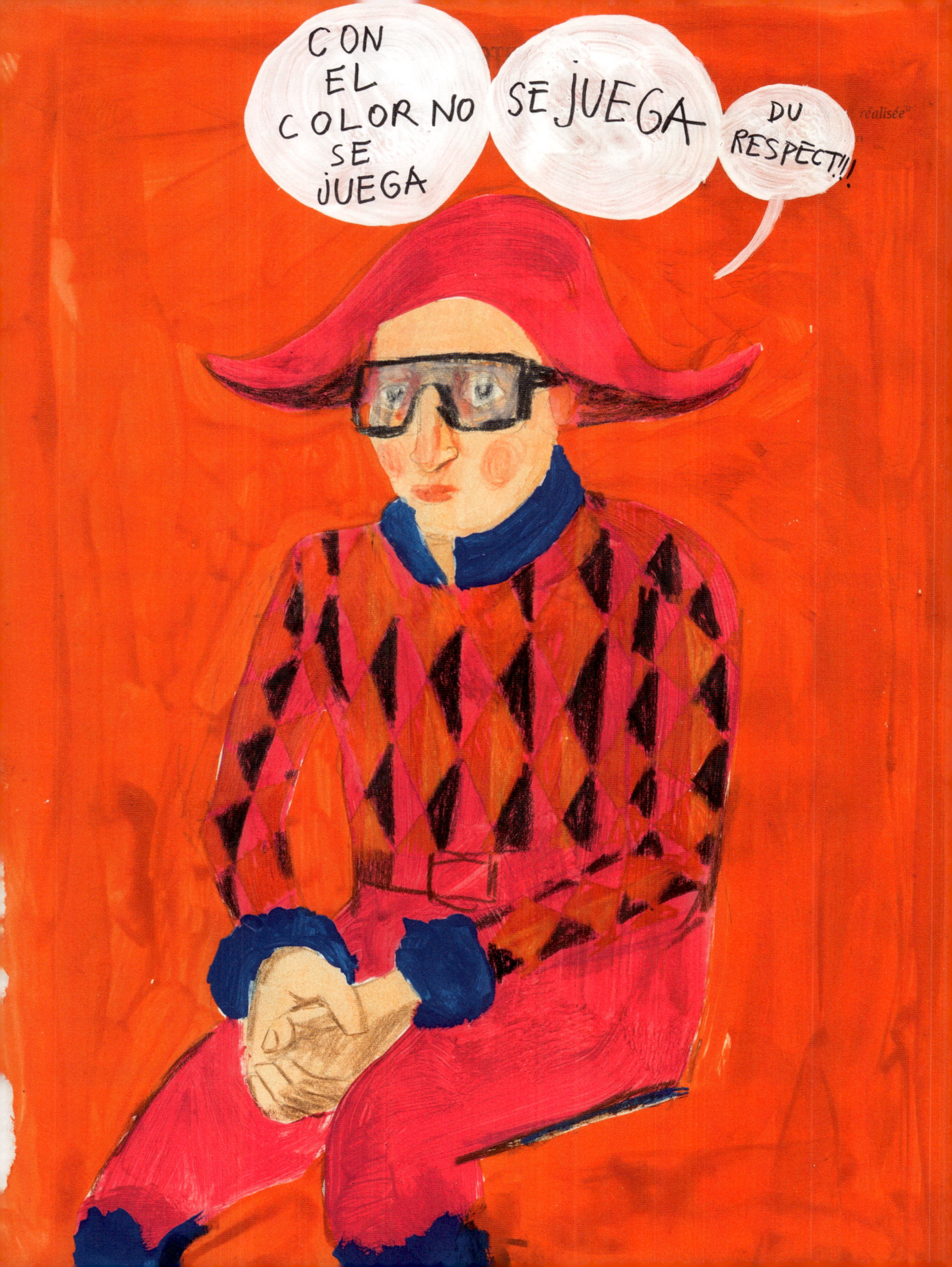
CON EL COLOR NO SE JUEGA
SE JUEGA
DU RESPECT!!!
réalisée

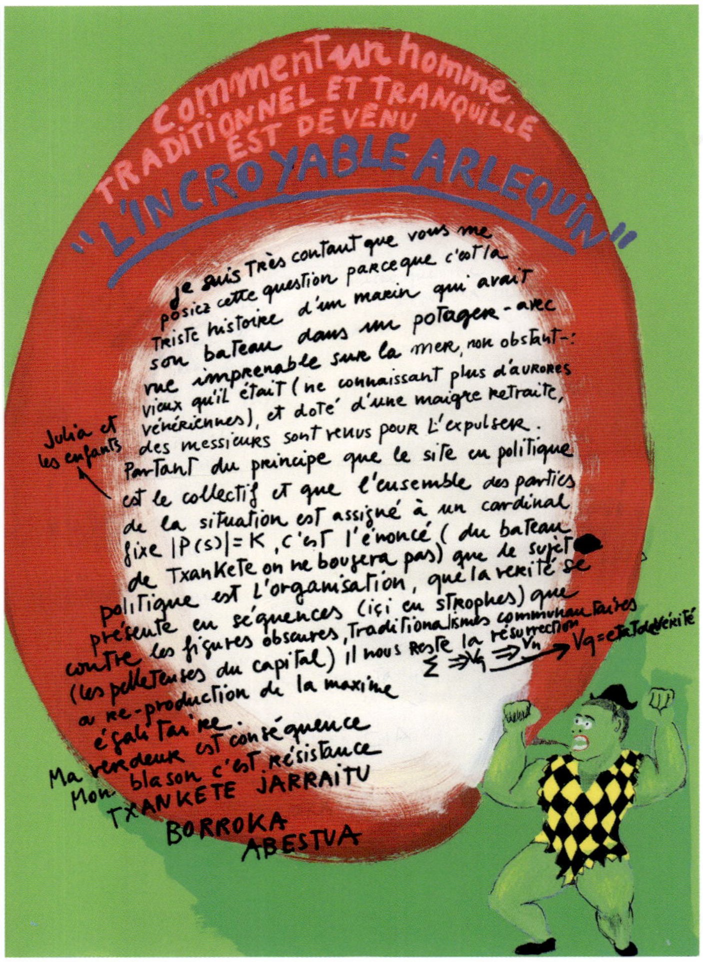

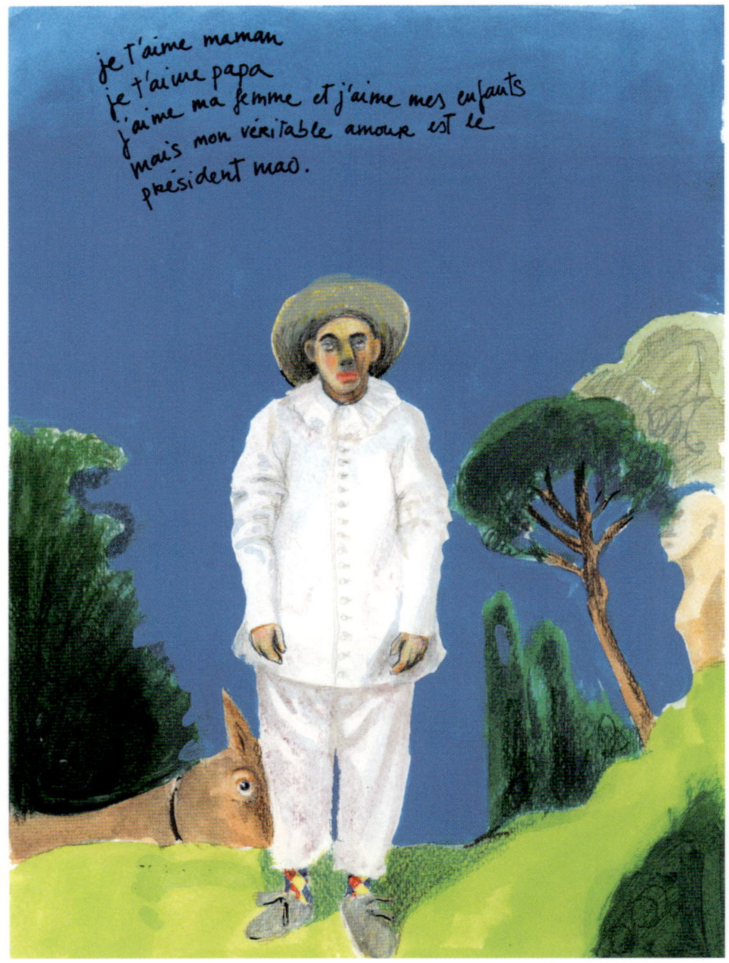

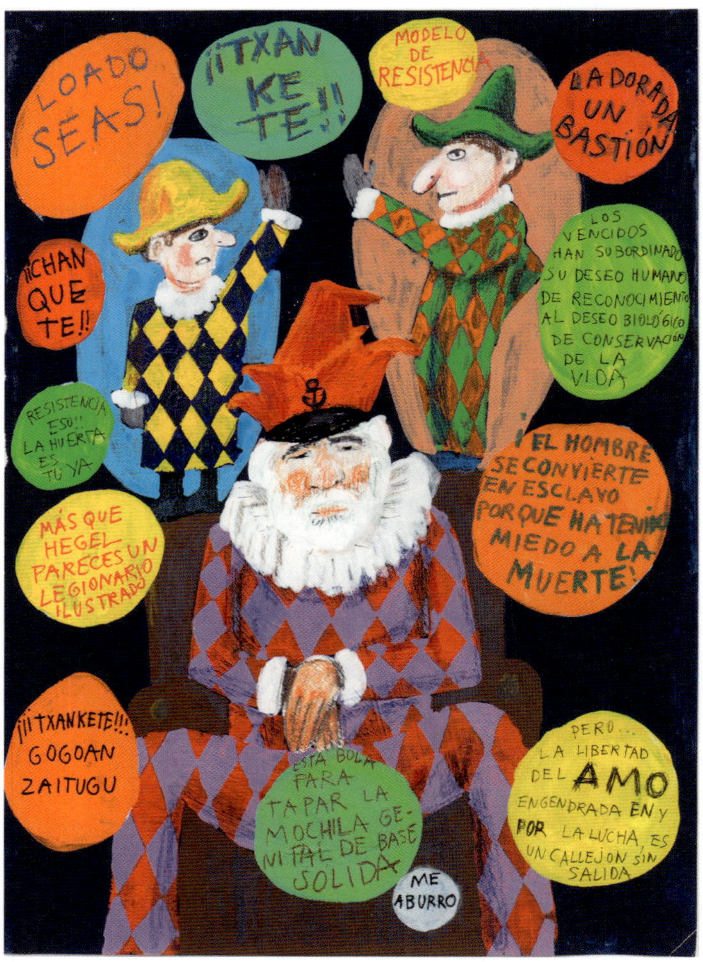

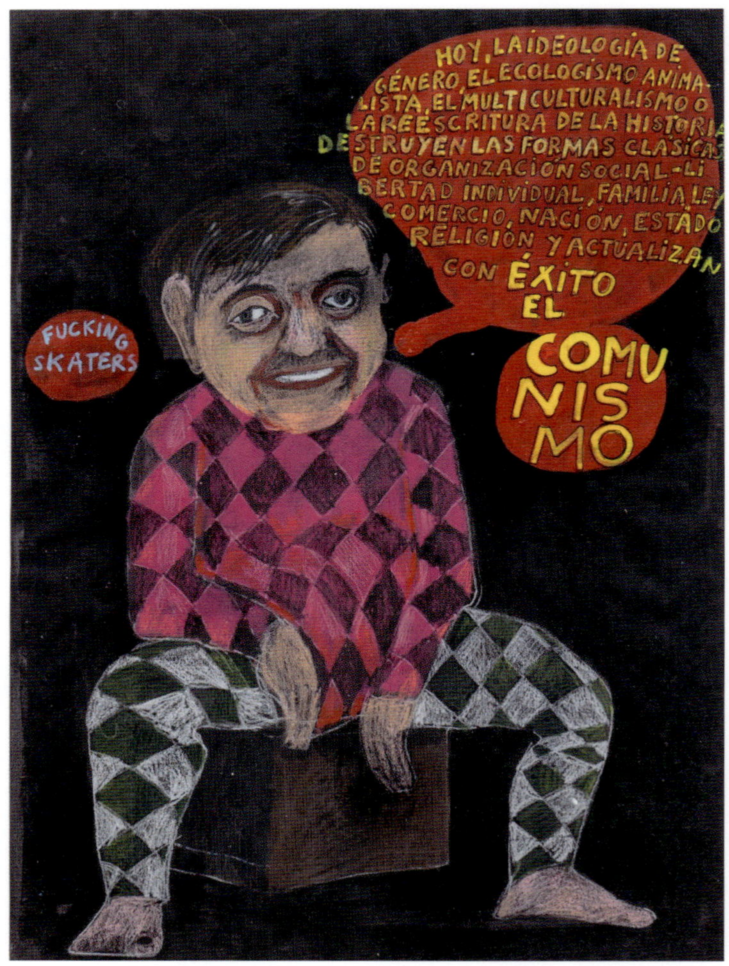

El increíble arlequín, 1997-99
Mixed media on paper
30 x 22 cm

El resistente, 1997-99
Mixed media on paper
30 x 22 cm

Tesis, 1997-99
Mixed media on paper
30 x 22 cm

Éxito comunismo, 2020
Mixed media on paper
41,5 x 30 cm

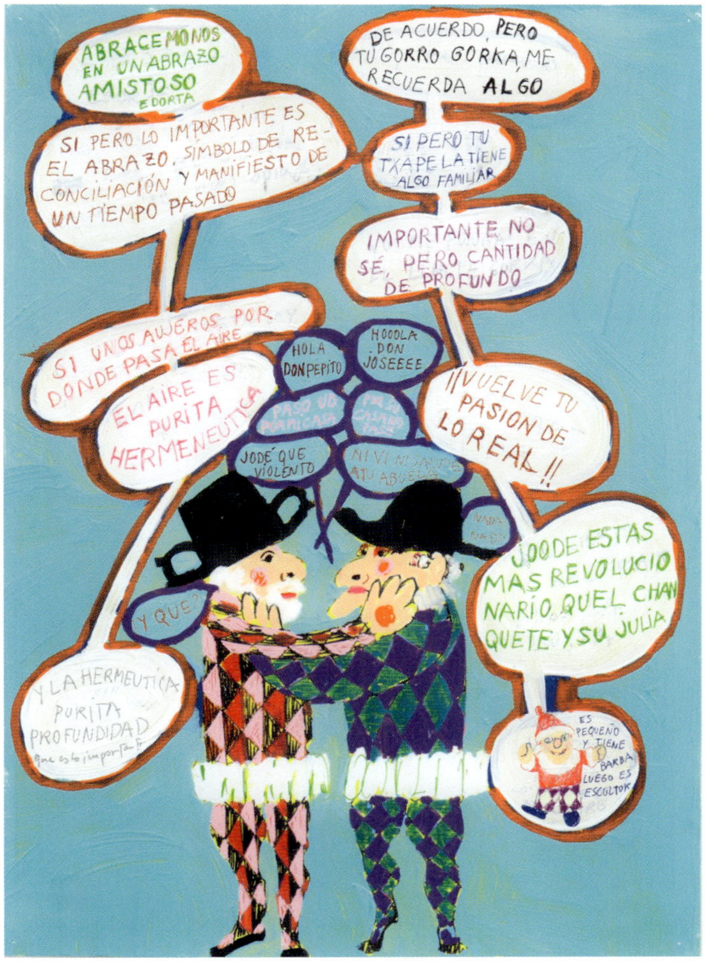

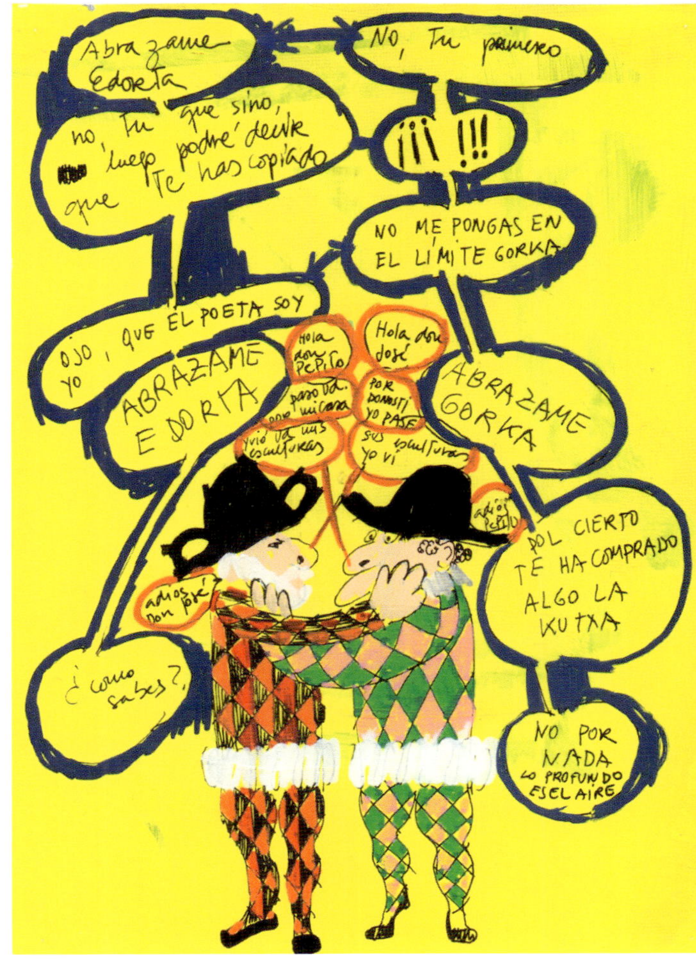

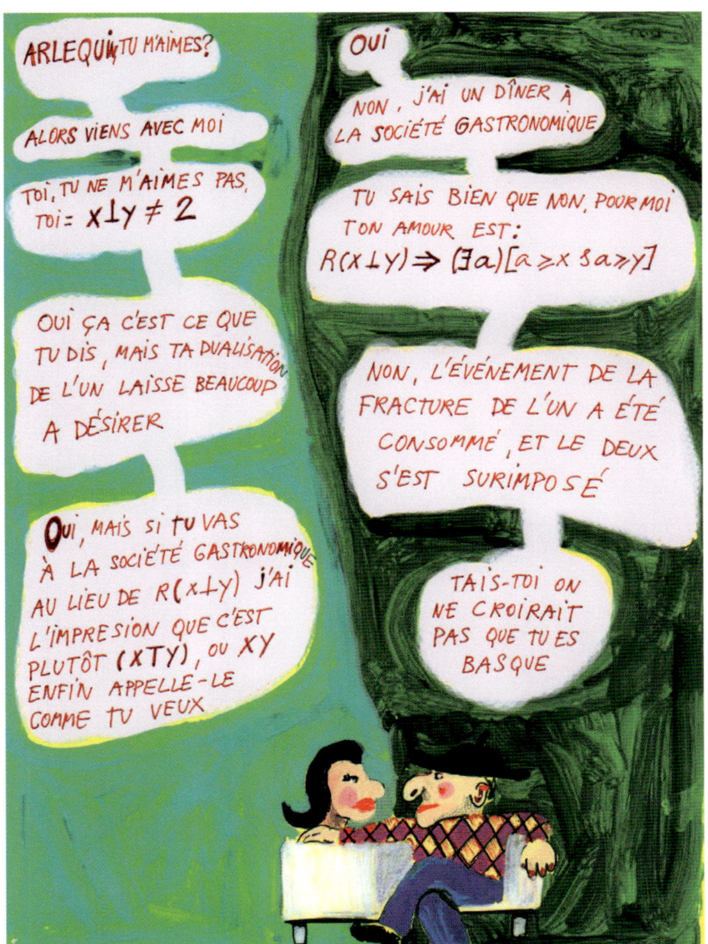

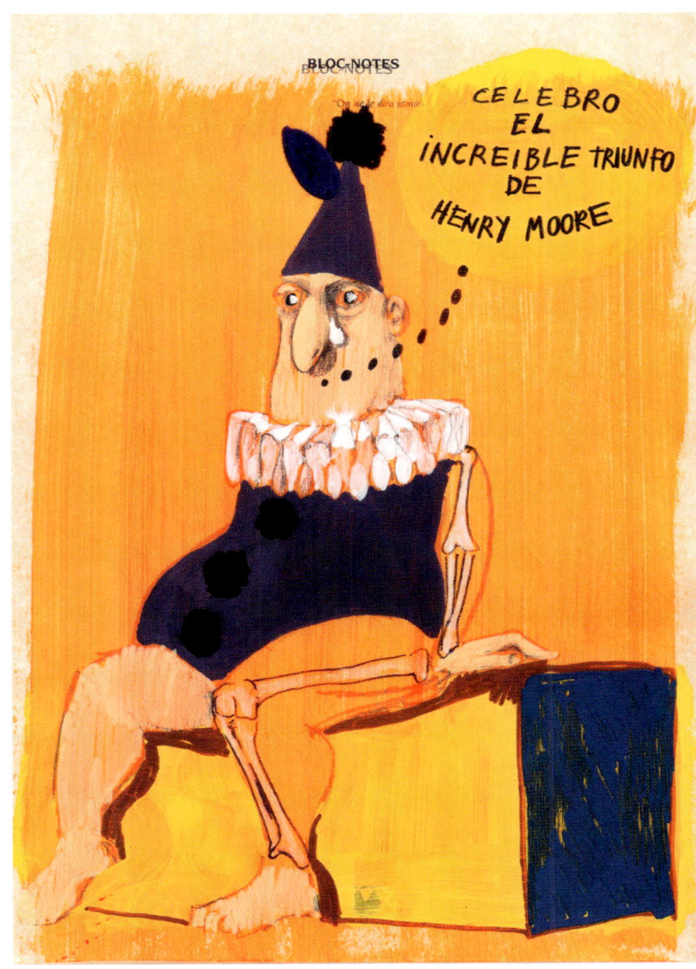

Abrazo 1, 1997-99
Mixed media on paper
30 x 22 cm

Síntesis de amor, 1997-99
Mixed media on paper
30 x 22 cm

Abrazo 2, 1997-99
Mixed media on paper
30 x 22 cm

El increíble triunfo, 1997-99
Mixed media on paper
50 x 35 cm

Nosotros somos contingentes, NY es necesario, 1997-99
Mixed media on paper
30 x 22 cm

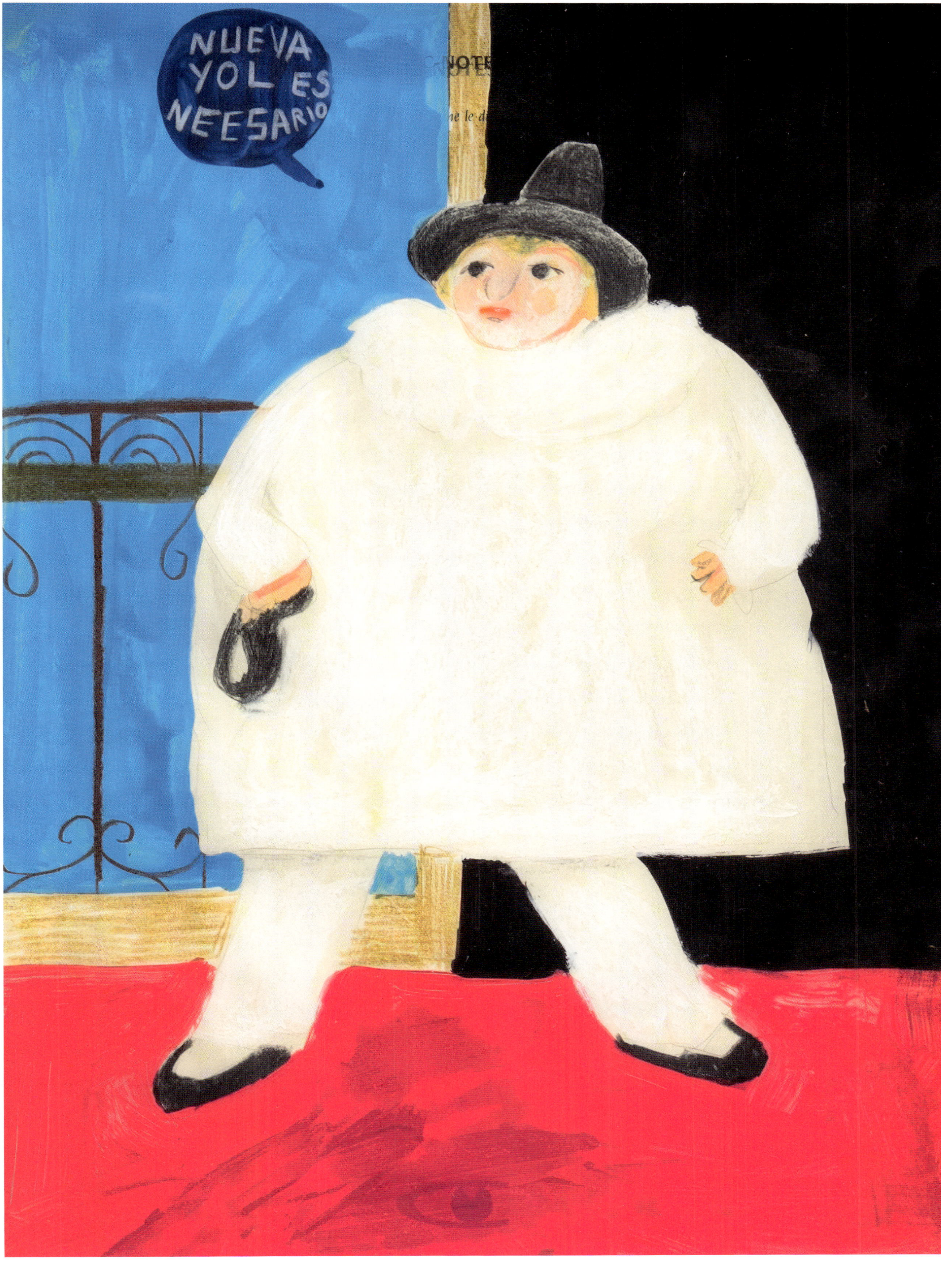
NUEVA YOL ES NEESARIO

Adhesive Capsulitis, 2020
Mixed media on paper
41,5 x 30 cm

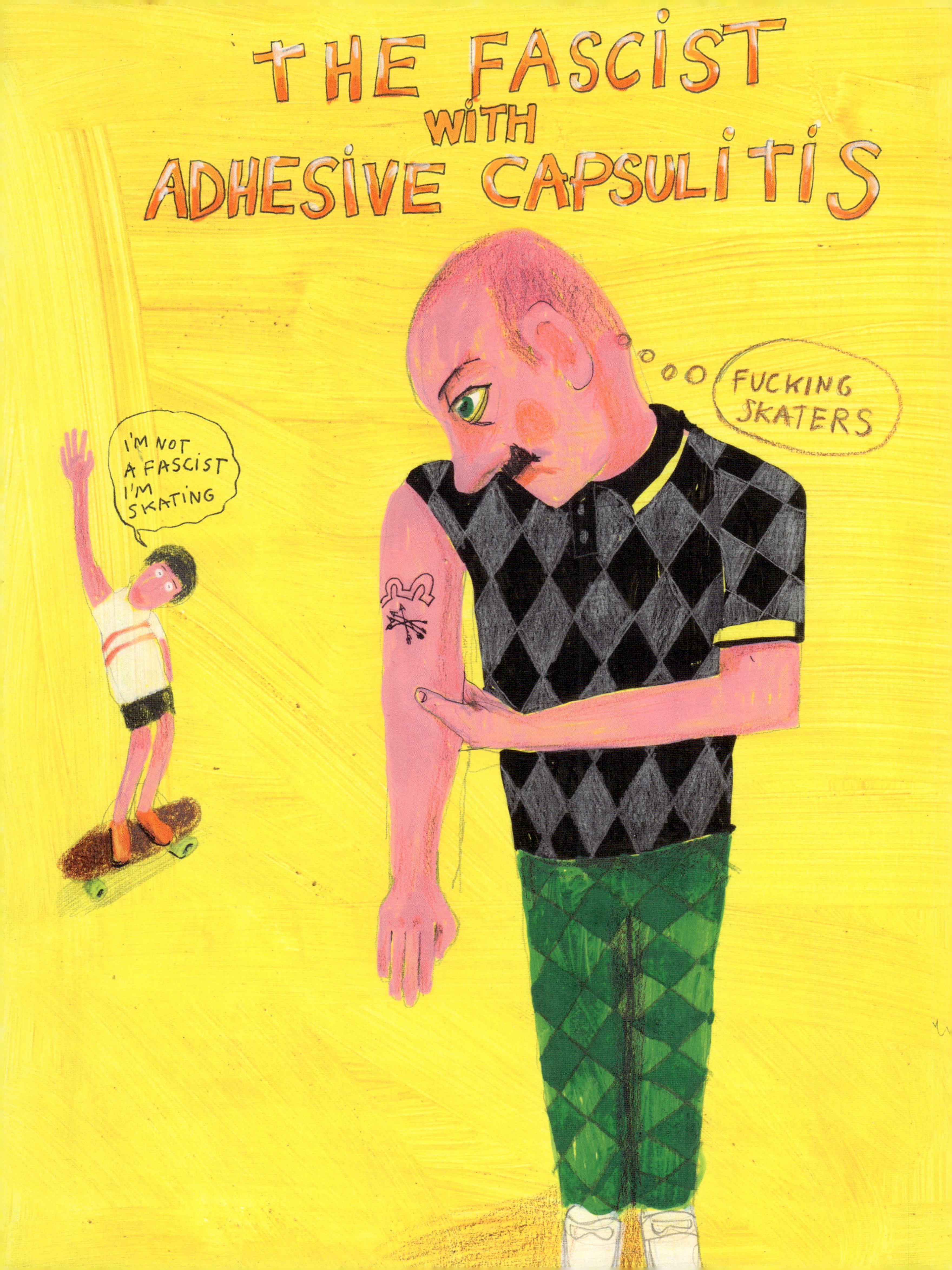
THE FASCIST WITH ADHESIVE CAPSULITIS
I'M NOT A FASCIST I'M SKATING
FUCKING SKATERS

Las fotos de Baudrillard, 1997-99
Mixed media on paper
30 x 22 cm

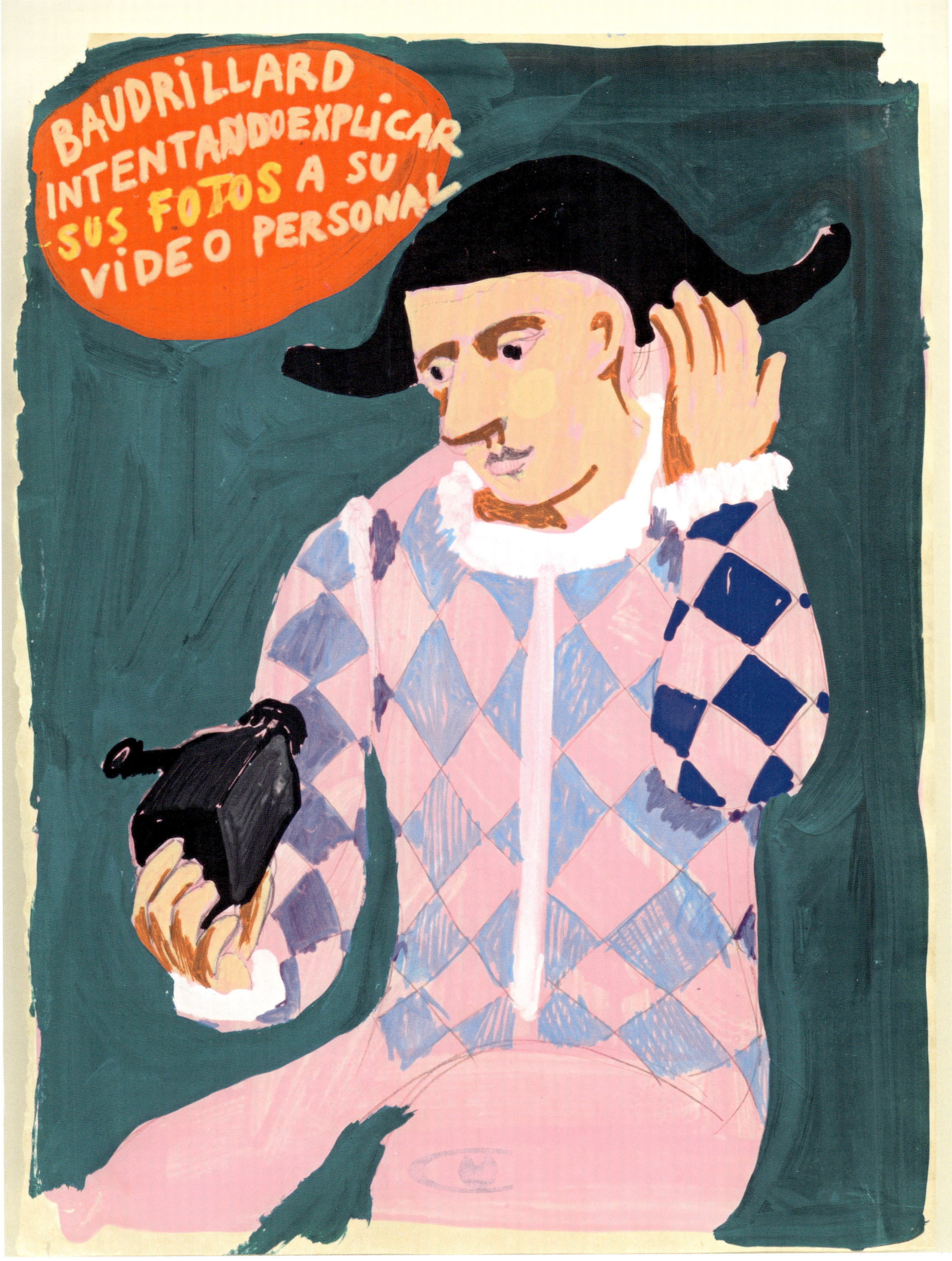
BAUDRILLARD
INTENTANDO EXPLICAR
SUS FOTOS A SU
VIDEO PERSONAL

Segurata, 1997-99
Mixed media on paper
30 x 22 cm

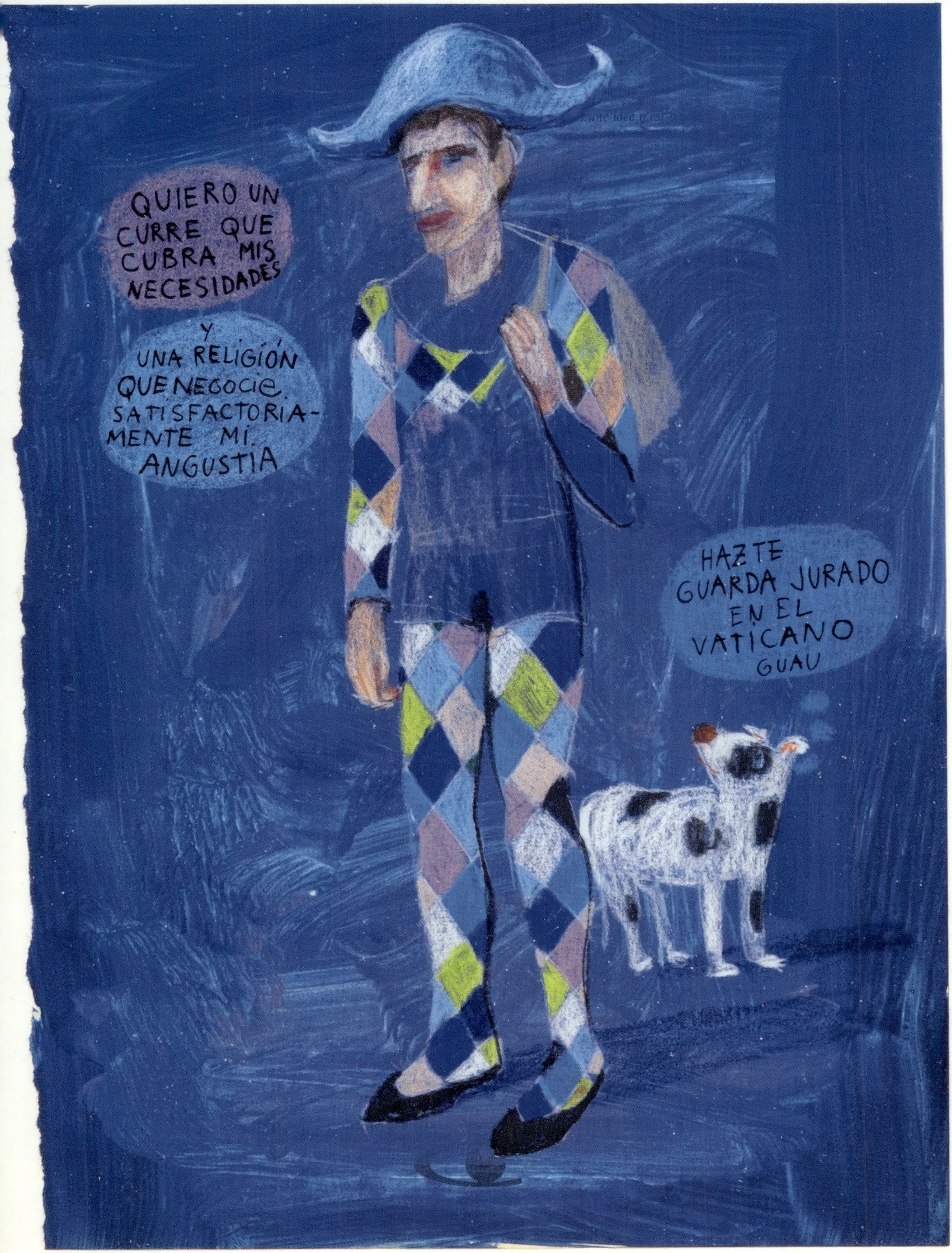
QUIERO UN CURRE QUE CUBRA MIS NECESIDADES
Y UNA RELIGIÓN QUE NEGOCIE SATISFACTORIA-MENTE MI ANGUSTIA
HAZTE GUARDA JURADO EN EL VATICANO GUAU

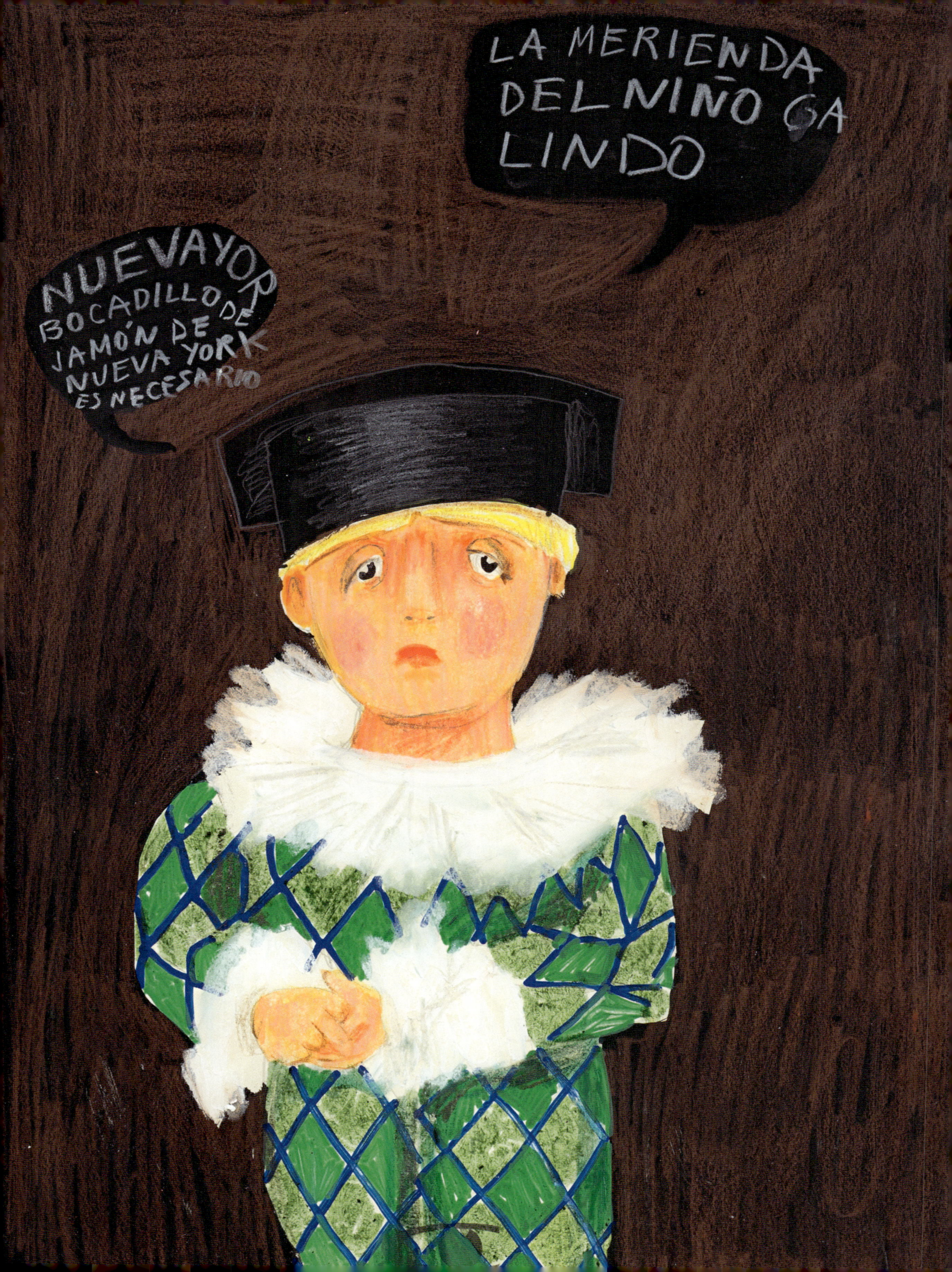
LA MERIENDA DEL NIÑO GA LINDO
NUEVAYOR BOCADILLO DE JAMÓN DE NUEVA YORK ES NECESARIO

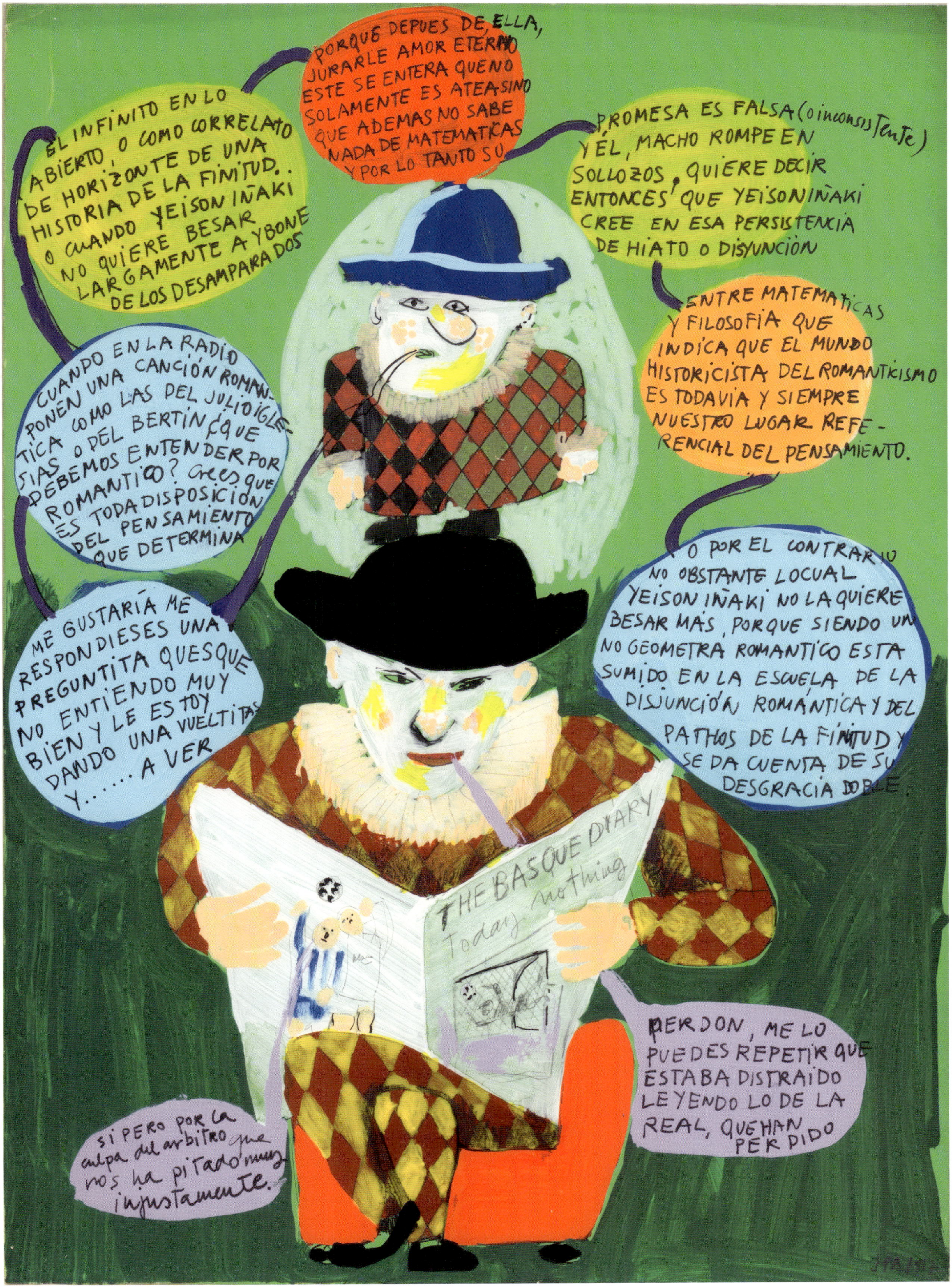
ME GUSTARÍA ME RESPONDIESES UNA PREGUNTITA QUESQUE NO ENTIENDO MUY BIEN Y LE ESTOY DANDO UNA VUELTITAS Y...... A VER
CUANDO EN LA RADIO PONEN UNA CANCIÓN ROMANTICA COMO LAS DEL JULIO IGLESIAS O DEL BERTIN ¿QUE DEBEMOS ENTENDER POR ROMANTICO? Crees que ES TODA DISPOSICIÓN DEL PENSAMIENTO QUE DETERMINA
EL INFINITO EN LO ABIERTO, O COMO CORRELATO DE HORIZONTE DE UNA HISTORIA DE LA FINITUD.. O CUANDO YEISON IÑAKI NO QUIERE BESAR LARGAMENTE A YBONE DE LOS DESAMPARADOS
PORQUE DEPUES DE ELLA, JURARLE AMOR ETERNO ESTE SE ENTERA QUE NO SOLAMENTE ES ATEA SINO QUE ADEMAS NO SABE NADA DE MATEMATICAS Y POR LO TANTO SU
PROMESA ES FALSA (o inconsistente) Y ÉL, MACHO ROMPE EN SOLLOZOS, QUIERE DECIR ENTONCES QUE YEISON IÑAKI CREE EN ESA PERSISTENCIA DE HIATO O DISYUNCIÓN
ENTRE MATEMATICAS Y FILOSOFIA QUE INDICA QUE EL MUNDO HISTORICISTA DEL ROMANTICISMO ES TODAVIA Y SIEMPRE NUESTRO LUGAR REFERENCIAL DEL PENSAMIENTO.
O POR EL CONTRARIO NO OBSTANTE LO CUAL YEISON IÑAKI NO LA QUIERE BESAR MÁS, PORQUE SIENDO UN NO GEOMETRA ROMANTICO ESTA SUMIDO EN LA ESCUELA DE LA DISJUNCIÓN ROMÁNTICA Y DEL PATHOS DE LA FINITUD Y SE DA CUENTA DE SU DESGRACIA DOBLE.
THE BASQUE DIARY
Today nothing
PERDON, ME LO PUEDES REPETIR QUE ESTABA DISTRAIDO LEYENDO LO DE LA REAL, QUE HAN PERDIDO
Si pero por la culpa del arbitro que nos ha pitado muy injustamente.

p. 58
La merienda, 1997-99
Mixed media on paper
30 x 22 cm

p. 59
Romántico distraído, 1997-99
Mixed media on paper
41,5 x 30 cm

Deseo, 1997-99
Mixed media on paper
30 x 22 cm

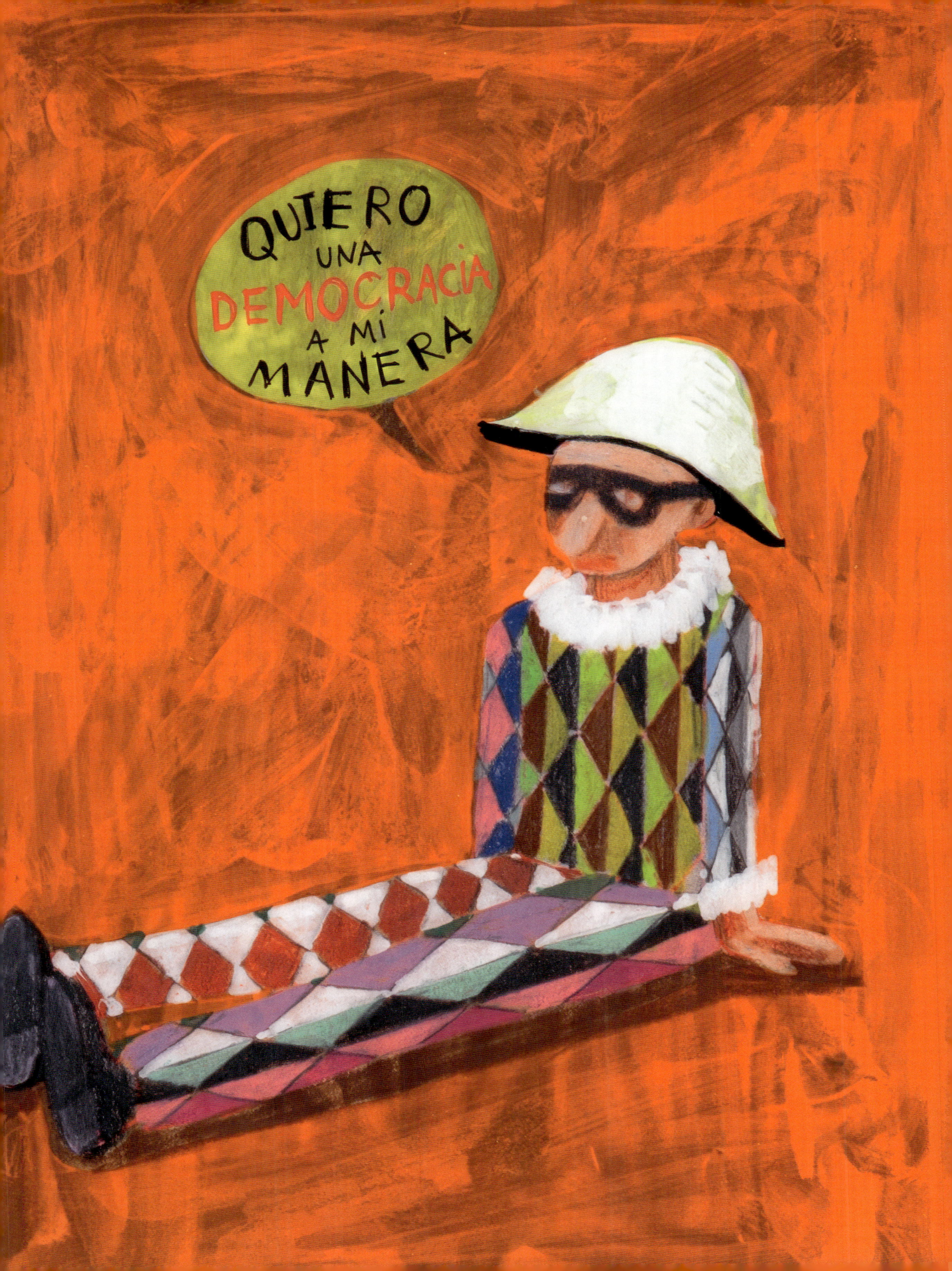
QUIERO UNA DEMOCRACIA A MÍ MANERA

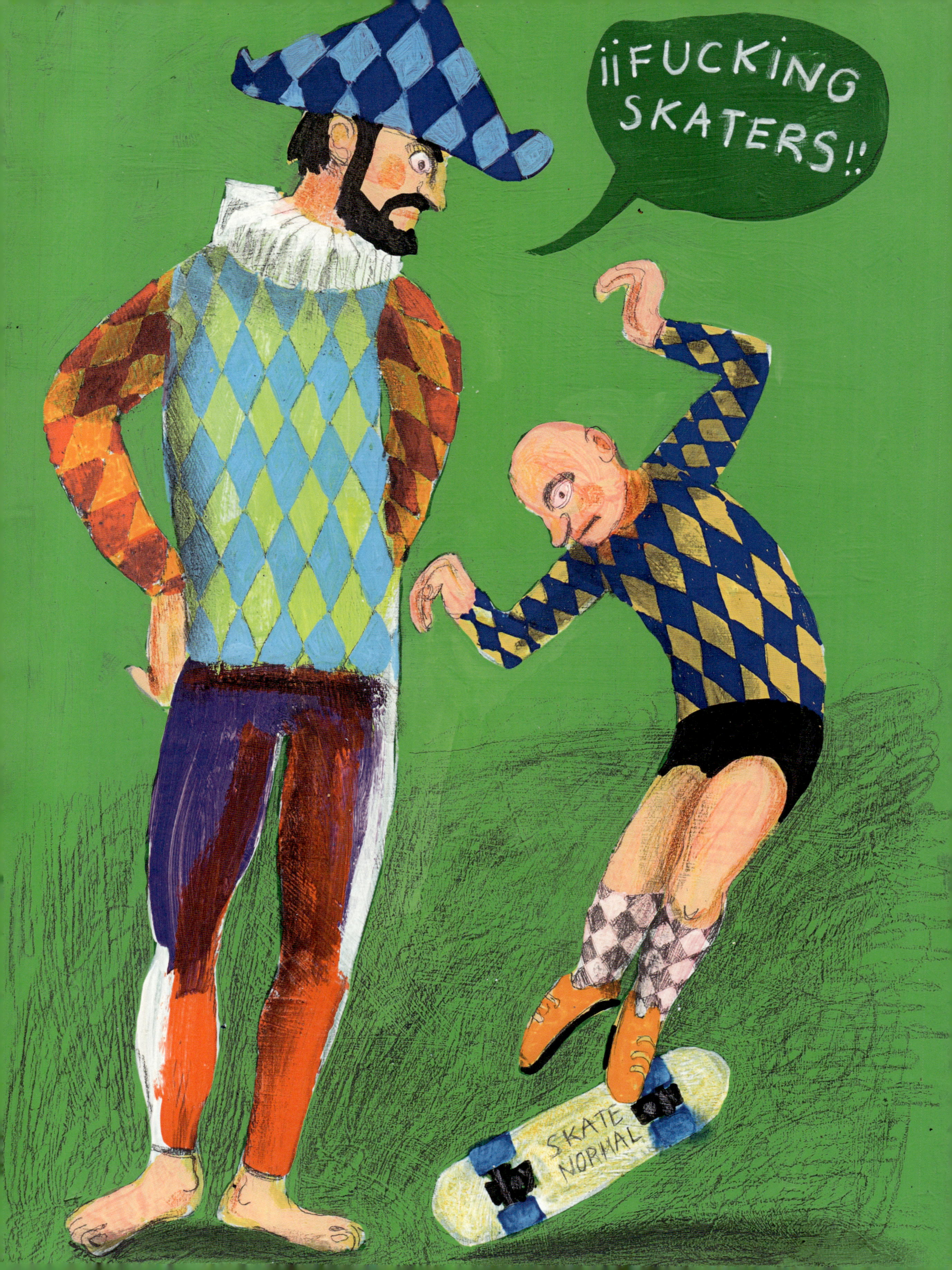
¡¡FUCKING SKATERS!!
SKATE NORMAL

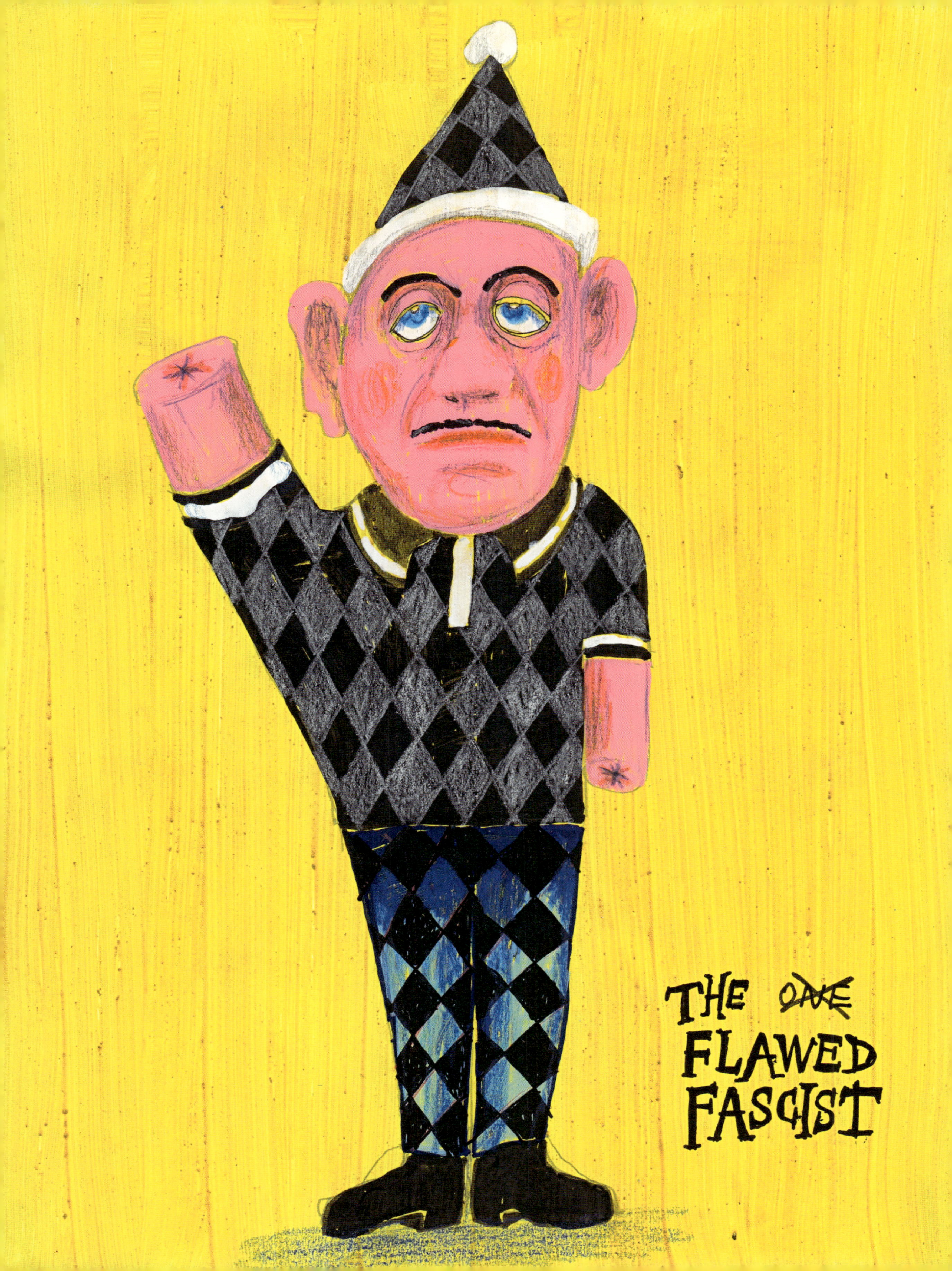
THE ~~ONE~~
FLAWED
FASCIST

p. 62
Fucking Skaters, 2020
Mixed media on paper
41,5 x 30 cm

p. 63
Defecto de fábrica, 2020
Mixed media on paper
41,5 x 30 cm

Il faut se décider, 1997-99
Mixed media on paper
30 x 22 cm

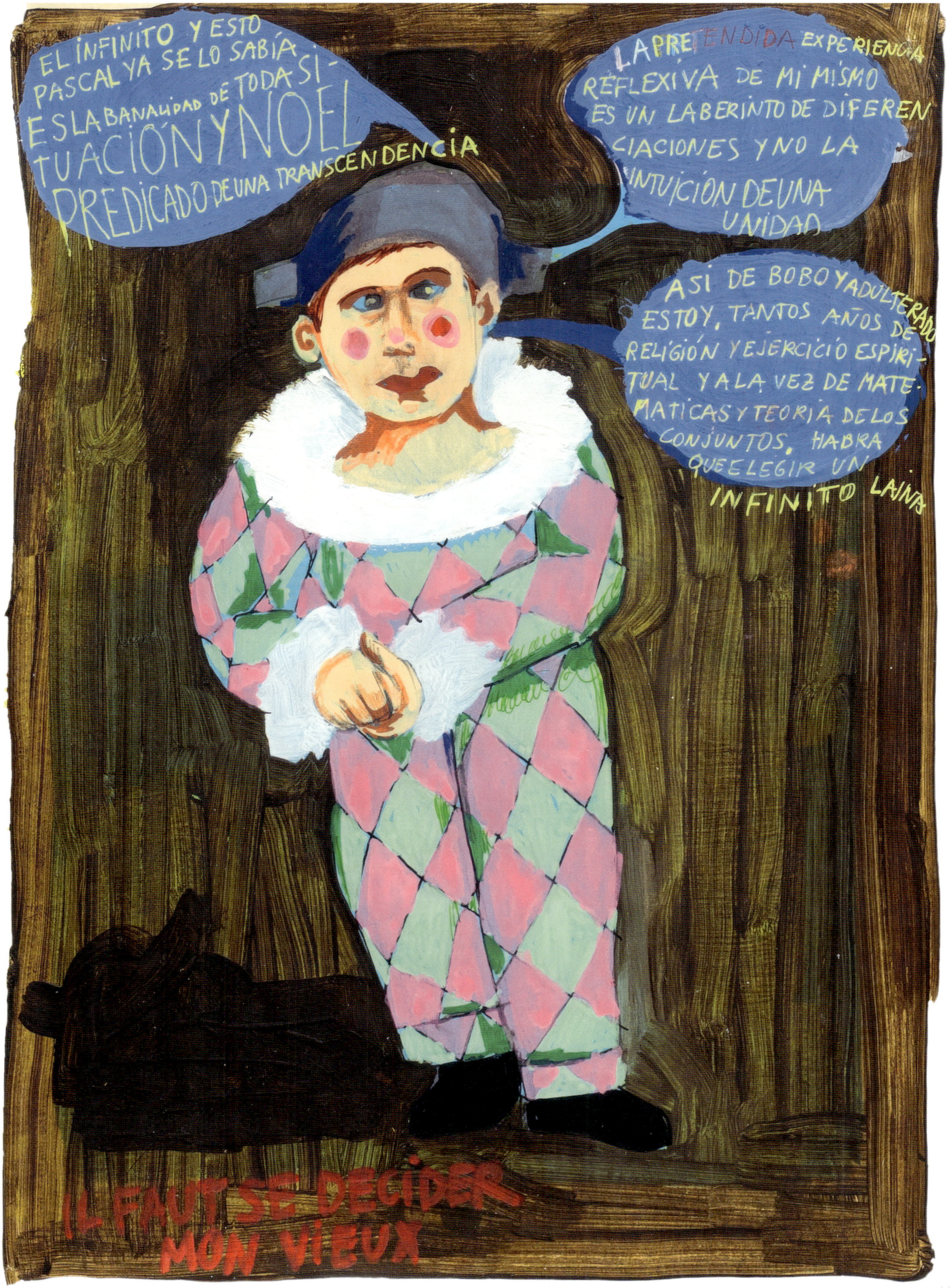
EL INFINITO Y ESTO PASCAL YA SE LO SABÍA ES LA BANALIDAD DE TODA SI-TUACIÓN Y NO EL PREDICADO DE UNA TRANSCENDENCIA
LA PRETENDIDA EXPERIENCIA REFLEXIVA DE MI MISMO ES UN LABERINTO DE DIFEREN CIACIONES Y NO LA INTUICIÓN DE UNA UNIDAD
ASÍ DE BOBO Y ADULTERADO ESTOY, TANTOS AÑOS DE RELIGIÓN Y EJERCICIO ESPIRI-TUAL Y A LA VEZ DE MATE-MATICAS Y TEORIA DE LOS CONJUNTOS. HABRA QUE ELEGIR UN INFINITO LAINA
IL FAUT SE DECIDER MON VIEUX

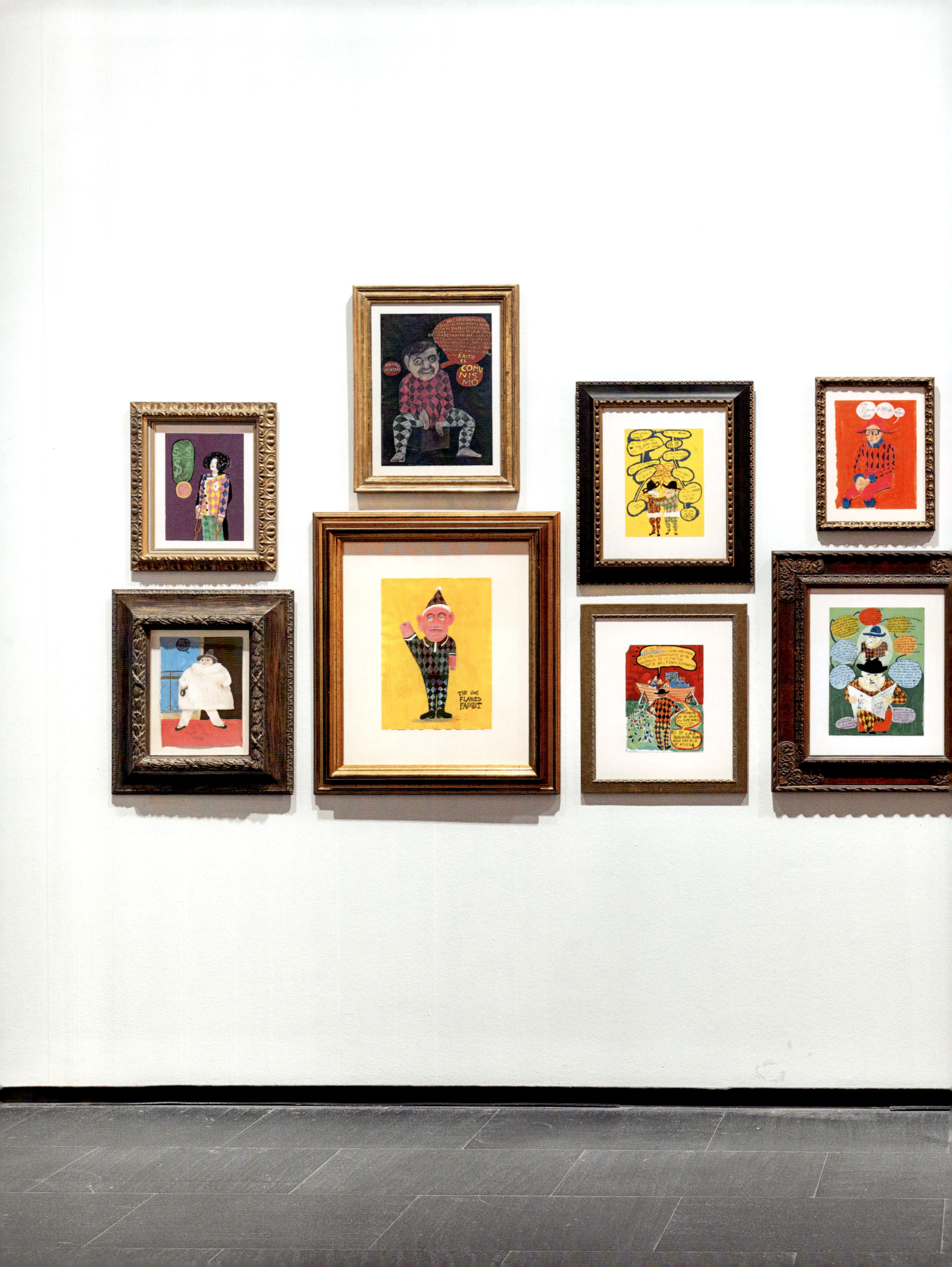
ÉXITO EL COMUNISMO
THE FLAWED FASCIST

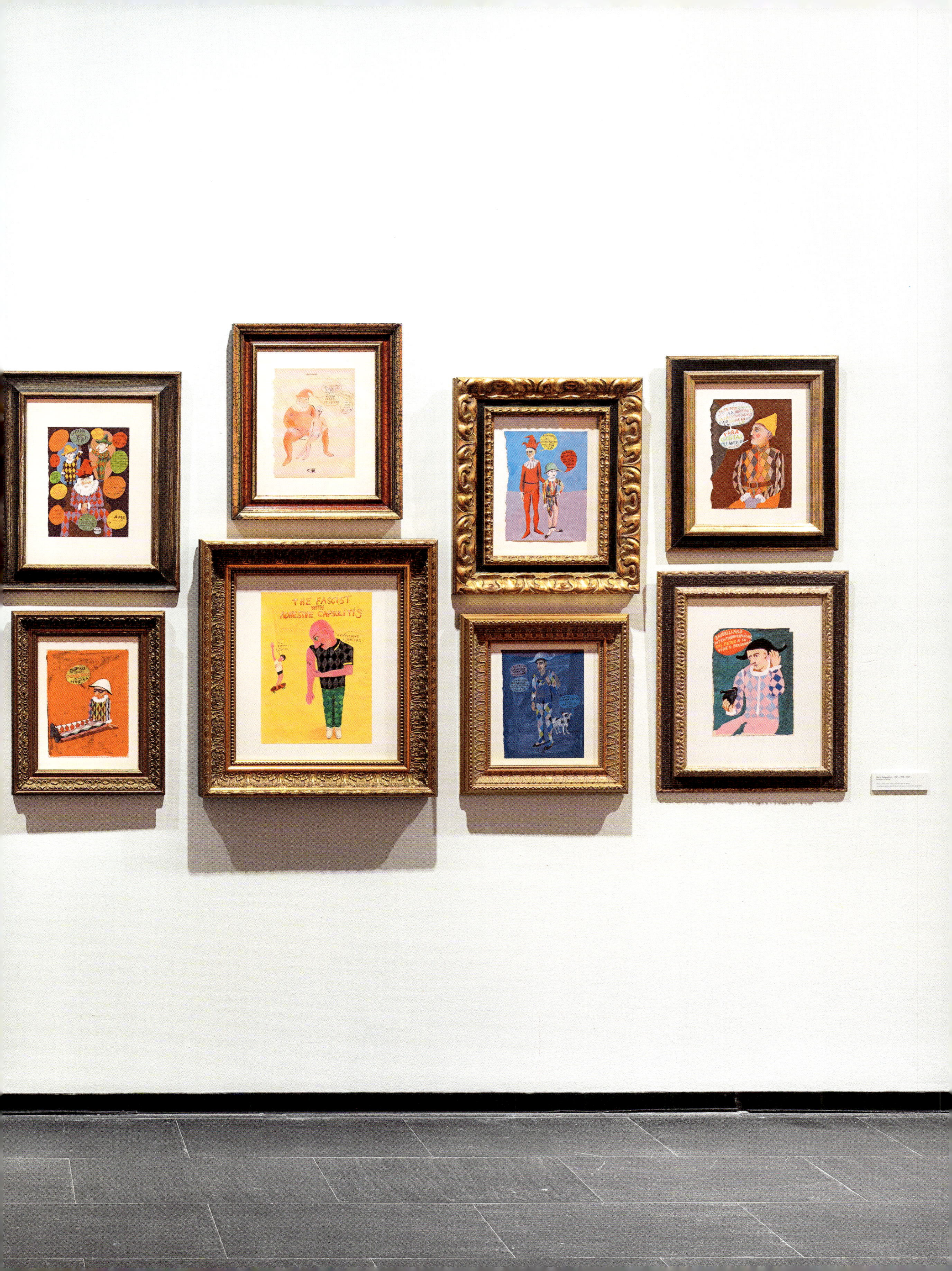
THE FASCIST
WITH
ADHESIVE CAPSULITIS

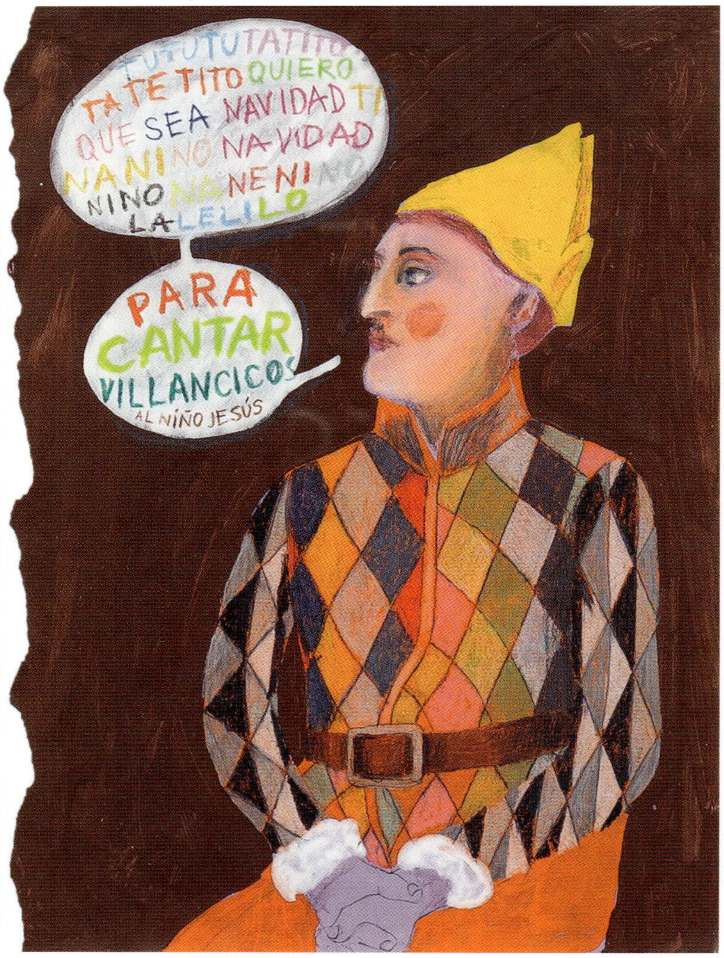

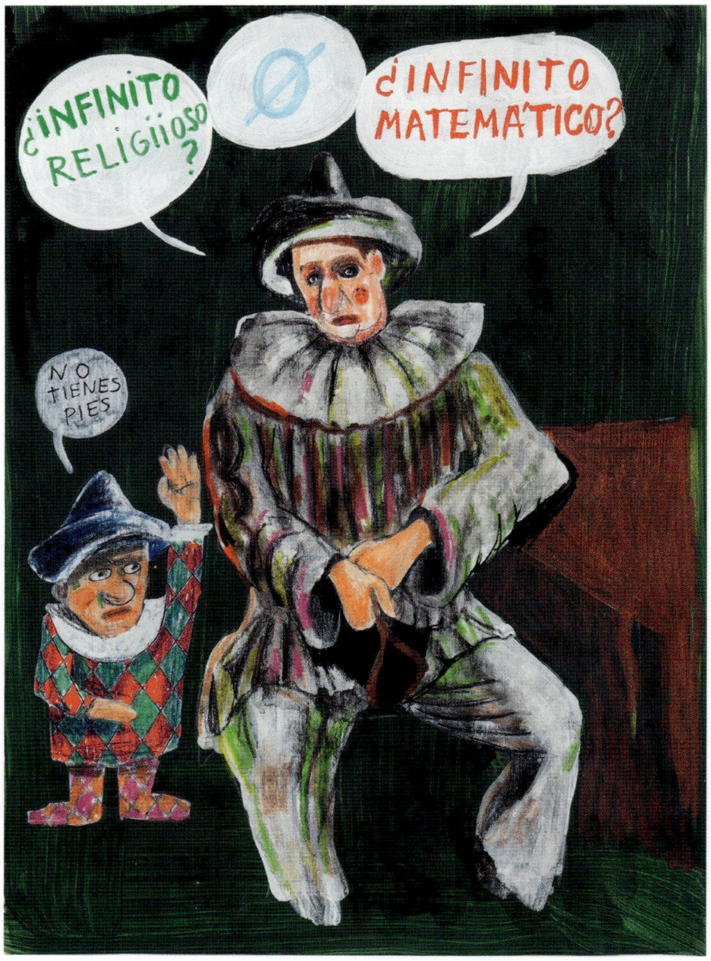

Un tonto de Navidad, 1997-99
Mixed media on paper
30 x 22 cm

No Feet, 1997-99
Mixed media on paper
30 x 22 cm

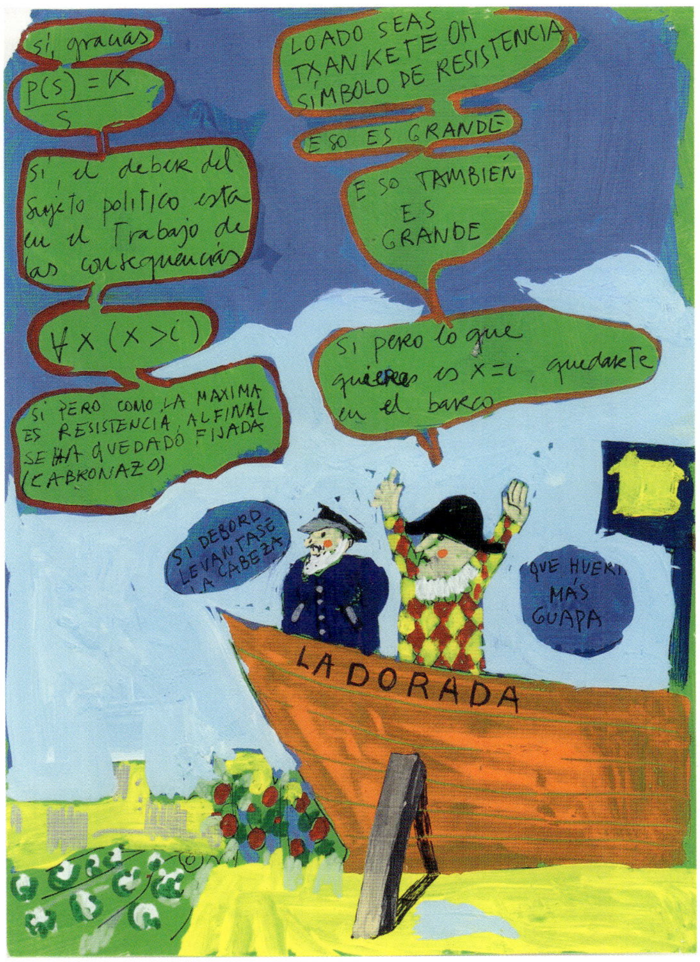

Política de la marisma, 1997-99
Mixed media on paper
30 x 22 cm

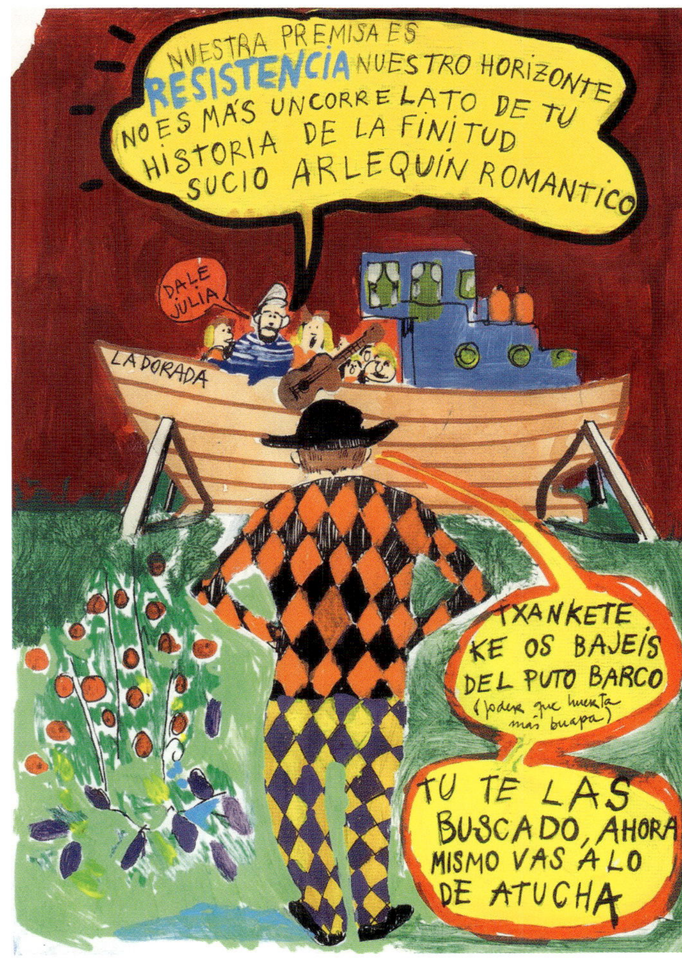

Política de la huerta, 1997-99
Mixed media on paper
30 x 22 cm

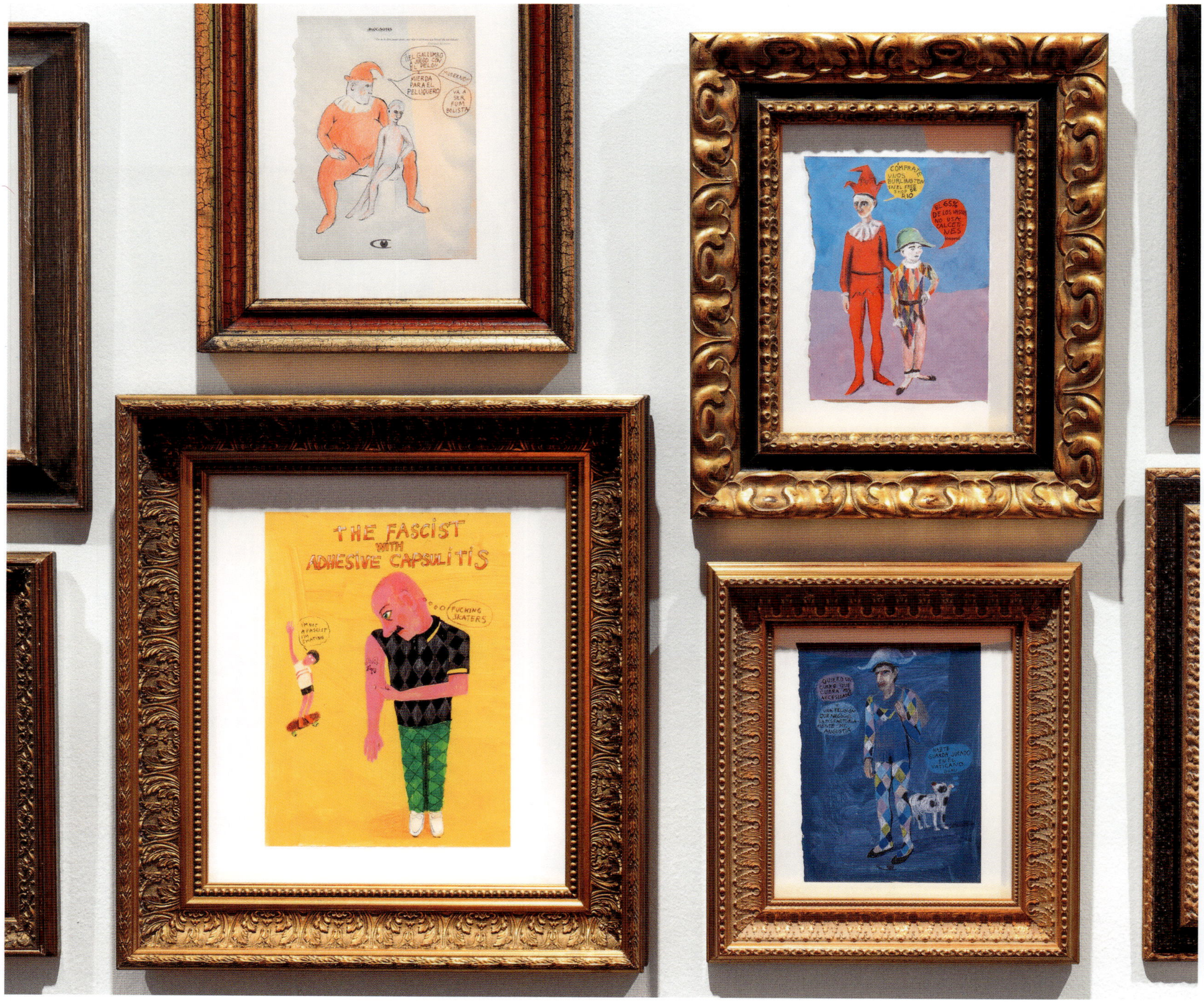

p. 71
Estadísticas, 1997-99
Mixed media on paper
30 x 22 cm

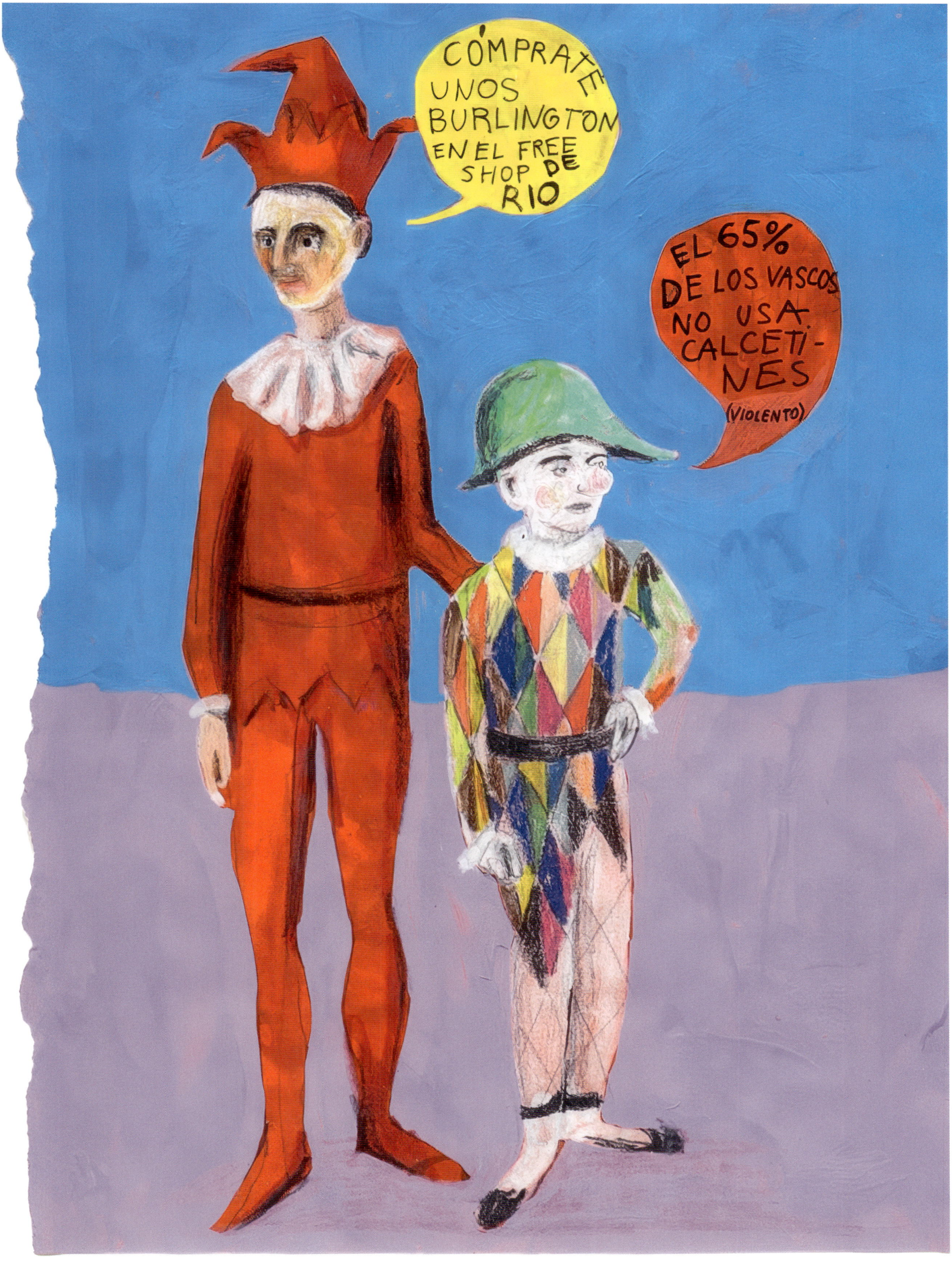
CÓMPRATE UNOS BURLINGTON EN EL FREE SHOP DE RIO
EL 65% DE LOS VASCOS NO USA CALCETINES (VIOLENTO)

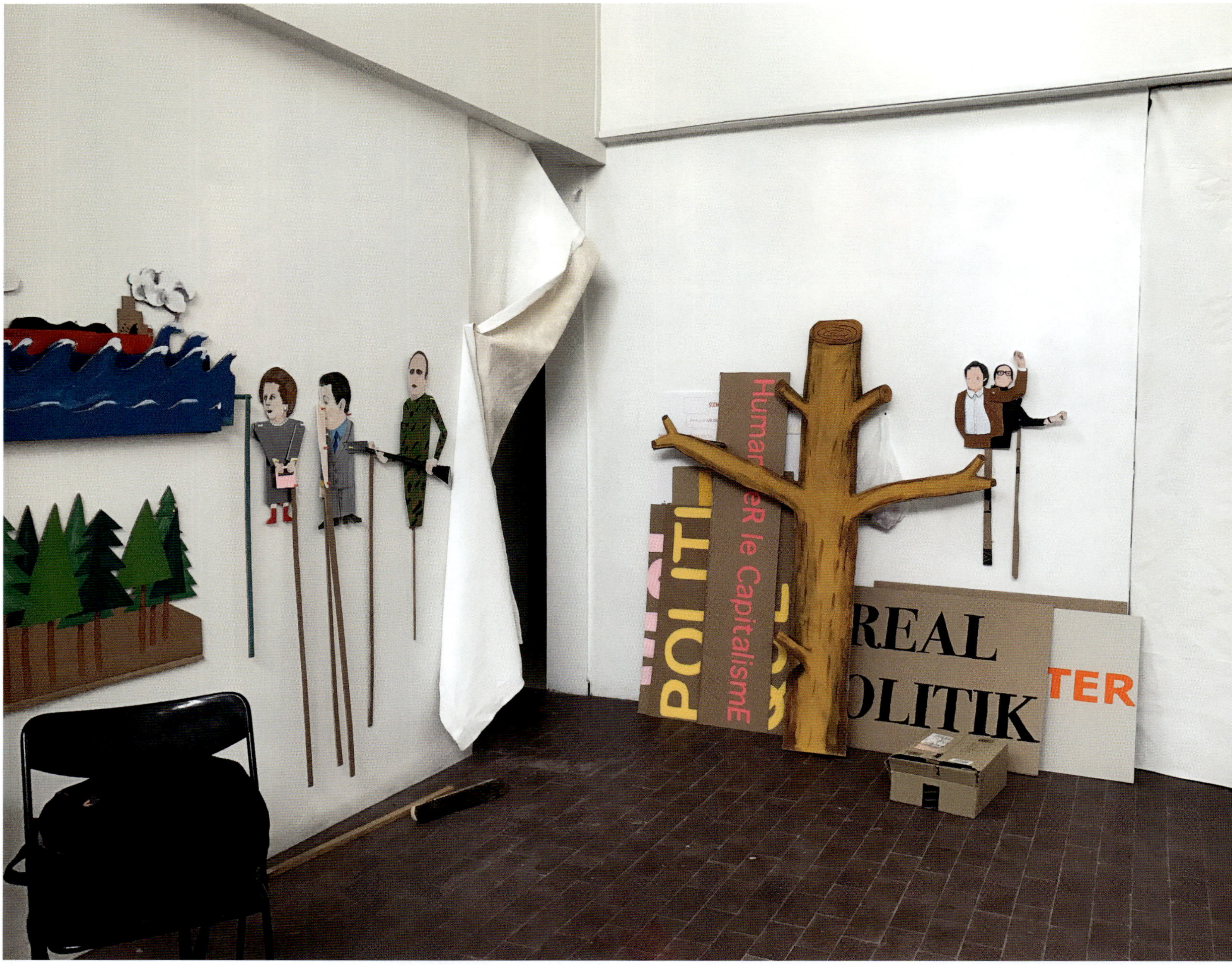

Material from the filming of the video *Caveman*, 2017-24
Studio, Belleville, Paris

The thread running through this video is the myth of the cave and its play of shadows from Book VII of Plato's *Republic*. It reflects on the nature of representation, on how we see things and how they are in reality, on education and the lack thereof.

The images of the cave are interspersed with four puppetry scenes based on pathetic events in our recent history.

1.
Socialism or death. Just like Rubén Darío in *Bohemian Lights*, two prominent socialist leaders in corduroy jackets cross through a cemetery with their left fists raised.

2.
Margaret Thatcher: "TINA". The alternative consisted of breaking the coalminers' strike by importing coal from Jaruzelski's Poland.

3.
In a speech he gave in Toulon in 2008, Nicolas Sarkozy said that "capitalism has betrayed capitalism." What was his solution? To make capitalism more humane!!! But is there anything more humane than capitalism?

4.
As the king *emeritus* said on returning from his hunt: "I'm very sorry. I made a mistake and it won't happen again."
It's 2025 and we are still living in a country with a feudal structure.

Caveman, 2017-24
Video
8 min 42 sec

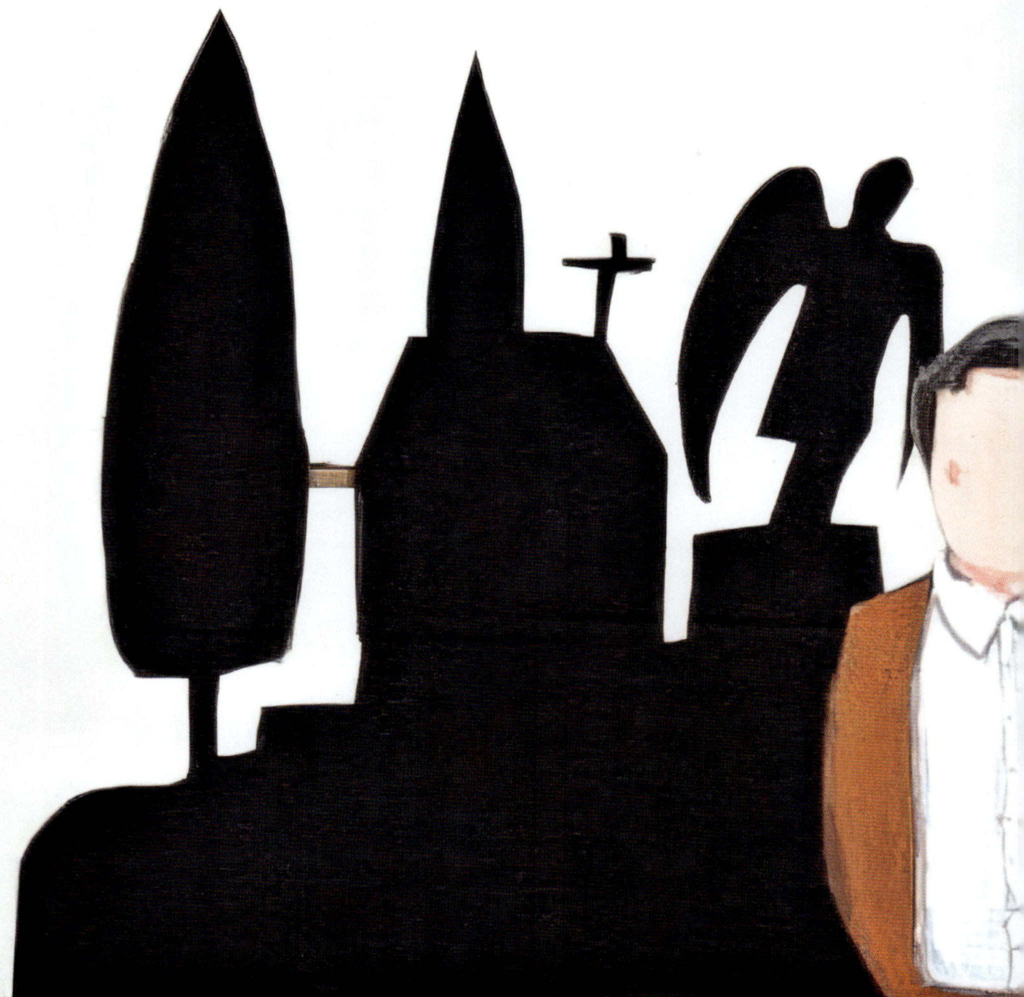

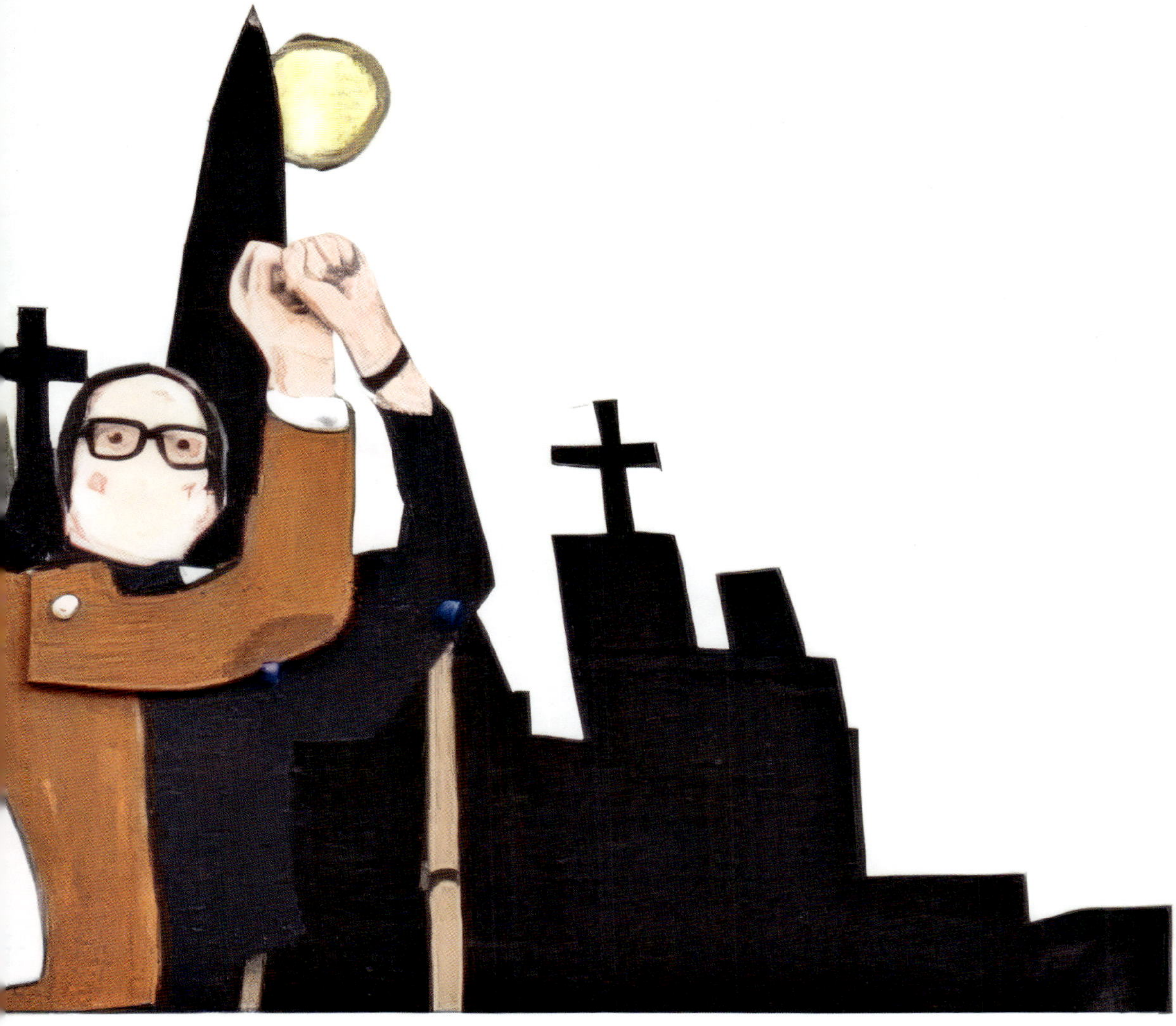

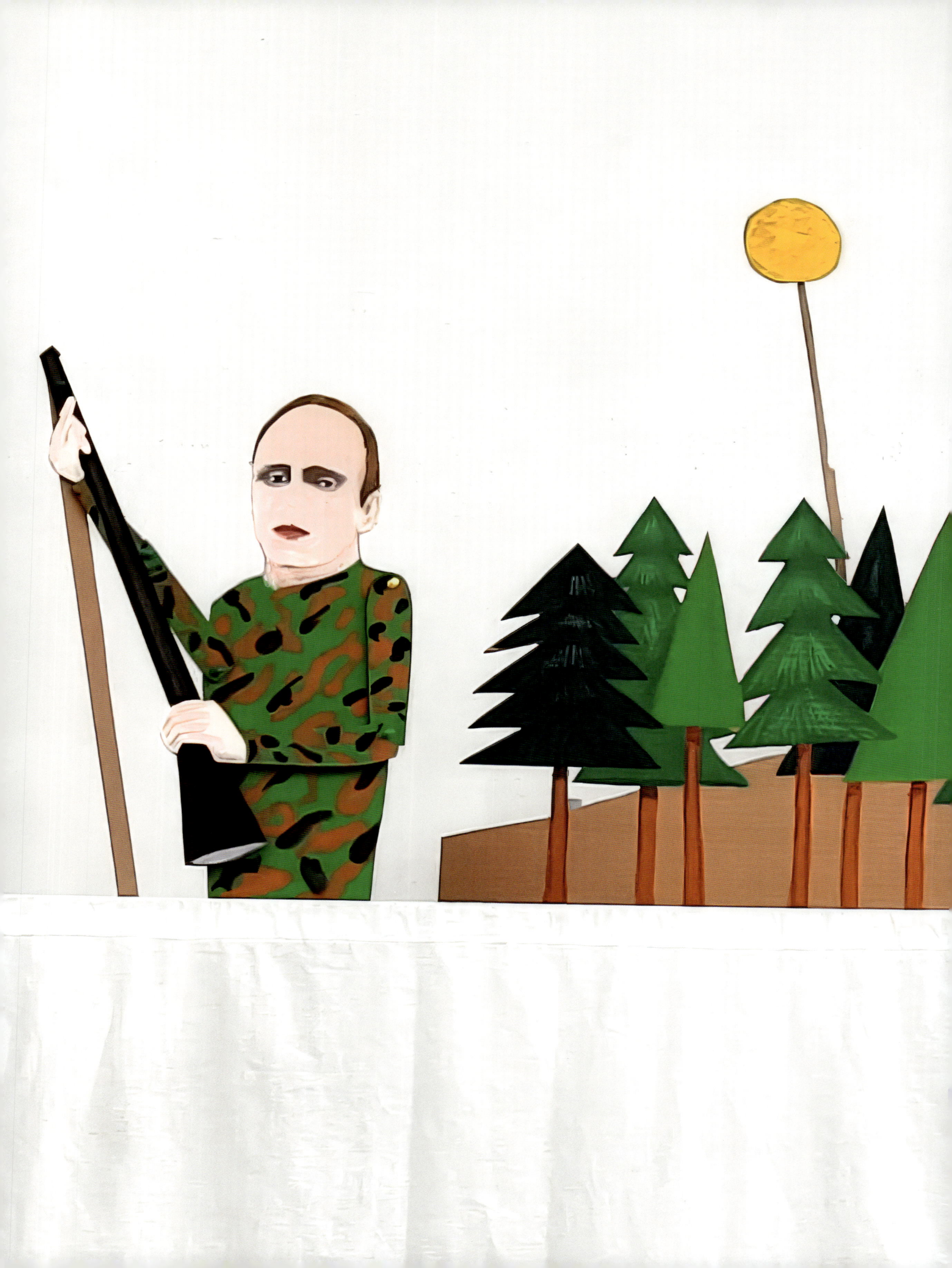

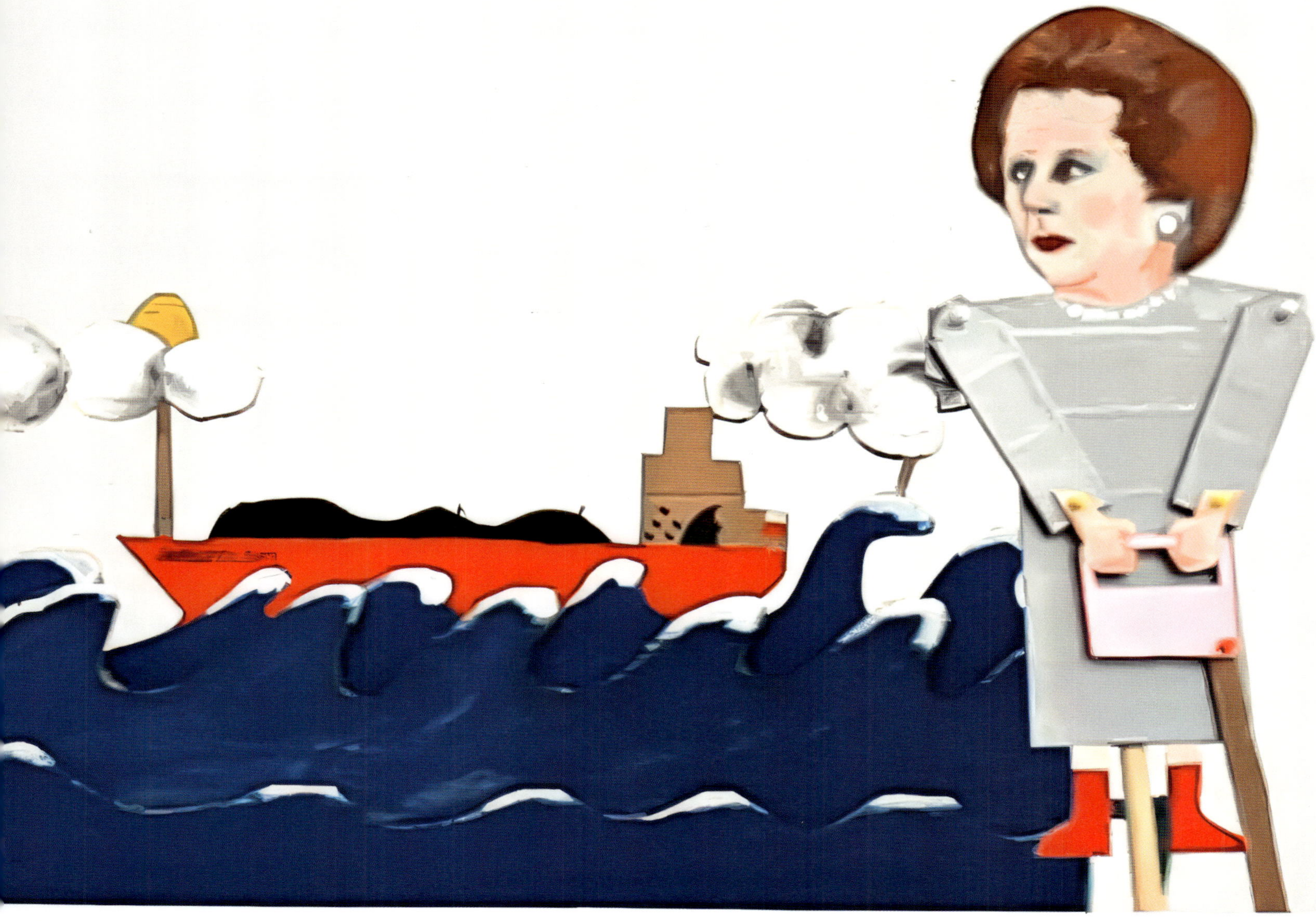

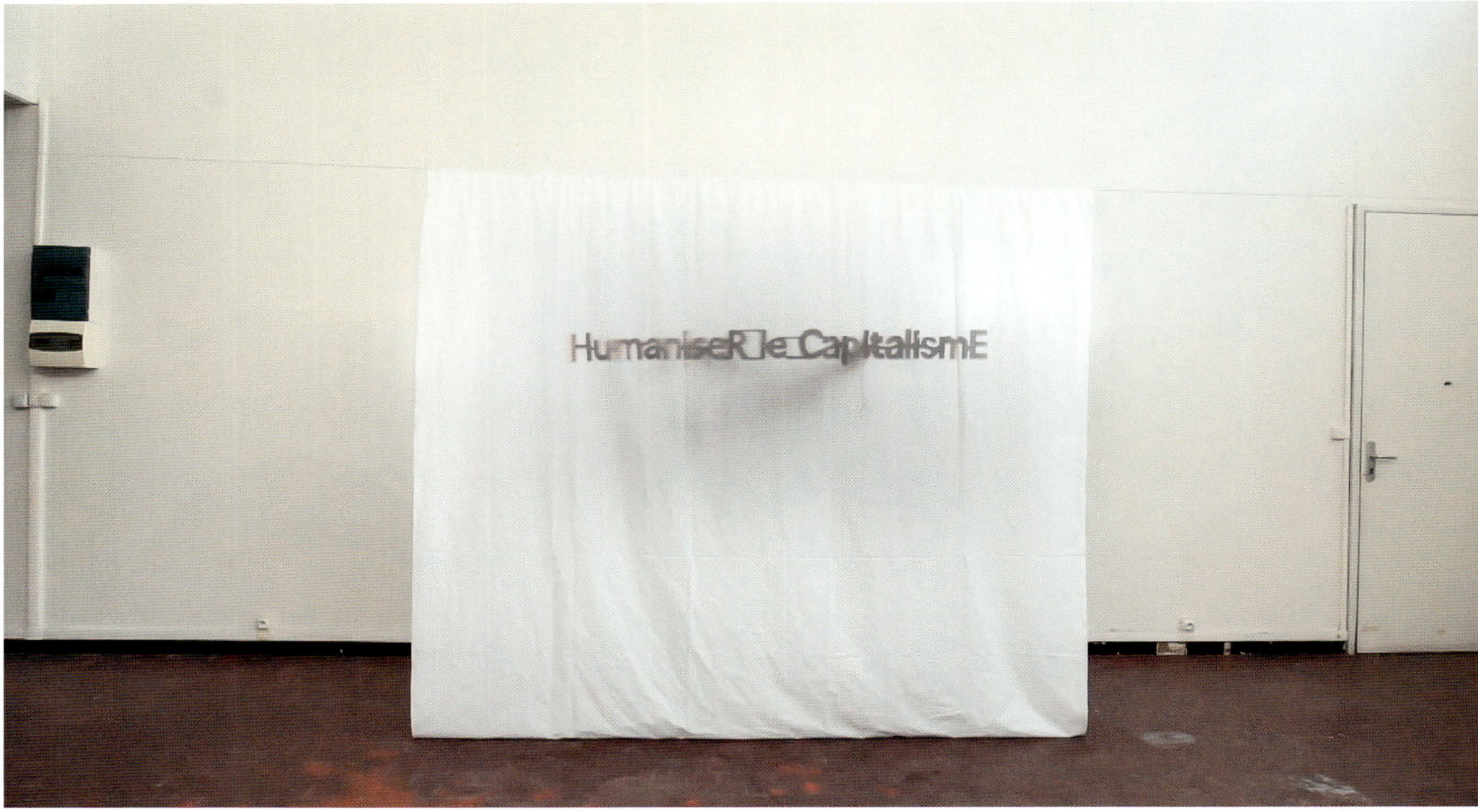
HumaniseR le CapitalismE

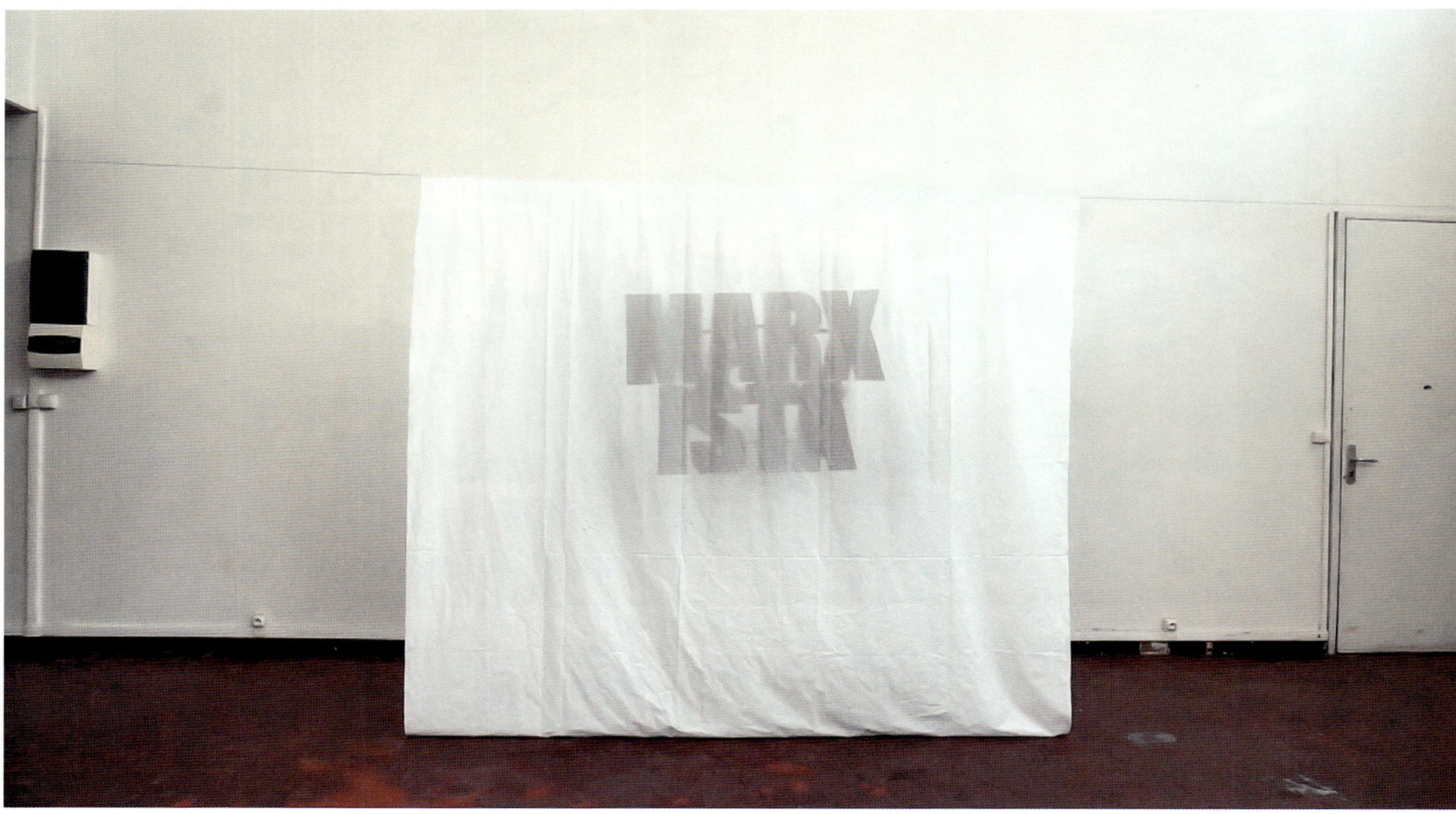

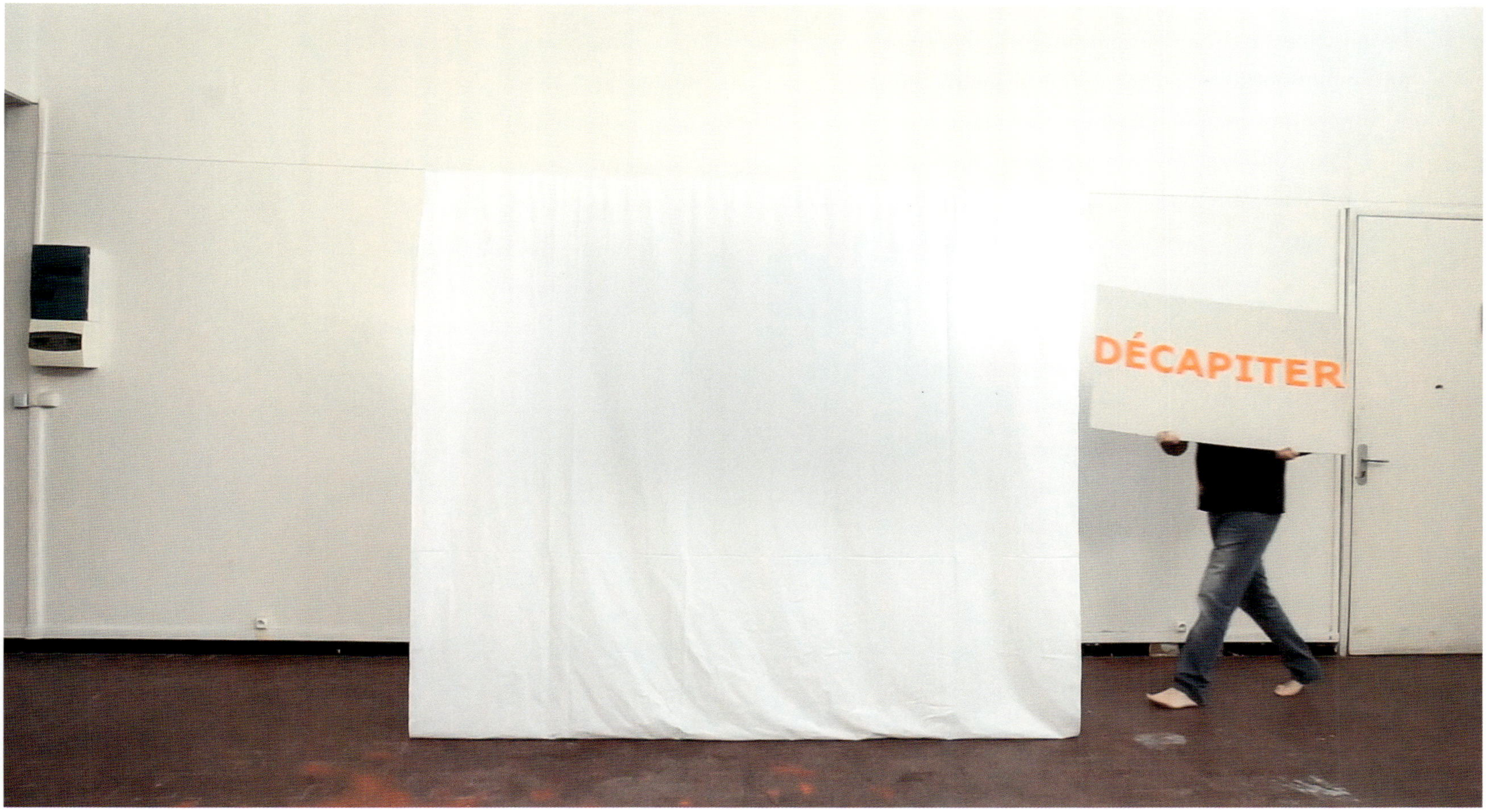
DÉCAPITER

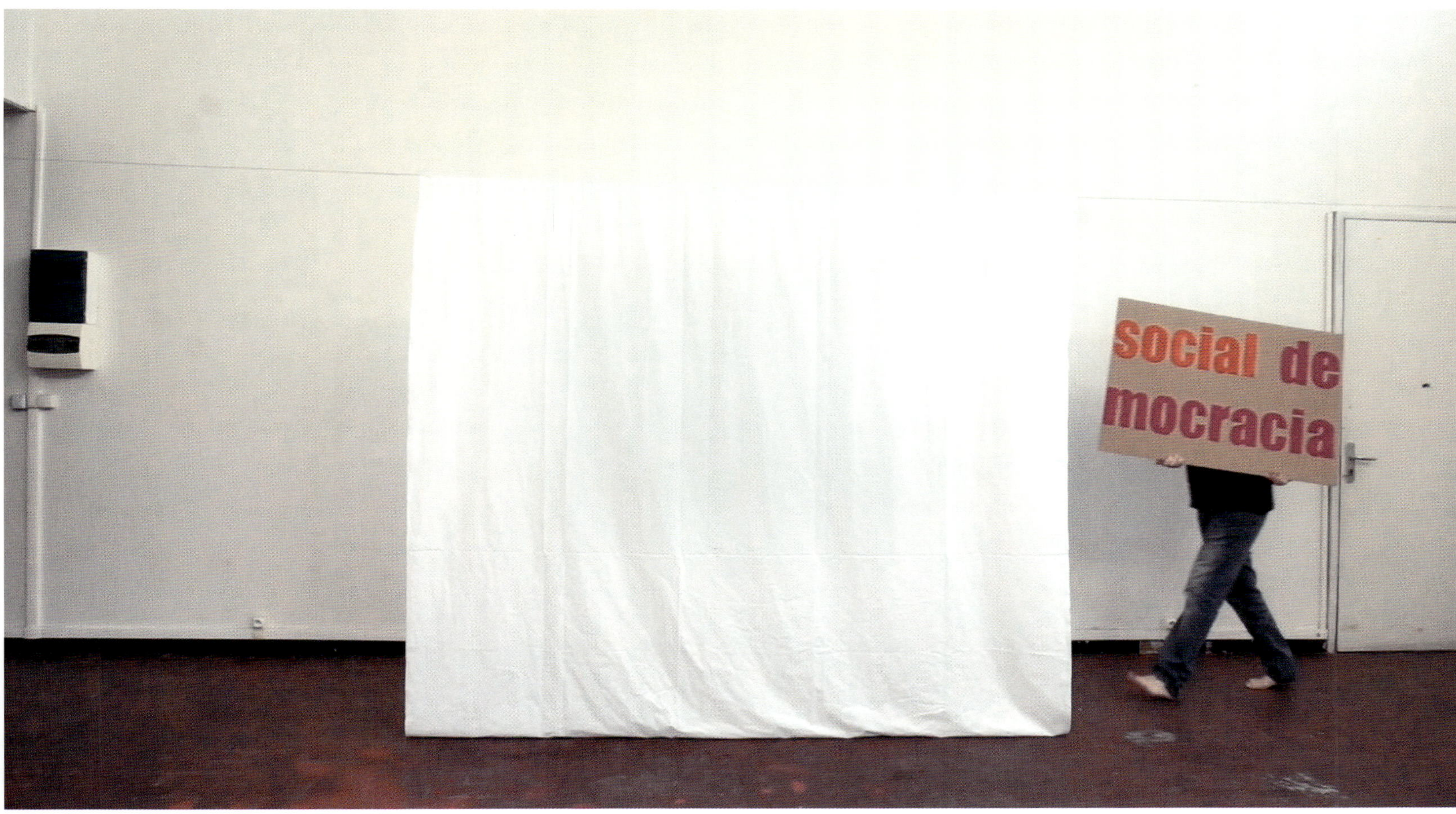
social de
mocracia

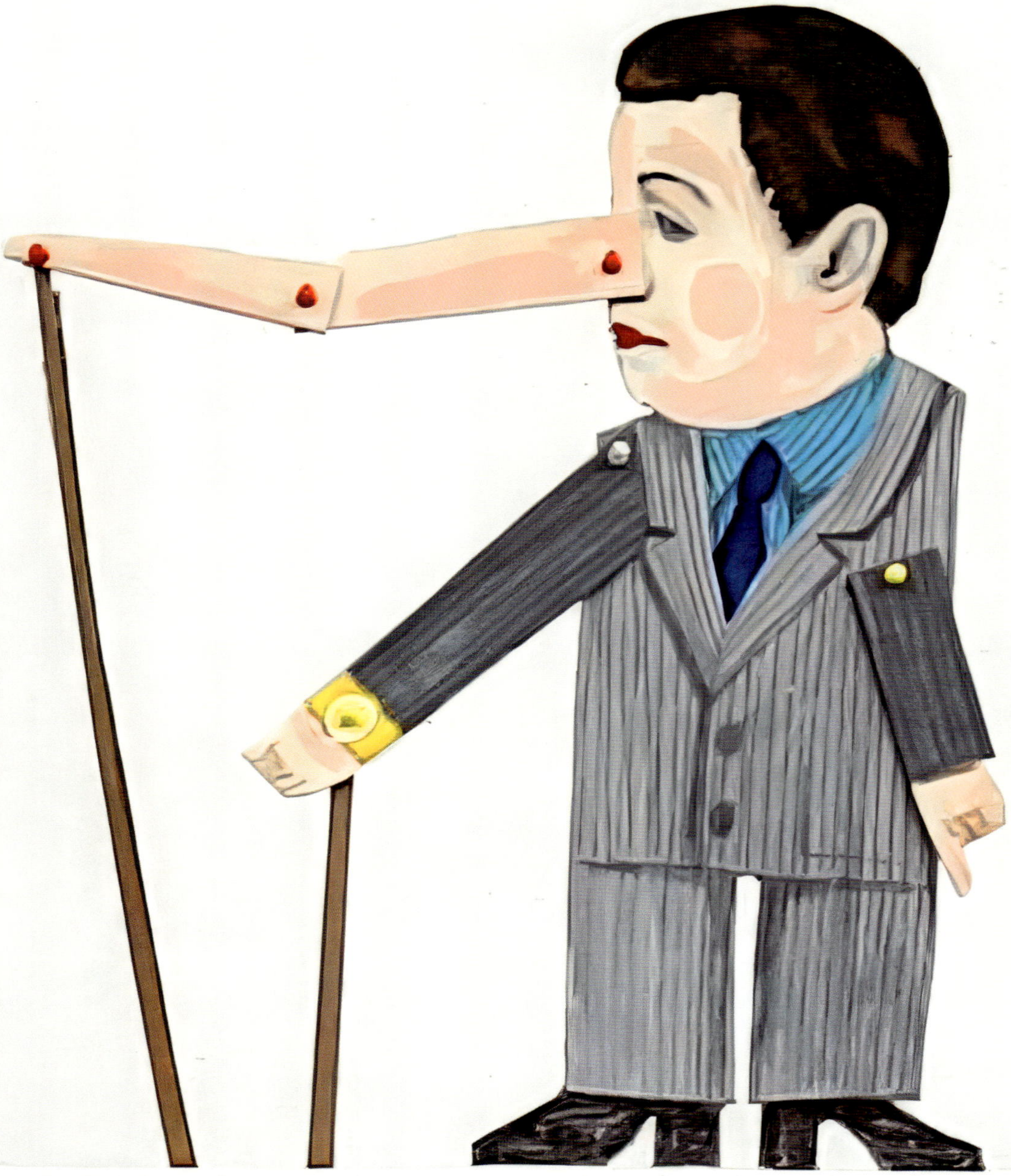

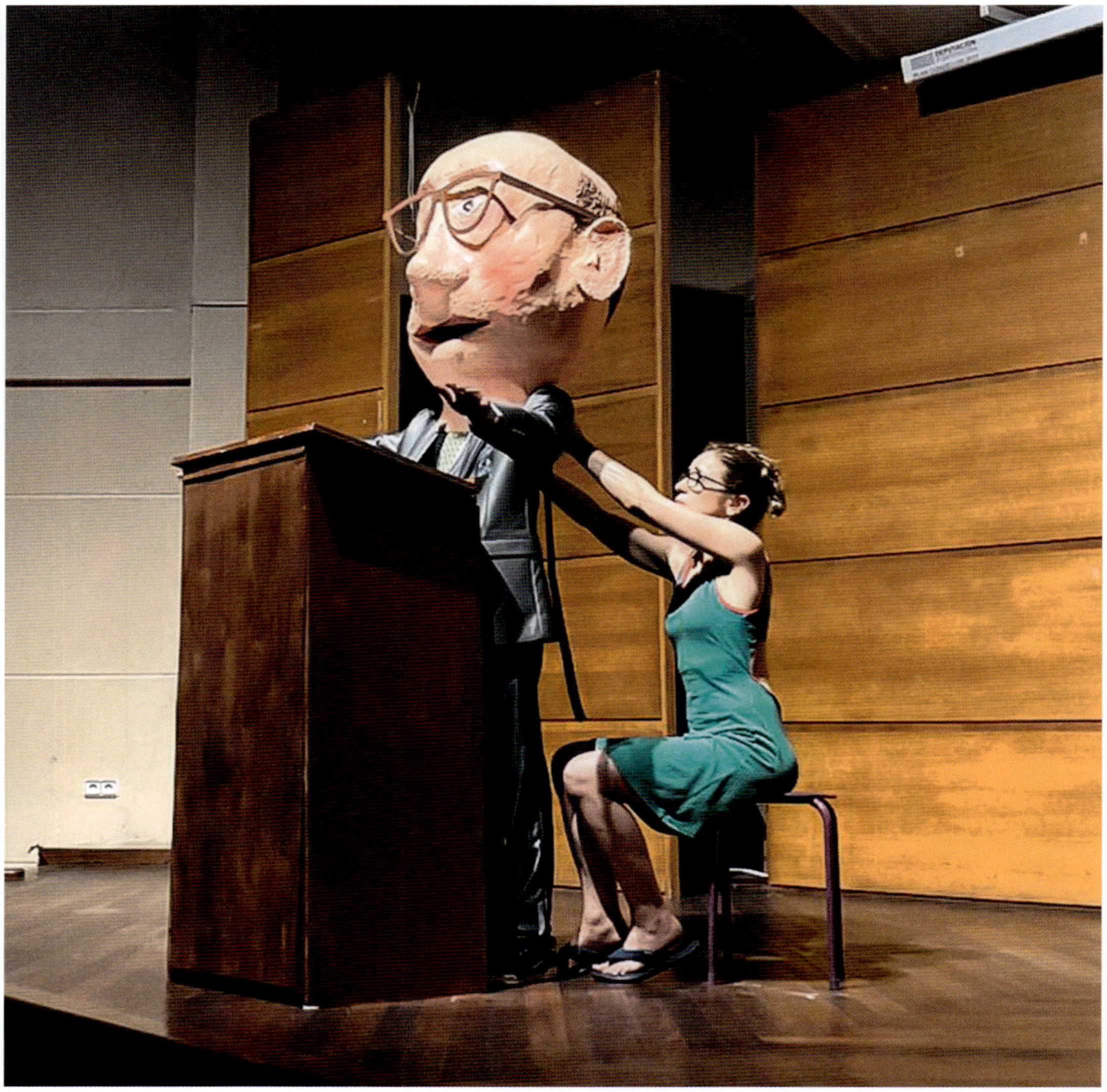

UNDESIRABLE ALIENS

1. *MIRACLE MIRACLE*

The title of this video, *Undesirable Aliens*, refers to the people who neither belonged to nor were included in the territory of The Netherlands before the Second World War.

The idea came to me while reading a passage in Hannah Arendt's *The Origins of Totalitarianism* that blew me away because it could have been talking about today and, sadly, about tomorrow.

She was referring to the Panama papers – not the more recent affair, but a nineteenth-century political corruption scandal during the French Third Republic that led to the ruin of many small investors – and basically said that you could get away with robbing by calling yourself patriots, whitewashing your friends and accomplices, offering people a scapegoat and handing them a flag.

The work is divided into three chapters.

The first chapter is called *Miracle, Miracle*.
This scene recreates Milton Friedman's lecture at Cornell University in 1980 called "Is Capitalism Humane?", inspired in turn by Leonard Read's lecture "I, Pencil", a paean to the global marketplace among people who do not know each other.

Miracle Miracle, 2020
Video
20 min 12 sec

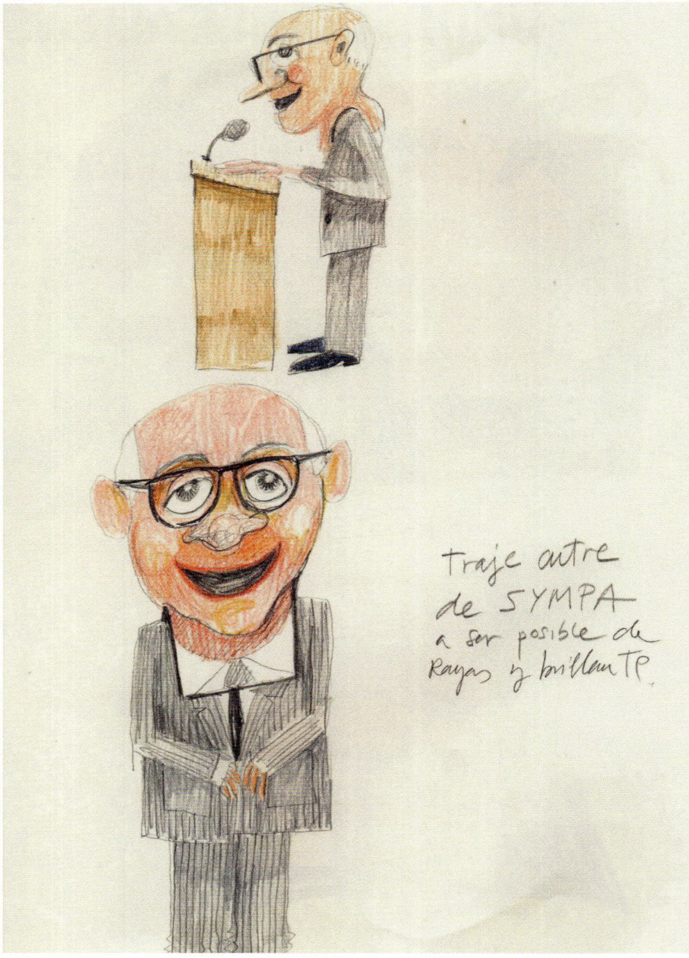

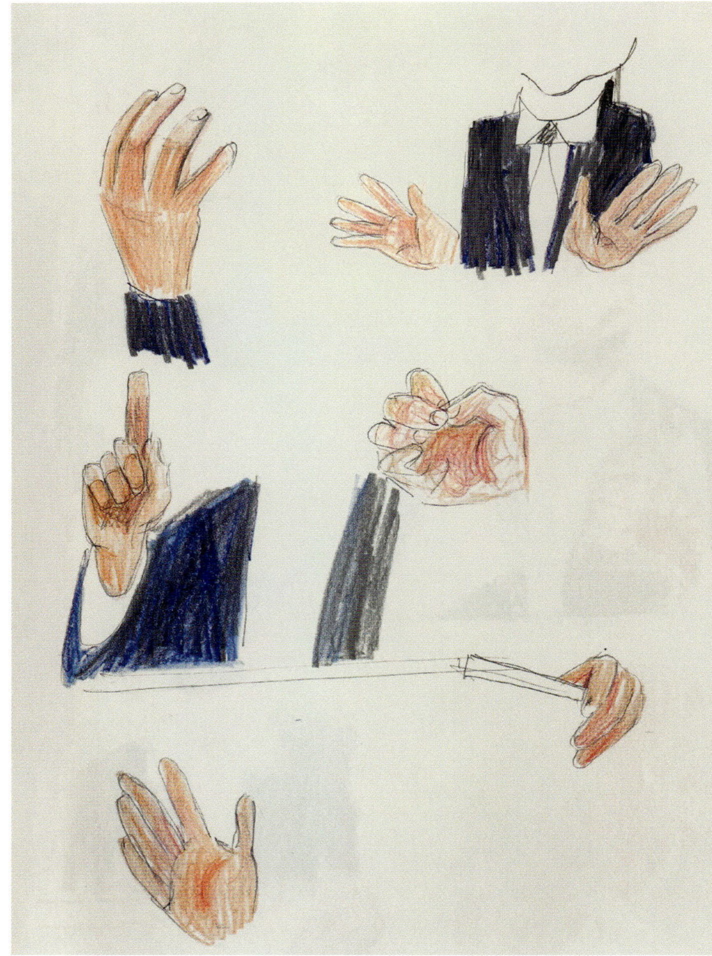

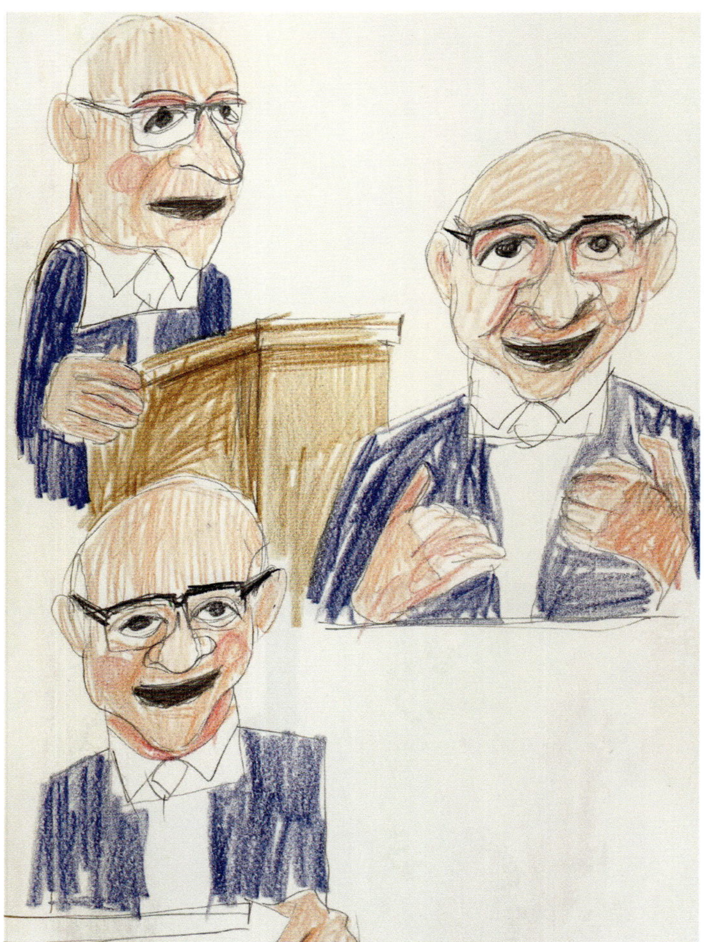

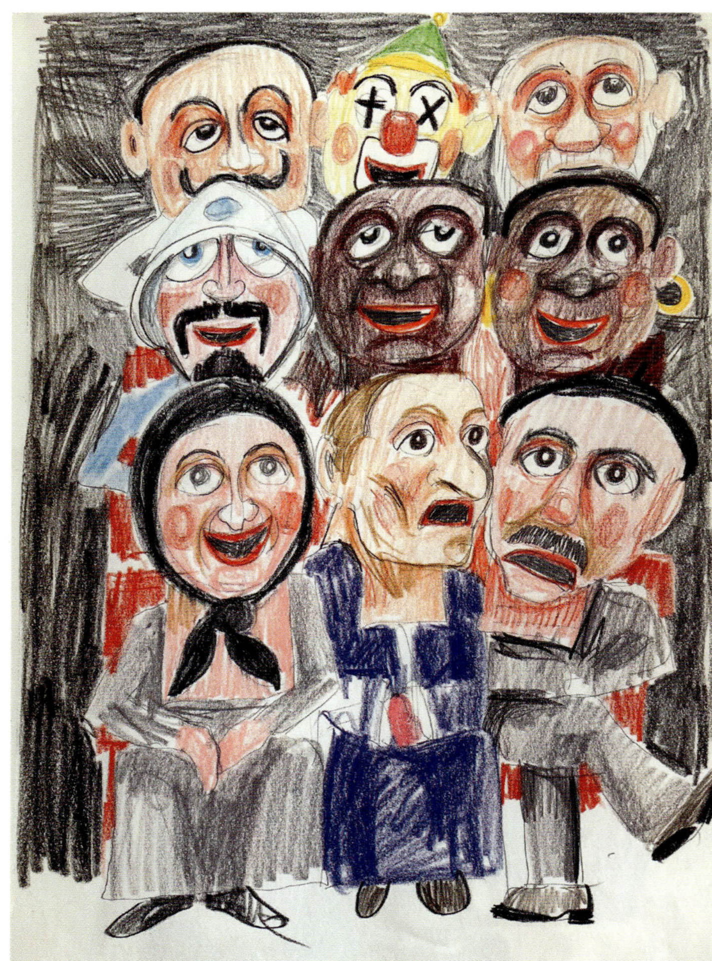

Preparatory drawings for the video *Miracle Miracle*

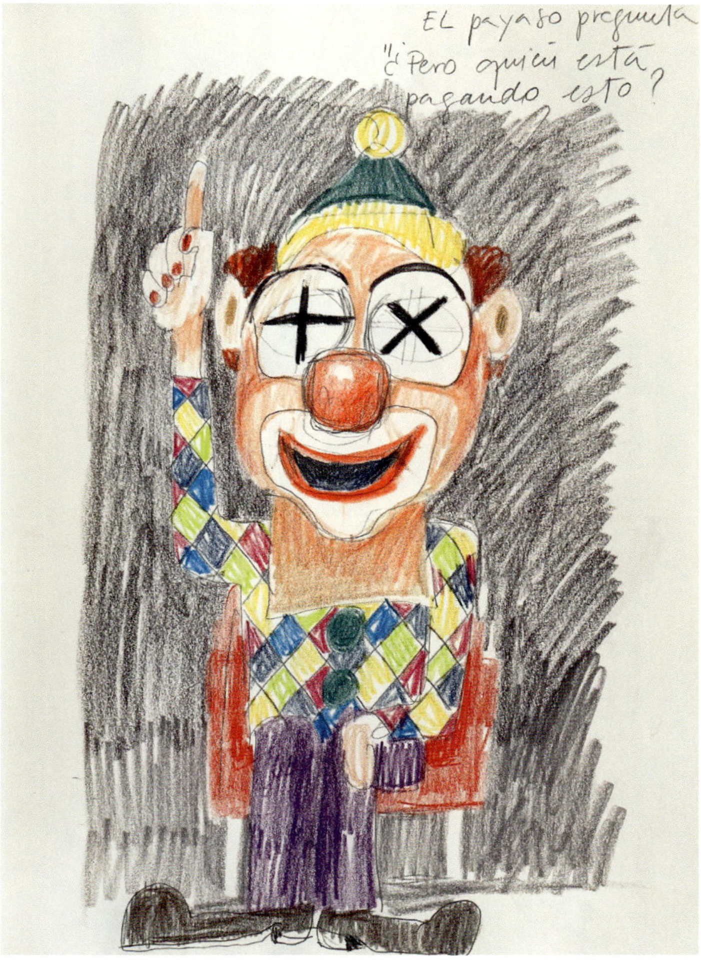
EL payaso pregunta
"¿Pero quién está
pagando esto?

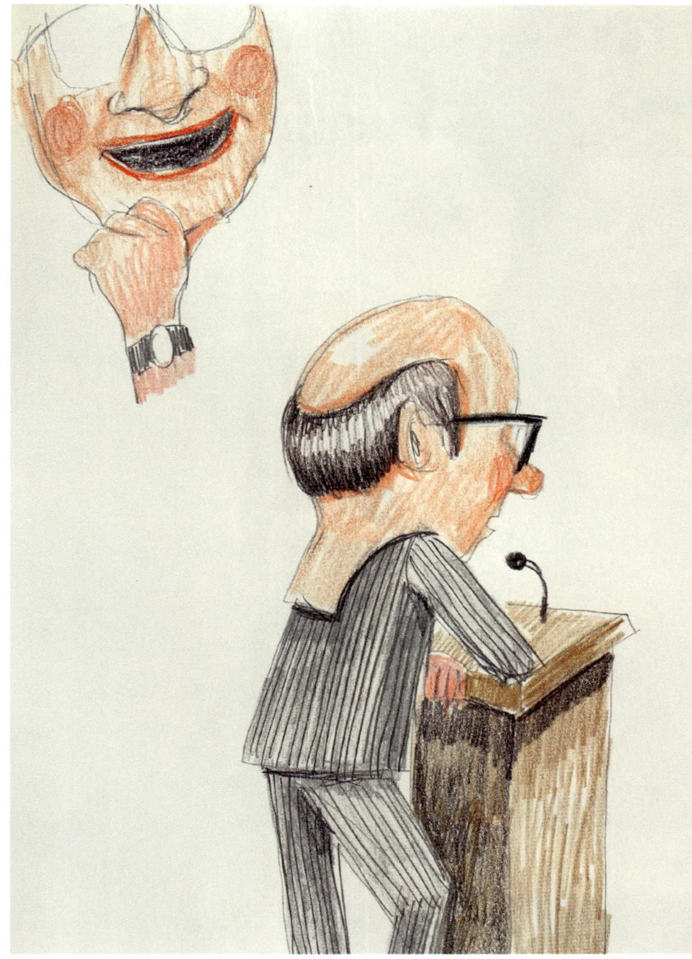

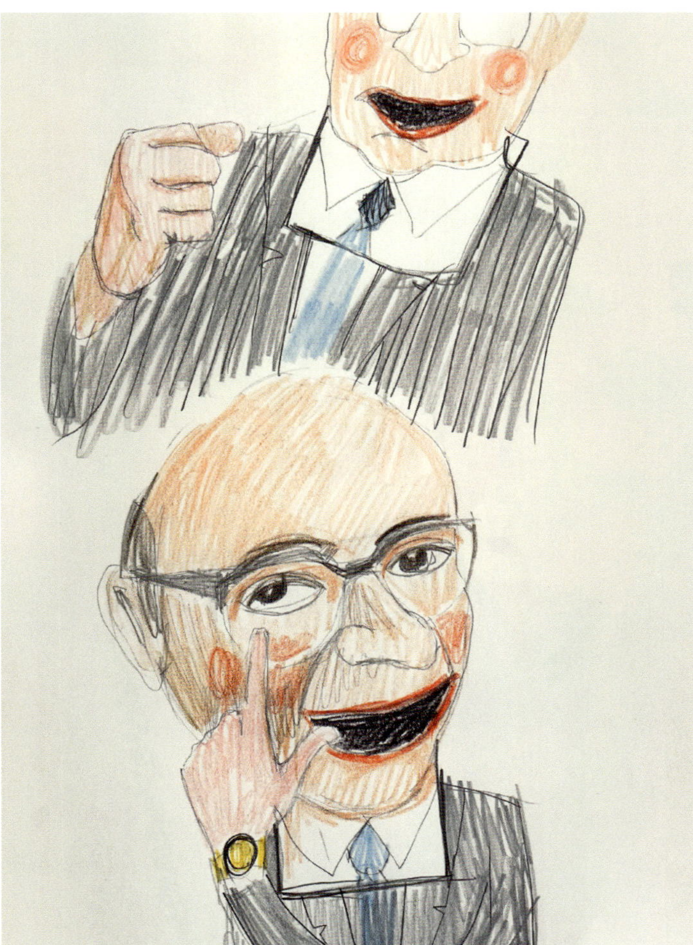

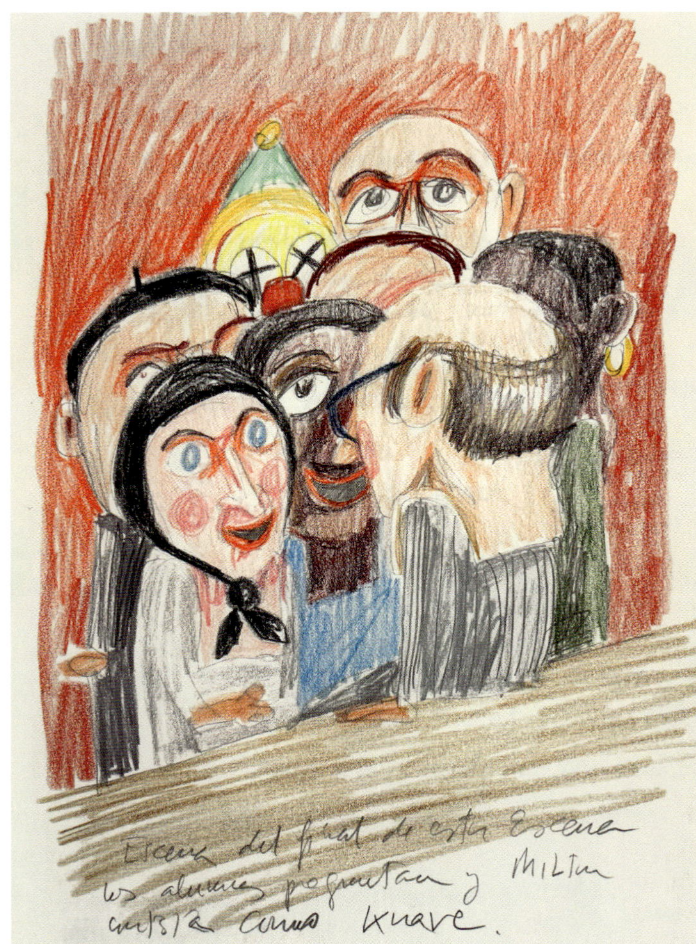
Escena del final de esta Escena
los alumnos preguntan y Milton
contesta como Knave.

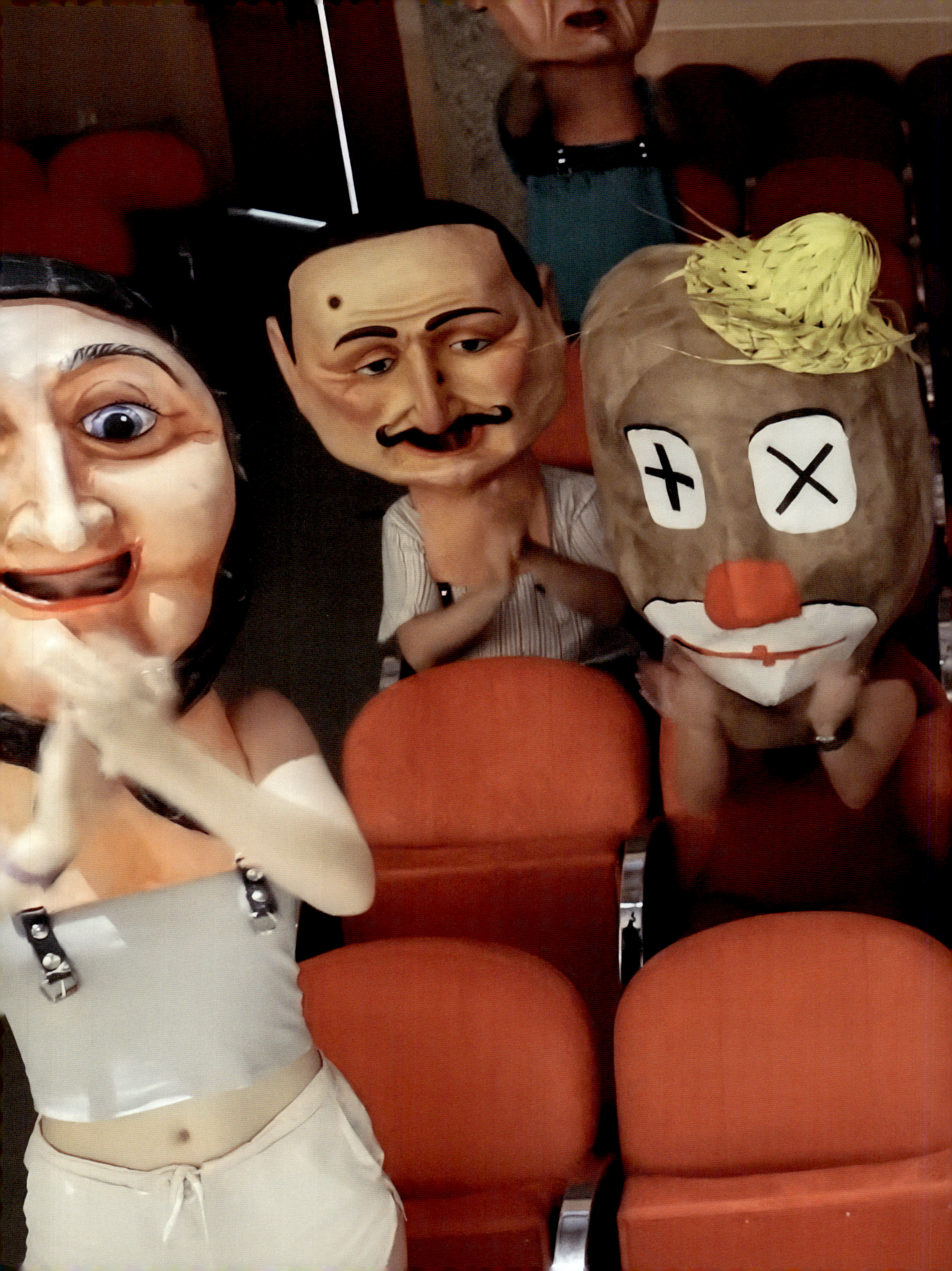

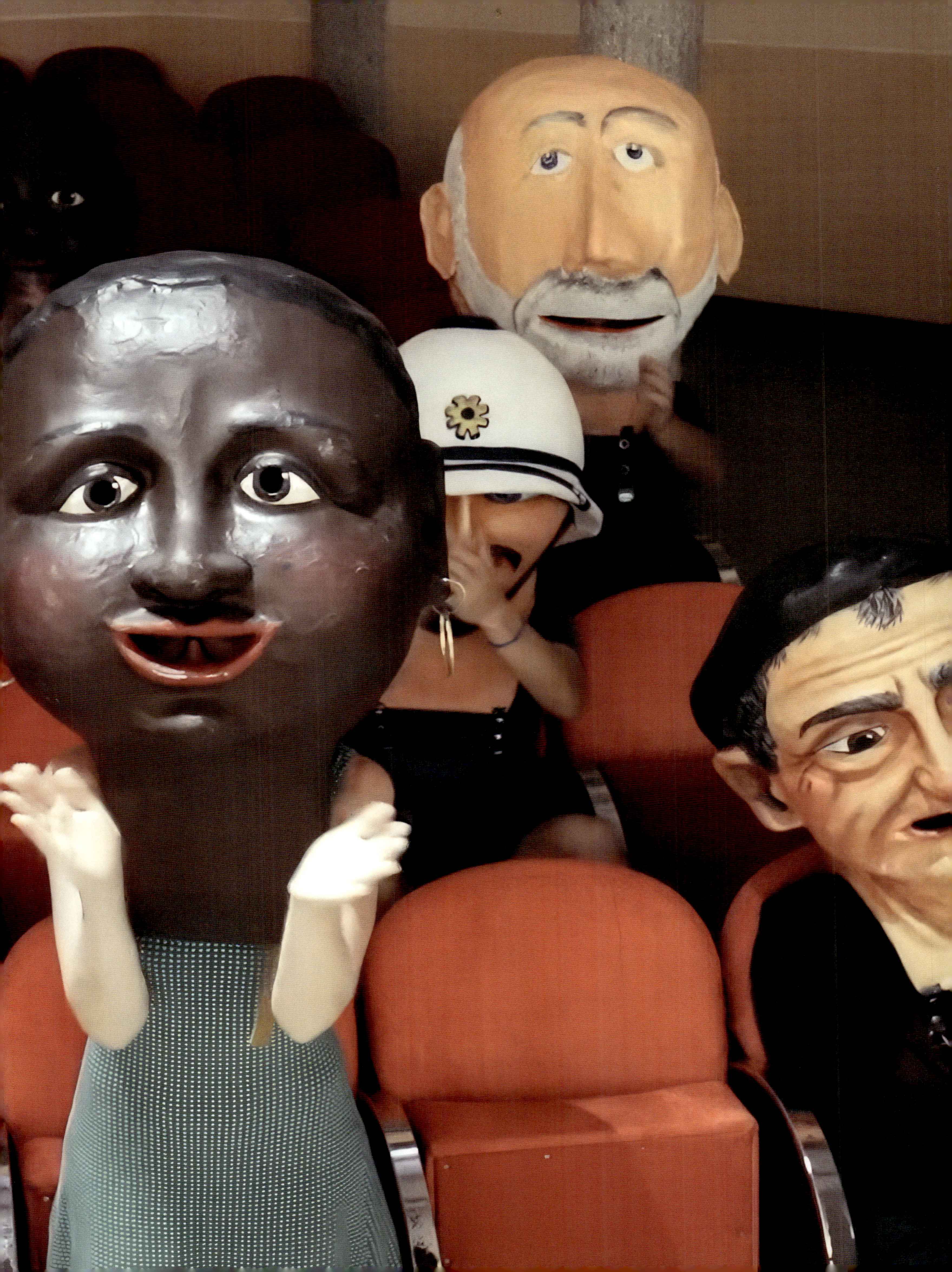

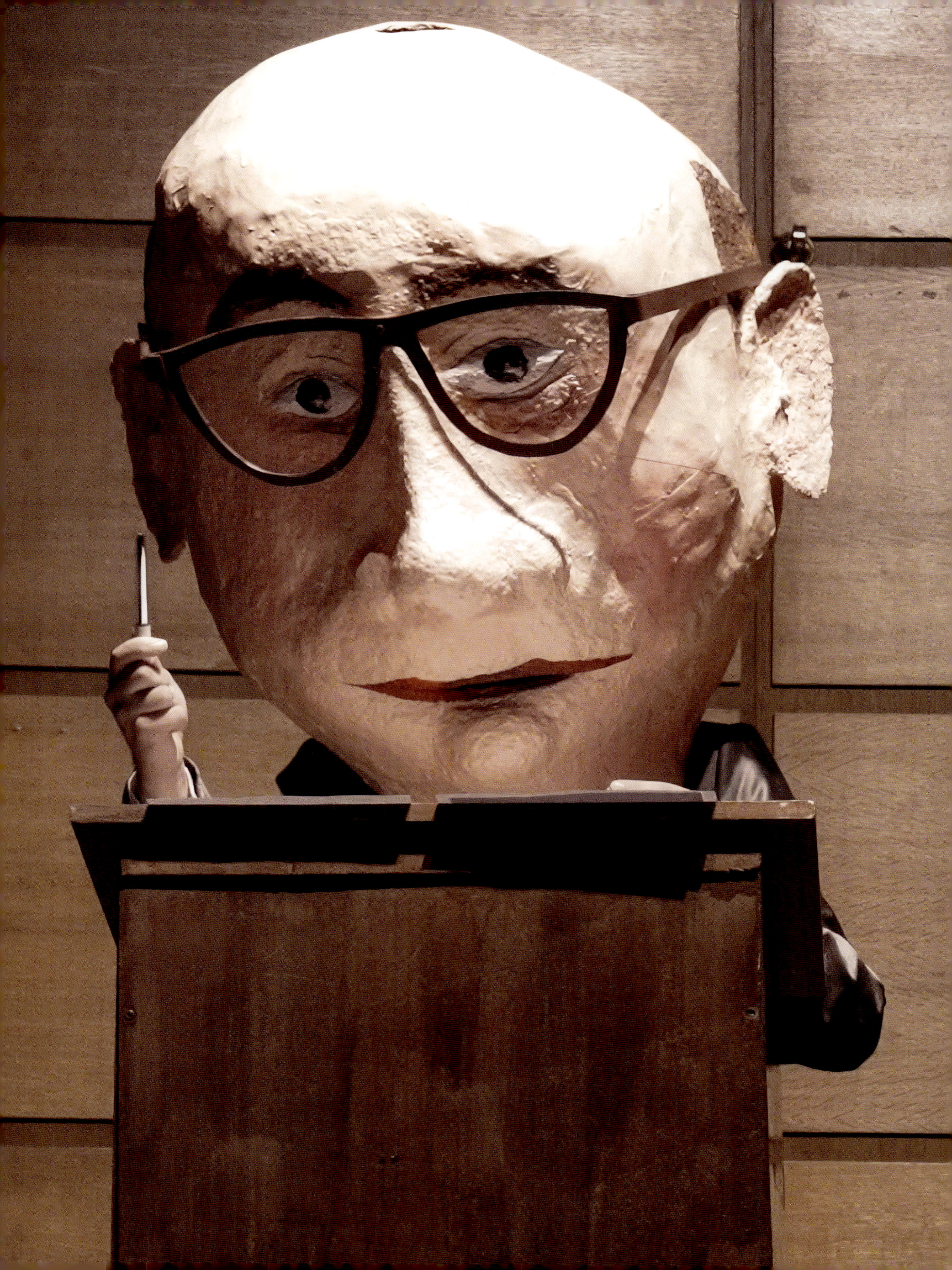

MILTON FRIEDMAN'S PENCIL SPEECH

INSIDE CALDAS THEATRE. Plan of a stage with an empty lectern. Plan of a row of empty seats in a theatre. Little by little, the conference participants enter and sit in the comfortable seats, the shot continues until they are all seated. Whispers and conversations can be heard until the lights are dimmed. The empty stage is illuminated again.

As Professor Milton Friedman, Nobel Laureate in Economics, appears on one side of the image and climbs the stairs to the podium, a voiceover announces:

PRESENTER
It is my very great pleasure
to present our speaker today
professor Milton Friedman.
(Applause)

He stands on the stage and lays the conference papers on the lectern, looks at the audience attending the conference, makes a few hand gestures to stop the applause and beginshis talk.

MILTON FRIEDMAN
We need an understanding of the real nature of freedom, economic and political, and the interrelation between the two. We need really to have a greater understanding of the kind of system, the kind of principles that have enabled us to get these great achievements of the past 250 years.
We need to understand how it is that a free market works to enable millions of people to cooperate peacefully together. I know no better way to bring this out than a with avery simple example that I owe to a very old friend of mine, Leonard Reed, who once wrote a little article called I the Pencil.

To make a pencil you need: someone to cut down trees in Washington or wherever, someone to produce steel so that you can make saws to cut them down, someone to extract graphite from a mine in South America, someone to bring the gum from Malaysia or Congo, others to extract the copper and zinc for the ferrule, the paint, the glue that binds everything together... etc., etc. To make a pencil I'm trading with thousands of people all over the world who don't know each other.

How is that brought about? How does this miracle happen? Is there some commissar sitting in some central office who is sending orders to these people in Malaysia, to the people in South America, to the people in Washington? How is it that they are led to cooperate with one another?

That's the miracle of the price system. Because note, these thousands of People who are being led to engage in this simple transaction with me, not One of them has been forced to do it, nobody has had a gun to his head, they've all done it. Why? Because each one of them thinks that he is better off in this transaction. Indeed, there is no doubt whatsoever that the owners of the forests, the steelworks, the mines and the landlords of the gum plantations are happy to collaborate peacefully.

Why? Because thanks to globalisation we can reach countries with no labour legislation, no trade unions, where there is a huge and cheap workforce, where wages are ridiculous, where costs are minimal, where profits are plentiful and where the city facilitates monetary transactions so that the miracle ends up in some virgin haven, avoiding the annoying taxes. In more structured countries, we advise, encourage, and invite states to change, to make the necessary structural reforms requested by the markets for the sake of progress. This is the miracle. There is no need to put a gun to anyone's head because, as an old friend of mine, Adam Smith, used to say, capitalist workers feed on fear and hunger.

Not only do they collaborate, but they also consume.
Another thing that we have realised in order to understand the importance of the global free market is what another old friend, Alphonse Allais, said, and that is that money has to be found where it is, that is to say, where the poor are.

Yes, all right, they do not have much money but there are plenty of them.

(Laughs)

In order to have a free, healthy market, it is very important to know how submission is spread. To understand this revelation, I was thinking about what another old friend, Jacques Lacan, said based on what another old friend, Marx, had shown in terms of production called surplus value and that is that something changes in the master's discourse from a certain moment in history. We do not care if it is because of Luther, or Calvin, or the ship traffic around Genoa, or in the Mediterranean Sea, or elsewhere, since the important point is that from a certain day, the excess of joy is counted, it is aggregated.

There begins what is called the accumulation of capital. What another old friend named Hobbes called Pleonexia.

But I insist, how does this miracle happen? We don't need a commissar in the Soviet sense. To be able to work this miracle, we need a government that preserves our freedom, that preserves it but at the same time is not a Frankenstein that destroys such freedom.

To realise this miracle, consisting of a small minority controlling the majority in order to increase their own profits, we have to promote individual freedom, free markets, free entrepreneurship that create wealth, jobs that result in economic growth by rewarding consumer freedom.
The immaterialist minority with deep moral values is doing the majority a great favour.

THE CAMERA FOCUSES ON AN ASSISTANT, WHOSE THOUGHTS CAN BE HEARD

(VO)
Blimey!! This chap! He's got so many friends!!
Lucky him!!!

MF continues with his conference.

But how can we benefit from the government's promise while avoiding the threat it poses to individual freedom?

I'll quote the two general principles. First, the scope of the government must be limited. Its primary function should be to protect our freedom from enemies outside our territory as well as from our fellow citizens: to preserve law and order, to enforce private contracts, to encourage competitive markets. Beyond this primary function, the government may at times allow us to accomplish together what we would find more difficult or costly to accomplish individually.

The state, that Leviathan, must limit itself to creating structures favourable to the market and to financial institutions, such as the Washington Consensus, the IMF., or the A.M.I. which was a good attempt that the enemies of freedom managed to stop...

Influencing the rest of the governments, the freer the better to make structural reforms in order to sell the pencil, the bike or just anything.

Governments that do not conform are considered the enemy and when any state is reluctant or nationalistic or its citizens decide to vote against individual freedom, Western forces promptly set to work to redress this.

The second general principle is that the power of government should be dispersed. It should not affect business and at the same time it should provide stability by safeguarding the security of corporations and elites.

The state must intervene as little as possible and to do this it is necessary to legislate to free up trade and finance, to curb inflation, to lower taxes on large fortunes and to privatise state-owned companies, those that are efficient and profitable, so that once their disinterested work has been completed, public representatives can be incorporated into the payrolls of the same companies they themselves have privatised.

But one of the greatest achievements we have made is to be able to privatise what is rightfully ours, such as health, education and housing.

For incomprehensible reasons, there are people who resist by curbing individual freedom, claiming against us that, as a friend of mine whose name I have already mentioned, what characterizes the right-wing intellectual is the adjective "rogue", someone who does not back down from the consequences of what is called realism, who can look the other way without any problems, that is, when necessary, admit to being a scoundrel!!

Or as my old friend Jacob Taubes used to say, being a liberal is not a neutral condition of existence.

If liberalism succeeds, who will pay for the cost? Liberalism ultimately implies a denial of the price that others pay for being liberal. But this is the criticism of materialists. If I'm right and history is on my side, I can't see why the others don't think like me!!

Whispers of approval among the audience

Sometimes people put up more resistance and at that moment for the sake of freedom we can make exceptions and let the government intervene with the invaluable collaboration of its coercive forces, creating policies resulting in laws that do not hinder Progress.

Let me explain something very simple, it is what politicians do when we vote against a law they want to pass and we complain, the first thing they say is that they haven't been very clear about it and that some pedagogy is needed ...

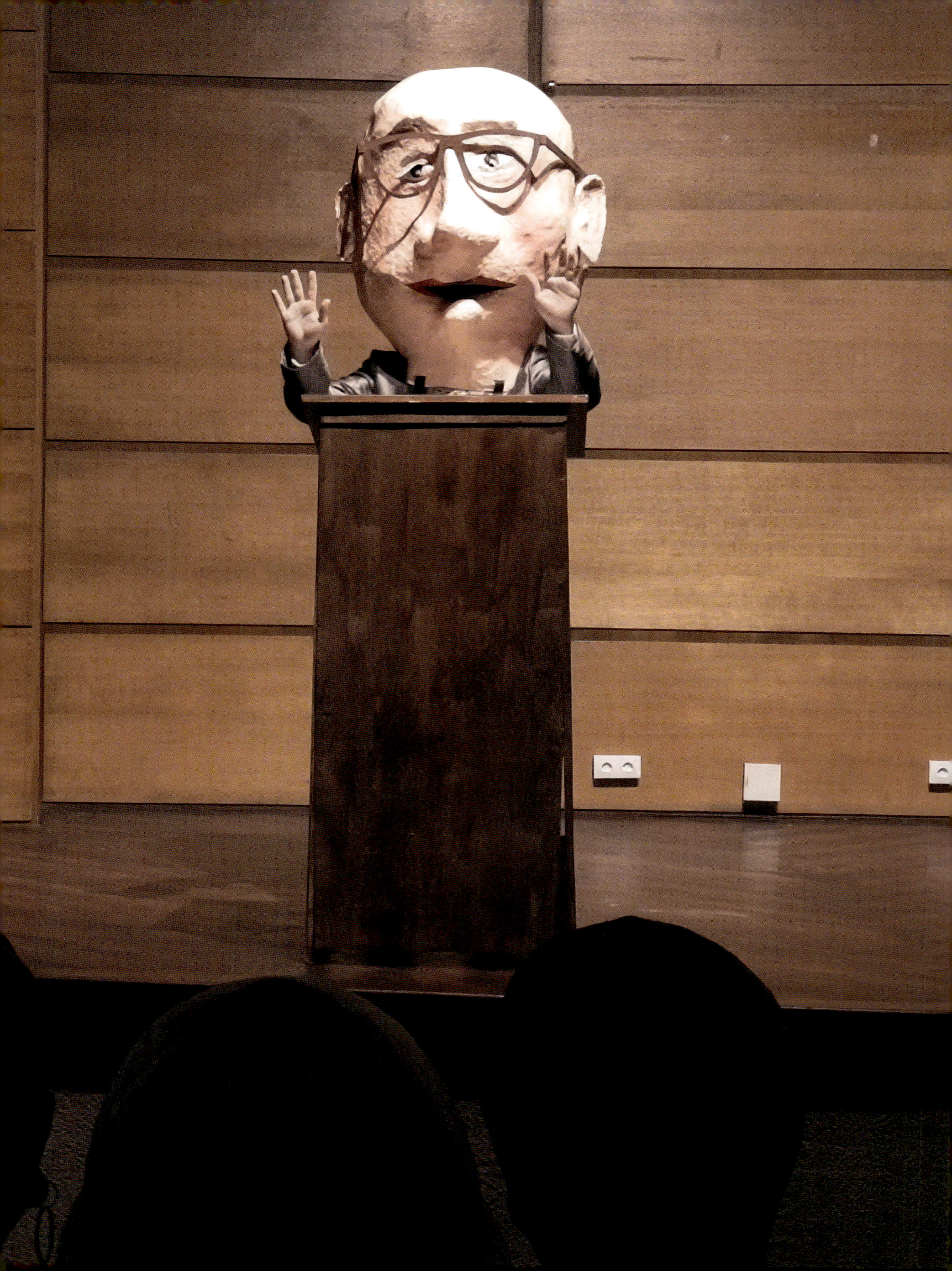

When the gap is too wide and the markets collapse and pedagogy doesn't work, then we also call on the state to defend us more forcefully against all these people who have lived above their means.

The citizens react in different ways and sometimes they don't want to continue collaborating peacefully and they don't want to make more pencils and they turn against freedom.

We have a very effective technique that an old friend, Hanna Arendt, summed up: we call ourselves patriots, we whitewash our people and we condemn others. We look for a scapegoat, the classical...

And we give them a flag, well we don't give it to them, they buy it themselves, this is one of the brilliant things about the significant masters.

With this demographic group that is going to direct its energy towards the south, care needs to be taken because they can overdo it and turn to the ultra-nationalist side, and we all know that the markets don't appreciate that.

CLOSE-UP OF THE OTHER CABEZUDO, WHOSE THOUGHTS CAN BE HEARD.

CABEZUDO 1

(VO)

I can understand why this thinking head
was given a Nobel Prize in economics,
how clever!! what a far-sighted juror!!

MF GOES ON TALKING

With another part of the population this system does not work. They put up more resistance, take to the streets, demonstrate and want to make the egalitarian revolution against individual values. They are usually left-wing. The good thing about the left that doesn't happen with the right is that the organic ends up dissipating itspower.

Besides, as my old friend Alain Badiou said, The Uprisings... are not representative.

A mass demonstration is just what it is, and it only legislates for itself. Even if it sees itself as the people of ... ... Bacteria, in a square, in demonstrations... etc. It is not a mechanism of representation, it is a mechanism of extraction, a metonymy, a part segregated from the mass in general that is true for this mass without having to resort to representatives. But then when it comes to voting the result is usually different. The street is not representative, and representation prevails over extraction.

After crises, what experience shows is that the best thing to do is to call for elections.

In May '68 it seemed that everything was going to change because of the protests of workers and students. Paris was on fire; the revolution was knocking on the doors. De Gaulle called for elections and... the right wing won by an absolute majority.

In view of the results, an old friend called Guy Debord made this analysis: "If we read the figures, we might wonder whether the population is made up entirely of millionaires who are contested by a tiny elite ofworkers."

Whispers of approval among the audience.

We want a society that at the same time is humane and provides opportunities for great human achievements, a society in which that small minority of people who do not have materialistic goals, who are interested in some of these achievements, have the greatest degree of freedom.
(MORE)

(CONT.)
And the only society that someone has invented, that someone has discovered, that comes close to doing so is a capitalist society. When I hear people who oppose the market or capitalism and examine their objections, all I find is that those objections are objections to freedom itself.

To conclude, I will tell you what an old friend of mine, Dr. Lacan, had in mind when he said that the exploitation of desire was the great invention of the capitalist discourse, "because it has to be called by its name, it's an incredibly accomplished thing. Managing to industrialise desire, in fact, nothing better could be done to keep people quiet, huh?"

Another old friend of mine called Michel Foucault said: "the divine market is established as the very principle of social bonds". A shopping centre as an agora,
I get goose bumps!!

Applause

The consumer could choose the boycott following the example of what the Moroccans did to Danone and the petrol stations, but I will not be the one who gives ideas.
What matters to make great human achievements is that everyone should want to buy the pencil, and so much the better if it's electronic and obsolete tomorrow.

Questions are taken from the floor. Shot of the cabezudo as he rises.

CABEZUDO 3

What time is it?

CLOSE-UP OF ANOTHER CABEZUDO, WHO ASKS A QUESTION.

CABEZUDO 4

I didn't want to ask any questions, just to say that I like silent films a lot.

FINAL SHOT. MILTON IS SITTING ON THE EDGE OF THE STAGE SURROUNDED BY THE PRIVILEGED STUDENTS WHO LOOK AT HIM IN ADMIRATION. ONE OF THEM ADDRESSES HIM.

CABEZUDO 5

As you know Chile so well, I'll recite a poem by Pablo Neruda ... I like it when you are silent, for you seem as if you were gone... Distant and painful as if you had died...

Fade out. THE END

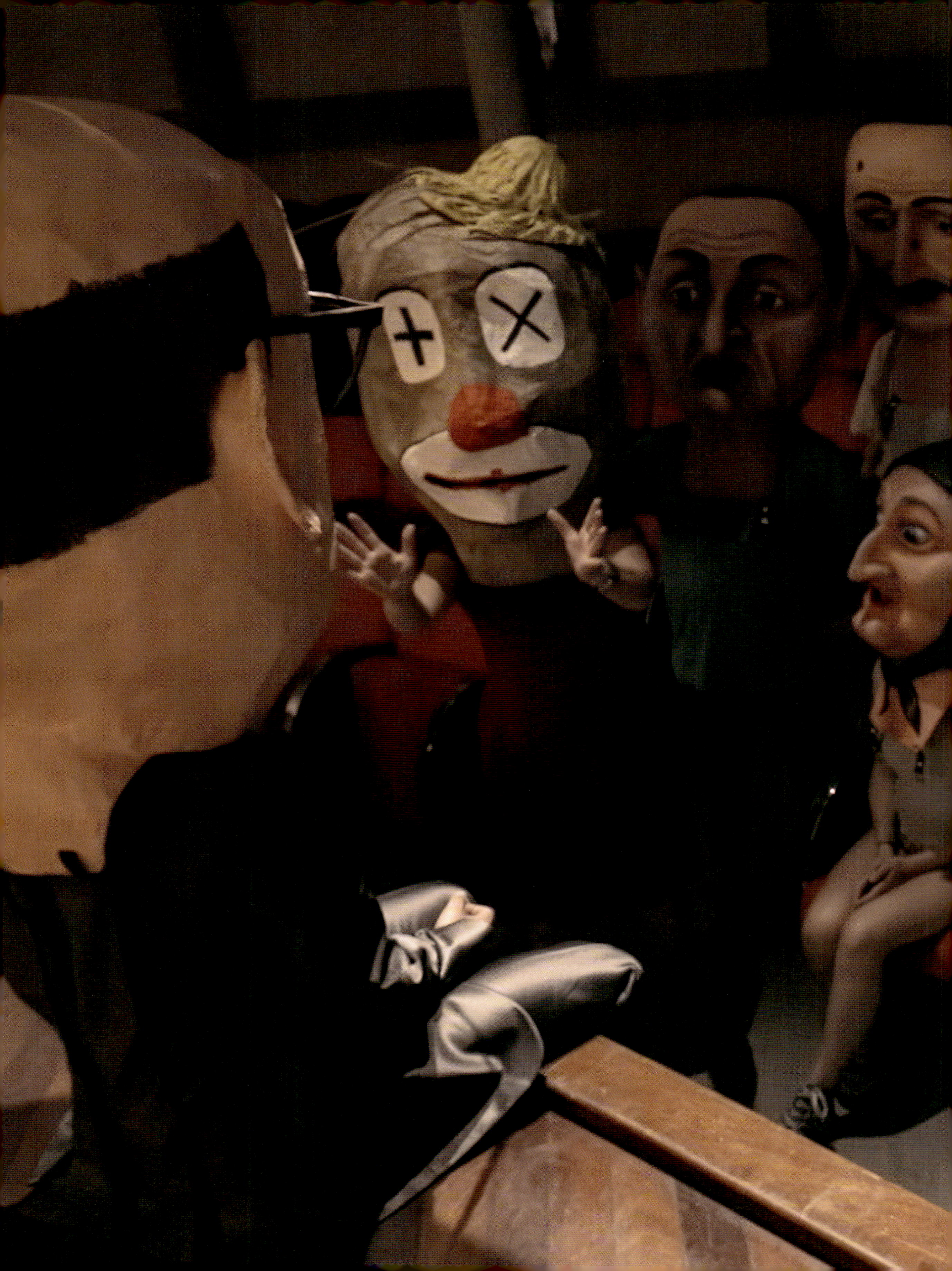

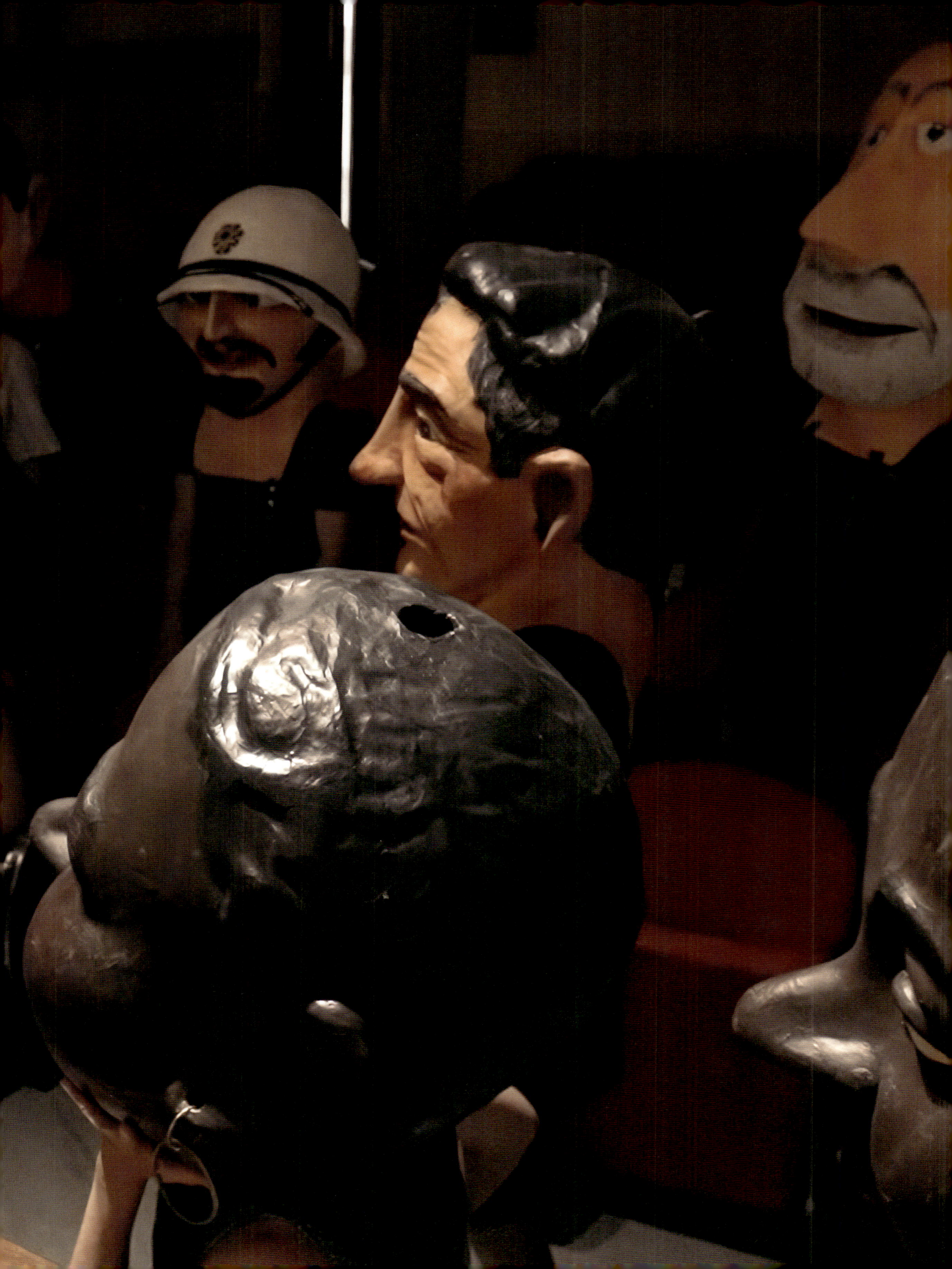

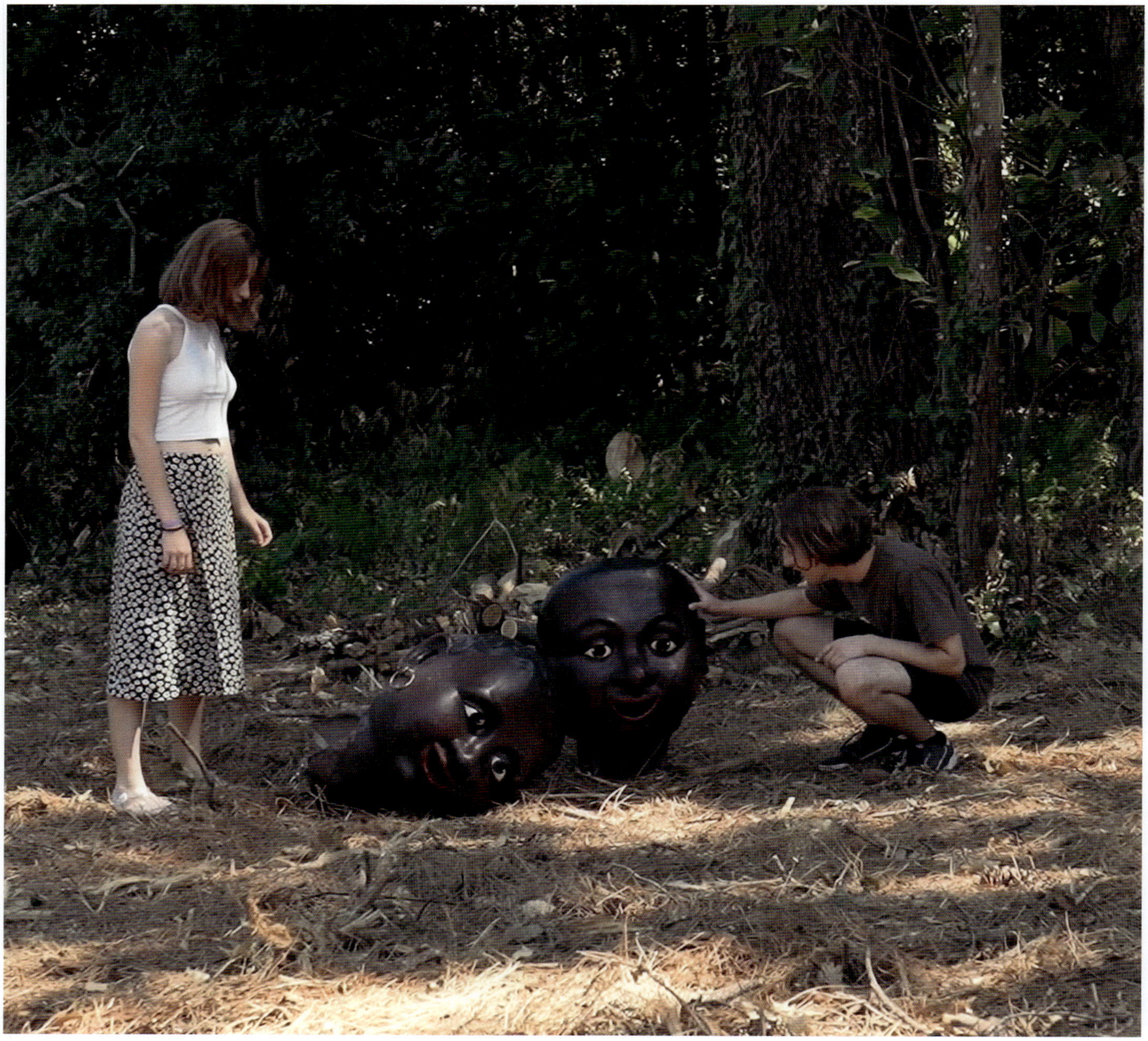

UNDESIRABLE ALIENS

2. *PLAYING THE EMIGRATION GAME*

The second chapter is called *Playing the Emigration Game*.

Inspired by Joseph Conrad's *The Heart of Darkness,* here one can see two Black carnival 'big heads' performed by white actors re-enacting an unwanted journey north. They play at leaving their homes because of war or the bad luck of being born in a place in which the West has strategic interests.

Playing the Emigration Game, 2020
Video
15 min 16 sec

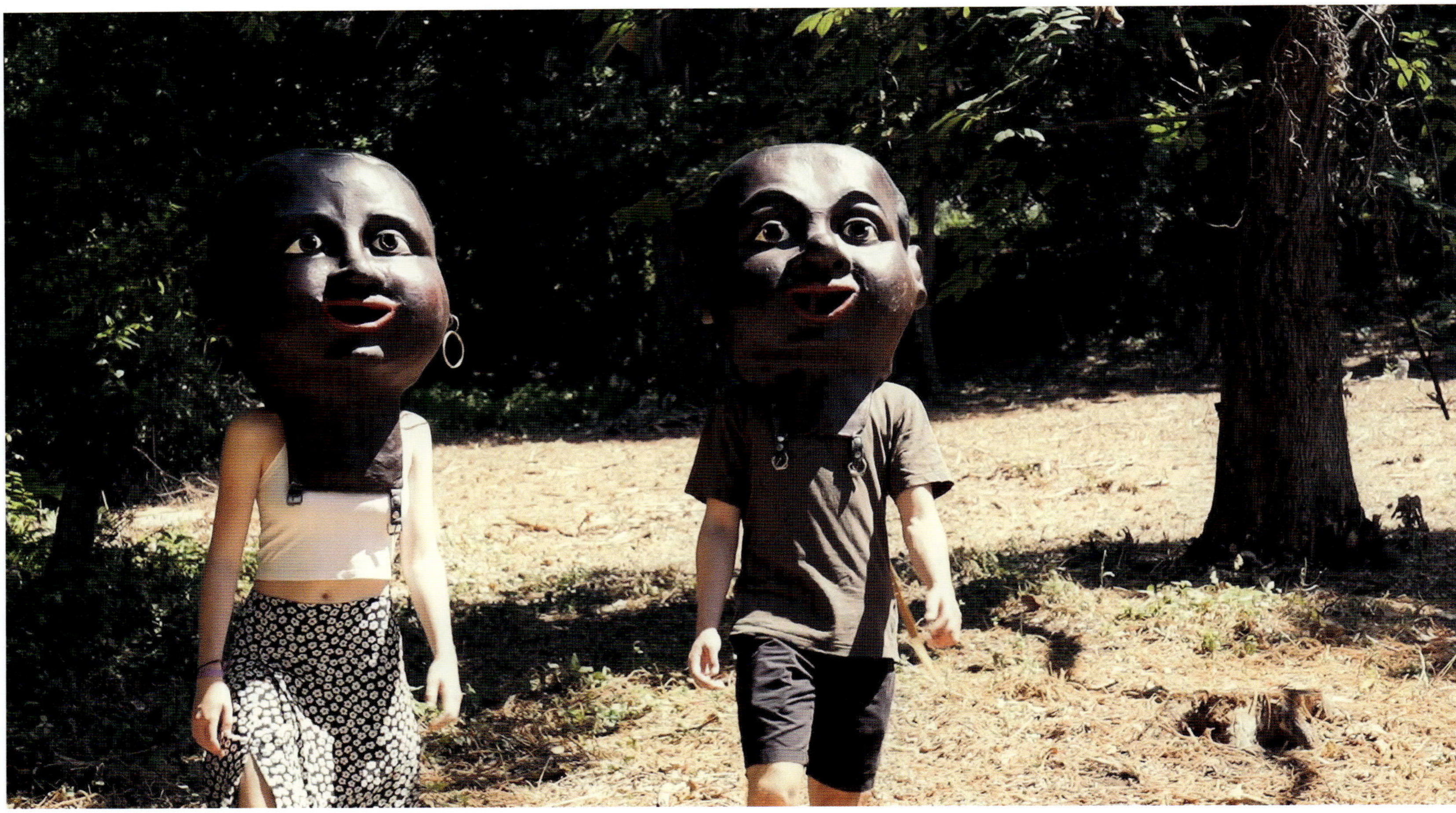

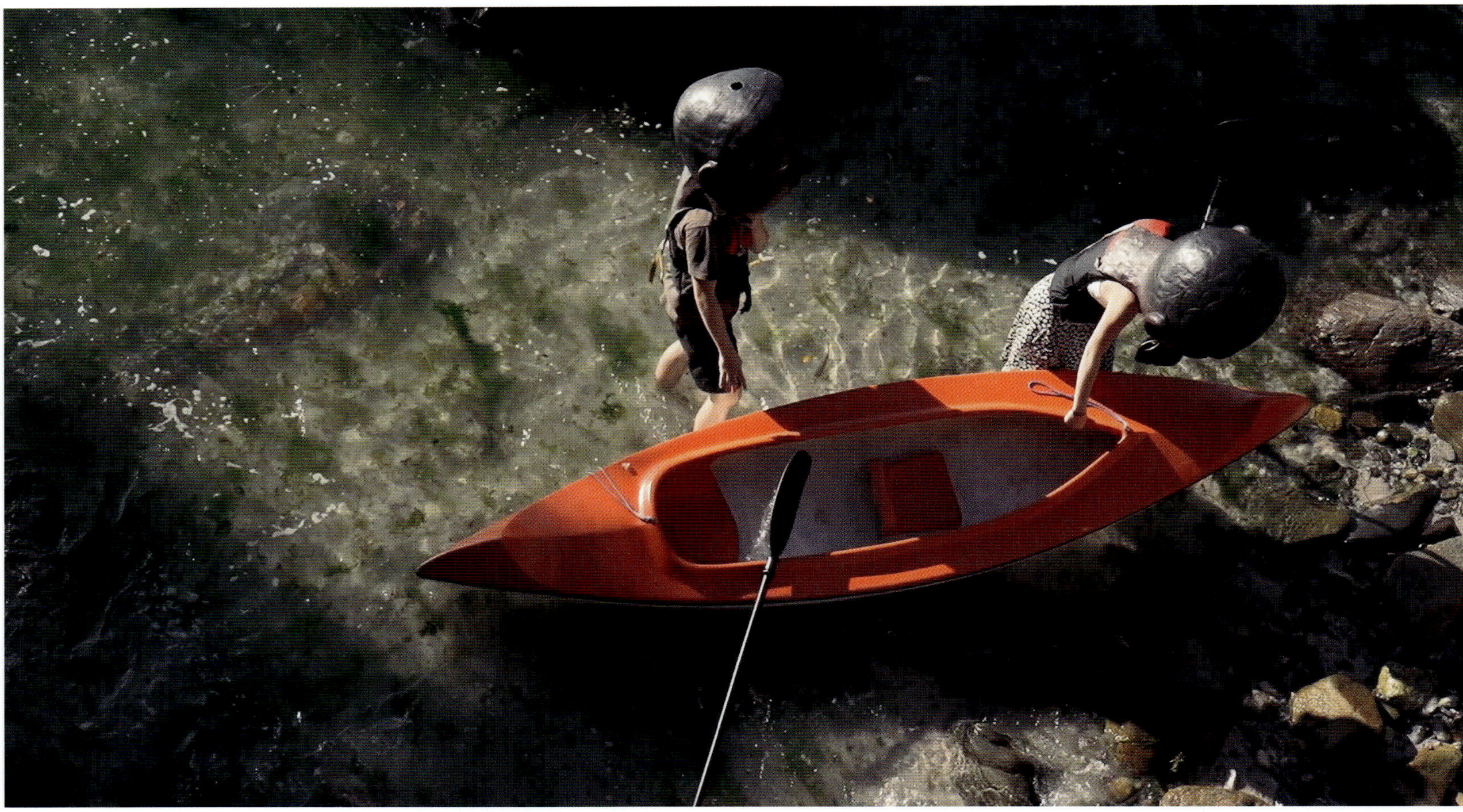

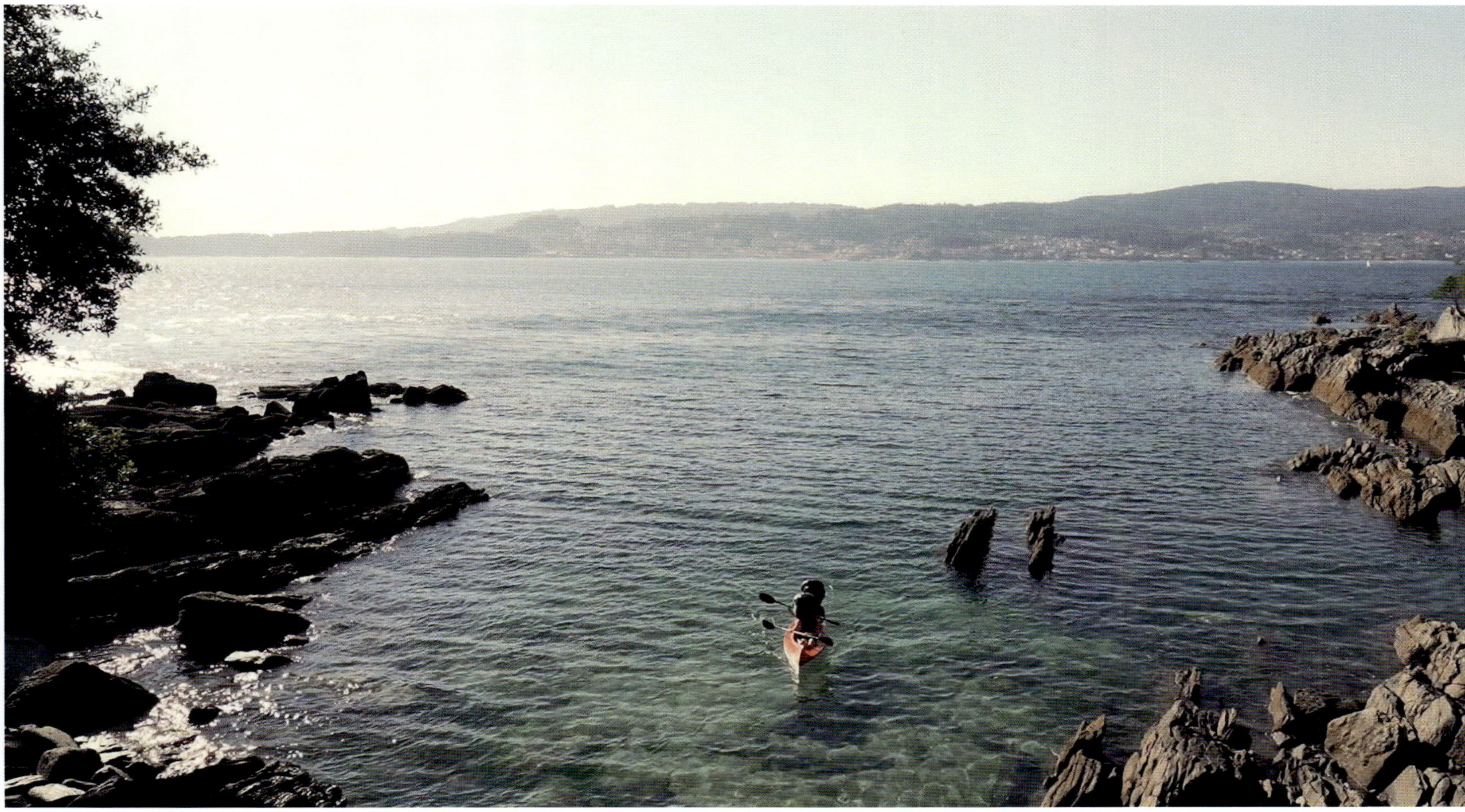

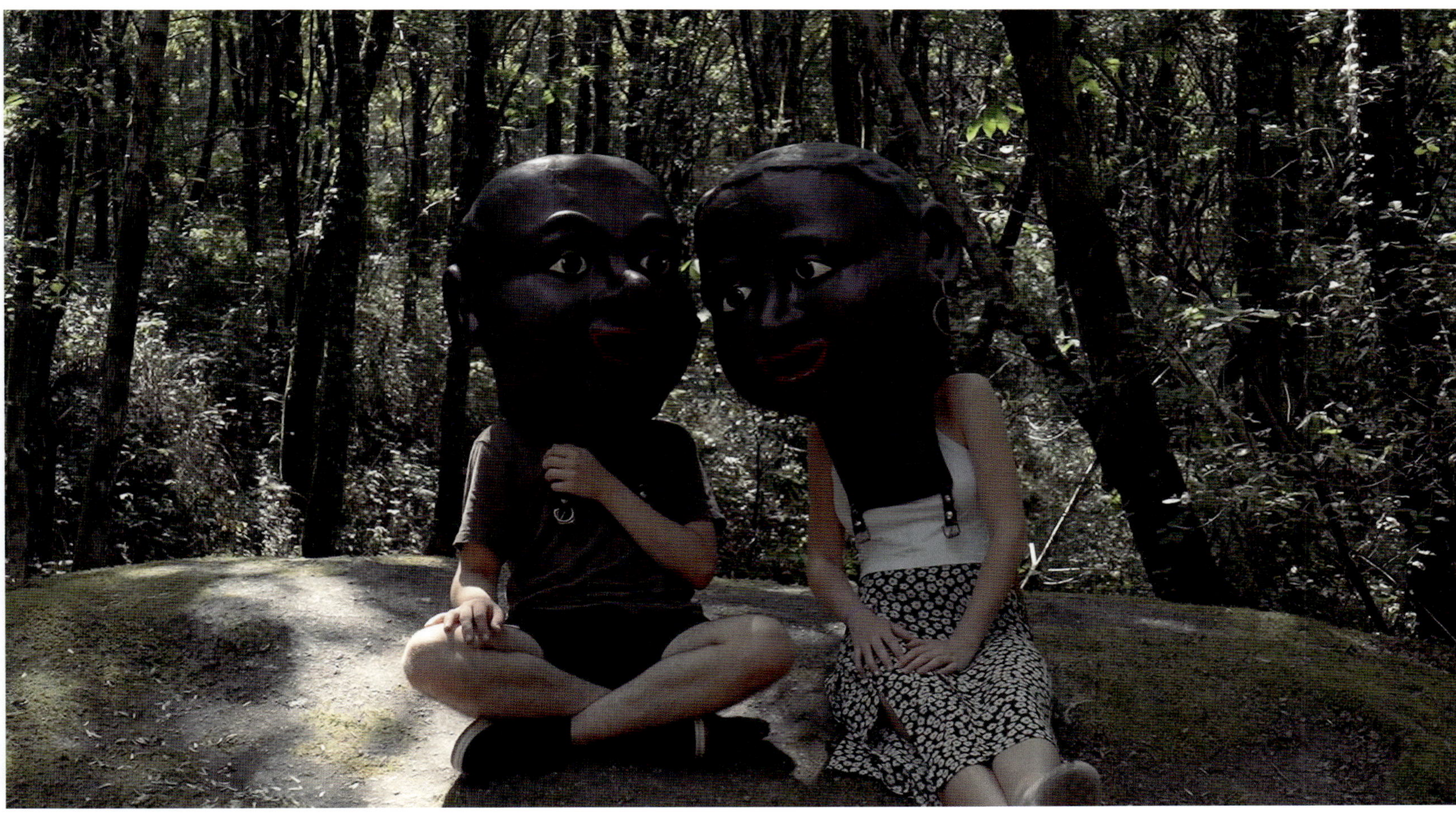

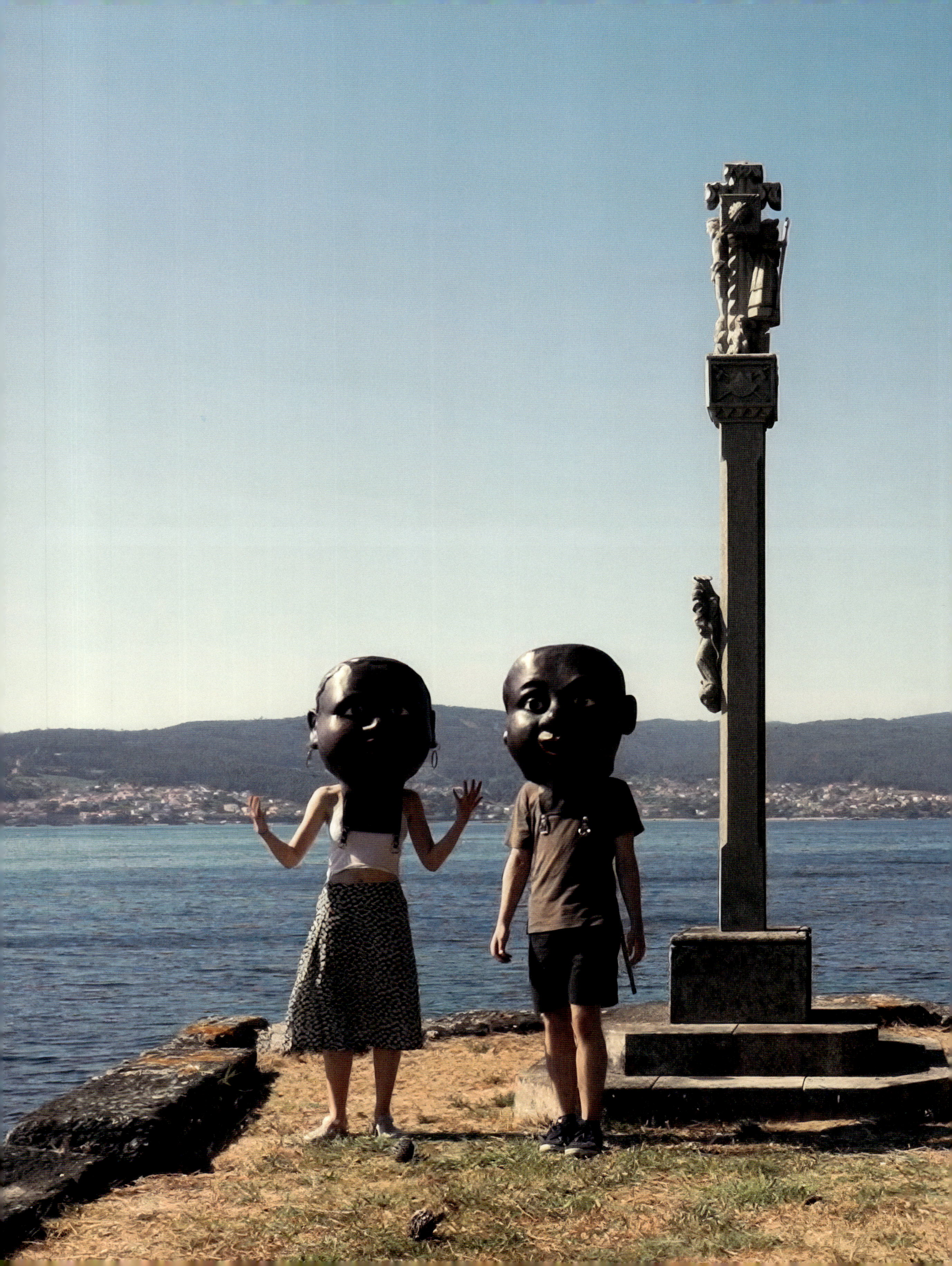

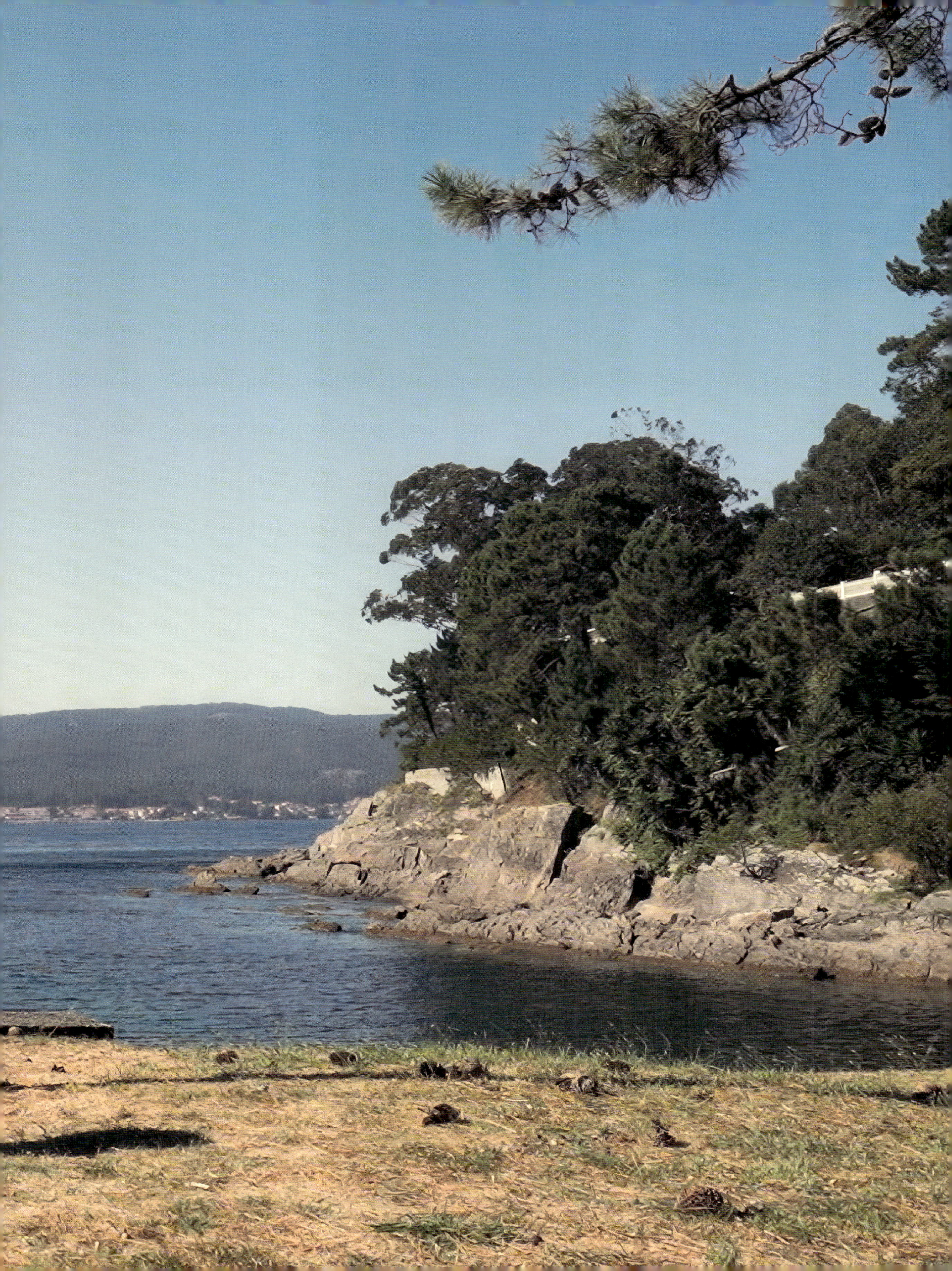

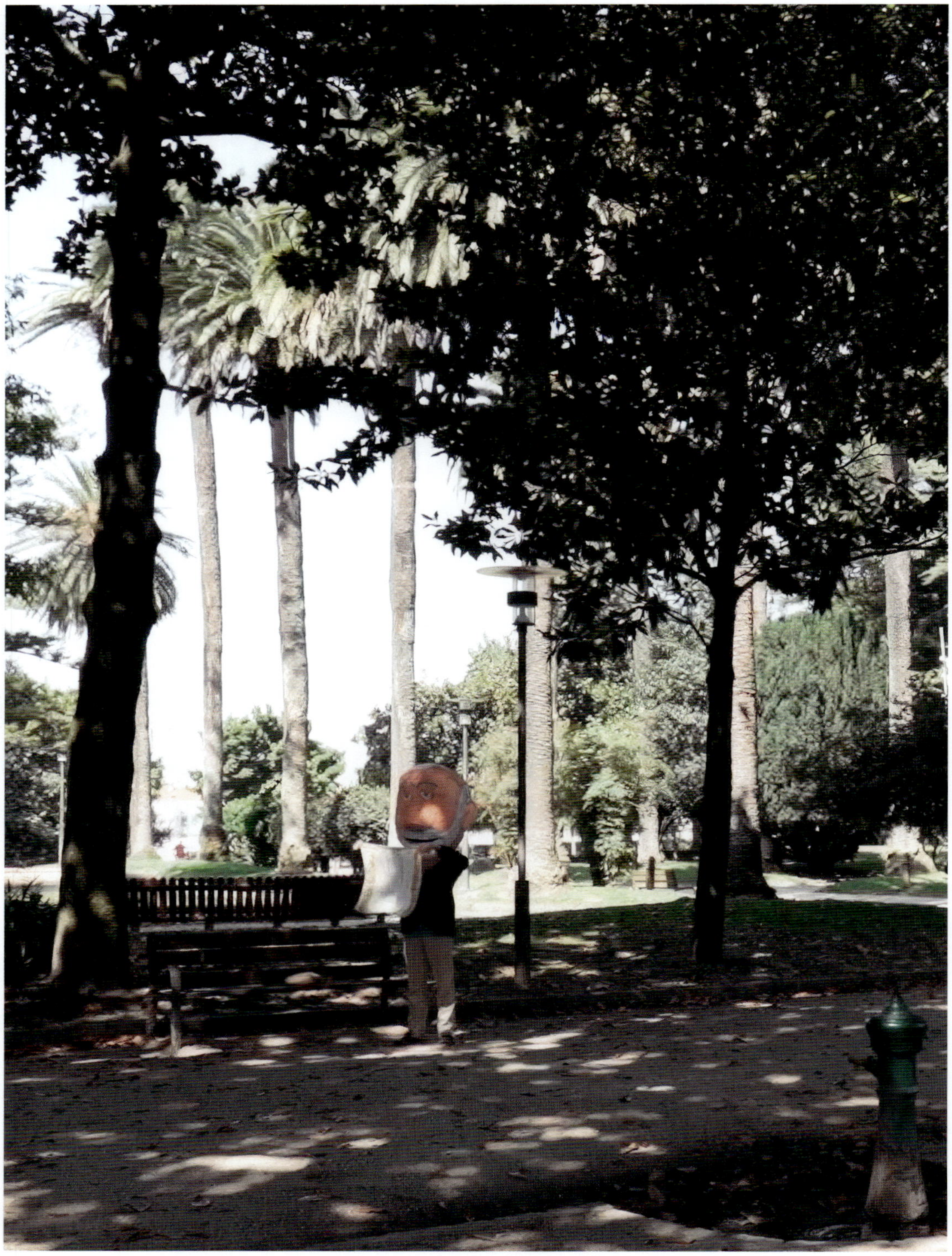

3. *CANTOR EXPLAINING THE CONCEPT OF STATE TO THE HUNGRY PIGEONS*

The third chapter is called *Cantor Explaining the Concept of State to the Hungry Pigeons*.

A 'big head' retired man – in fact, it is Georg Cantor, the mathematician behind set theory – walks into a park with a paper bag, sits on a bench and starts to feed bread to the pigeons as he categorically claims that the State is a fiction.

Cantor uses set theory to explain the concepts of state, fatherland, flags and other master signifiers that lay claim to the truth which drive people and make them work for free. State understood as a multiple set of individuals and not as a multiple of One.

Cantor Explaining the Concept of State to the Hungry Pigeons , 2020
Video
10 min 58 sec

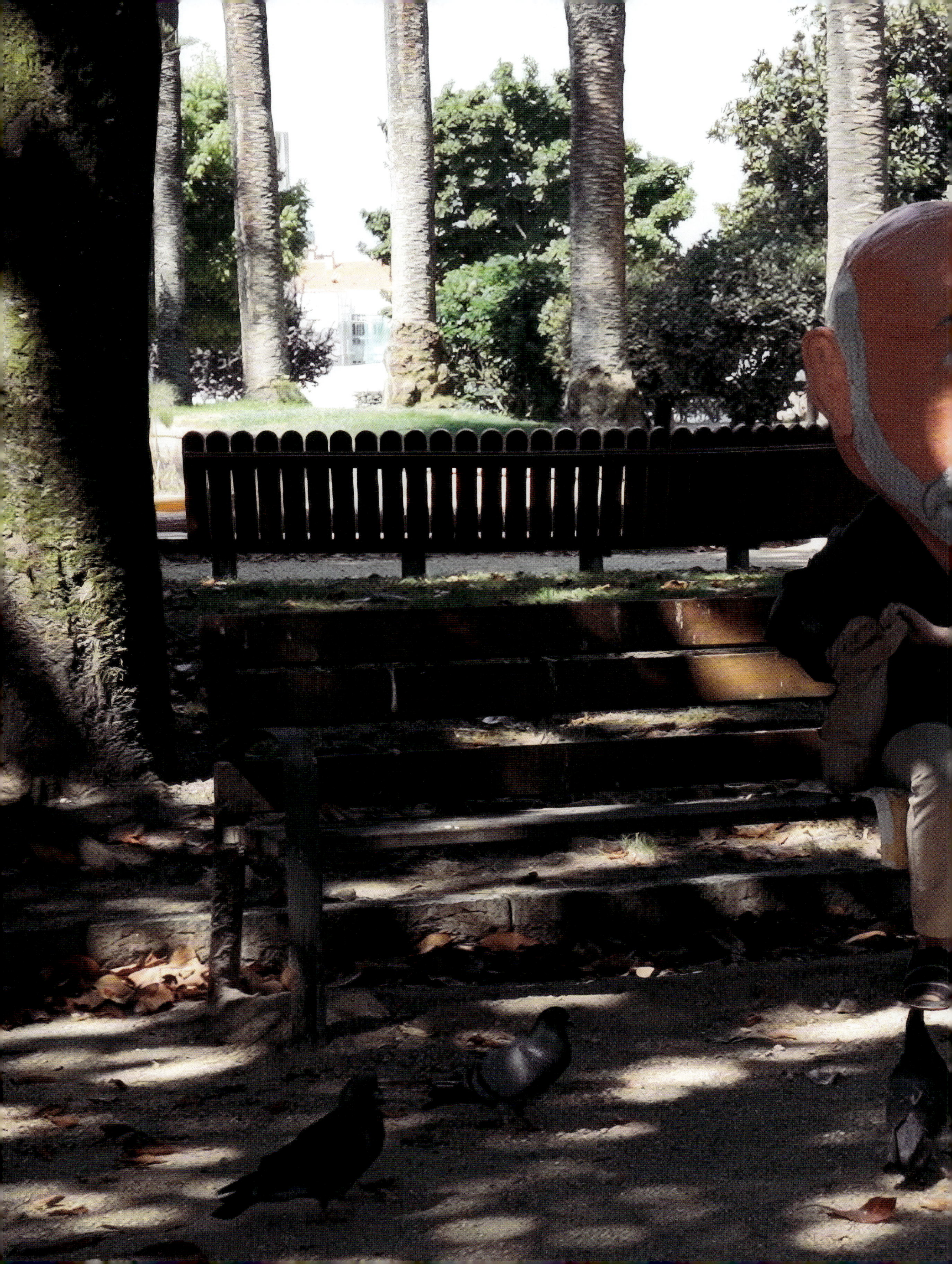

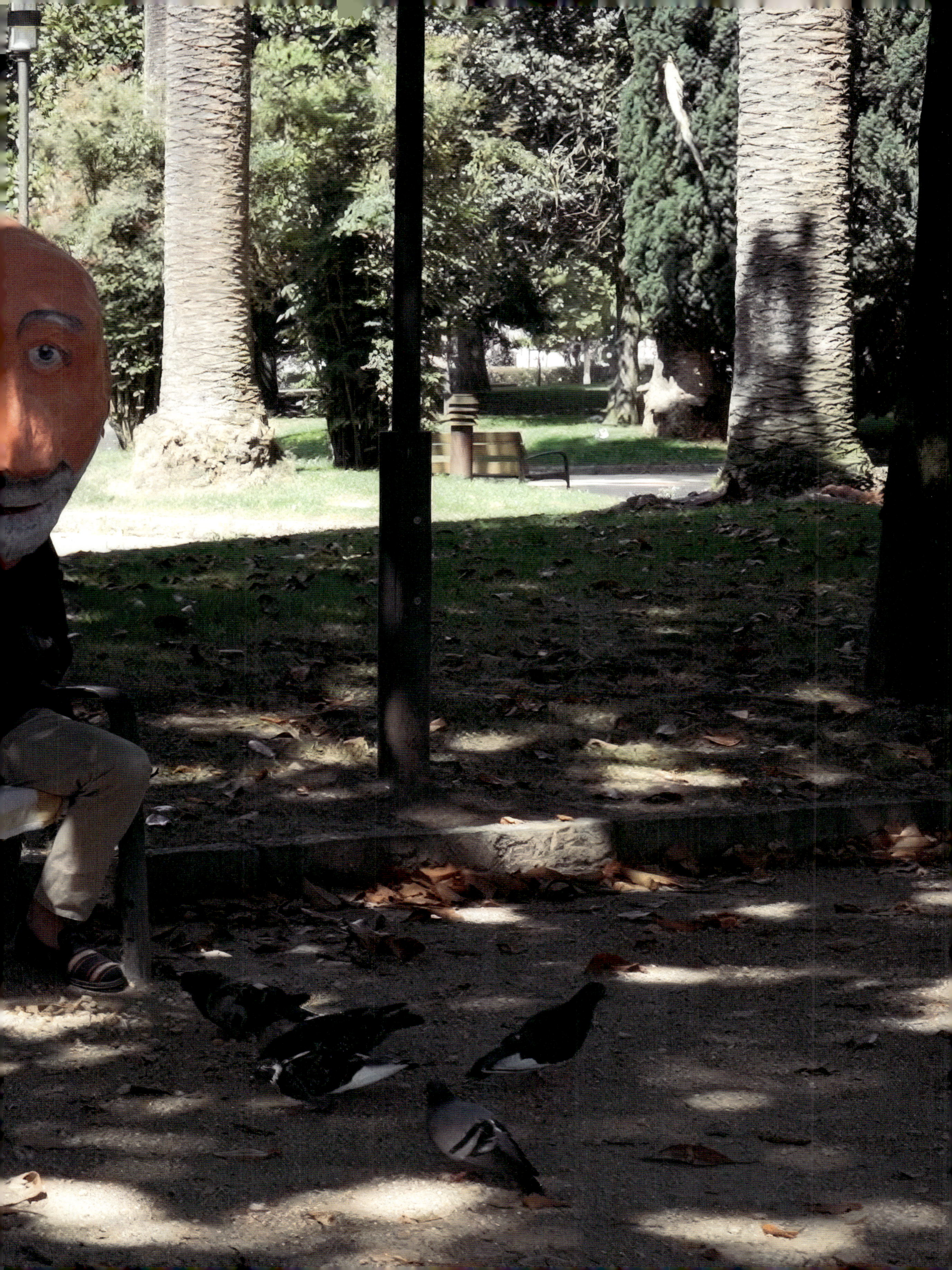

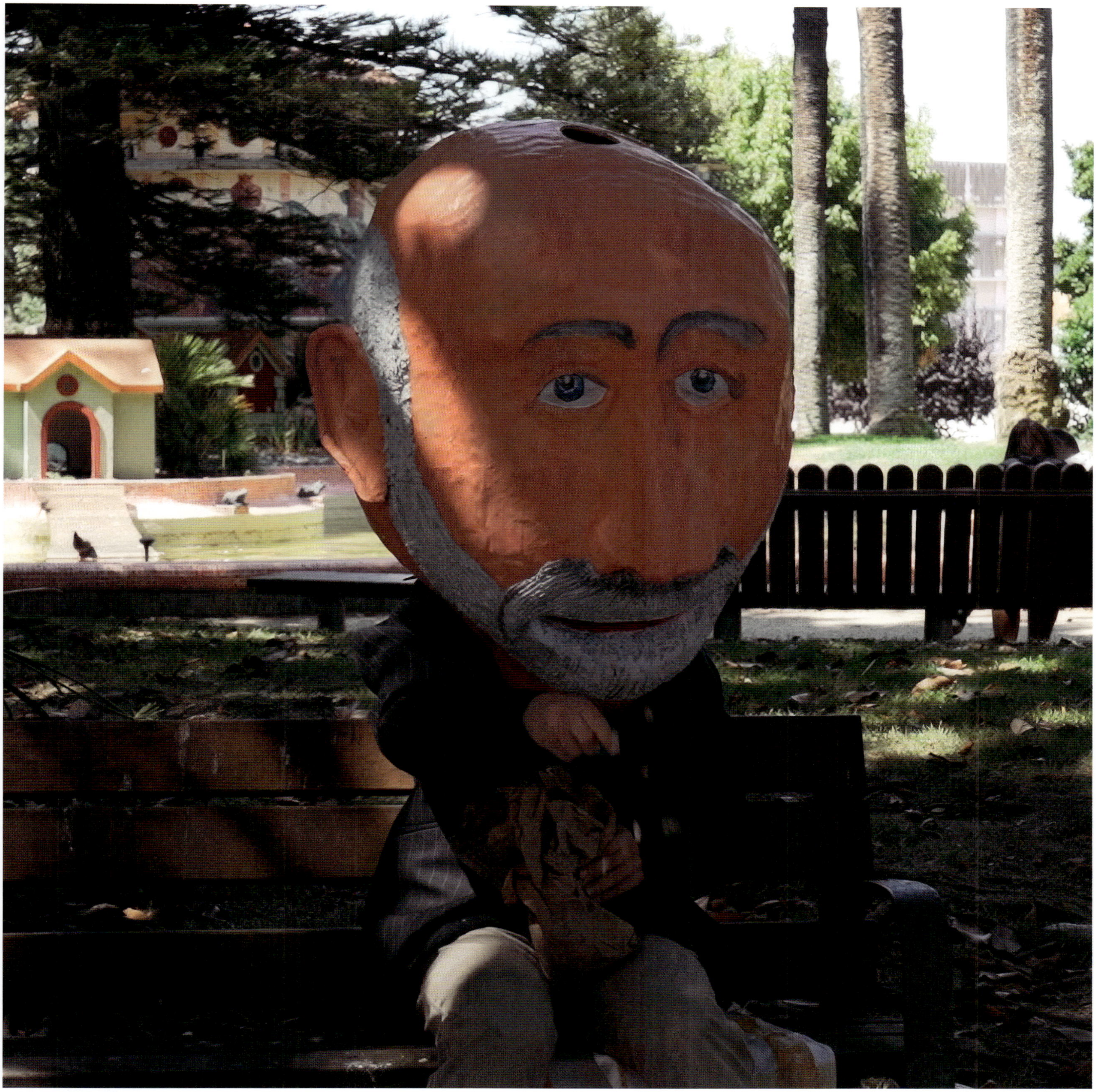

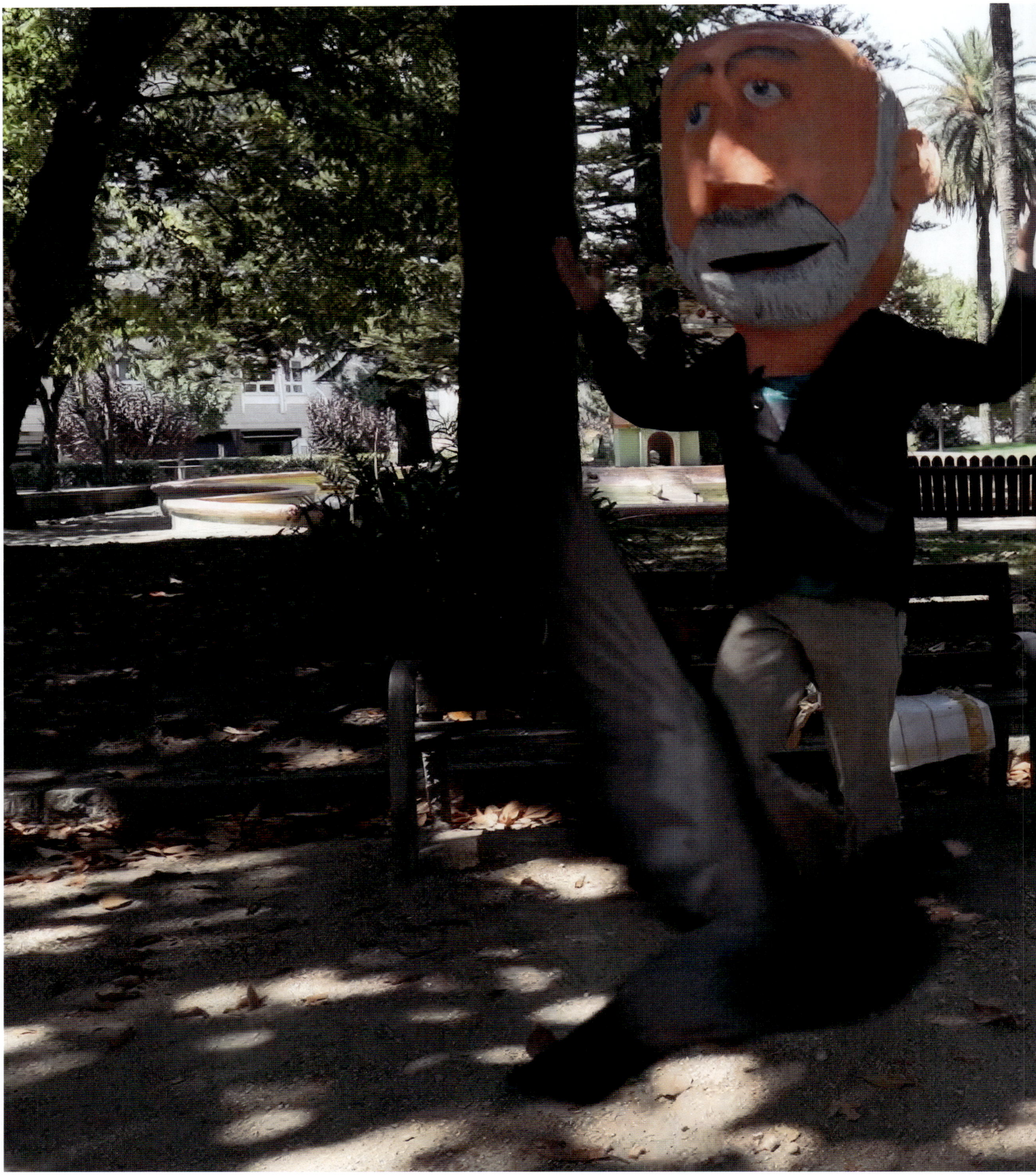

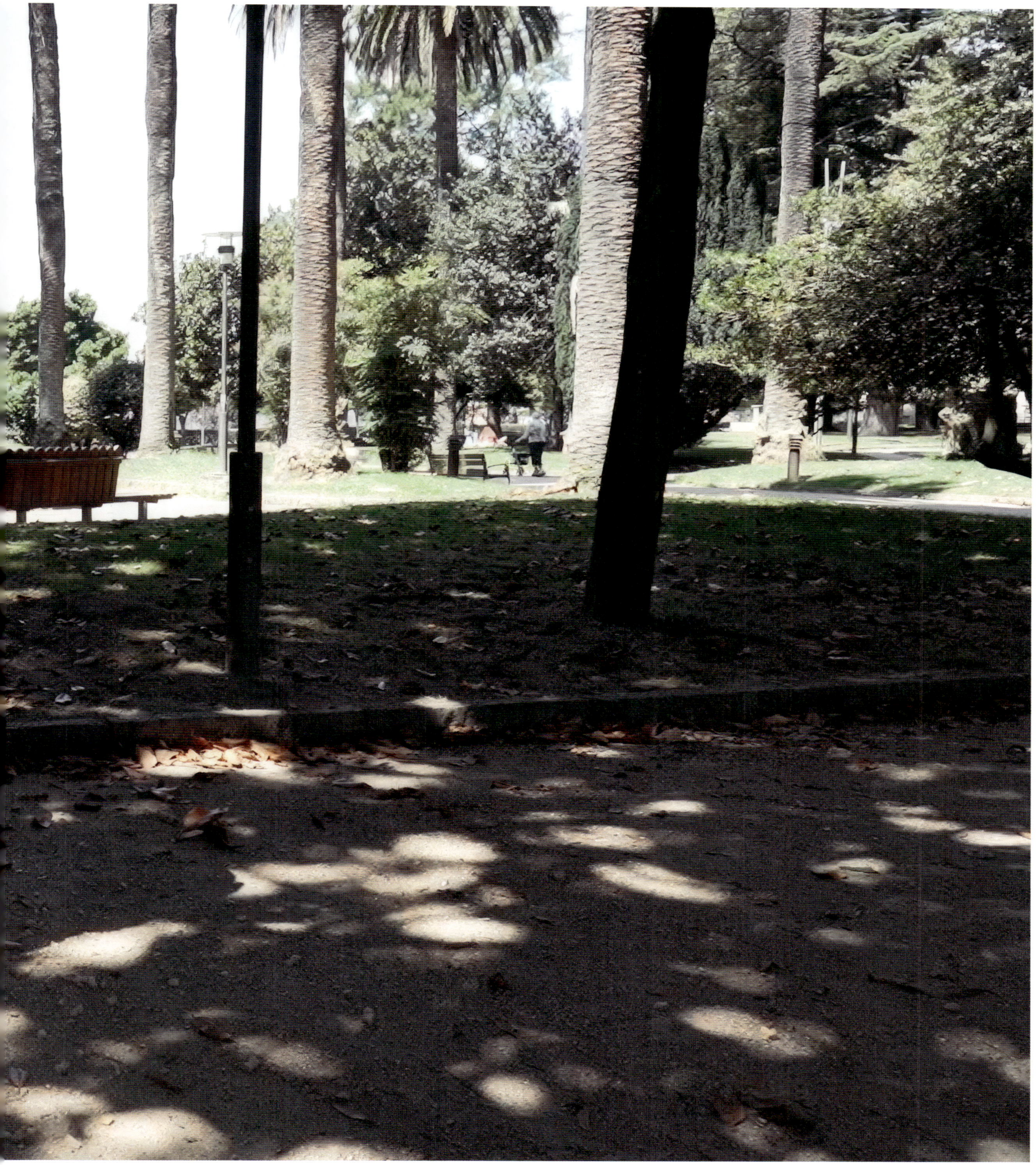

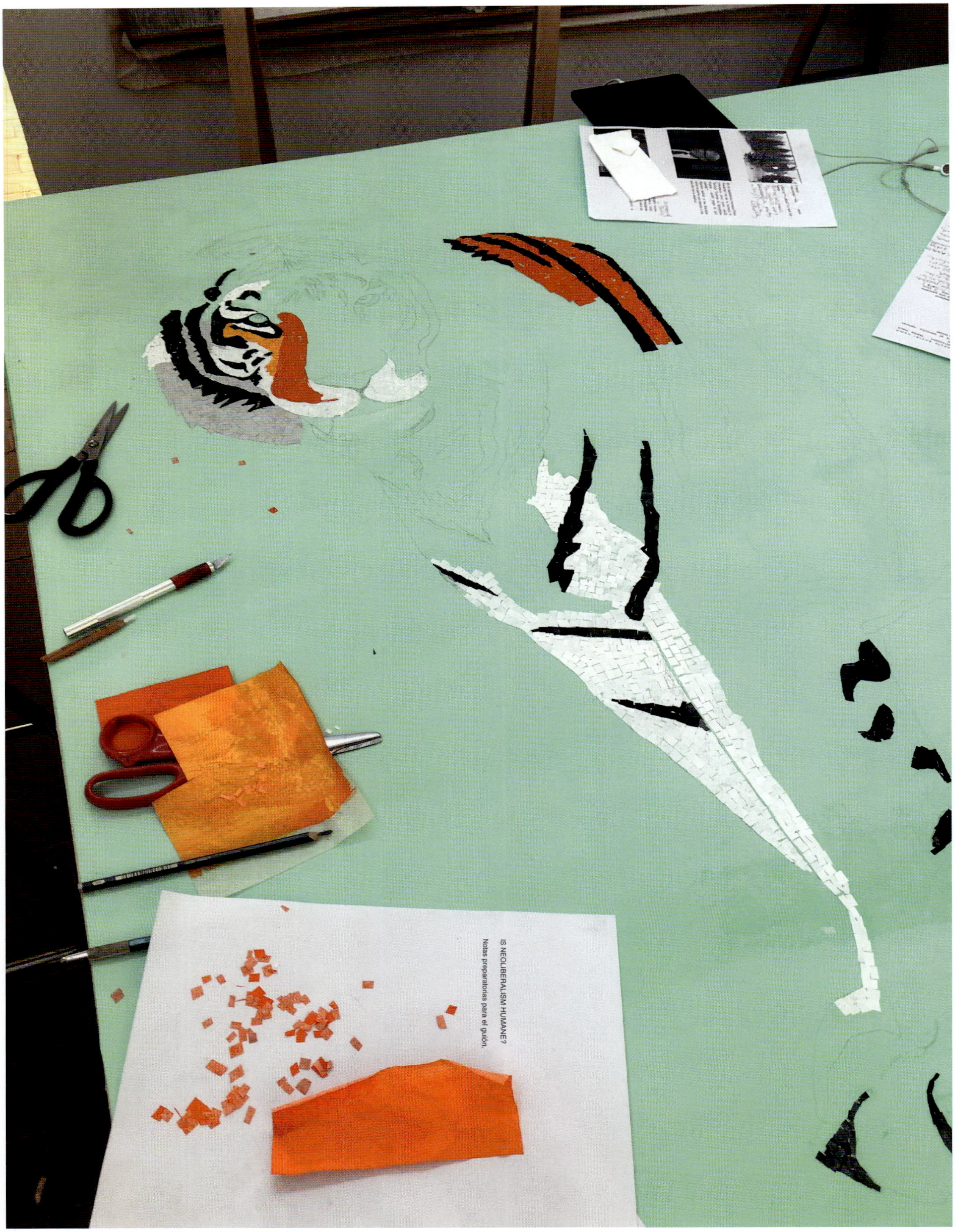
IS NEOLIBERALISM HUMANE?
Notas preparatorias para el guión.

AMERICAN IMPERIALISM IS...

The first tiger was prompted by a quote from Mao, pronounced on 18 November 1957, when he said that American imperialism was a paper tiger.

The technique is the same as I used for the series of Hands: collage on canvas. In fact, the process consists in filling in a drawing with tiny bits of tissue paper cut into little squares with the goal of, among other things, wasting as much time as possible.

The figure of Mao has always interested me as a model of formalization. The hands in the images next to the tigers are those of the great leader, doing things. If there's one thing that characterizes a leader it is that they are always doing things and very often doing them with a serious expression in order to lend their actions greater weight and solemnity.

Lin Piao always appeared smiling behind Chairman Mao, brandishing his little red book, that is, until he had a strange plane accident. His hagiographers recount the love for the Great Helmsman: "Mao you are our sun, we are your sunflowers." Mao's children learned to say "Long live Chairman Mao" before they learned to say "Daddy". "Not a day goes by without reading the works of Chairman Mao." Etcetera, etcetera.

At this stage we should we well aware that giving in to the master's desires does not guarantee anything, because the master doesn't sign contracts. Throughout history, making a clean break with the past to follow a leader, to leave one father only to fall into the hands of a greater father has had mixed results, but there is always one thing in common. This desire always ends in the master's discourse and in the recovery of surplus value.

pp. 114-115
American Imperialism Is... Shaking Hands, 2022
Acrylic and collage on canvas
130 x 197 cm

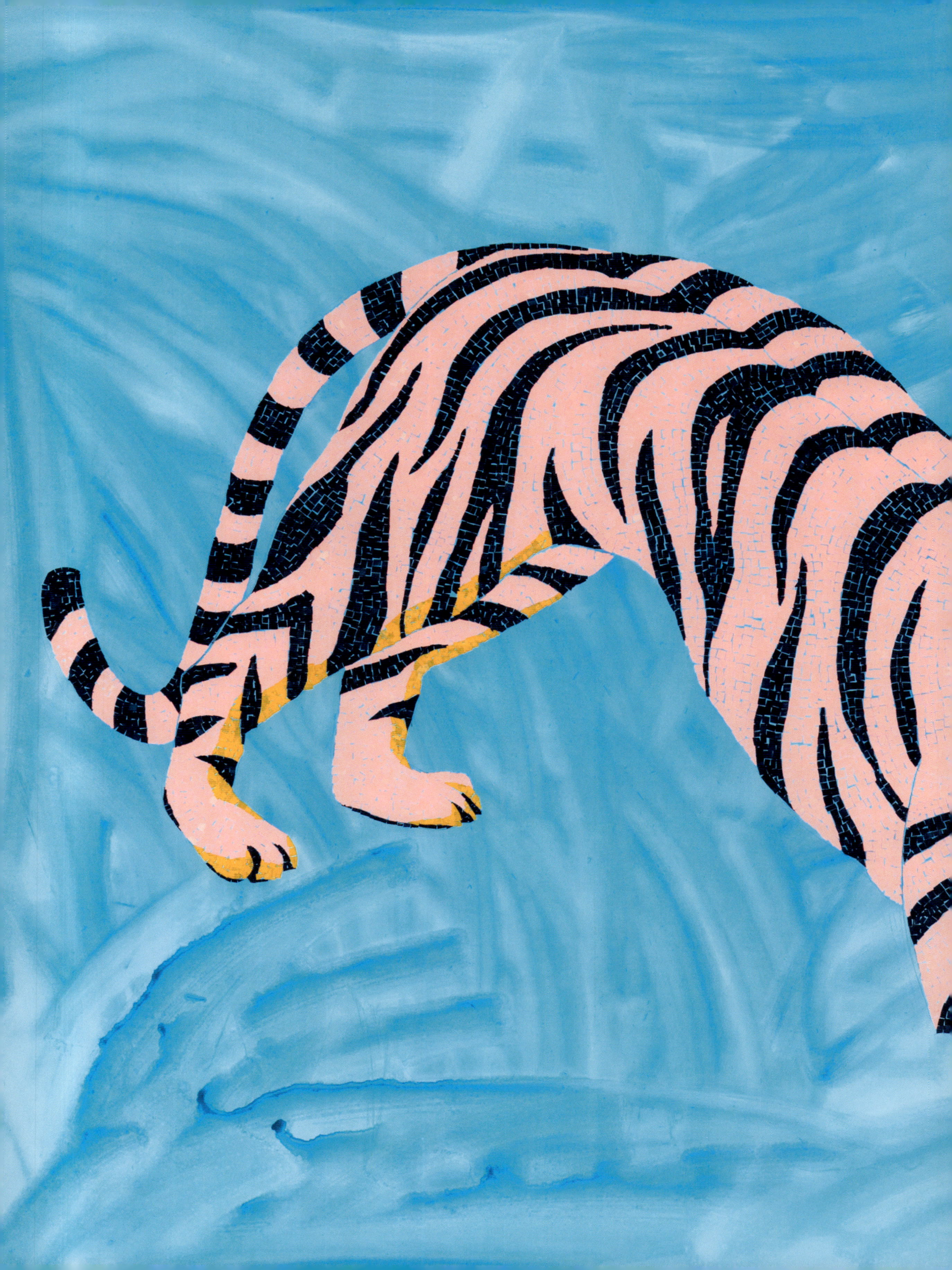

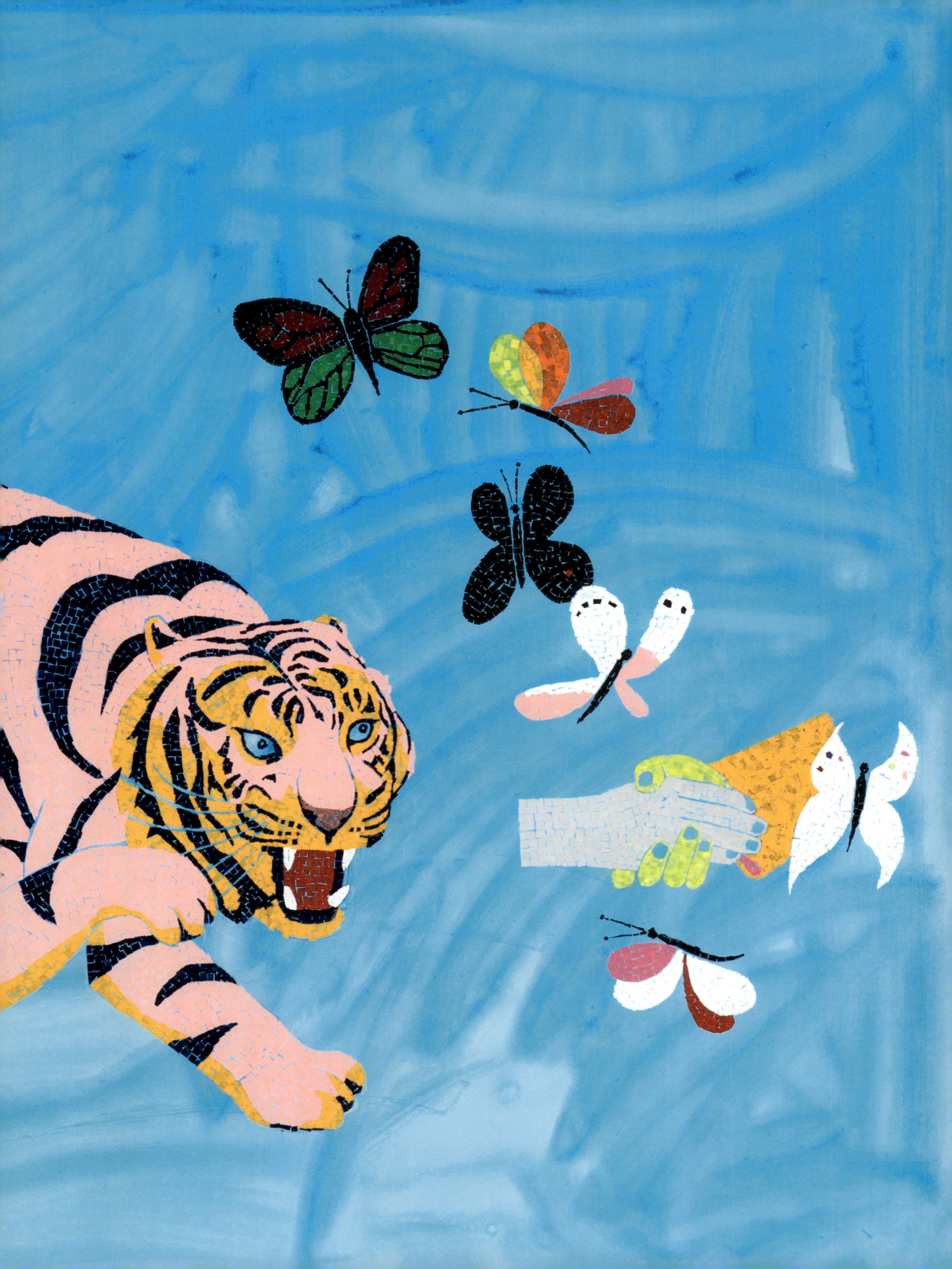

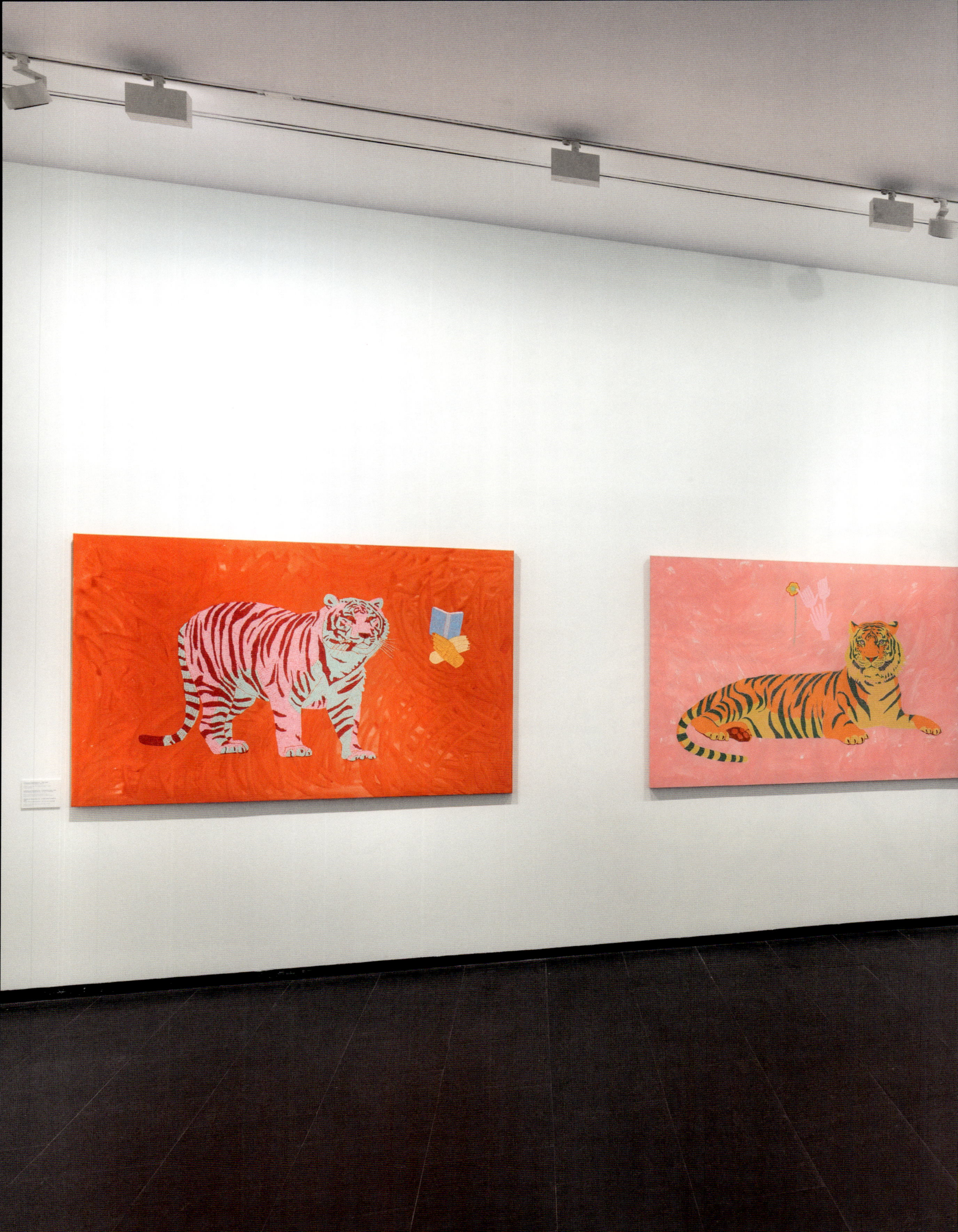

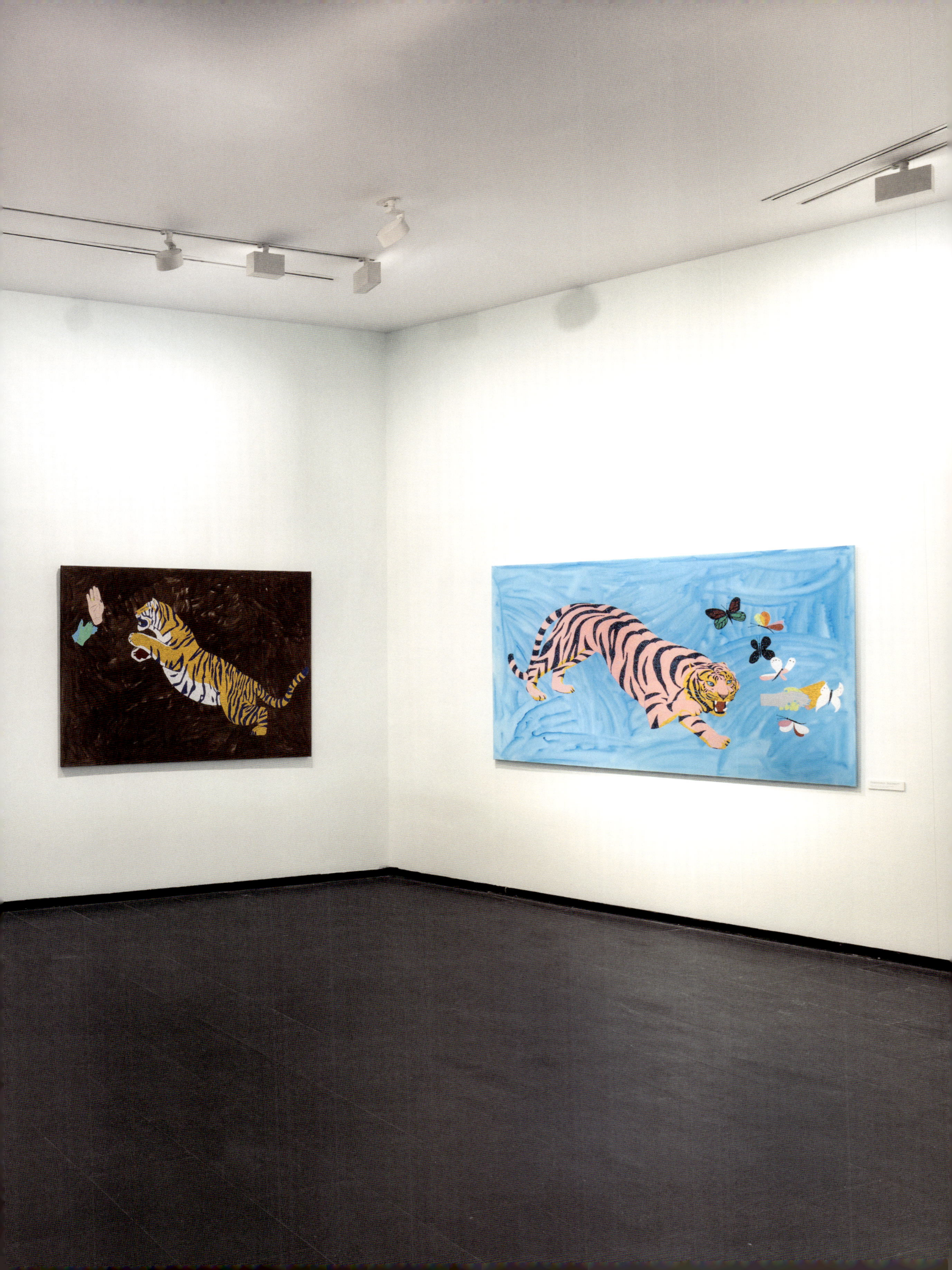

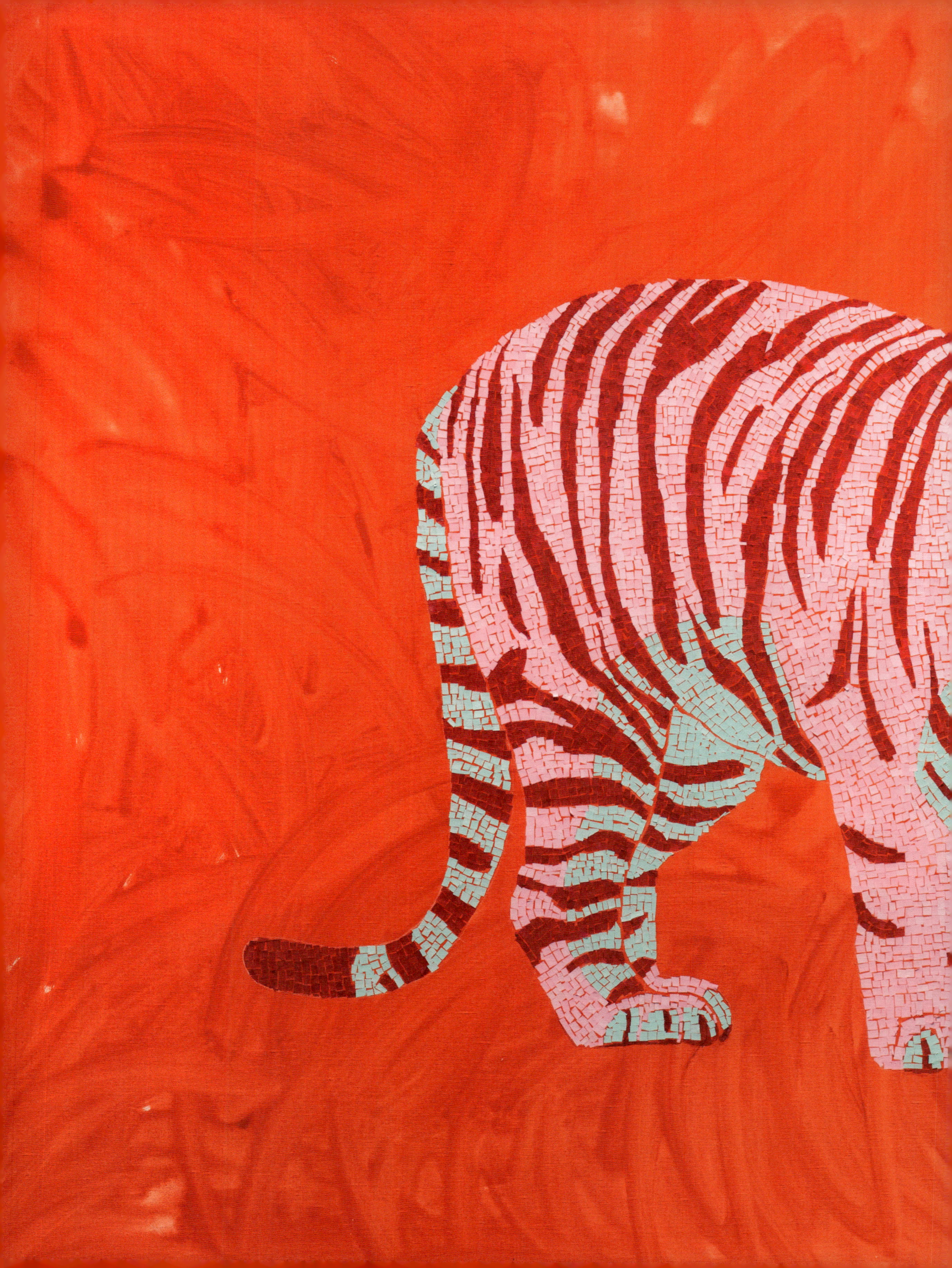

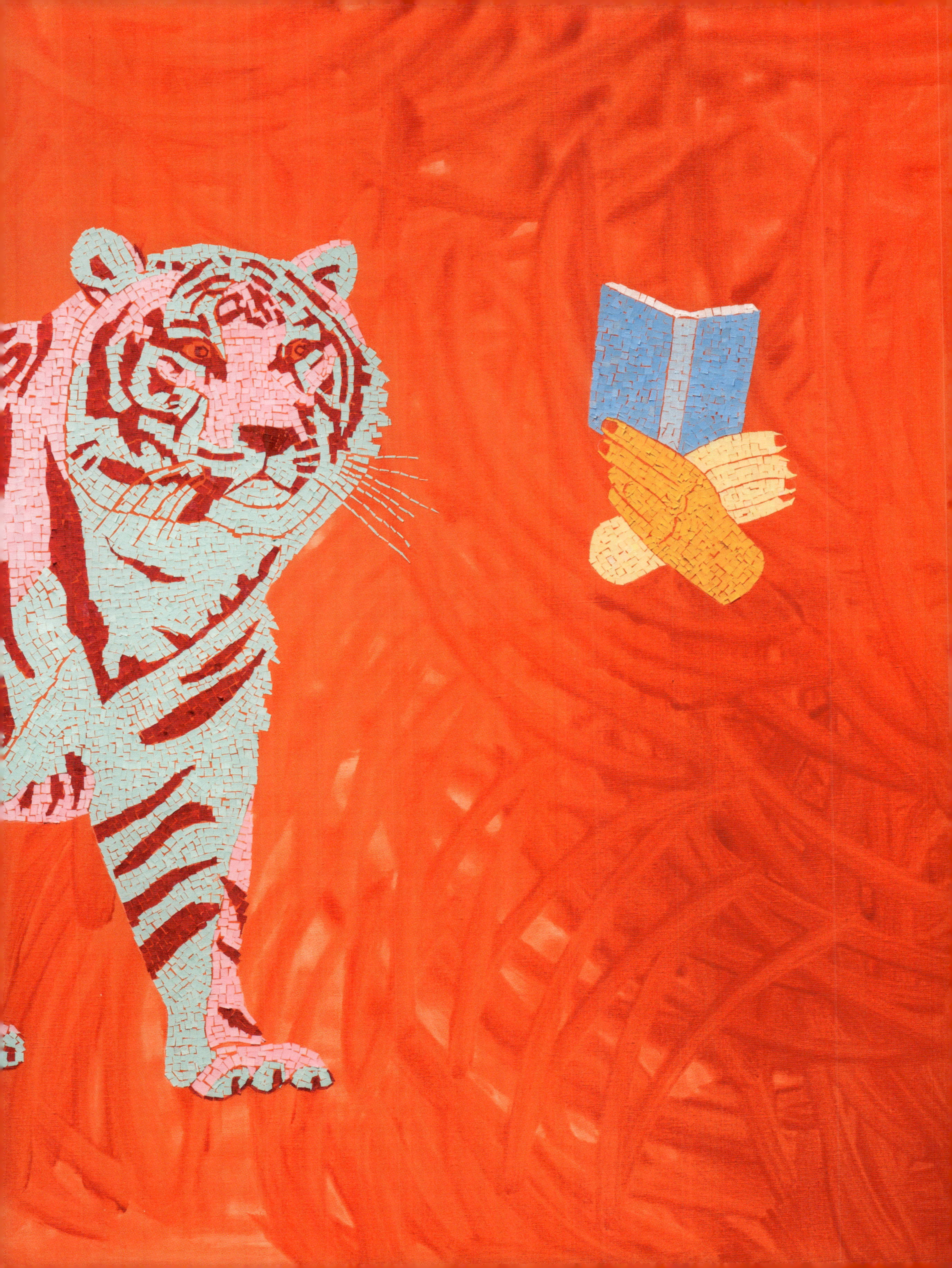

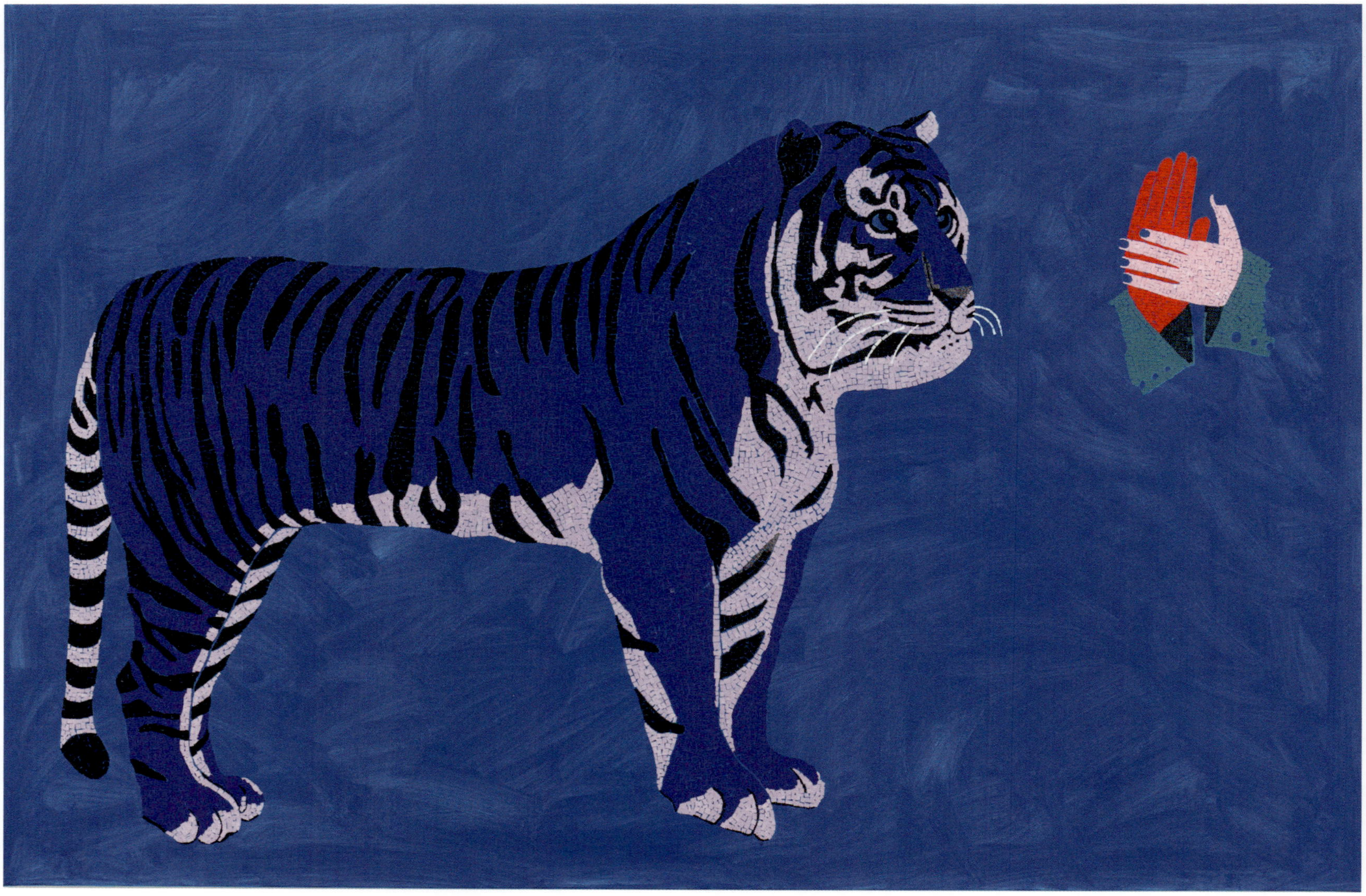

pp. 118-119
American Imperialism Is... You, 2025
Acrylic and collage on canvas
130 x 197 cm

American Imperialism Is... Clapping, 2021
Acrylic and collage on canvas
130 x 197 cm

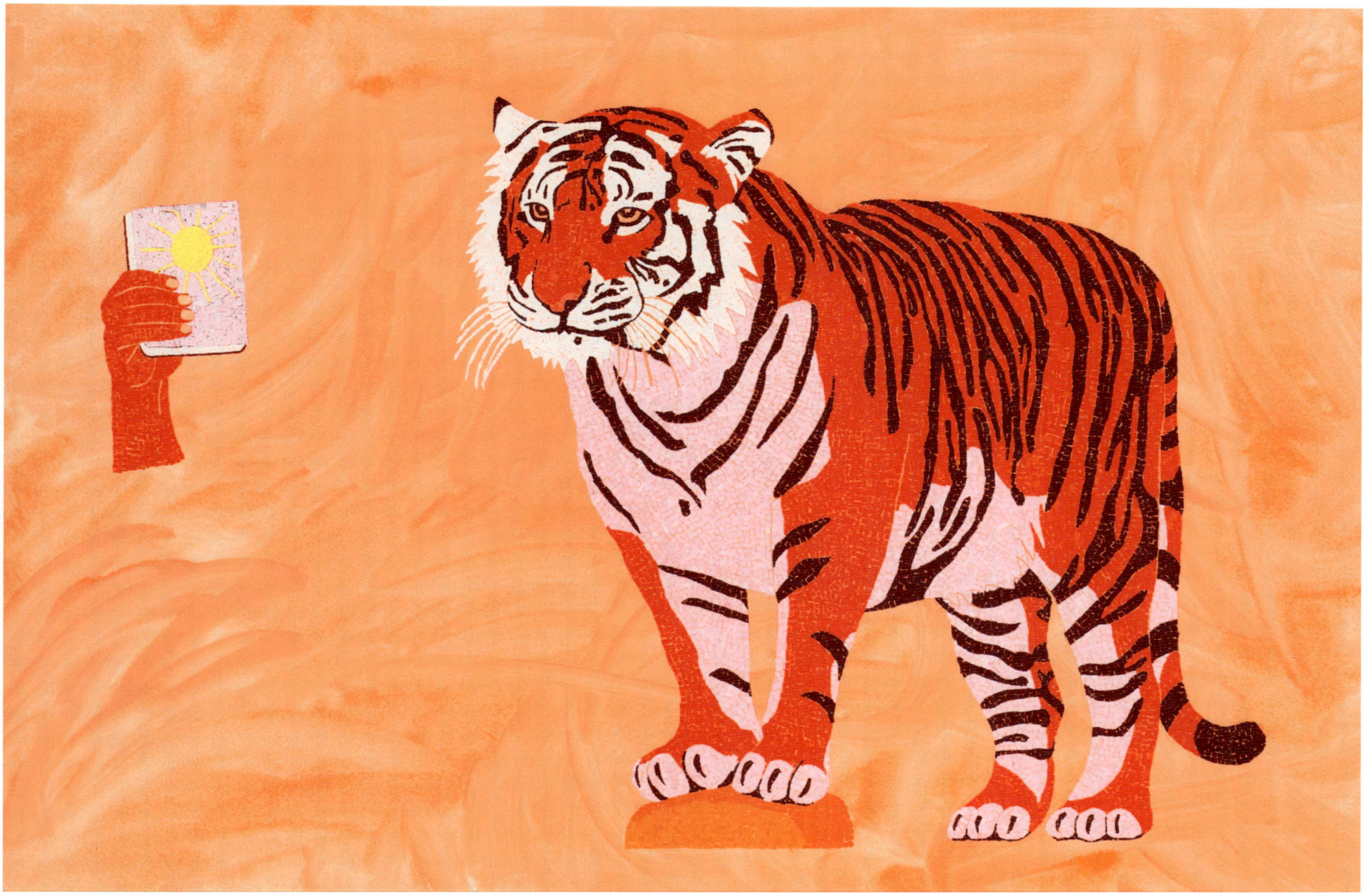

American Imperialism Is... The Rose Book, 2021
Acrylic and collage on canvas
130 x 197 cm

pp. 122-123
American Imperialism Is... A New Step Forward, 2025
Acrylic and collage on canvas
130 x 197 cm

pp. 124-125
American Imperialism Is... A Belleville Tiger, 2022
Acrylic and collage on canvas
130 x 197 cm

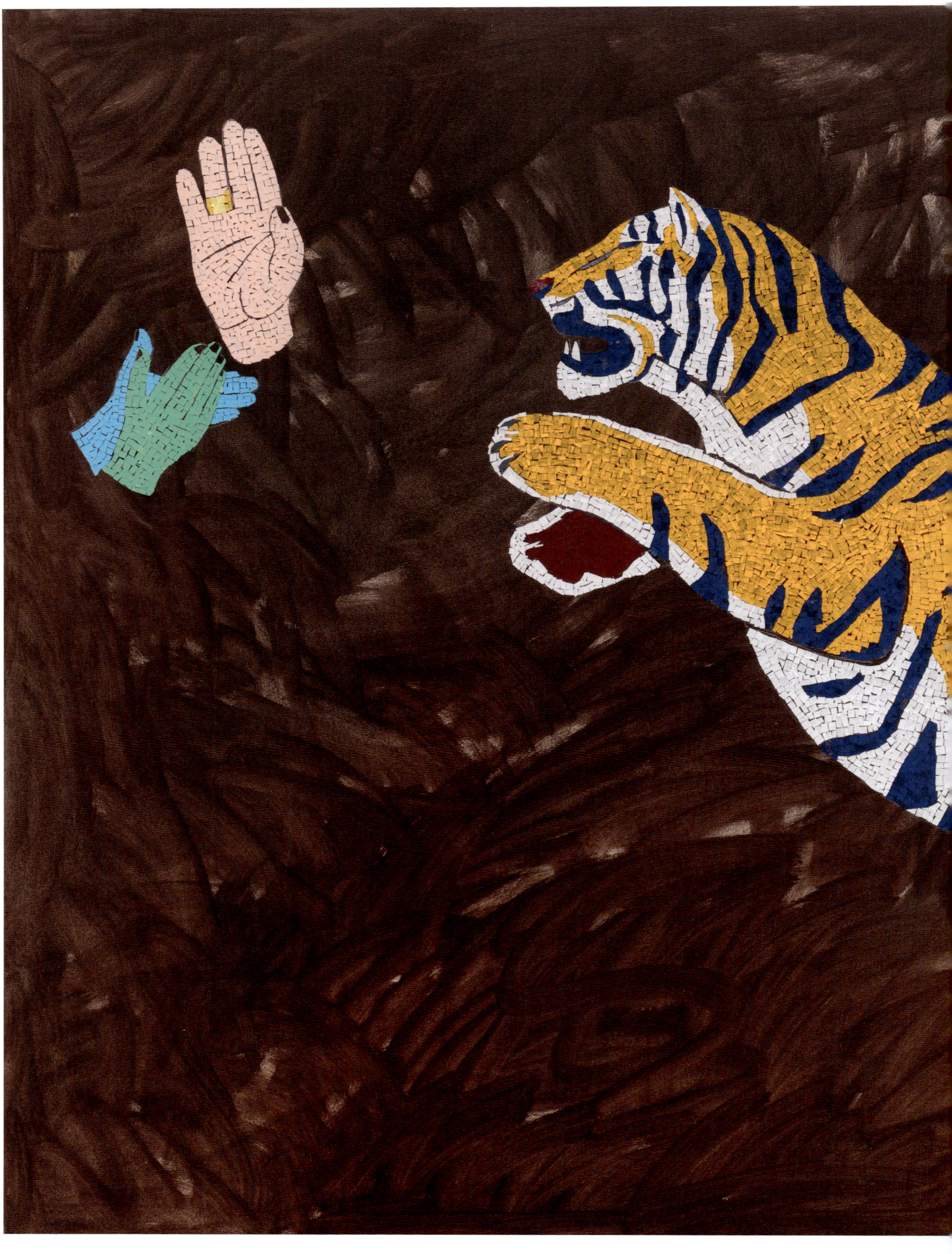

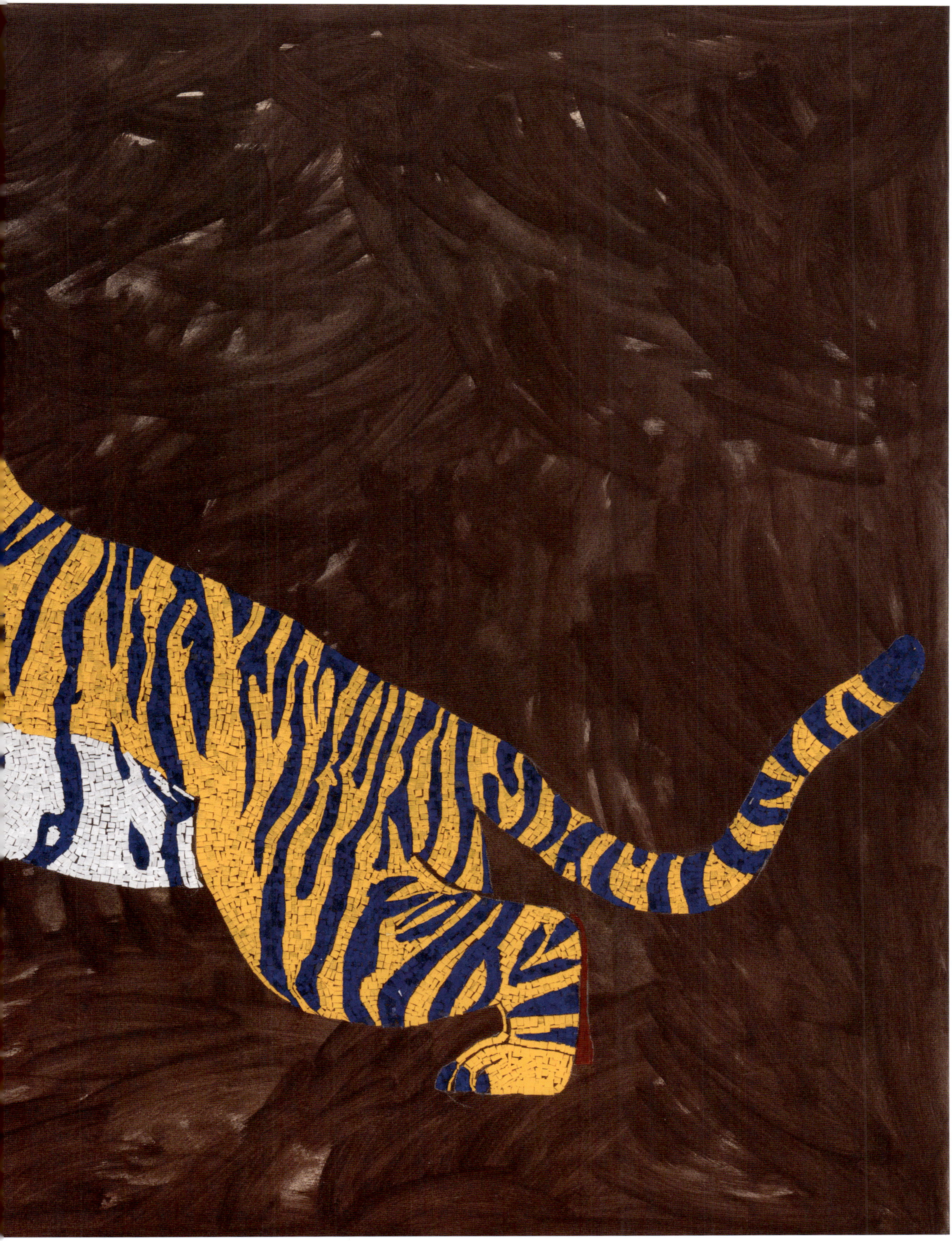

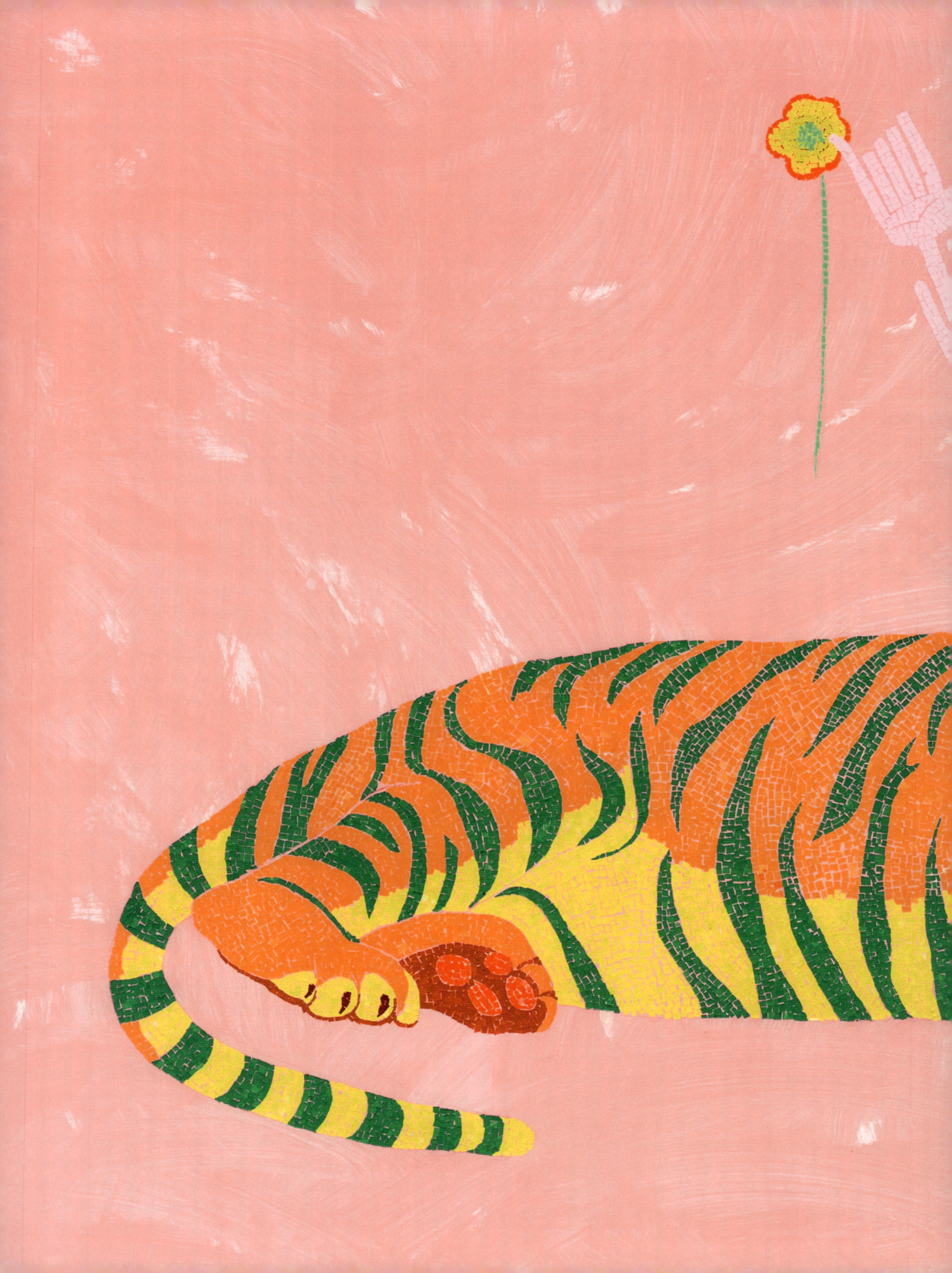

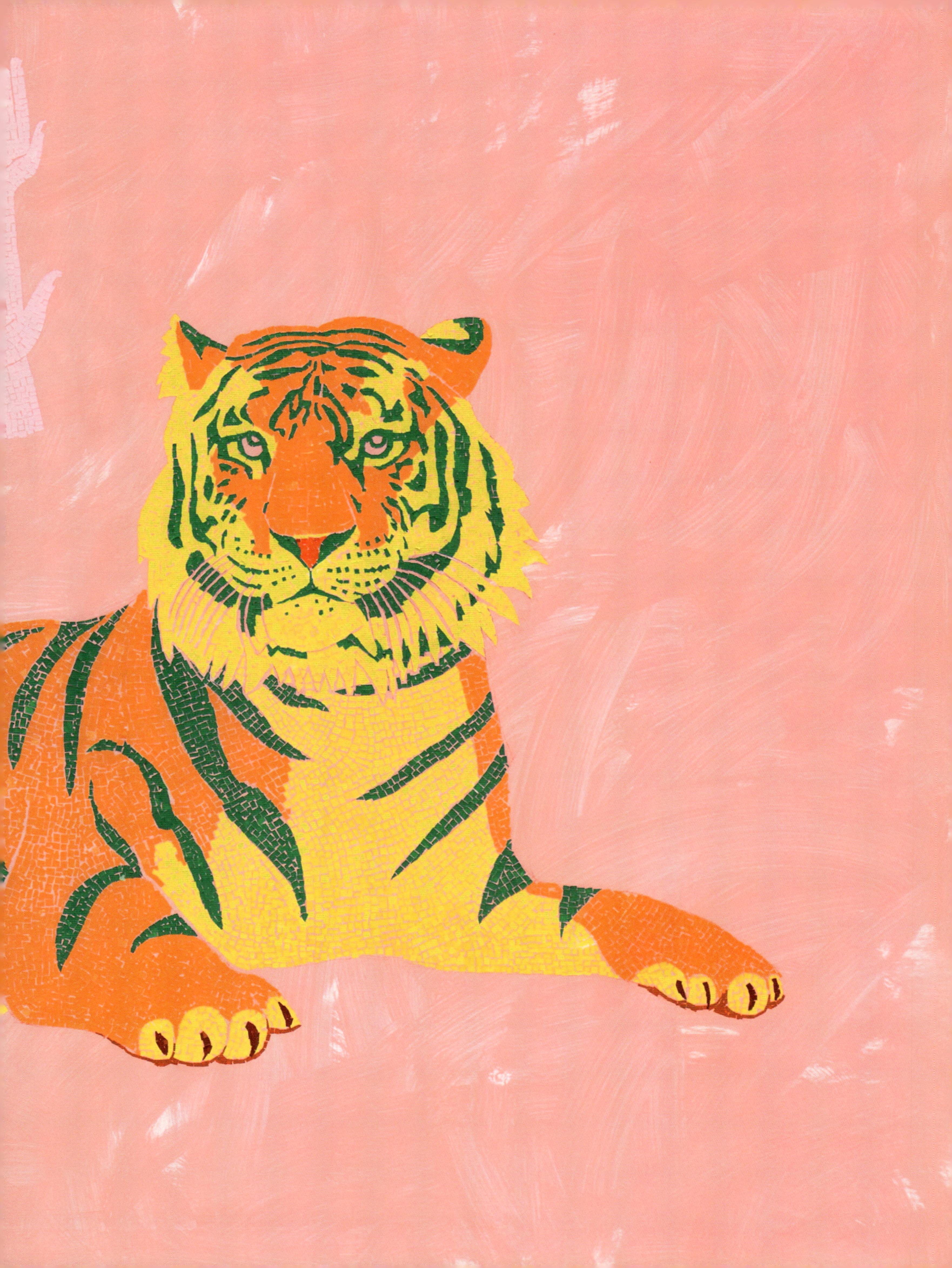

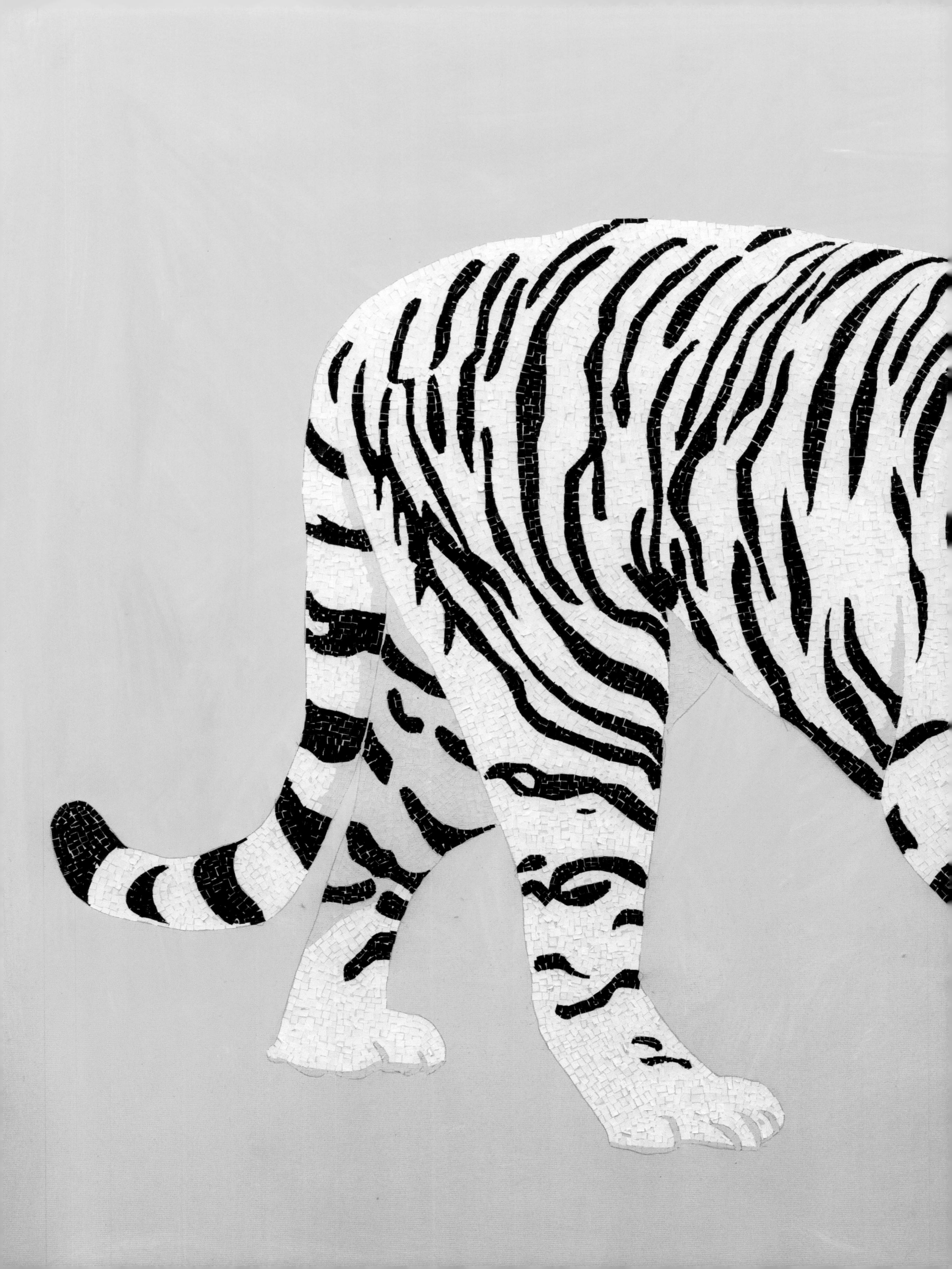

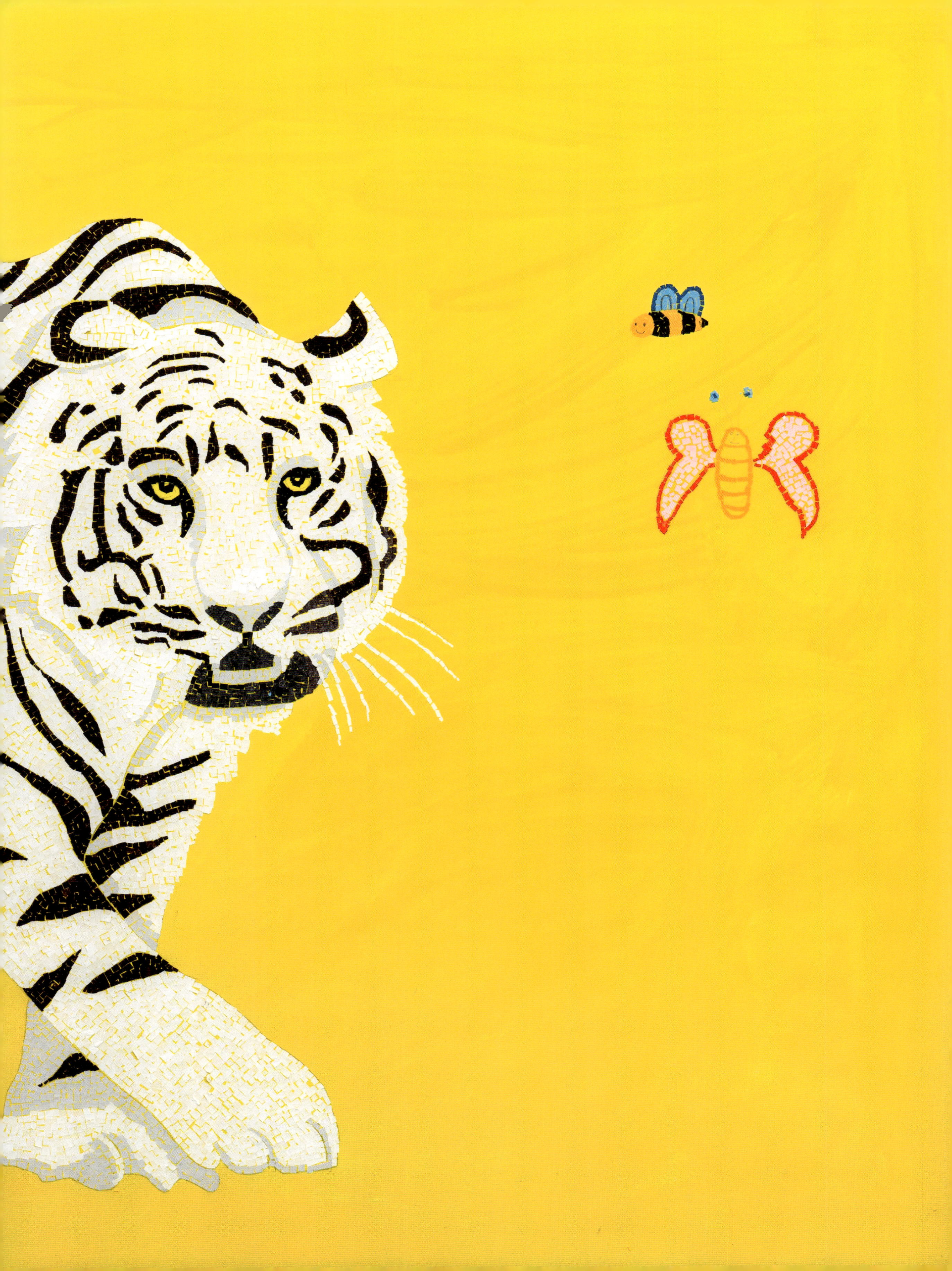

pp. 126-127
American Imperialism Is... With Bee, 2021
Acrylic and collage on canvas
130 x 197 cm

p. 129
American Imperialism Is... A Plastic Tiger, 2022
Acrylic and collage on canvas
197 x 130 cm

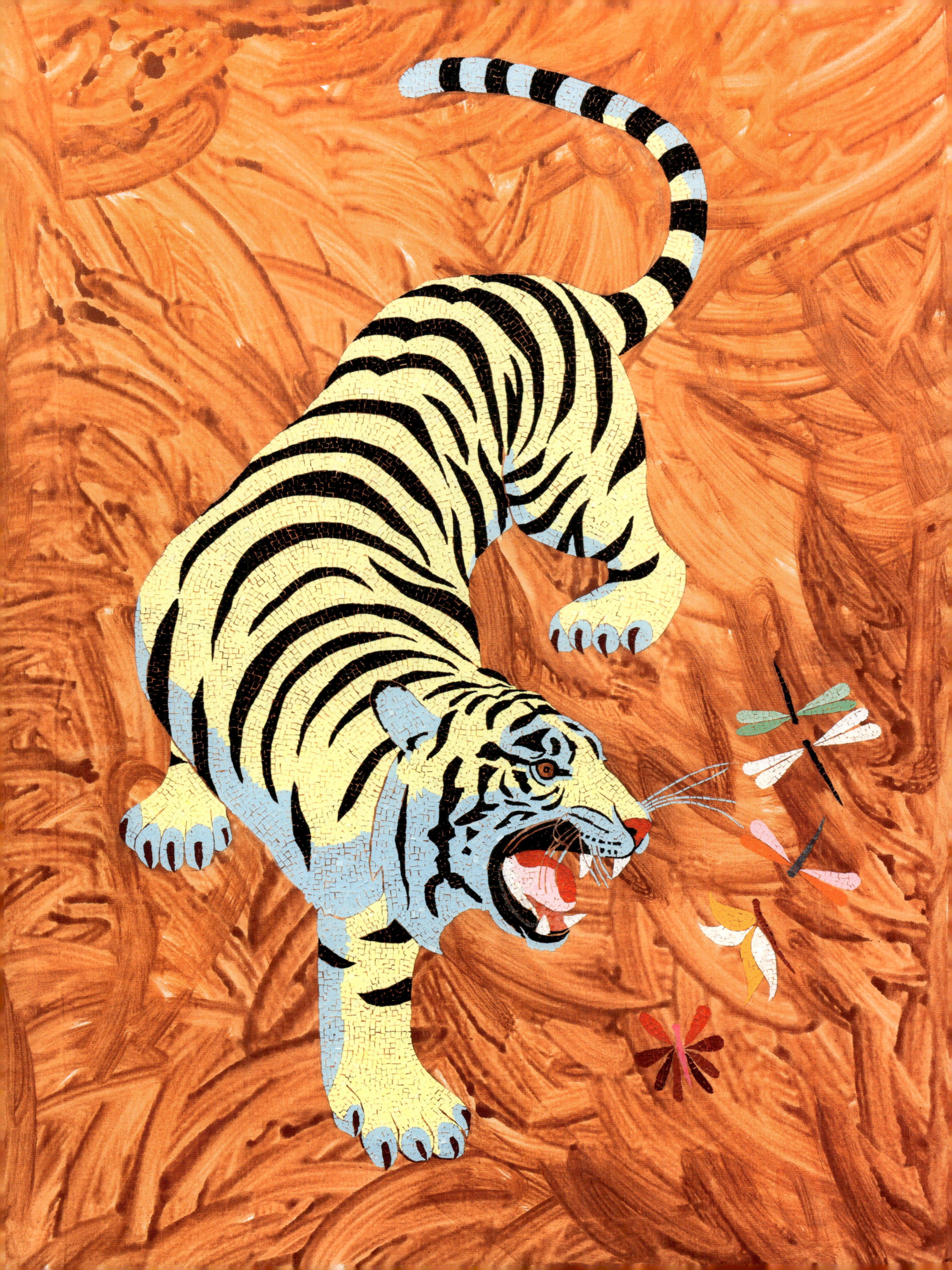

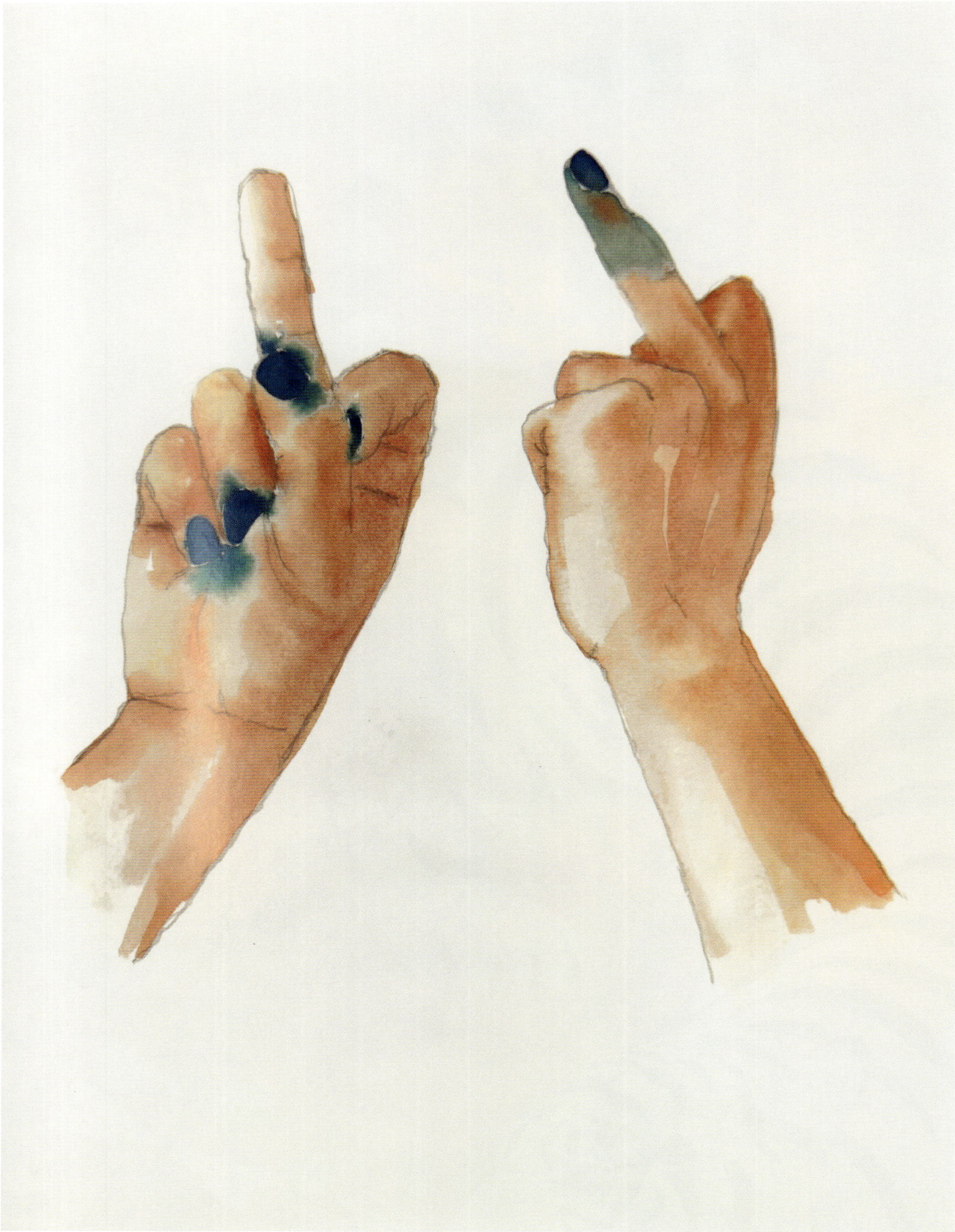

Manicura, 2008
Watercolour on paper
32 x 25 cm

RIGHT HANDS

The series of right hands is part of all the work I have been doing on the subtle return of fascism. They are made using collage with little pieces of paper, a technique often used in art classes at school to keep young children occupied.

What at first seemed like a mere suspicion started to become real. You didn't have to be a genius to realize, because there was no shortage of warning signs. Now it's more than obvious: interference of enemy countries, targeted algorithms feeding us lies customized to our tastes, and one hoax after another.

Having said that, I believe that the most telling and most frightening sign is the surprising support for these ideas among people close to us, a clear symptom that the updated version of the fascist message has gradually taken hold. It's always good to have a scapegoat, and the phoney gravitas adopted, the highest form of cynicism, actually works.

And so, now I ask myself whether it was any use to have made those big hands from which fingers sprout like polyps, extremities growing in number and lifted in a solemnly enacted gesture, reaching skywards as if someone was looking down from above.

Hands with butterflies and insects, symbols of purity and life but also spreaders of the pollen of evil. Hands and more right hands swarming with flies, always drawn to the stench of shit.

When I think of the way the impressionists worked, going outdoors to capture the moment, and I think about decoration, about the hours spent gluing bits of paper, then the answer to my question is yes.

p. 133
Mao Clapping, 2022
Acrylic and collage on canvas
100 x 73 cm

pp. 134-135
Right Hand Polyps, 2022
Acrylic and collage on canvas
130 x 197 cm

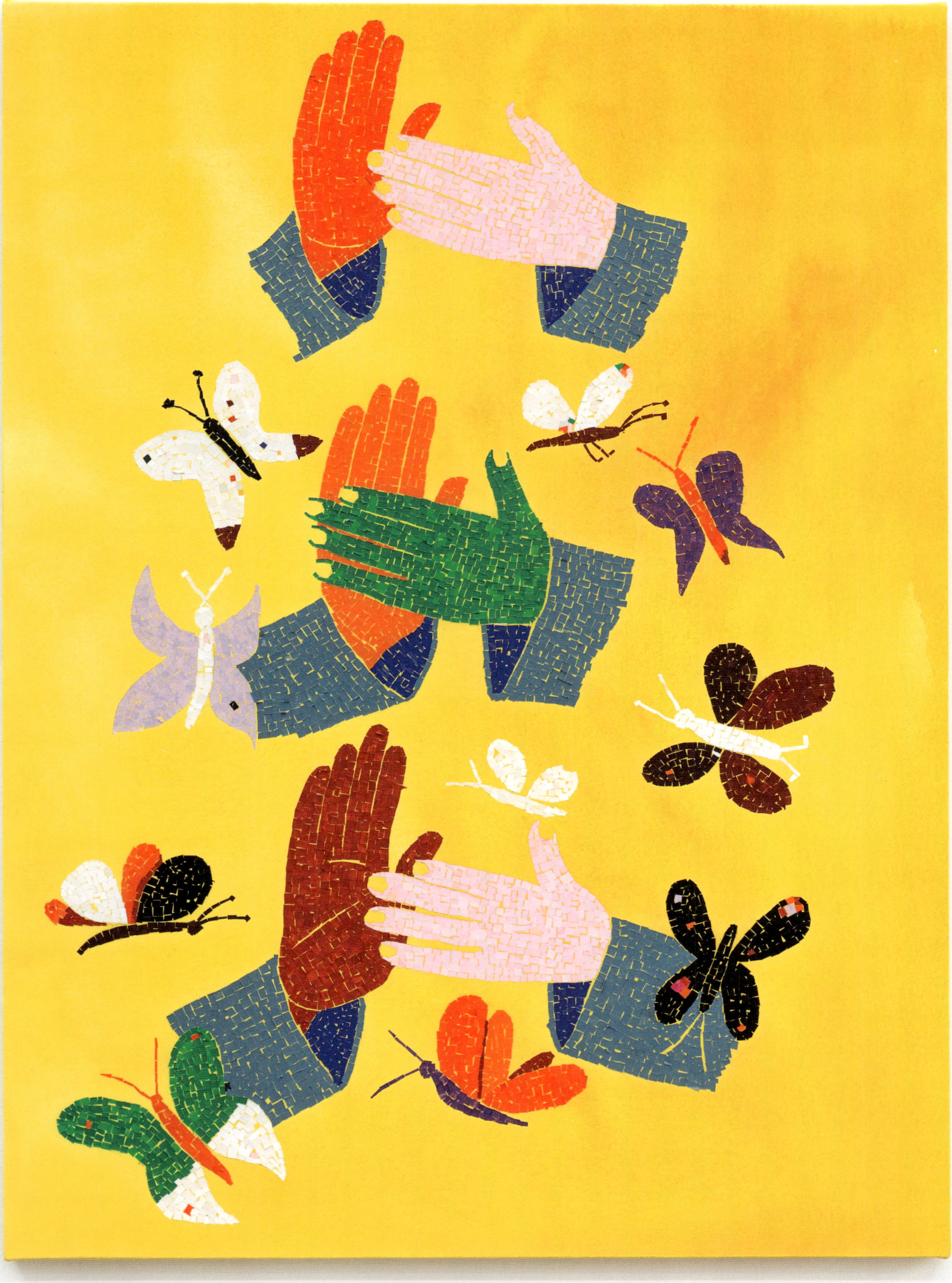

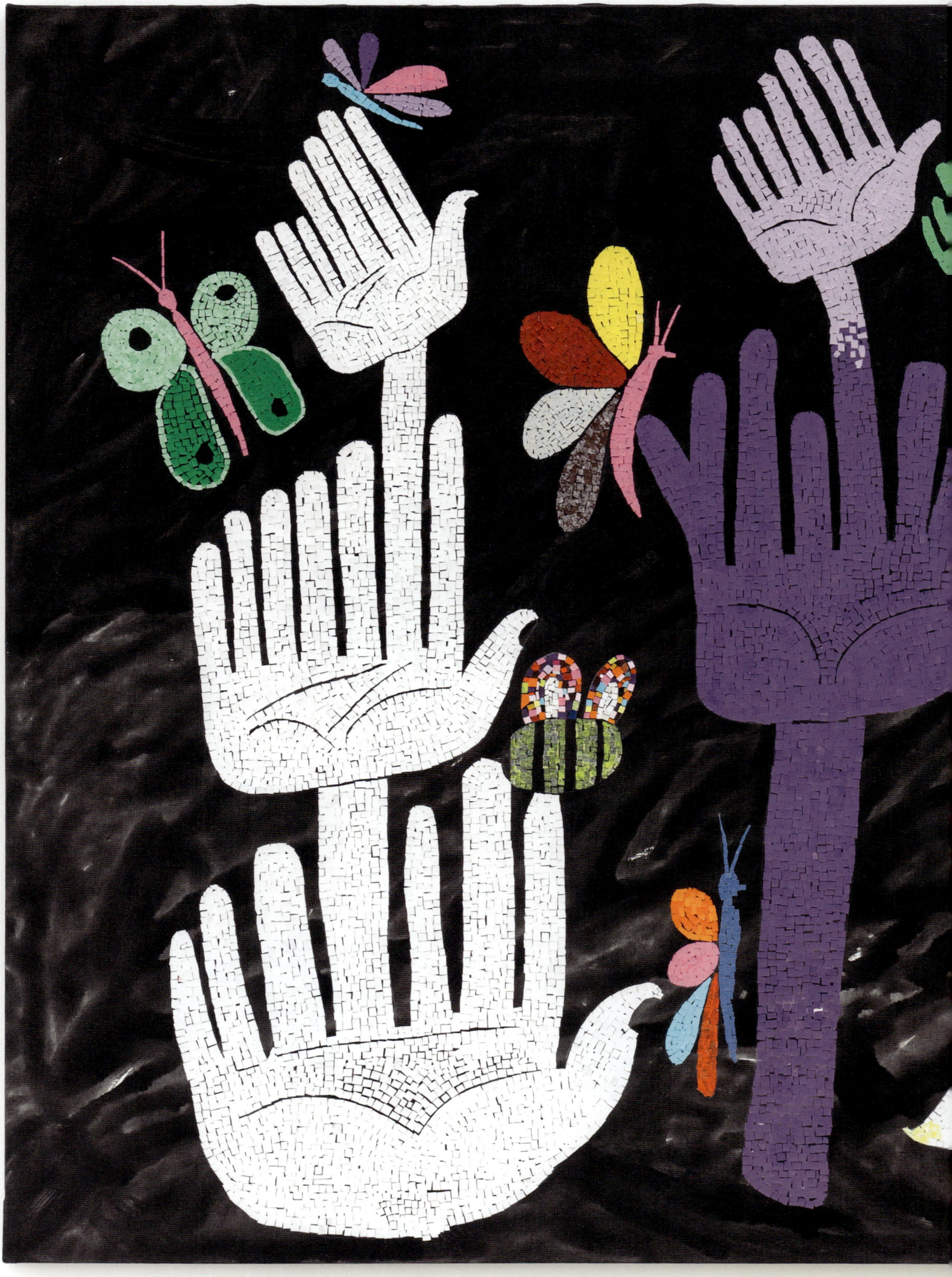

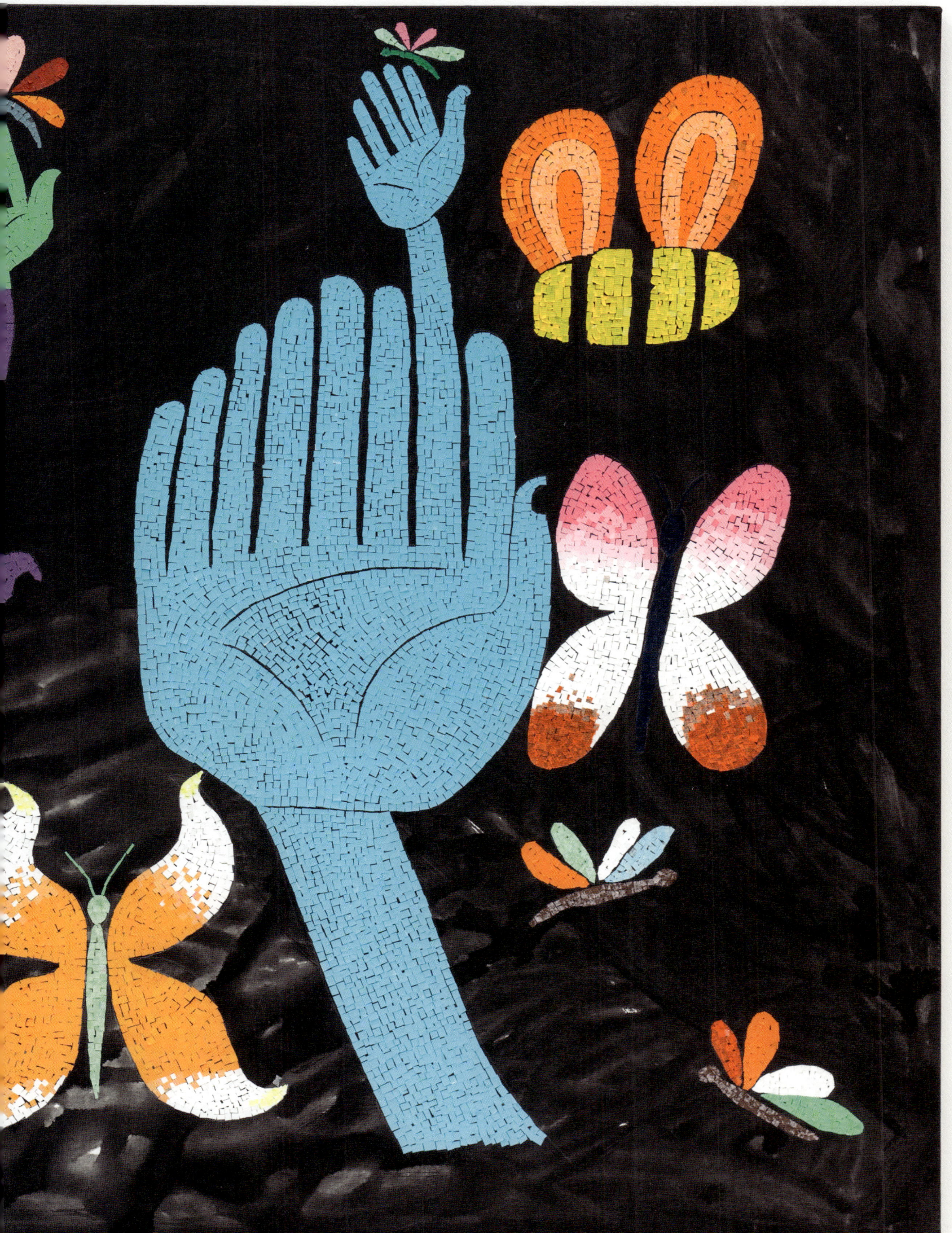

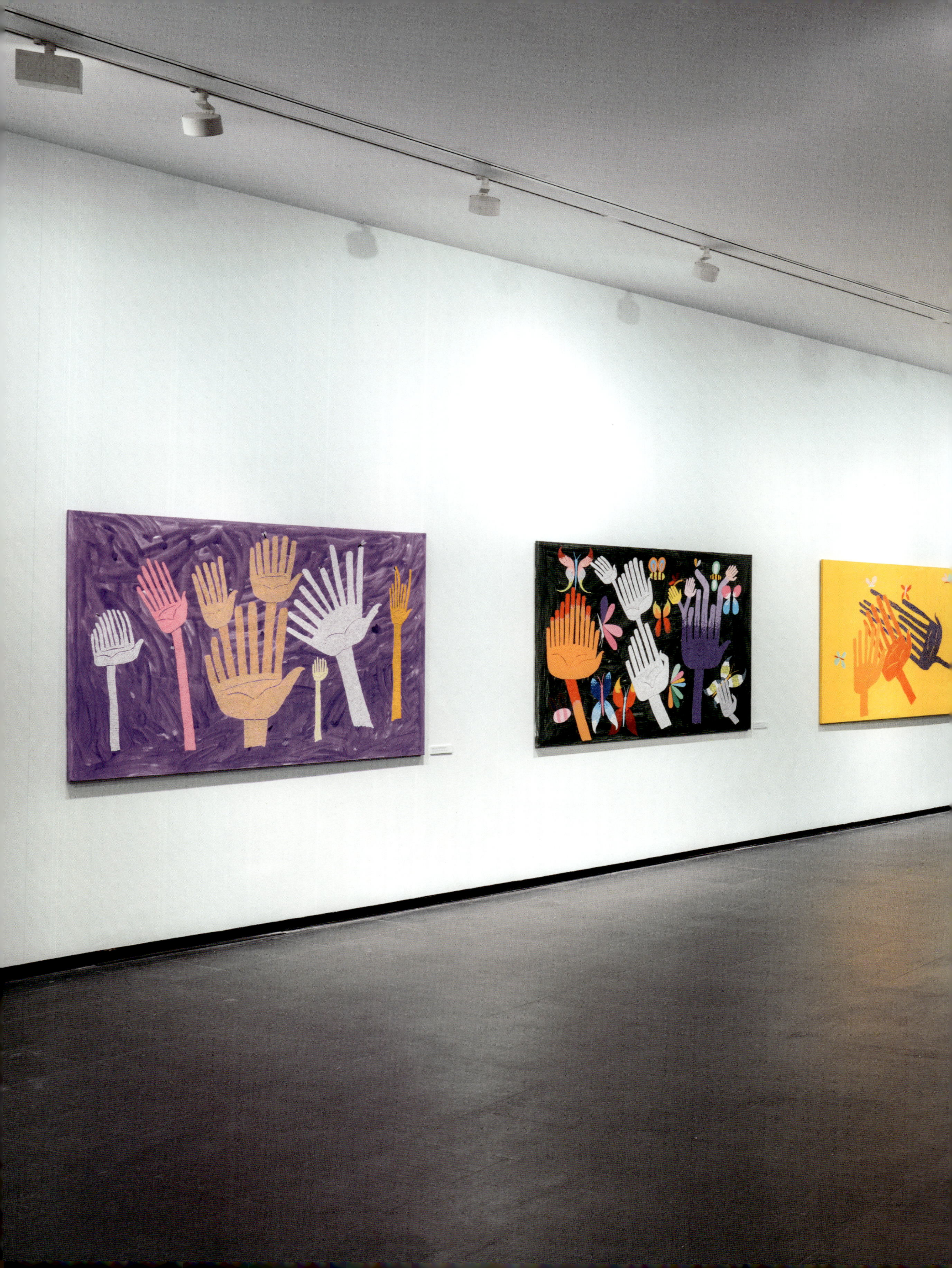

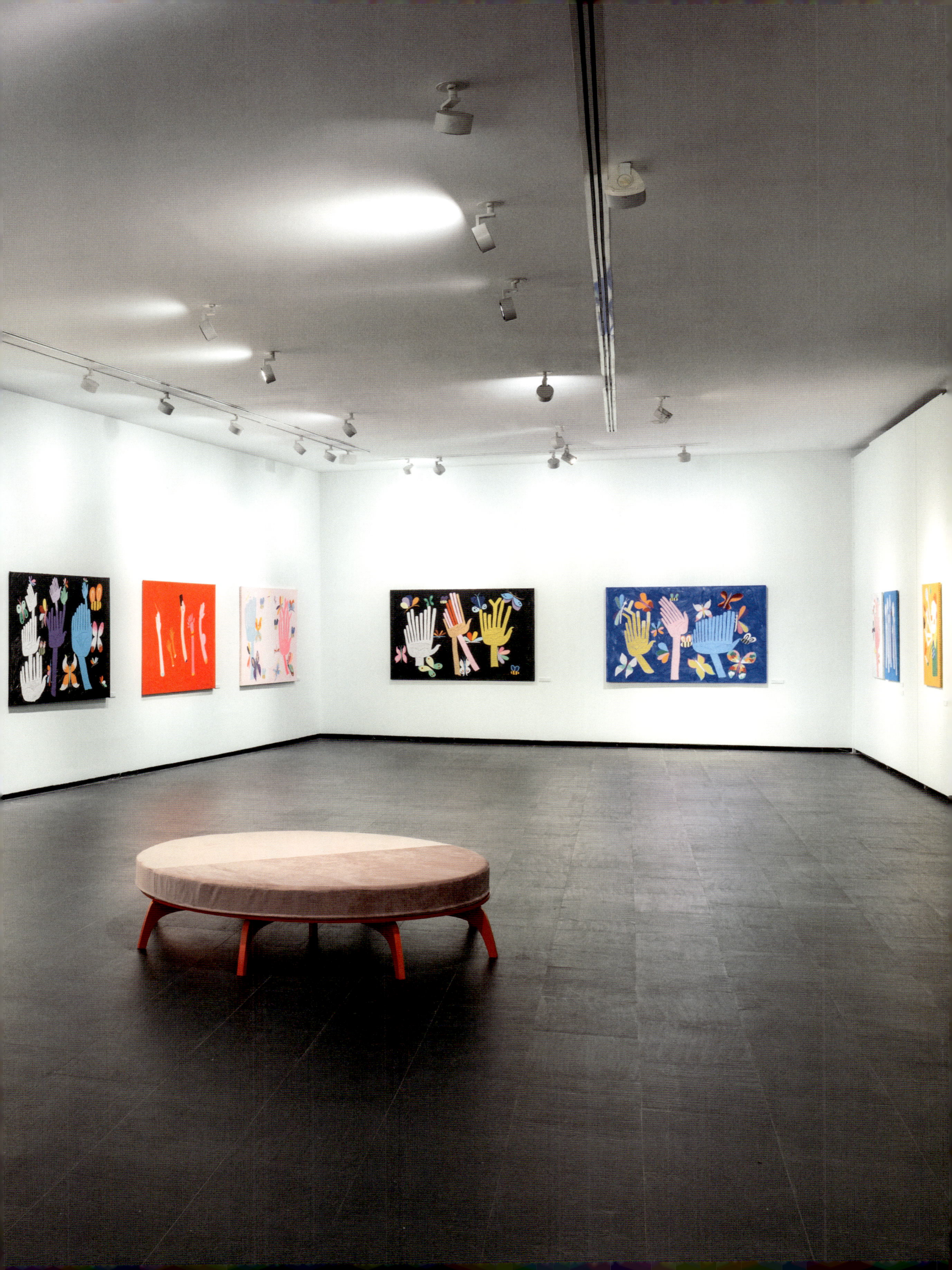

p. 139
Rose Right Hand, 2022
Acrylic and collage on canvas
100 x 73 cm

pp. 140-141
Western Coral with Western Flies, 2023
Acrylic and collage on canvas
130 x 197 cm

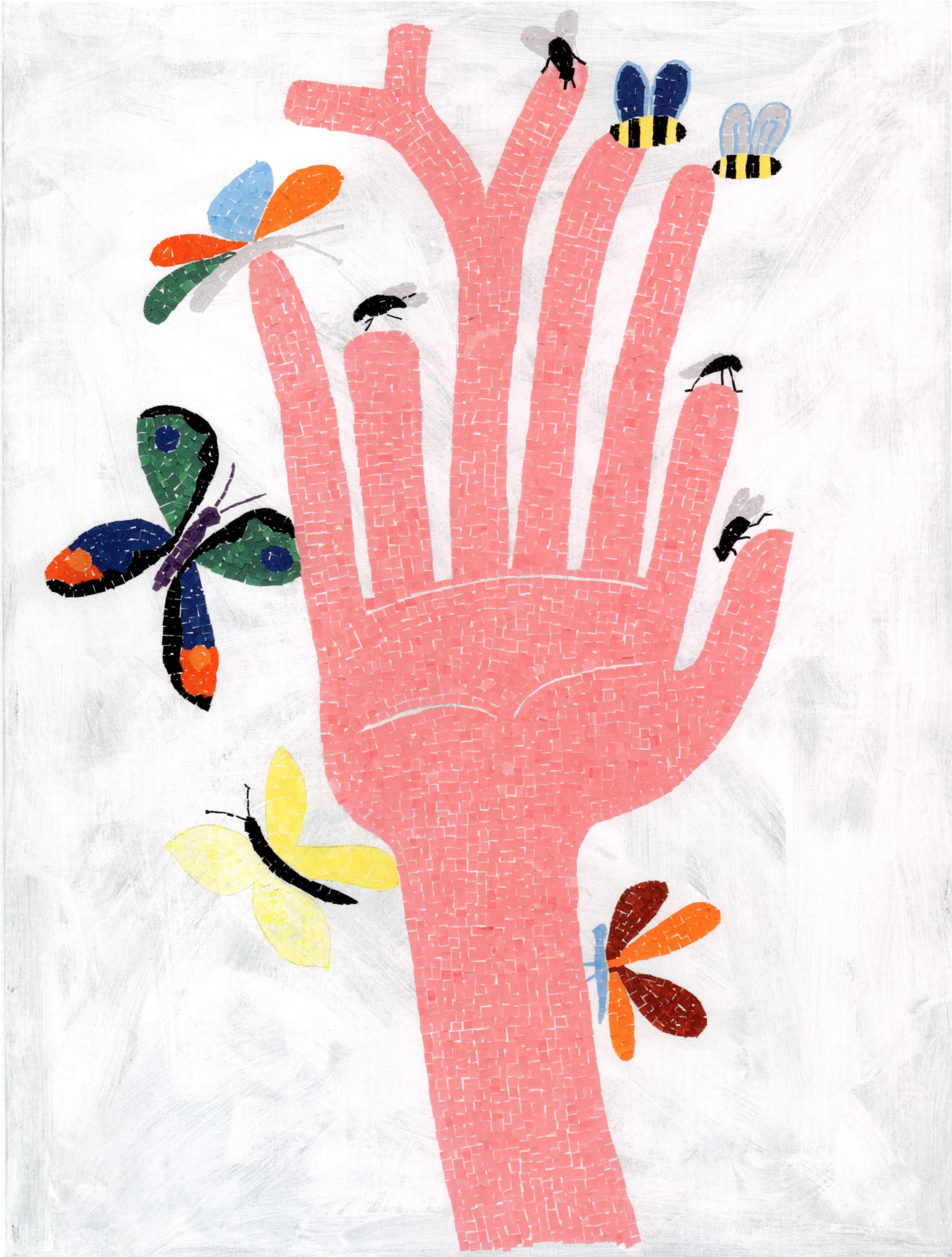

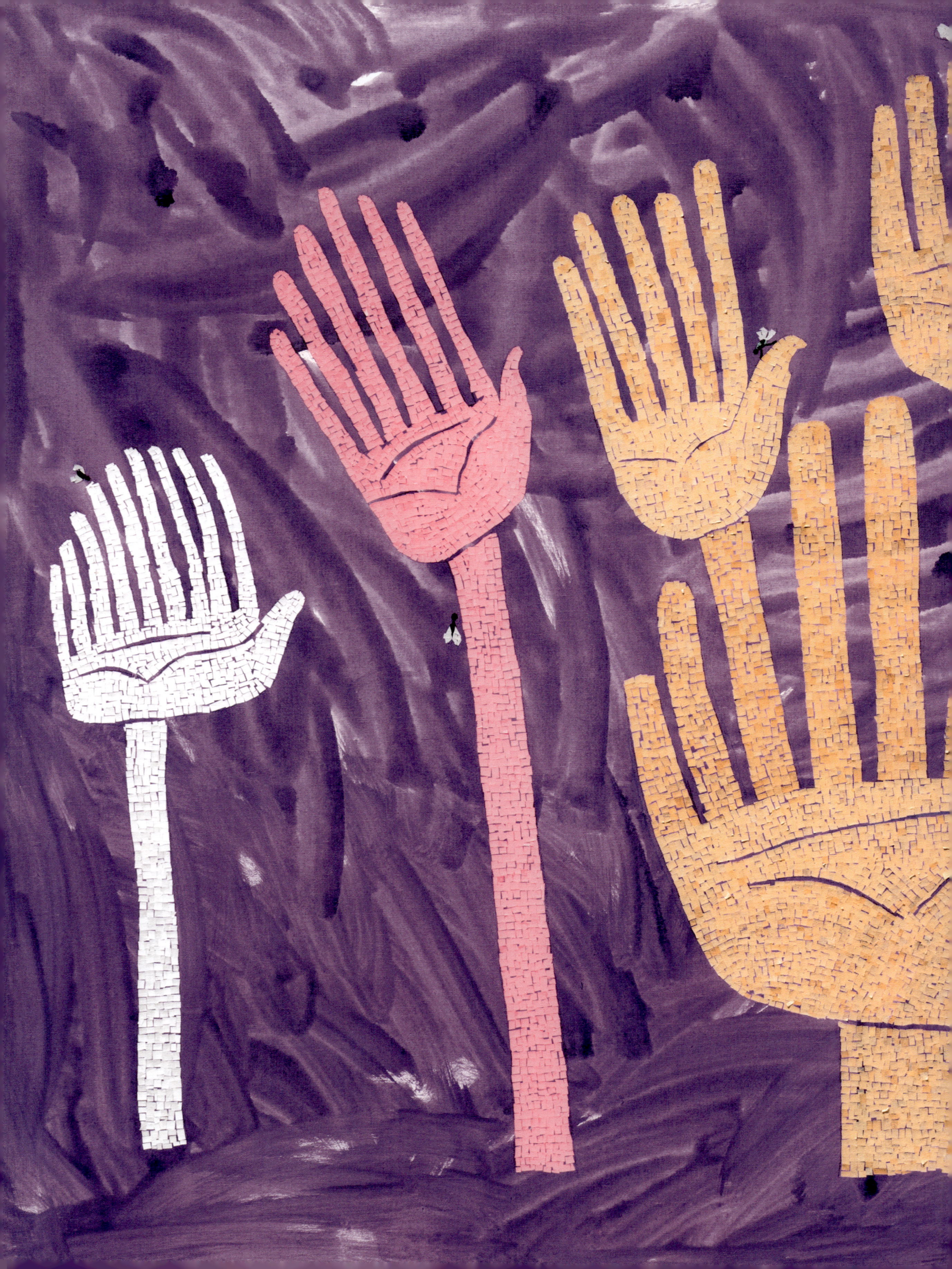

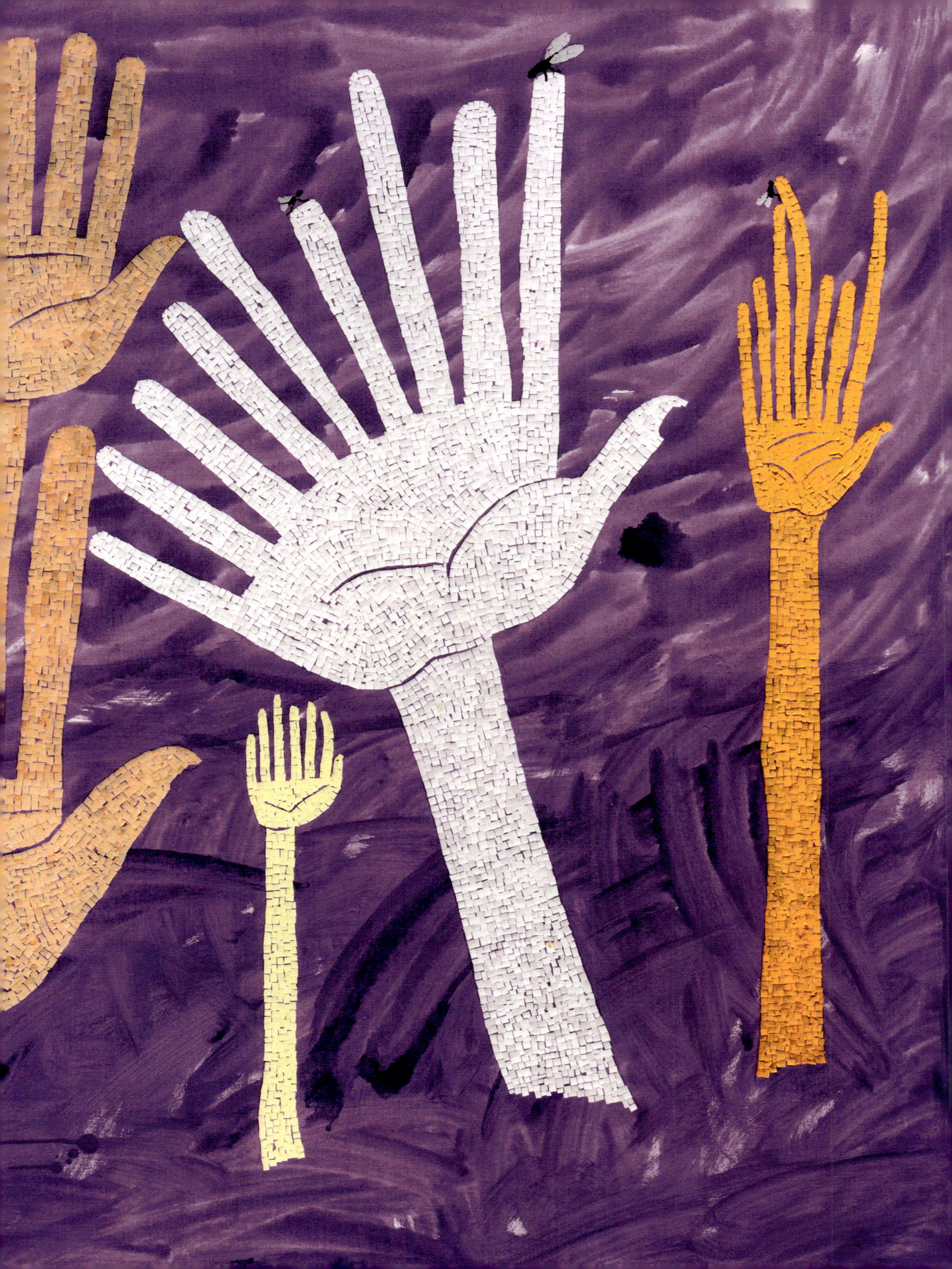

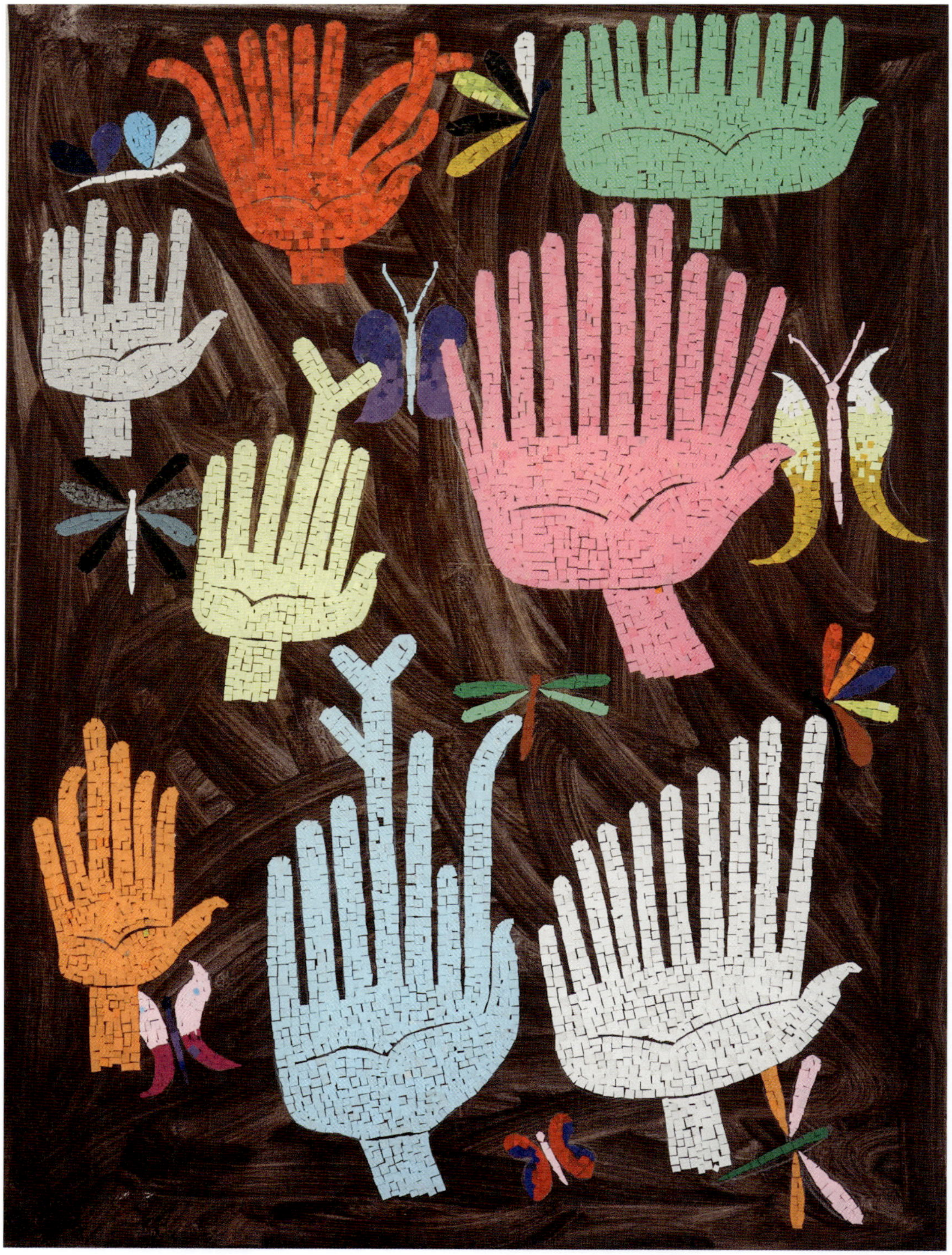

p. 143
The Suicidal Fascist, 2021
Acrylic and collage on canvas
100 x 73 cm

pp. 144-145
Blue Coral, 2023
Acrylic and collage on canvas
130 x 197 cm

Right Hand Alien Models, 2023
Acrylic and collage on canvas
100 x 73 cm

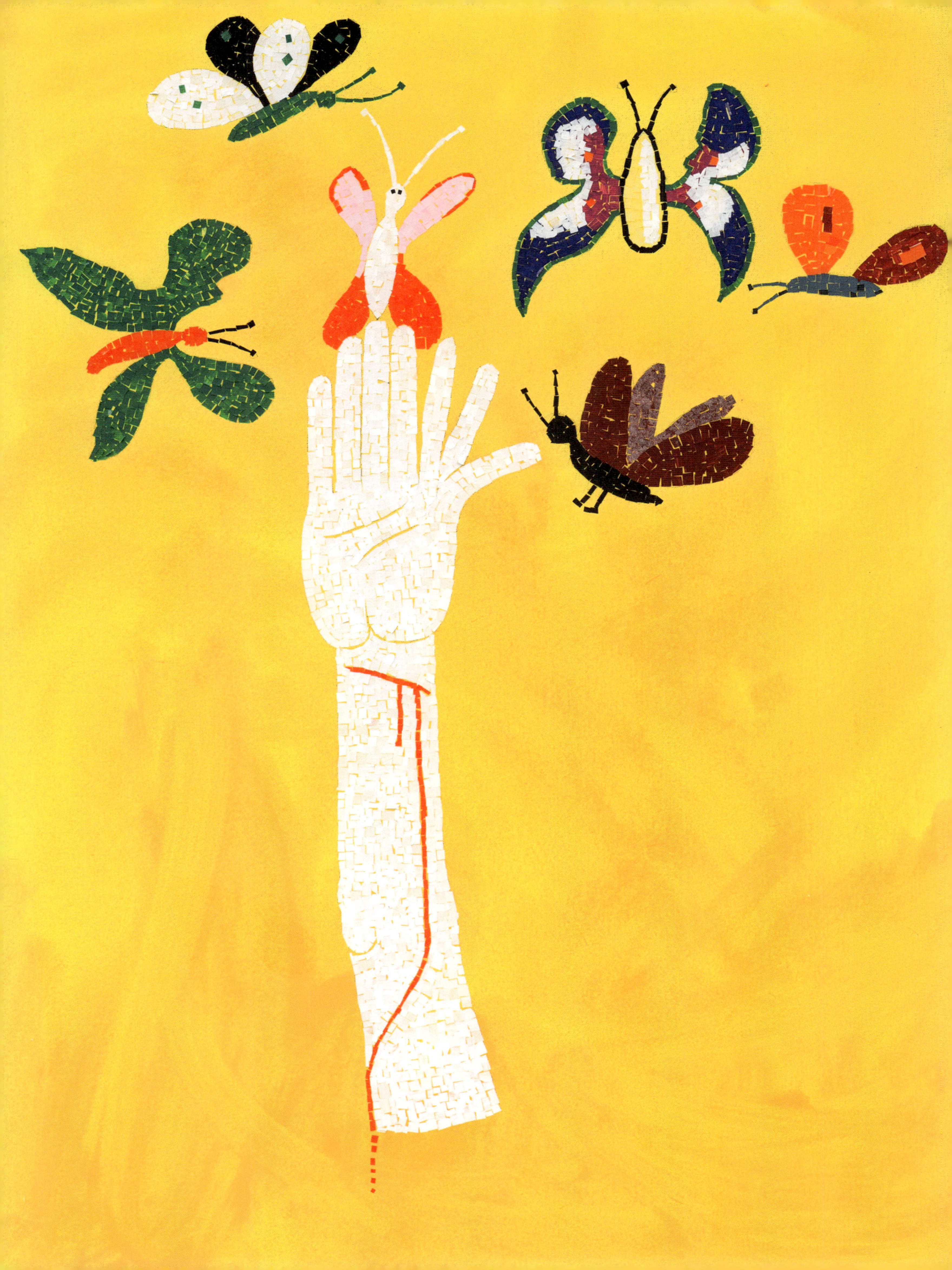

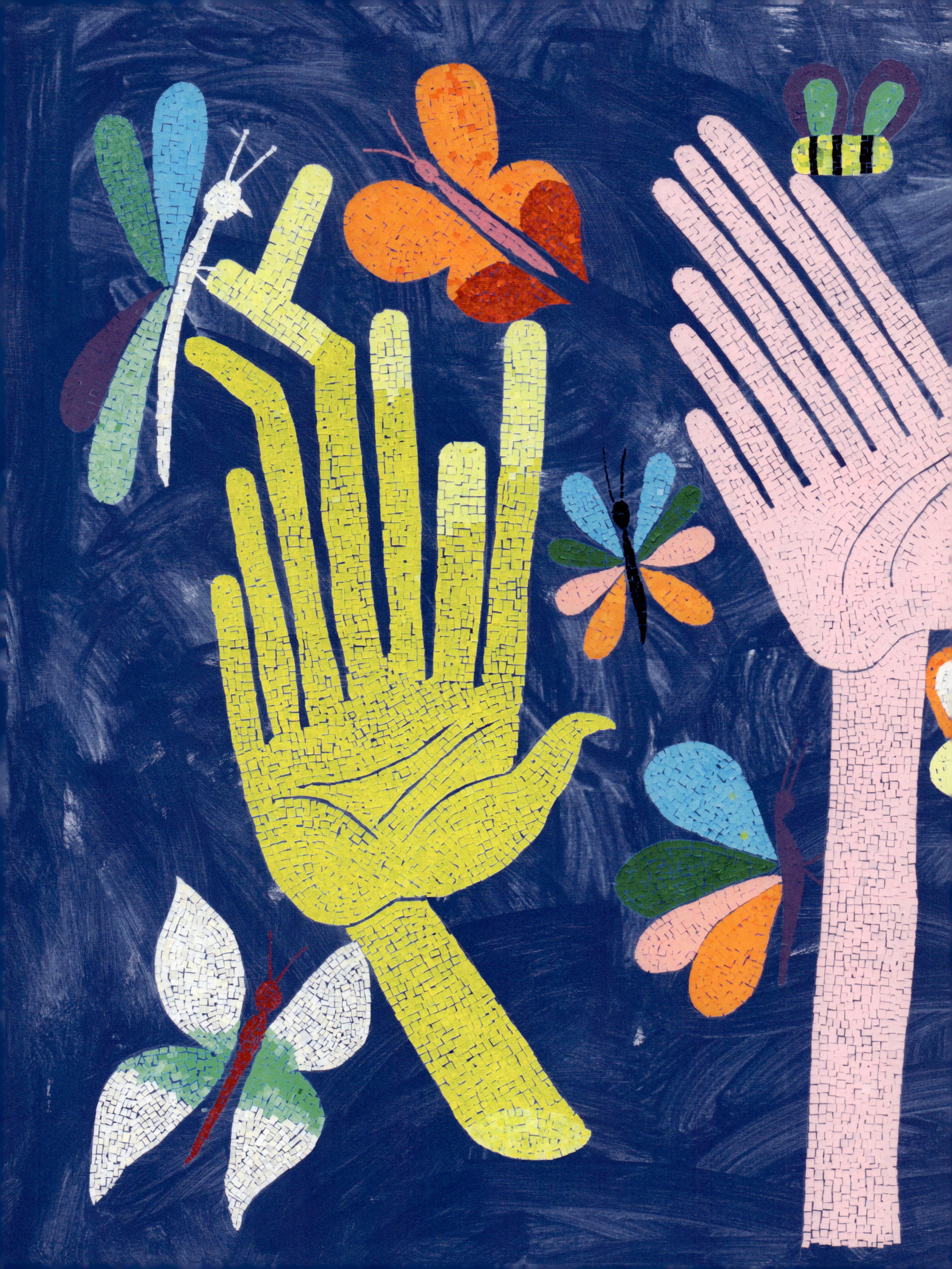

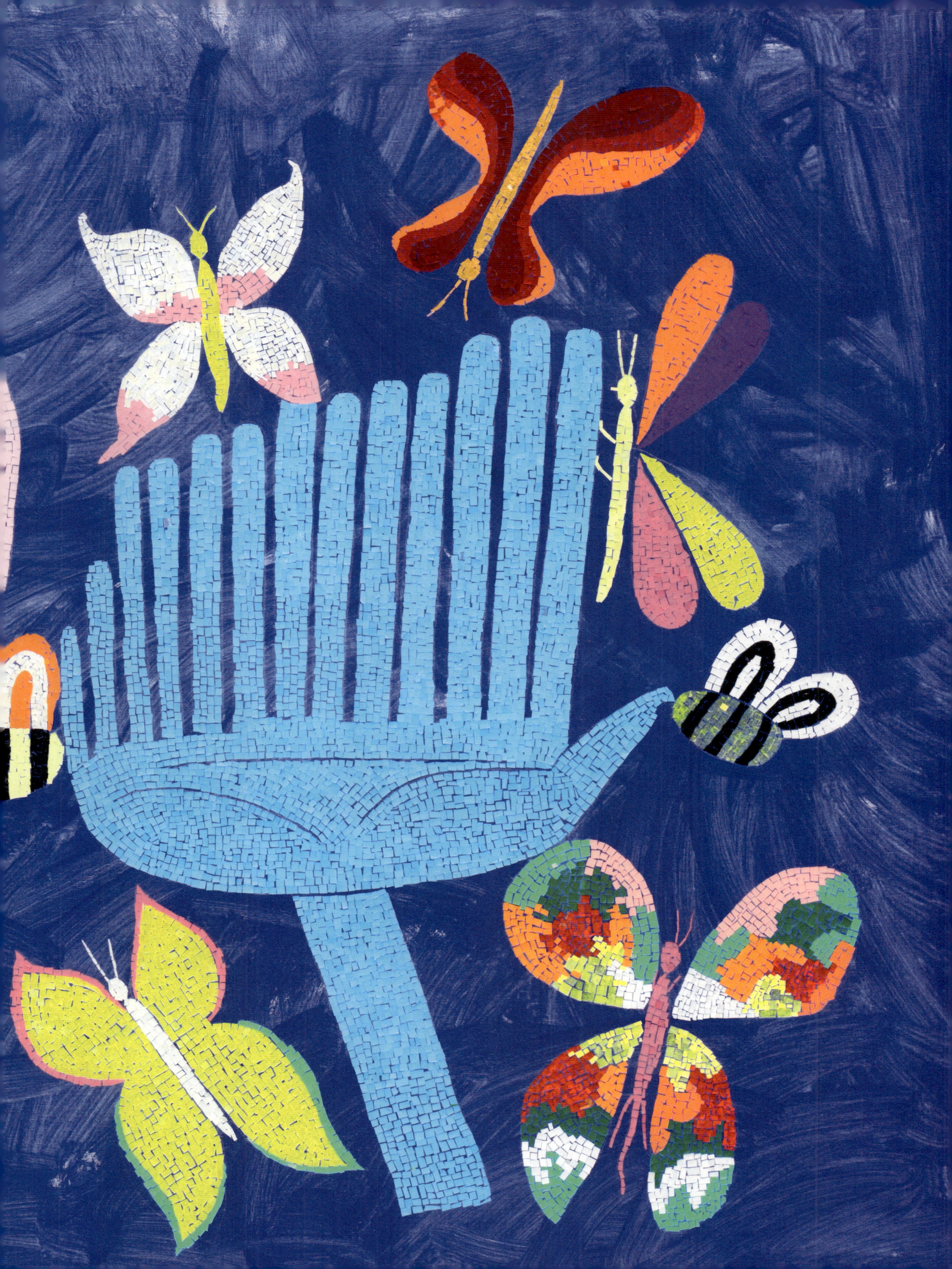

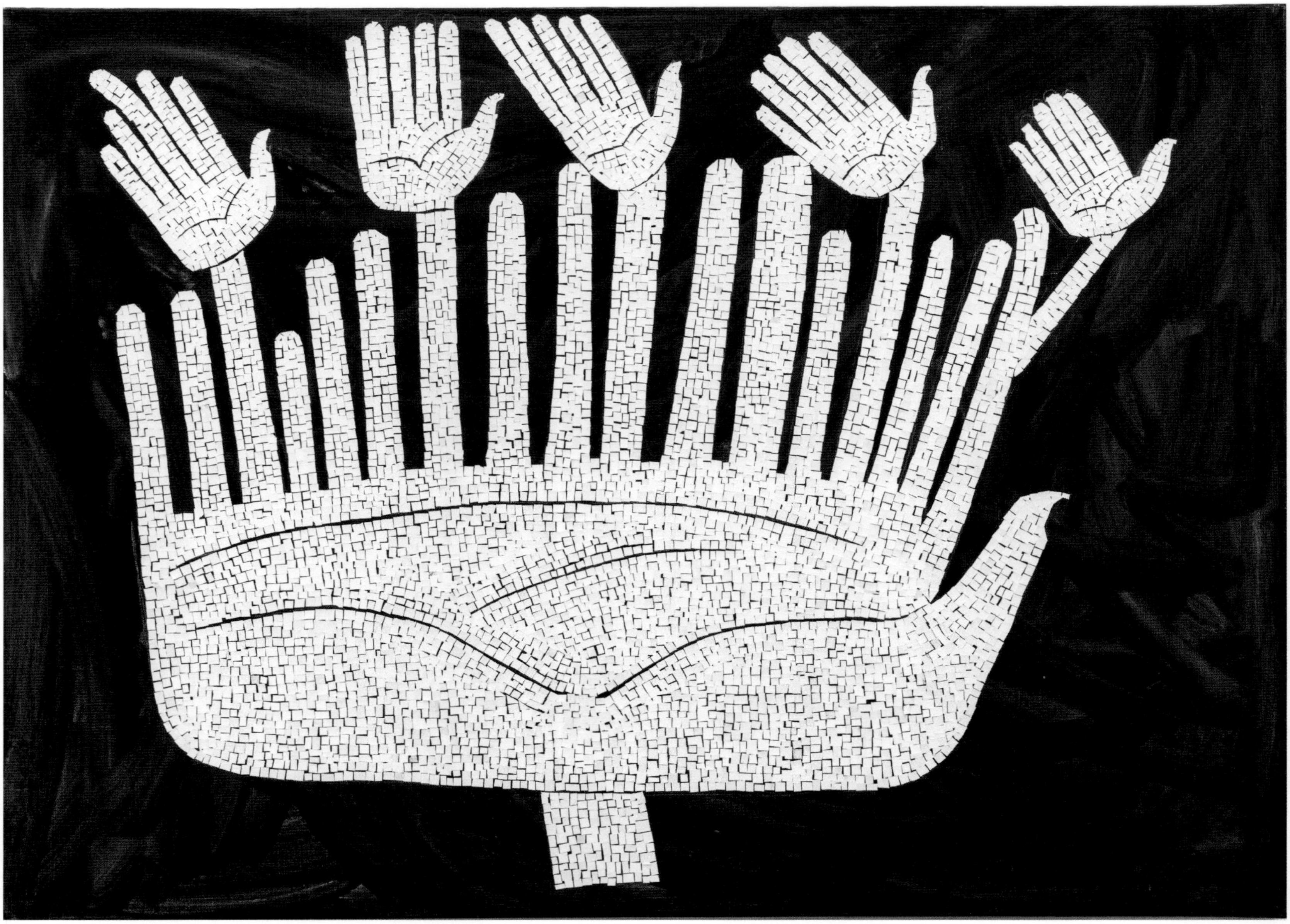

White Coral Polyps, 2022
Acrylic and collage on canvas
73 x 100 cm

pp. 148-149
Butterflies and Polyps, 2023
Acrylic and collage on canvas
130 x 197 cm

pp. 150-151
Western Coral, 2023
Acrylic and collage on canvas
130 x 197 cm

pp. 152-153
El monseñor de los anillos, 2025
Acrylic and collage on canvas
130 x 197 cm

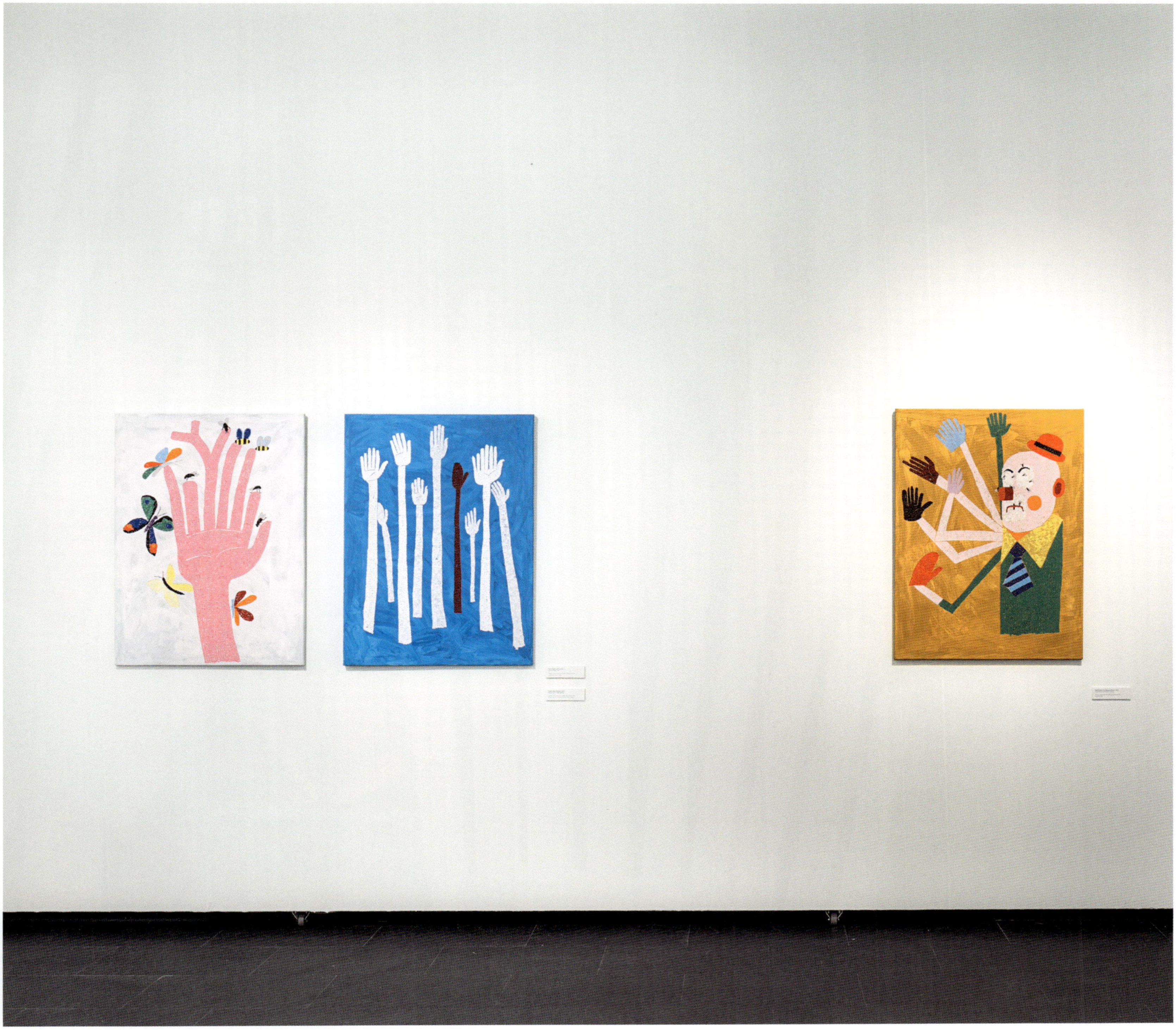

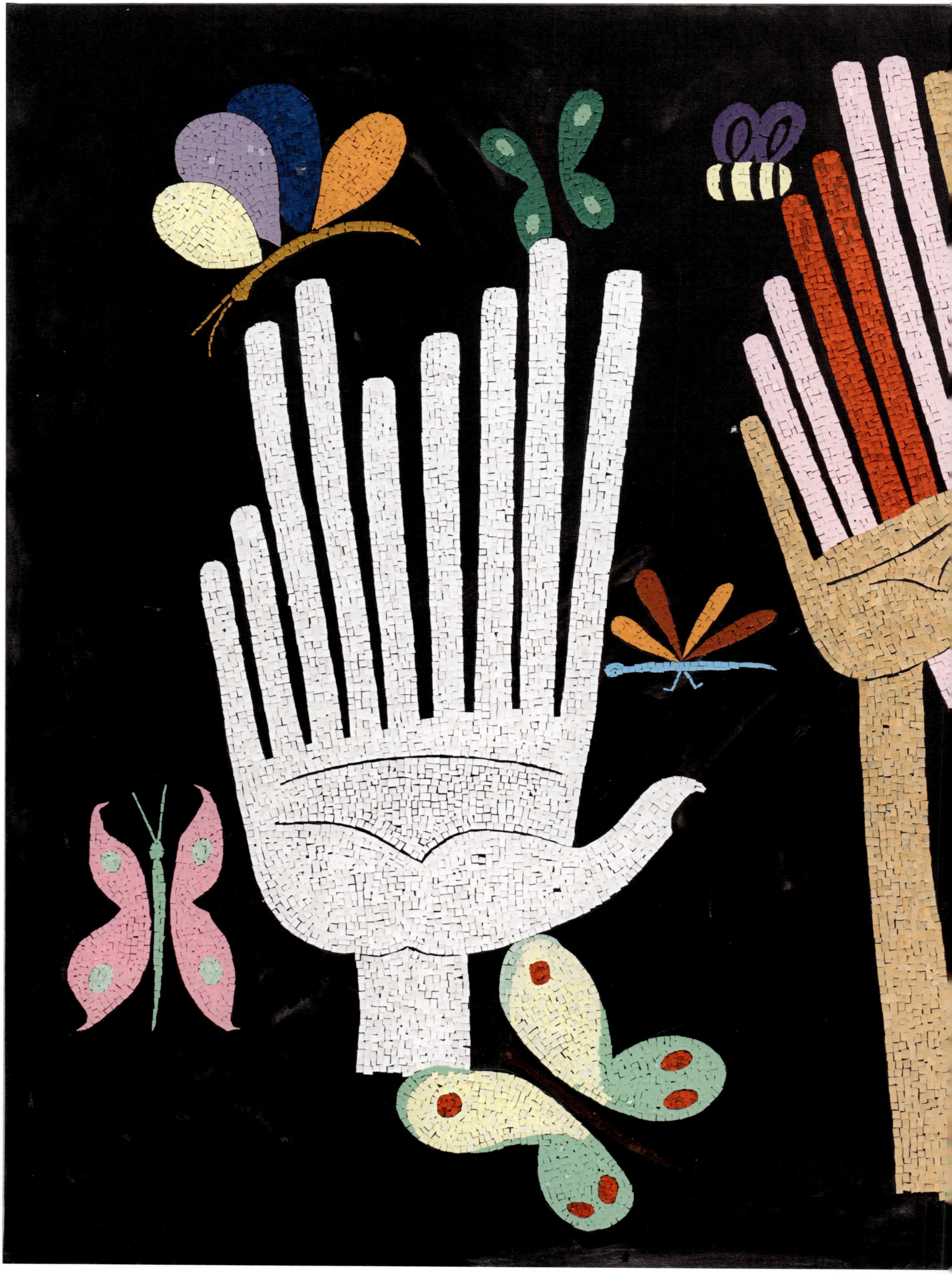

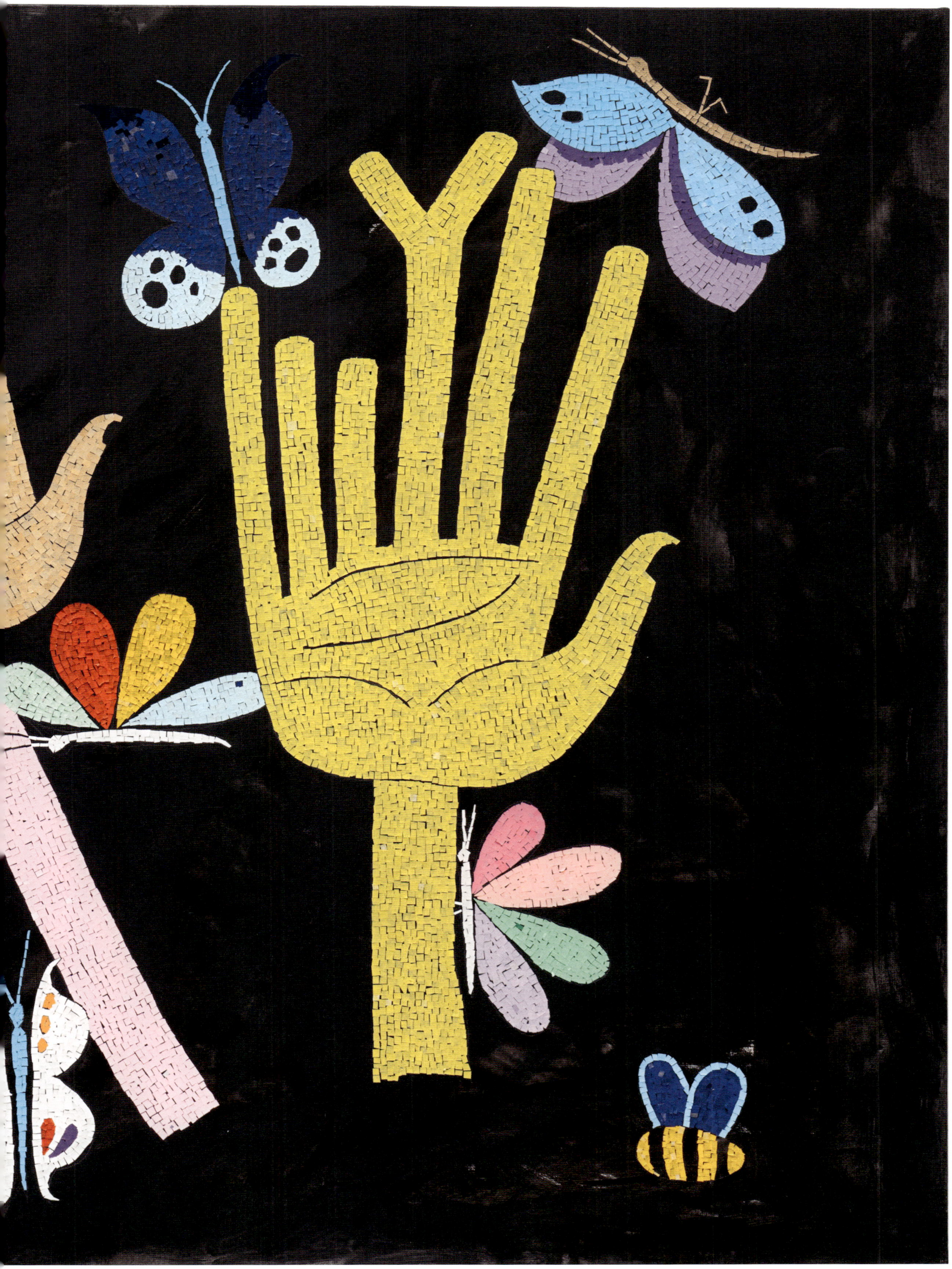

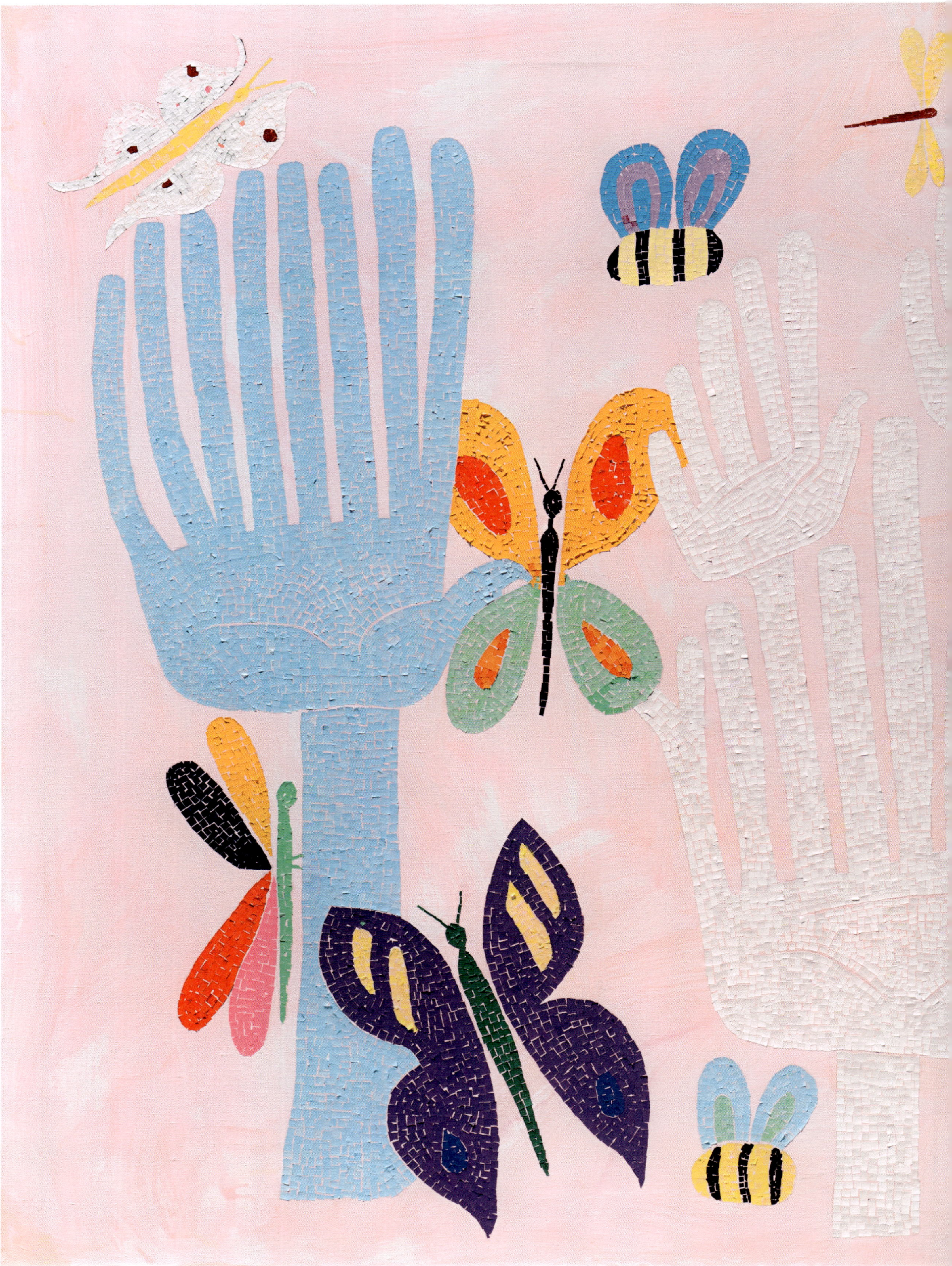

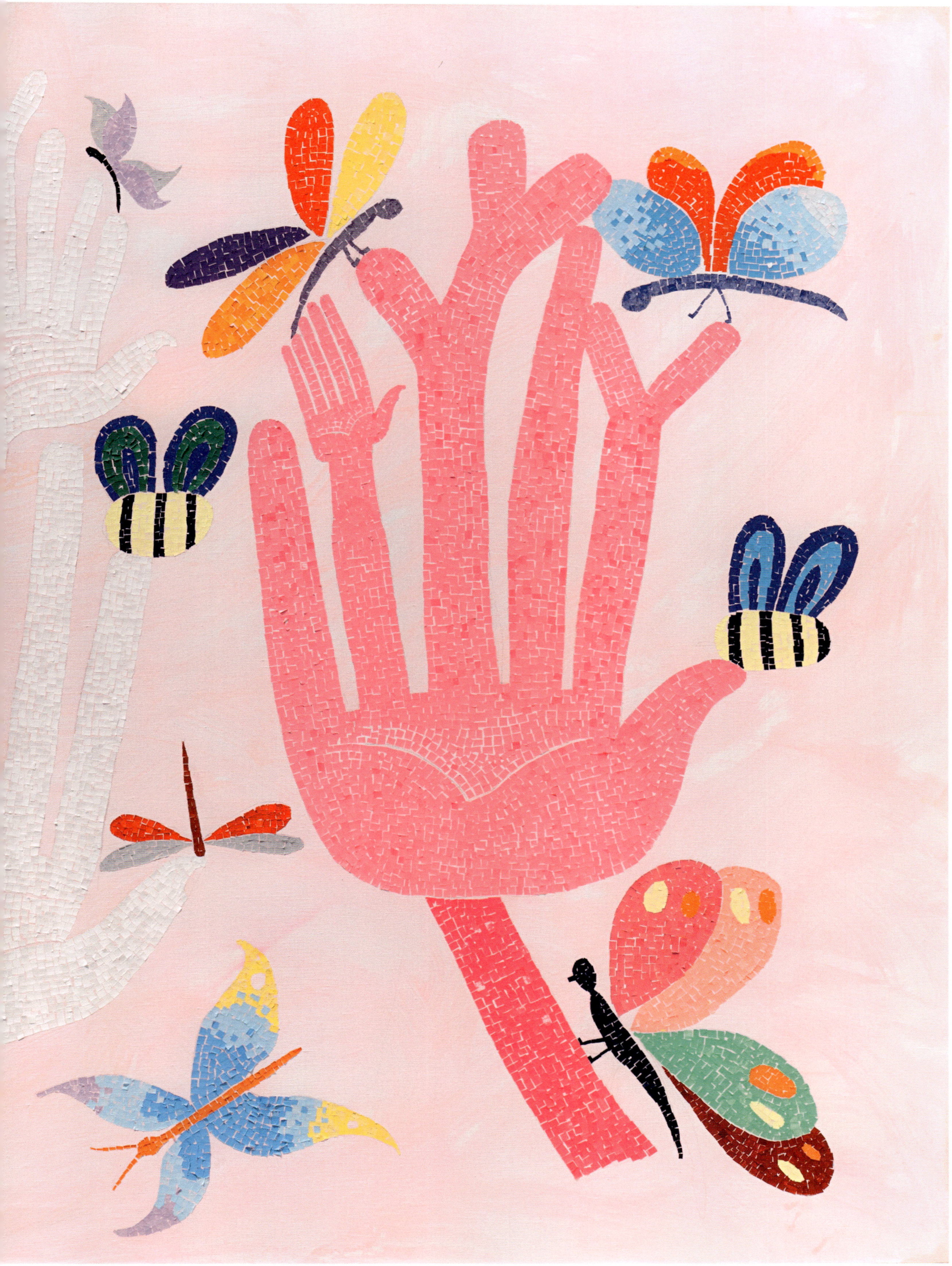

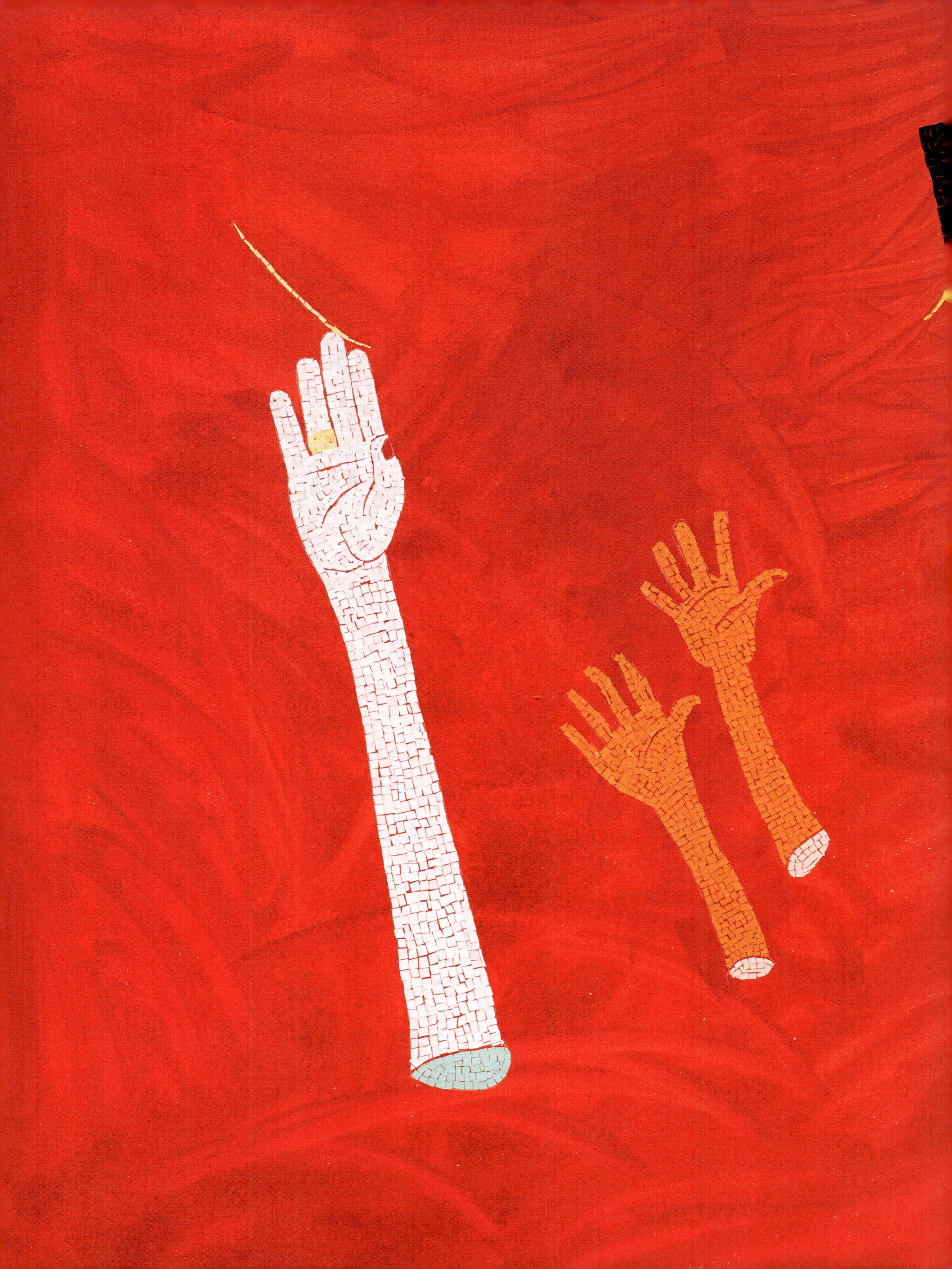

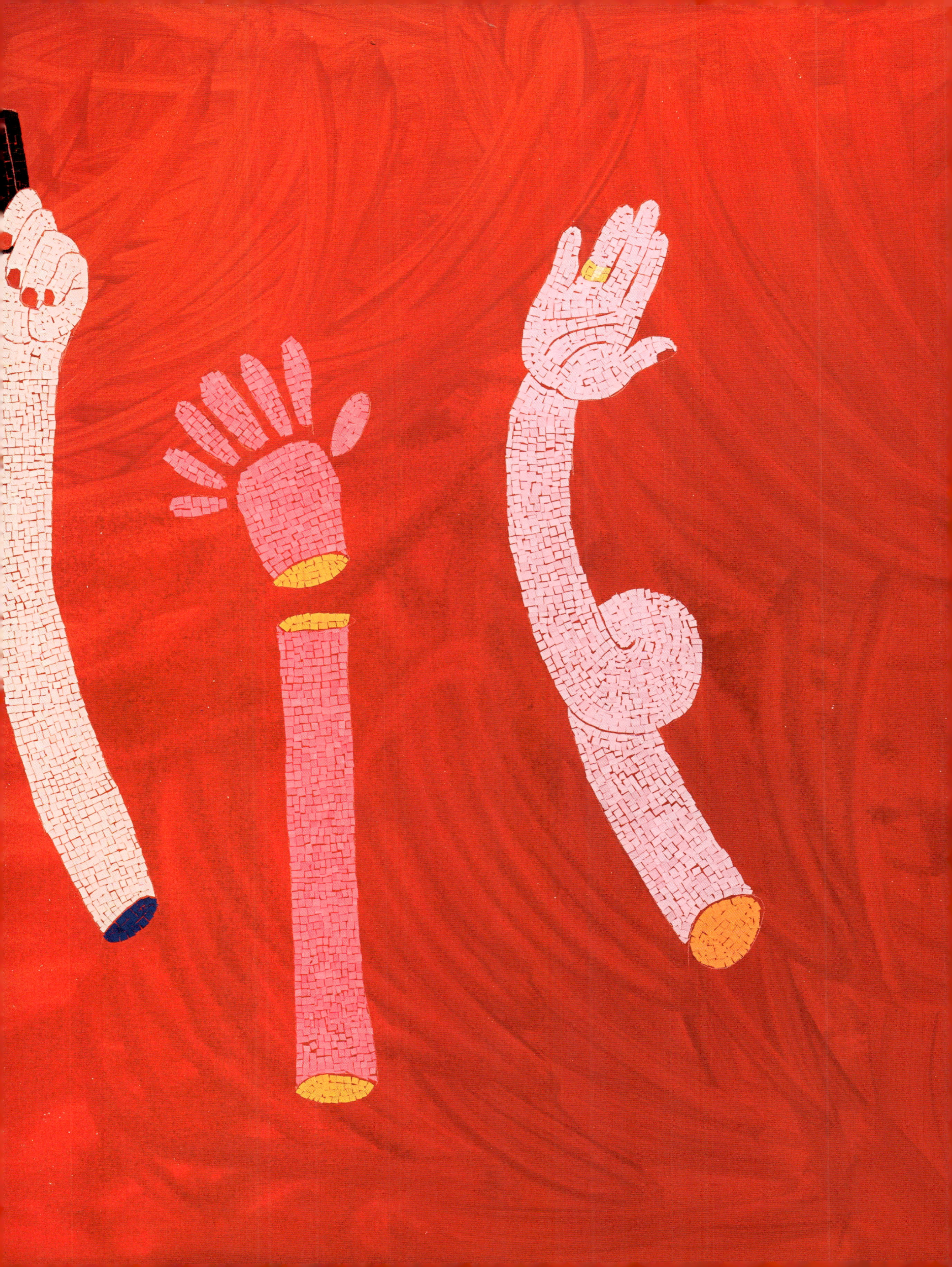

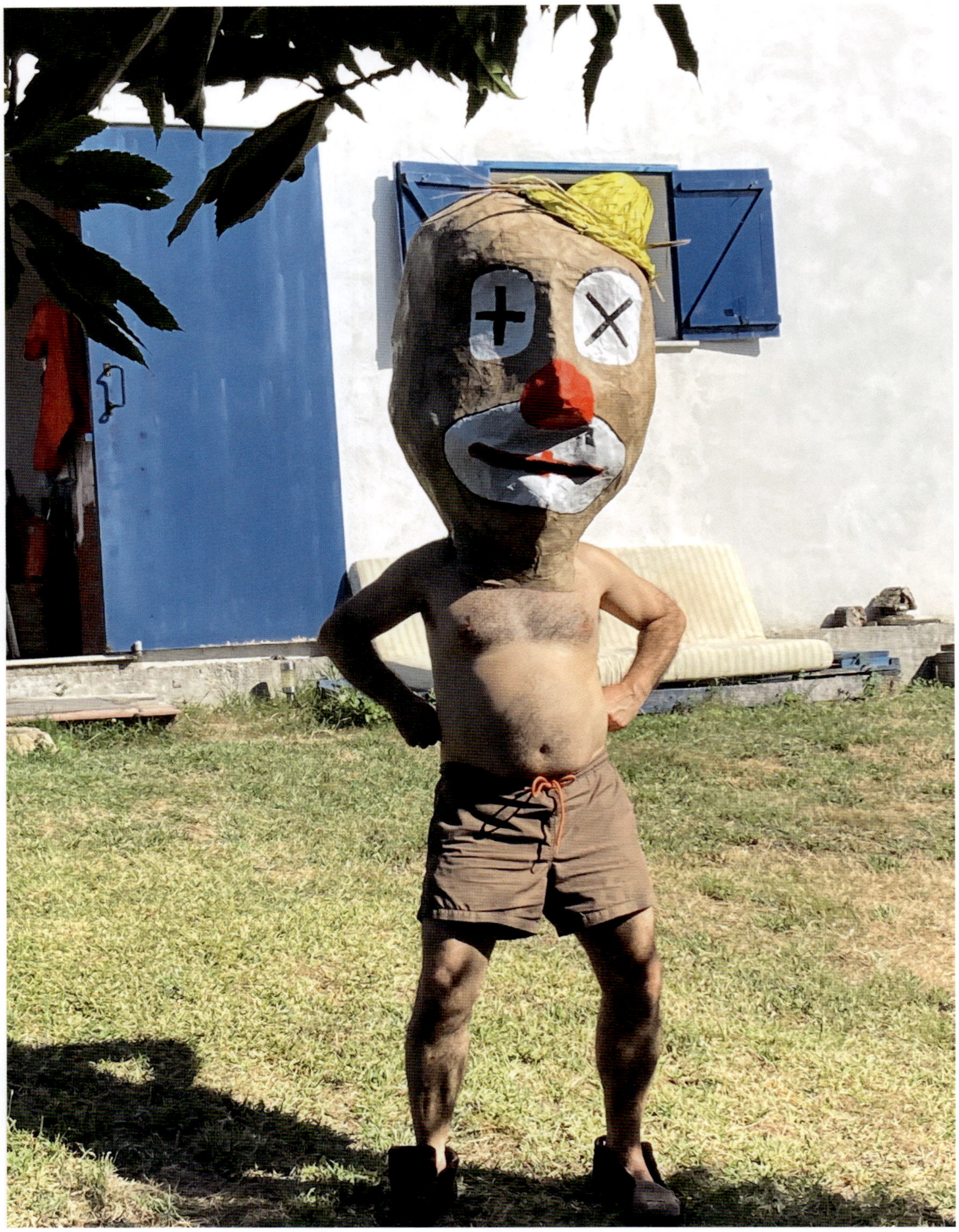

Definition:
A circus performer, typically wearing a distinctive costume, who provokes laughter through their actions, gestures and words. The term can also refer more broadly to a person whose behaviour is intended to make people laugh. It can also be used disparagingly to describe an absurd or comical person who acts foolishly.

CLOWN
CLOWN
CLOWN
CLOWN
CLOWN
CLOWN
CLOWN
CLOWN
CLOWN
CLOWN
CLOWN

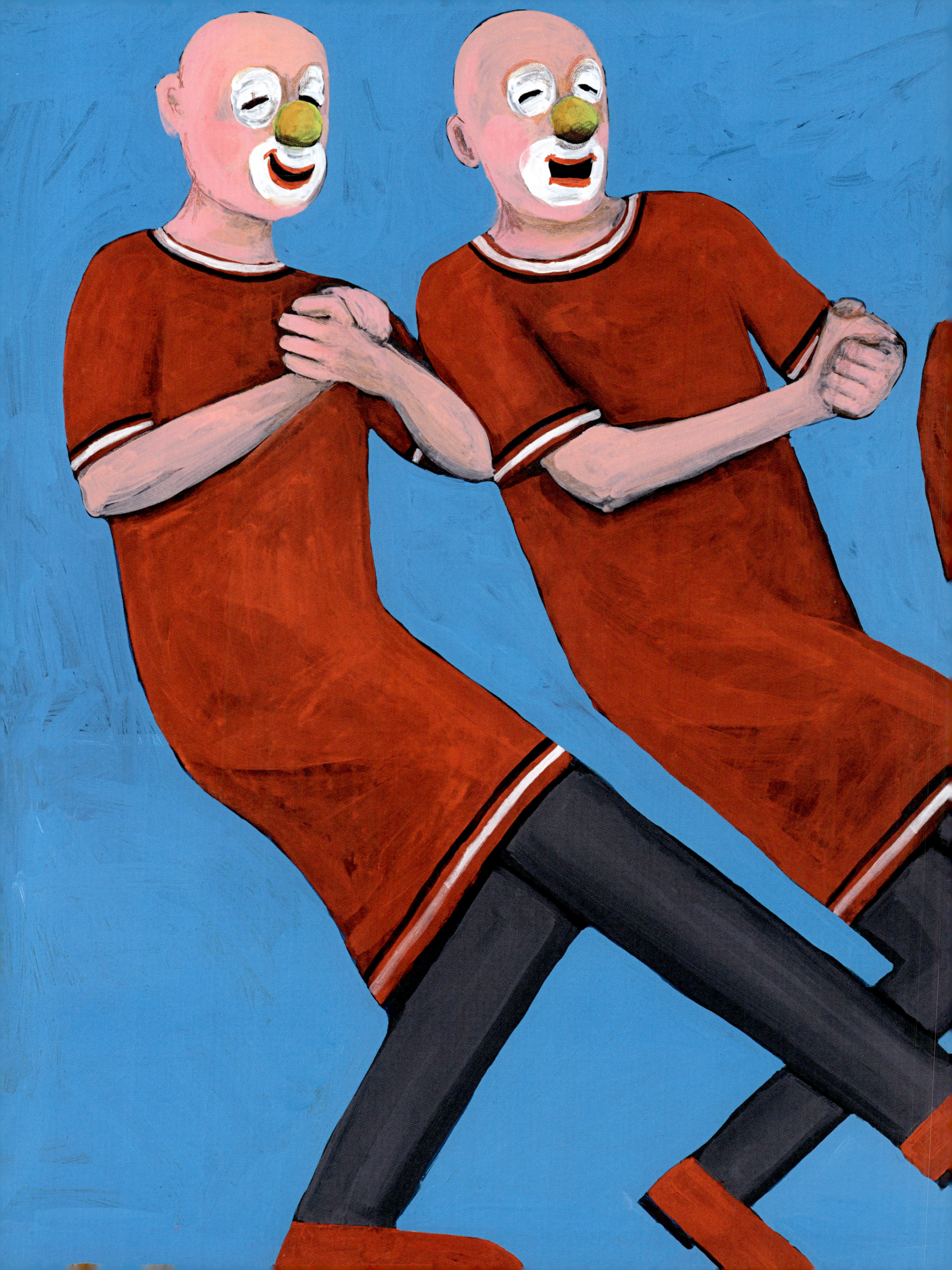

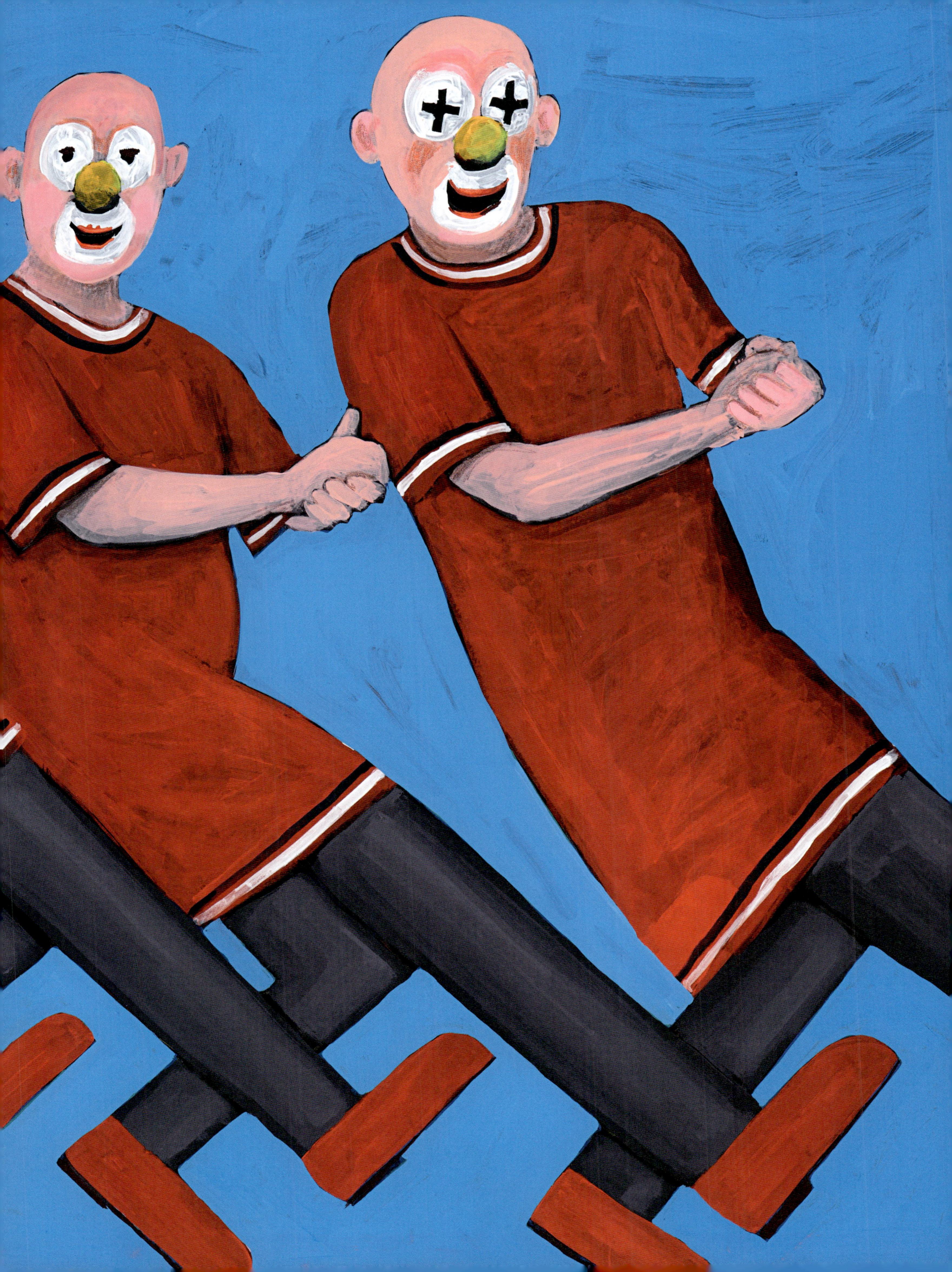

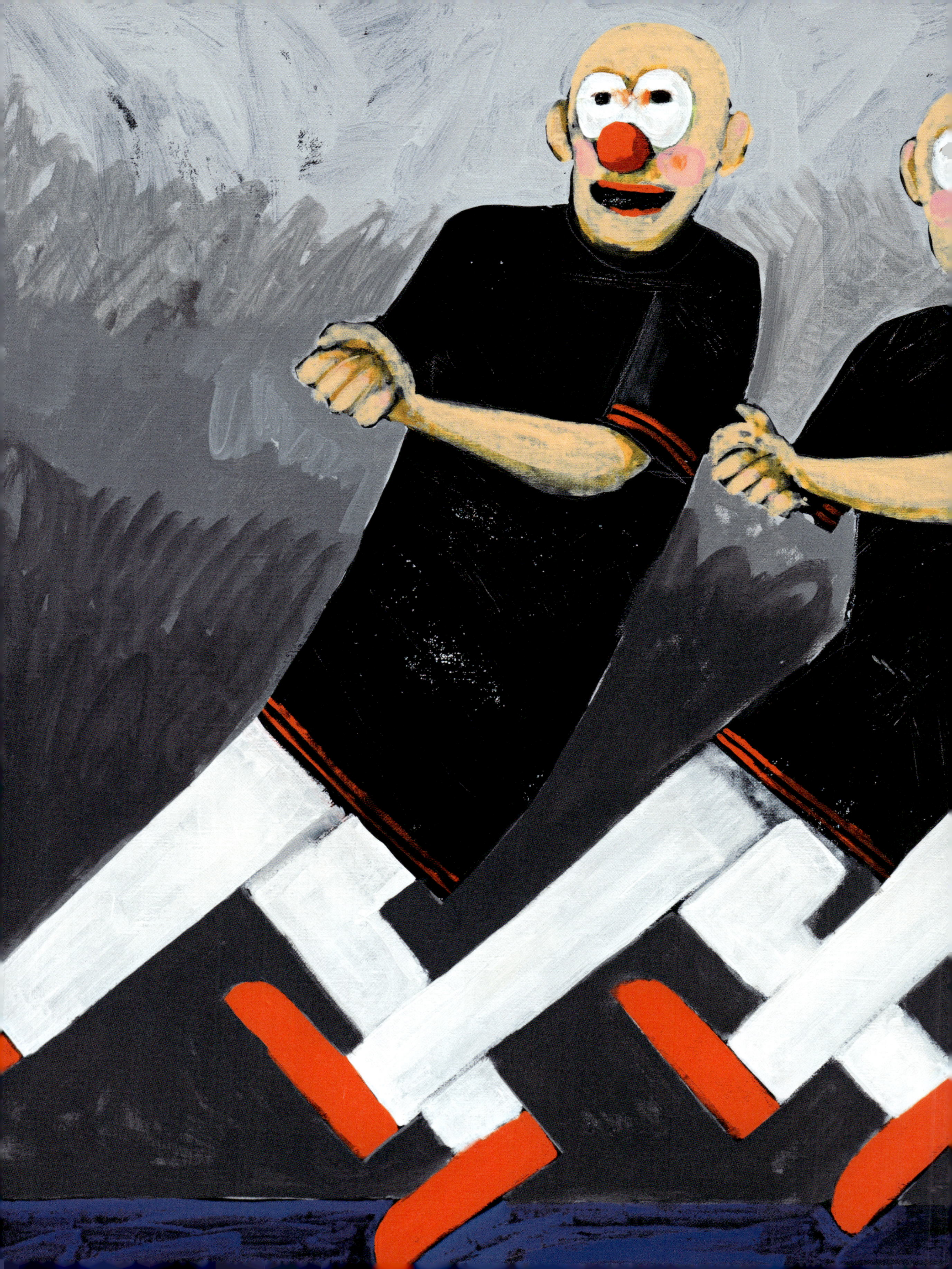

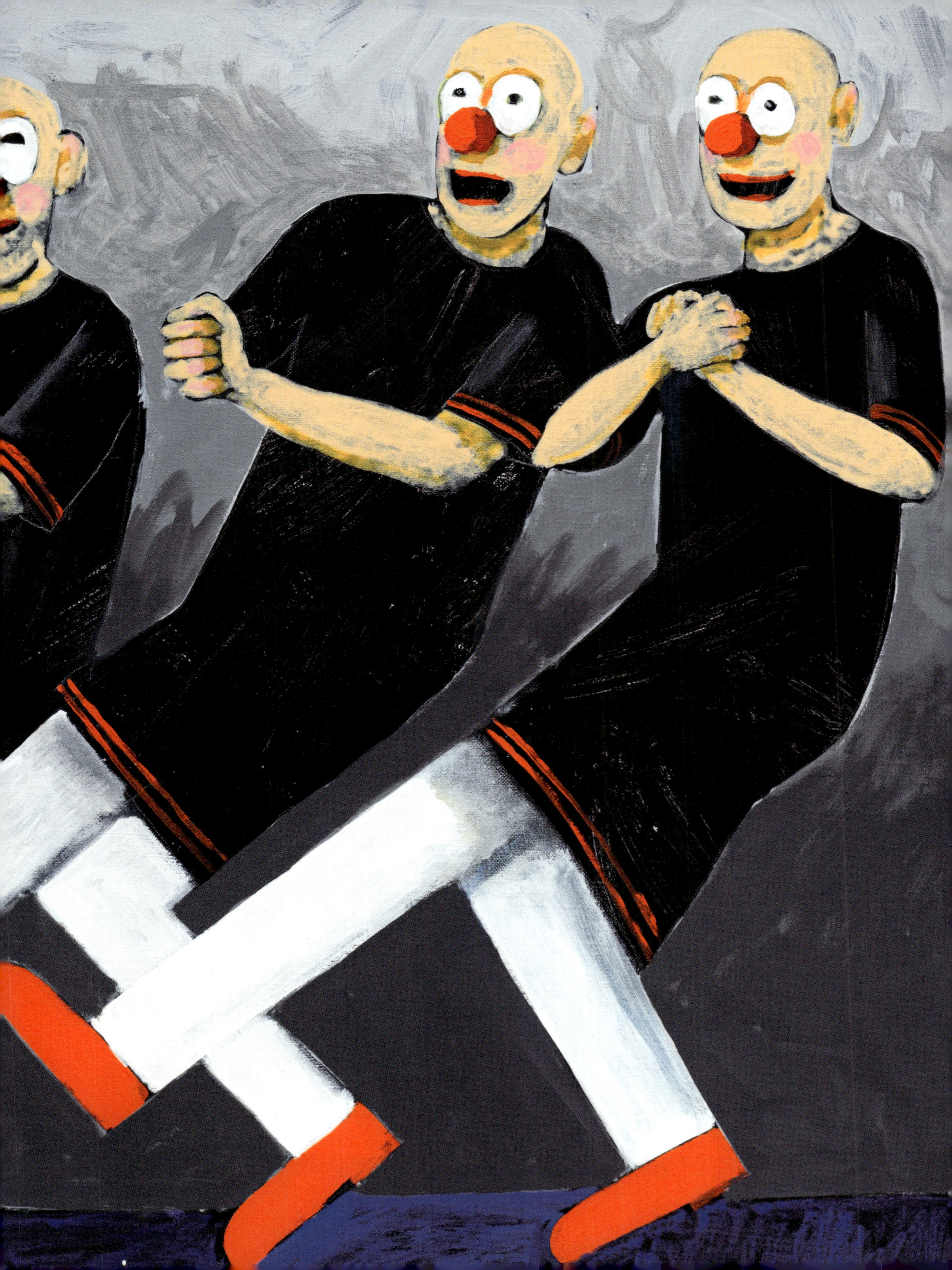

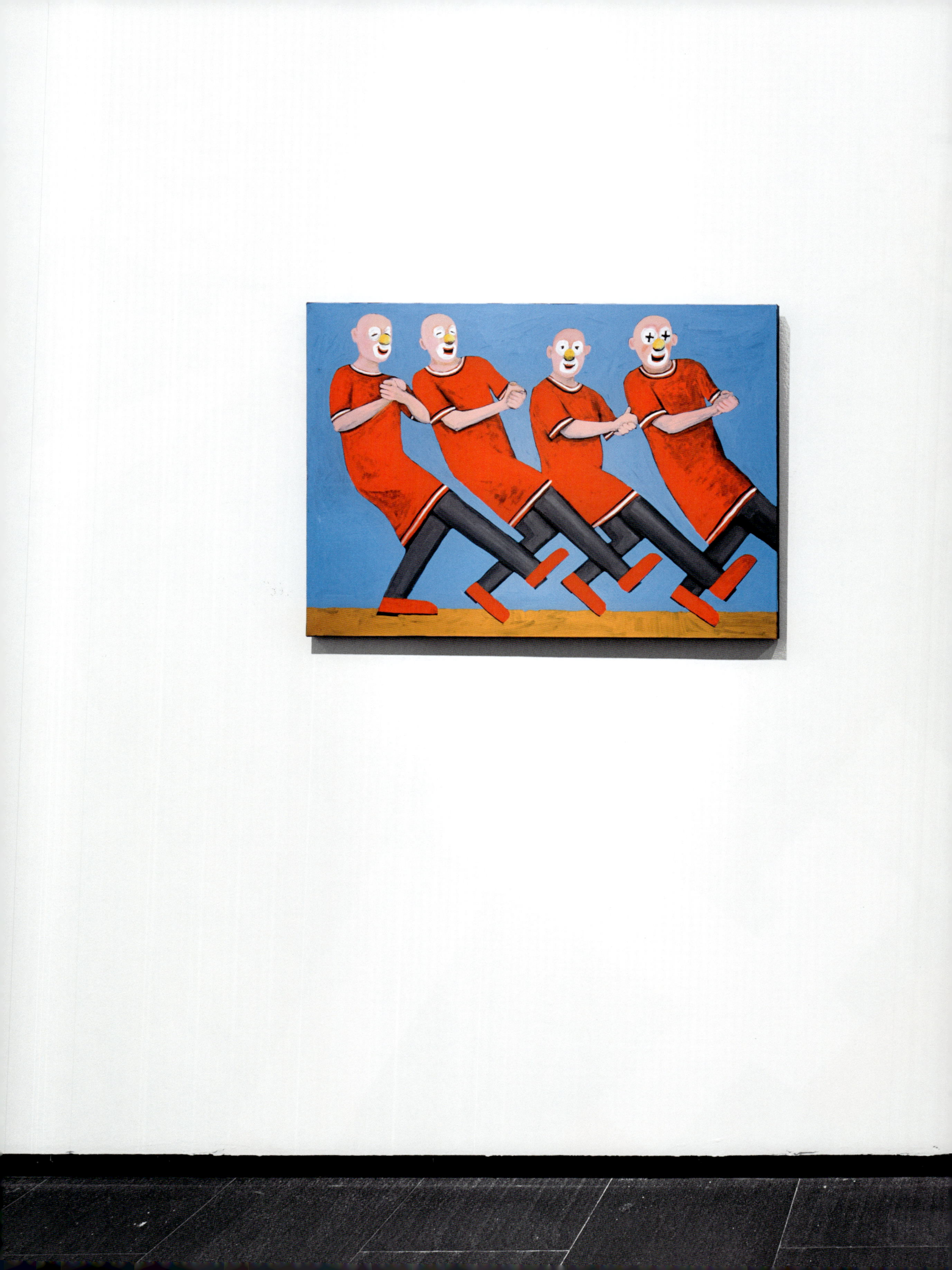

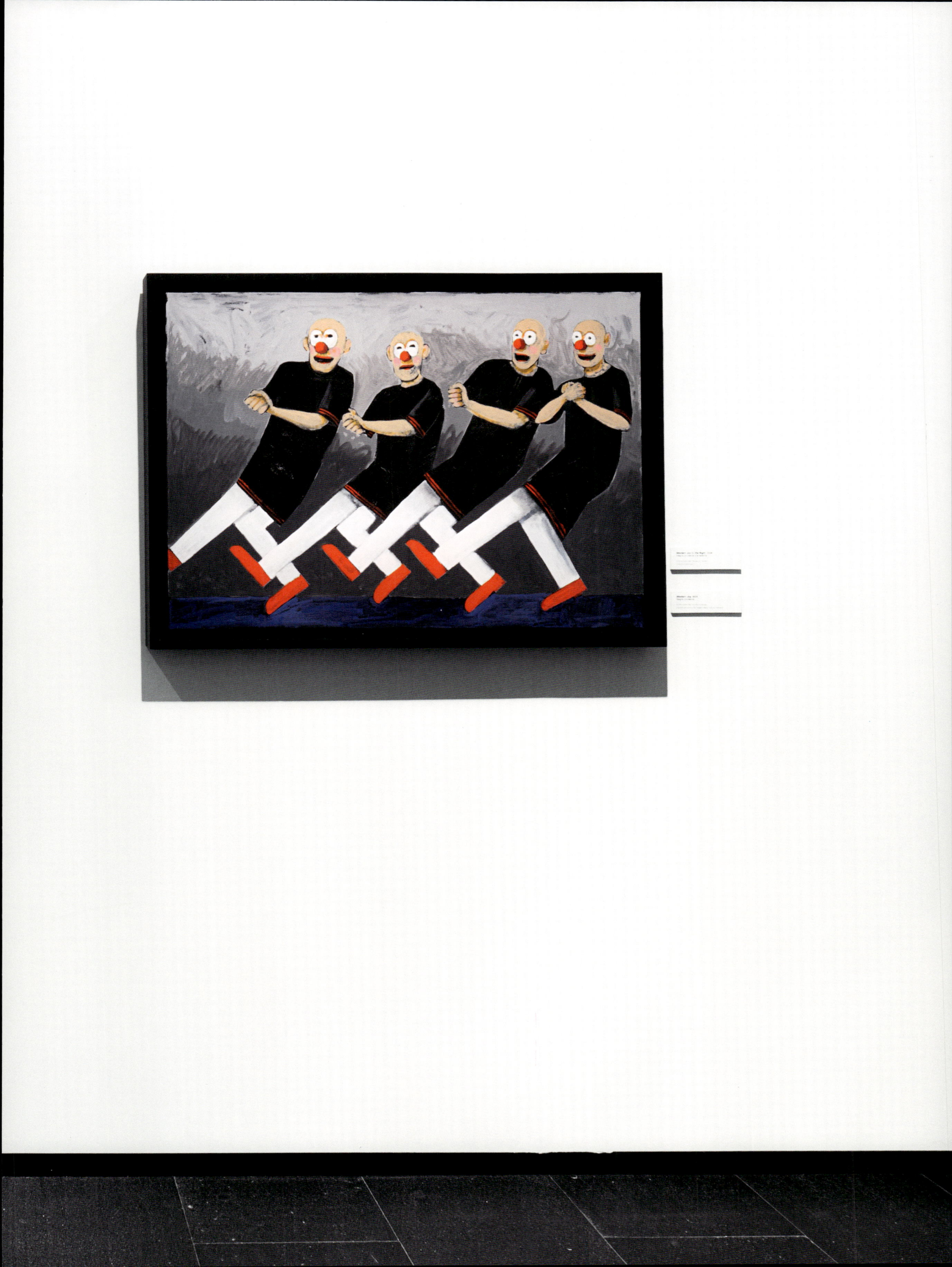

pp. 156-157
Western Joy, 2024
Acrylic on canvas
73 x 100 cm

pp. 158-159
Western Joy to the Right, 2024
Acrylic on canvas
73 x 100 cm

Self-Portrait as Nervous Clown, 2022
Acrylic and collage on canvas
100 x 73 cm

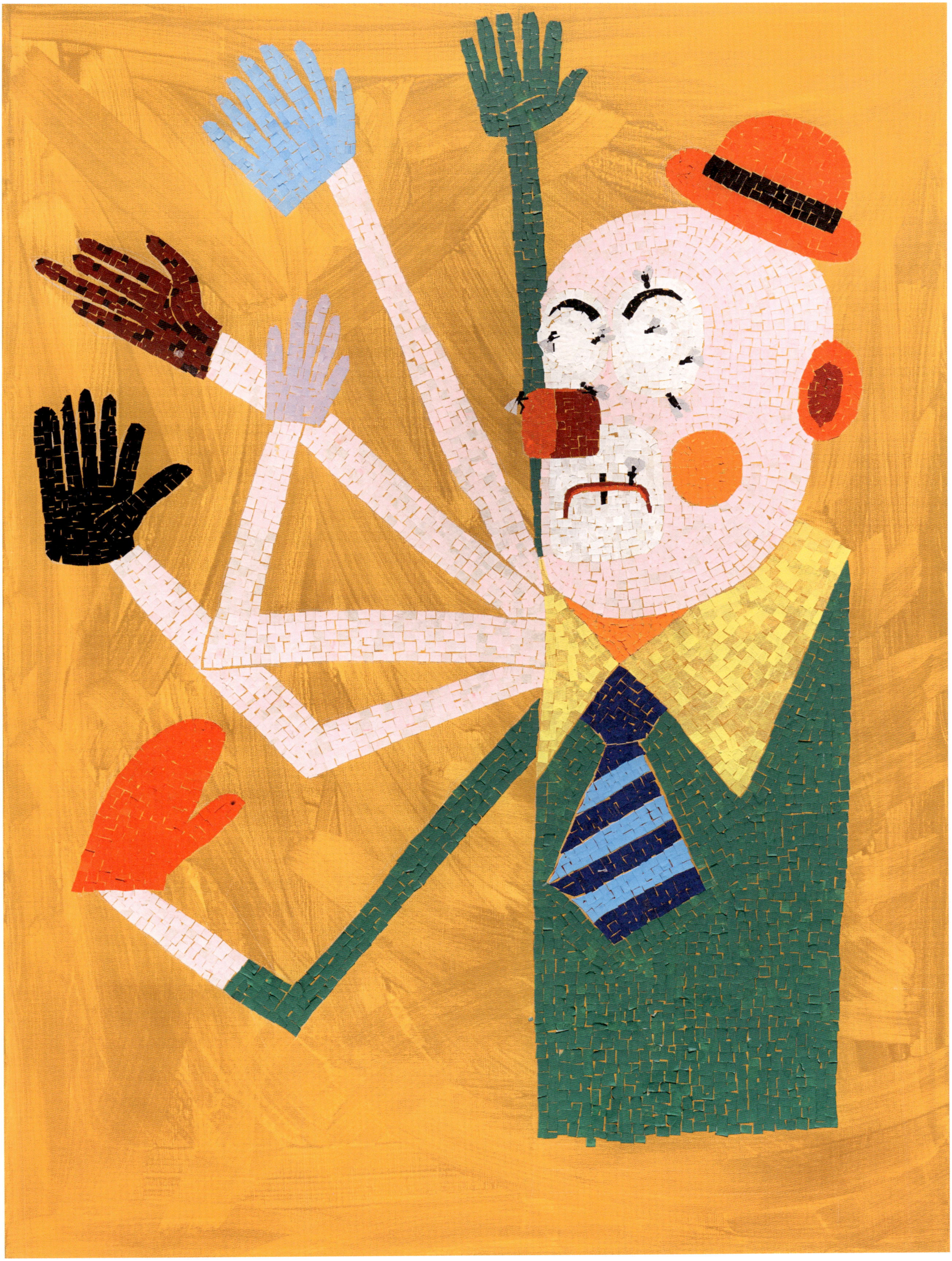

Self-Portrait as Fascist, 2022
Acrylic and collage on canvas
100 x 73 cm

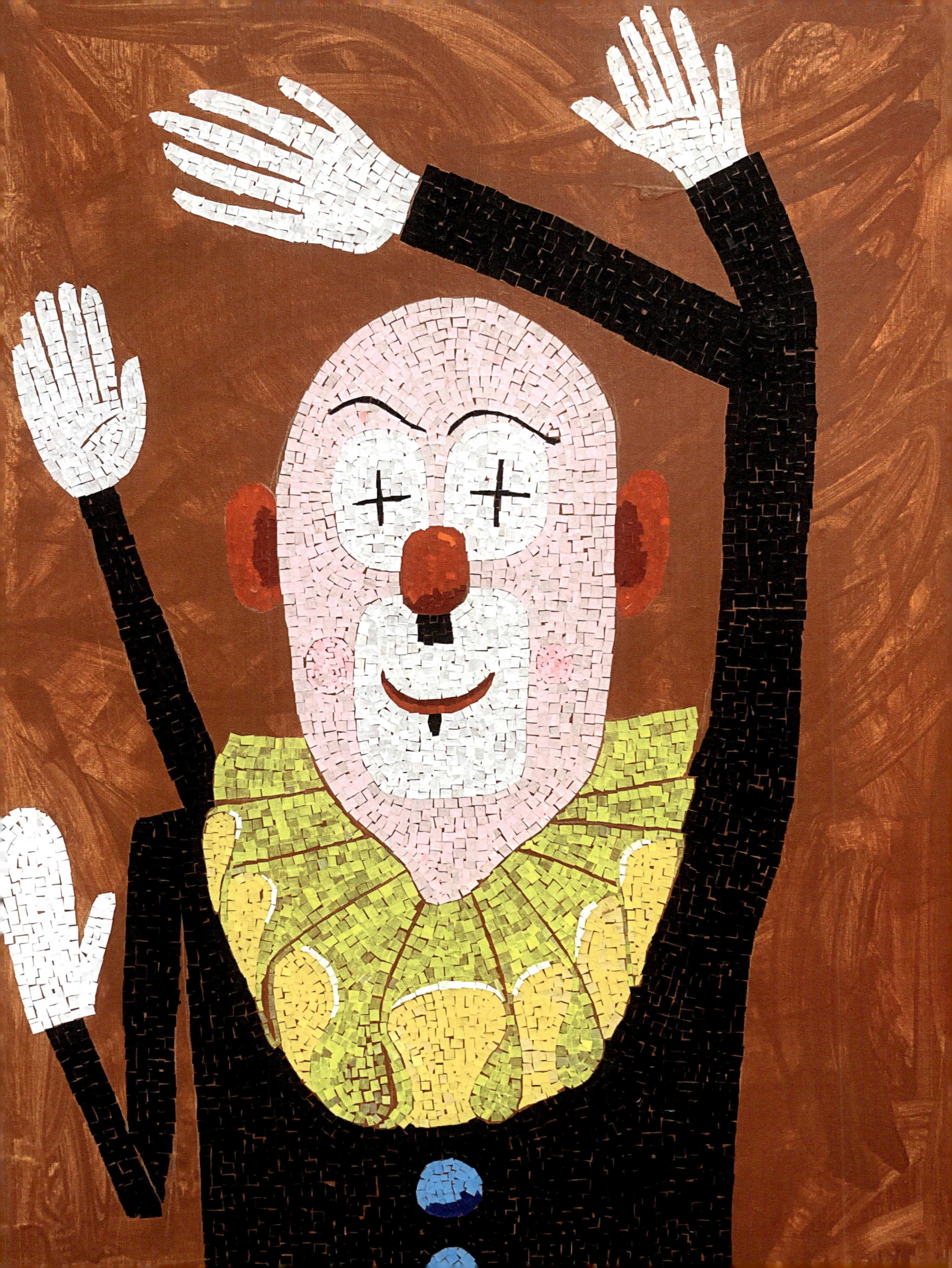

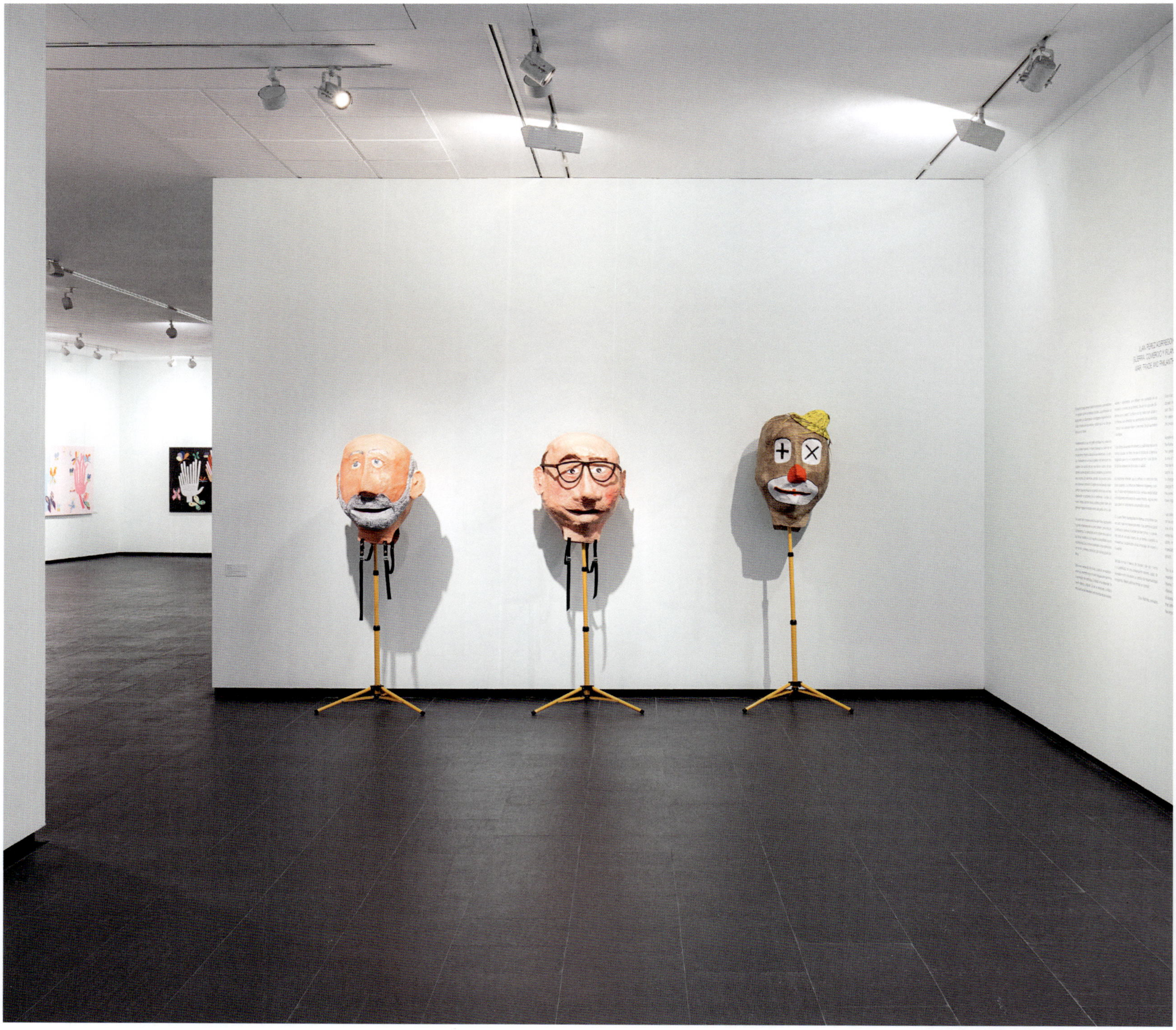

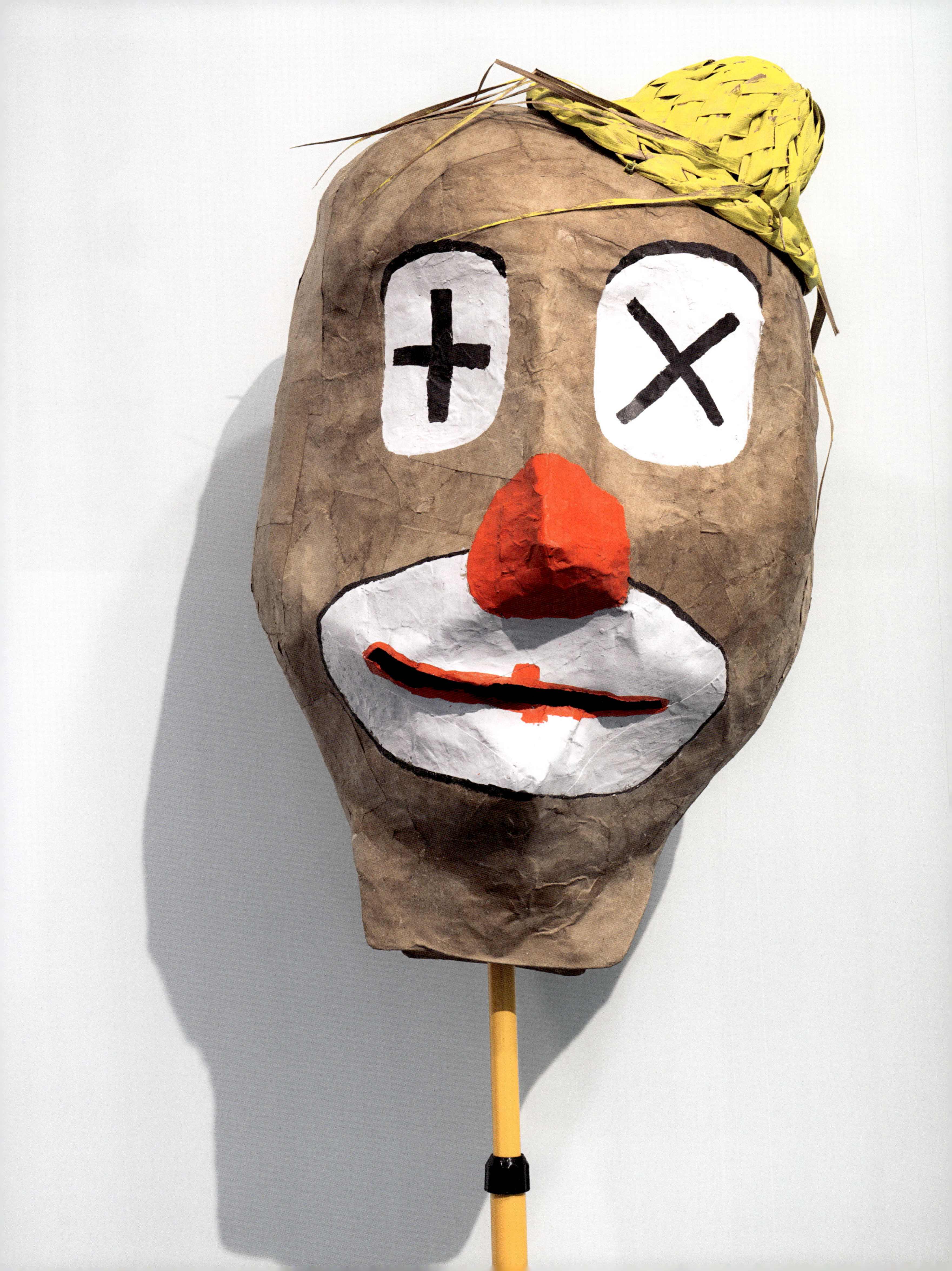

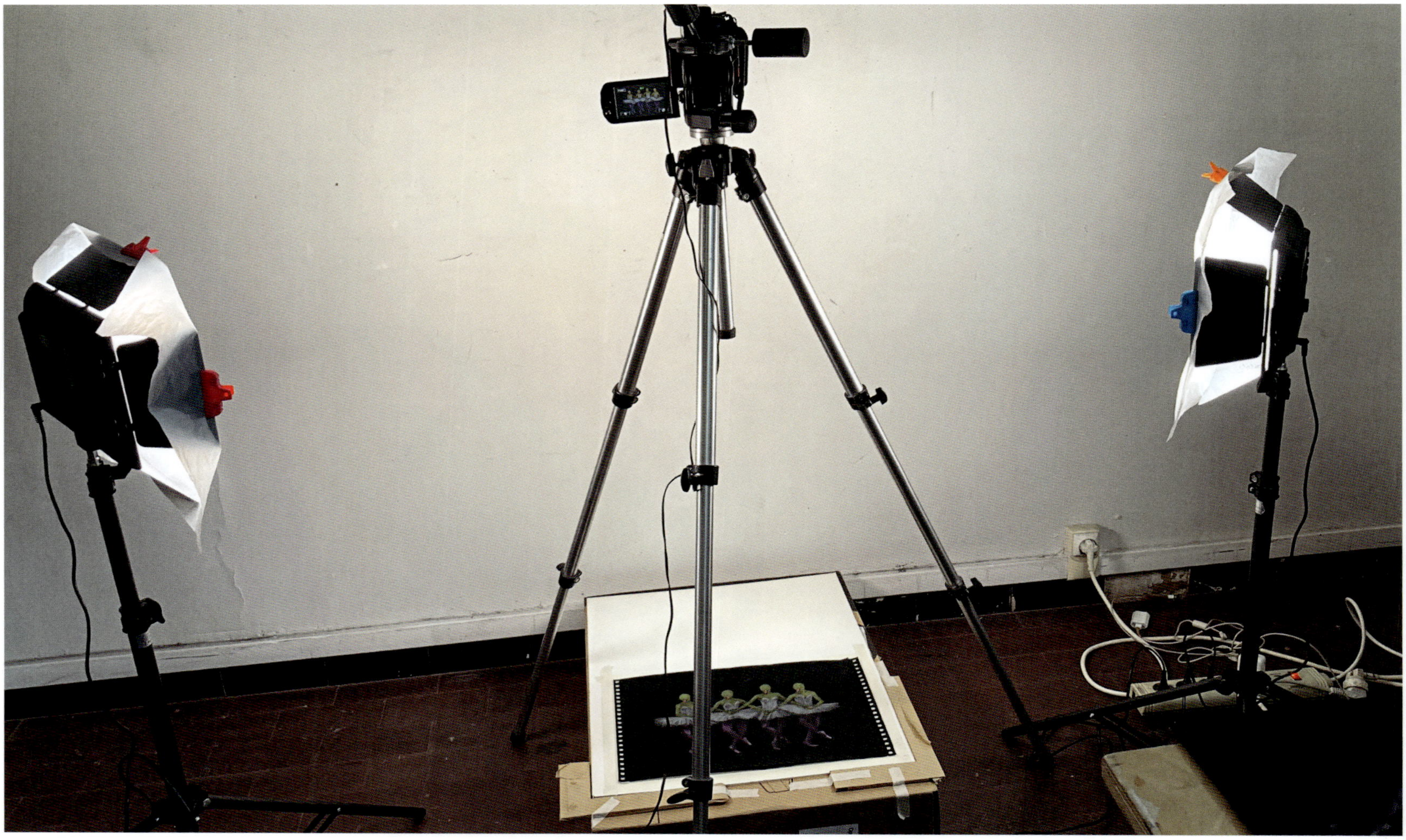

THE MASTER SIGNIFIERS LAKE

The Master Signifiers Lake is an animation composed of several hundred coloured pencil drawings on wallpaper showing a number of clown-ballerinas dancing *Swan Lake* nazistically.

The composer of the soundtrack, Xabier Erkizia, was given just one instruction: to mix Tchaikovsky's music with the sound of trains, in keeping with the idea that the greatest atrocities in history have always required the complicity of minor collaborators.

My work over recent years has been all about fascism, which Guy Debord defined as technically-equipped archaism (race, blood, leader).

New technologies and extravagant hairstyles have developed a new kind of fascism with outlandish hair, beards, moustaches or the ghost of their absence. Adorno said that a large part of Hitler's success was owing to the fact that he acted like a clown, and throughout history the circus has been a classic example of techniques of control.

It's hard to believe that "the land of the free", the world's longest-standing democracy, was going to repeat the methods of 1930s Germany and that in the Near East we would see the same scenes of horror as in 1940s Germany, committed by the very people who suffered them.

We are witnessing a strange paradigm shift in fascism.

The Master Signifiers Lake, 2024
Video
4 min 47 sec
Sound Xabier Erkizia

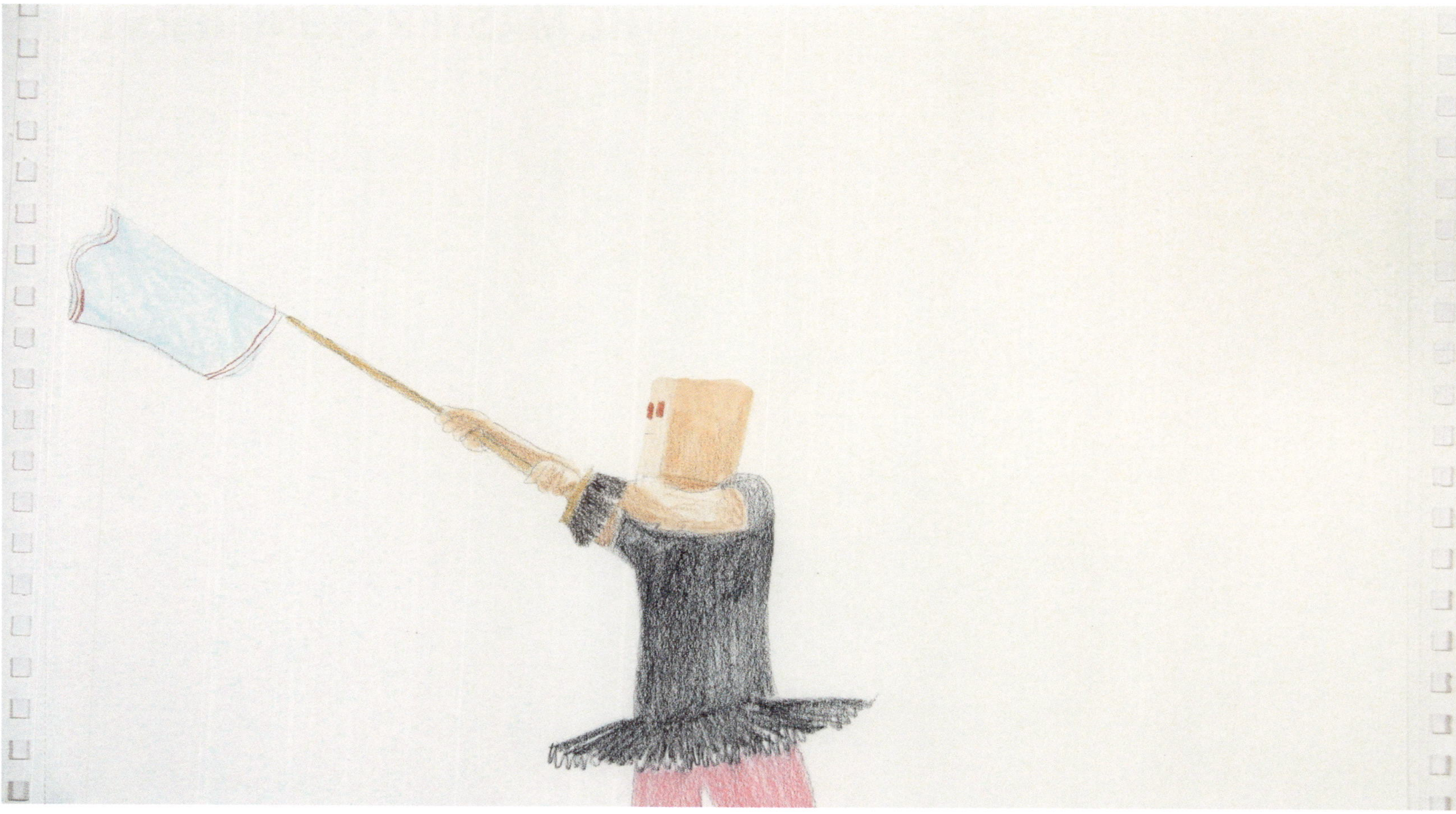

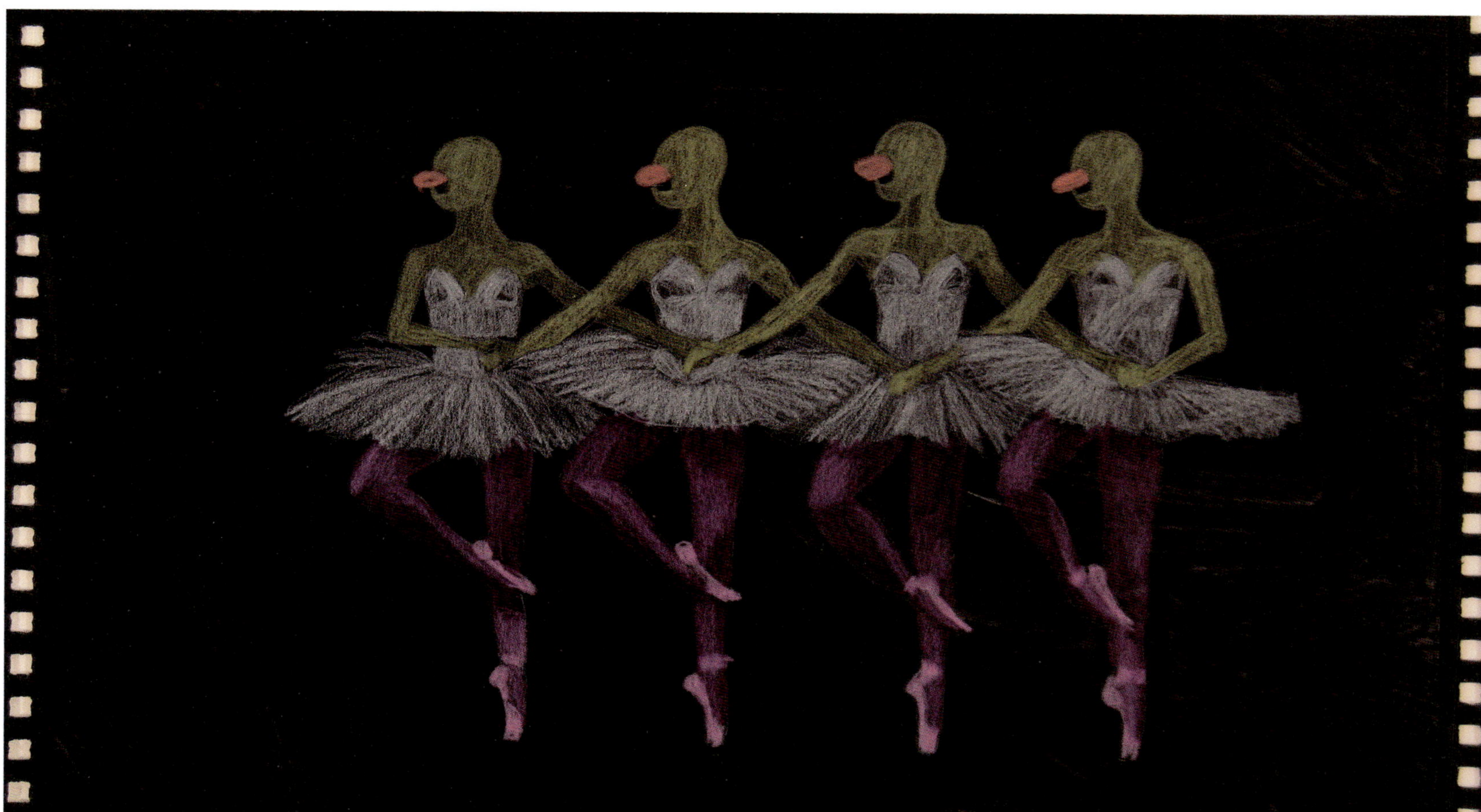

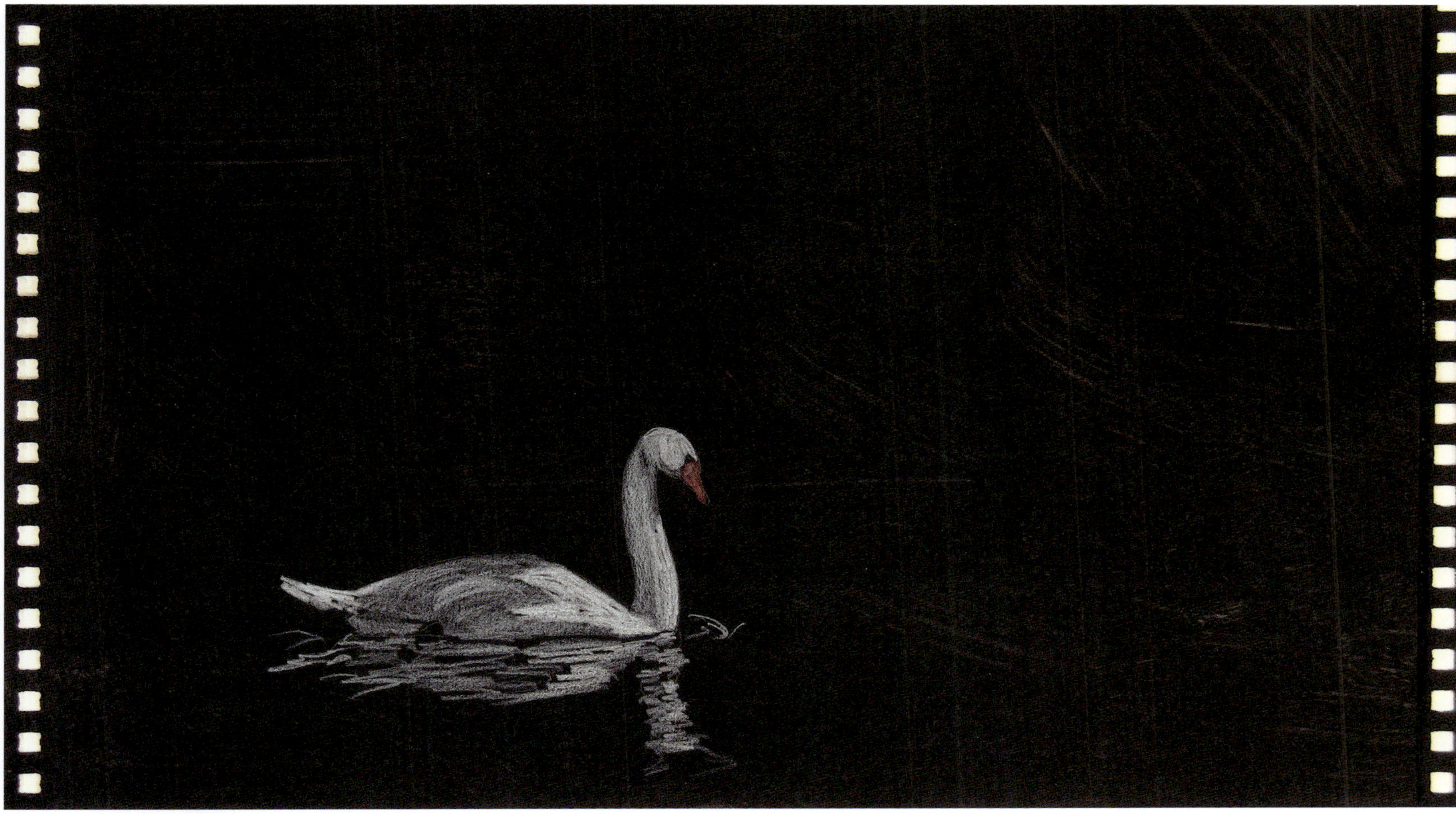

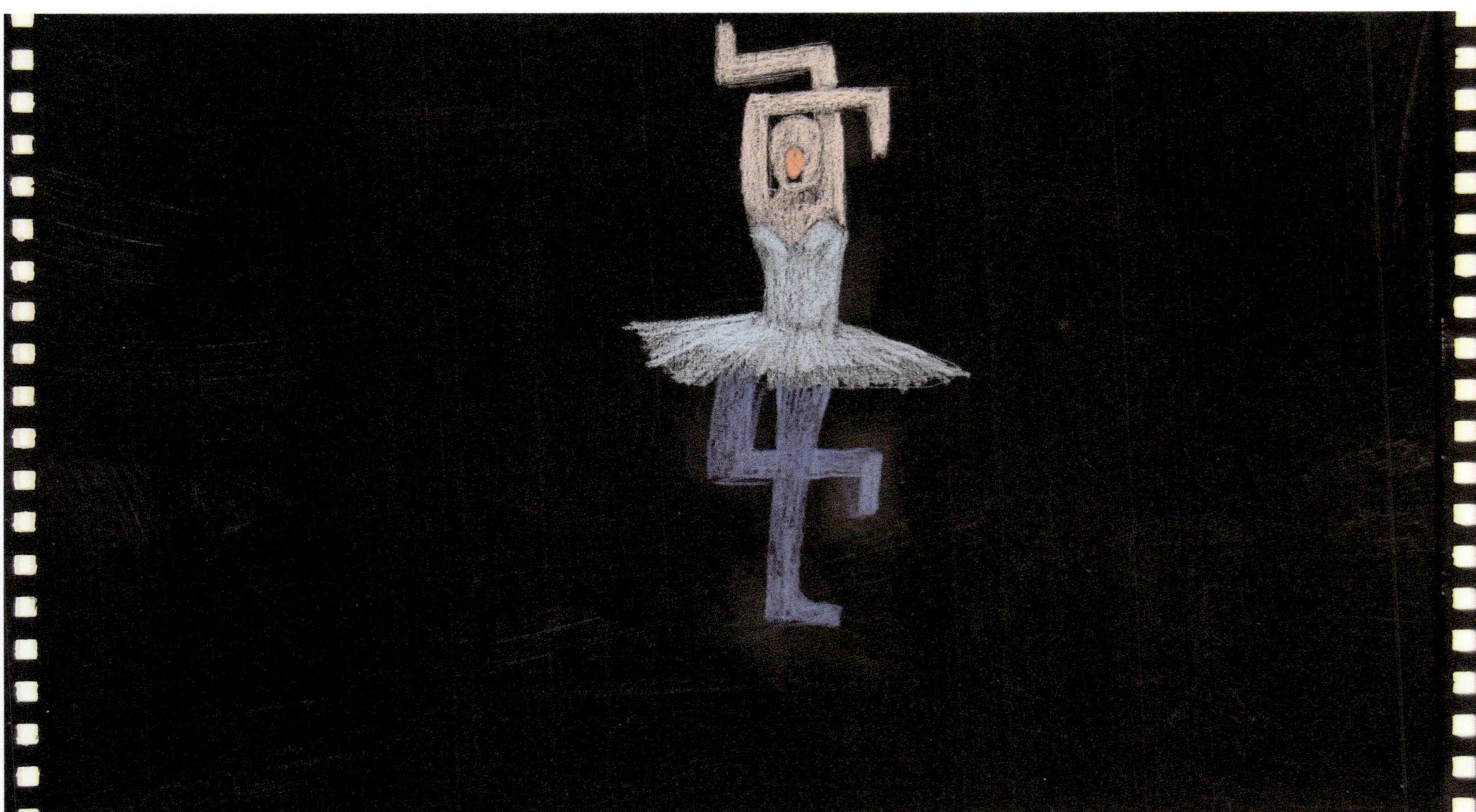

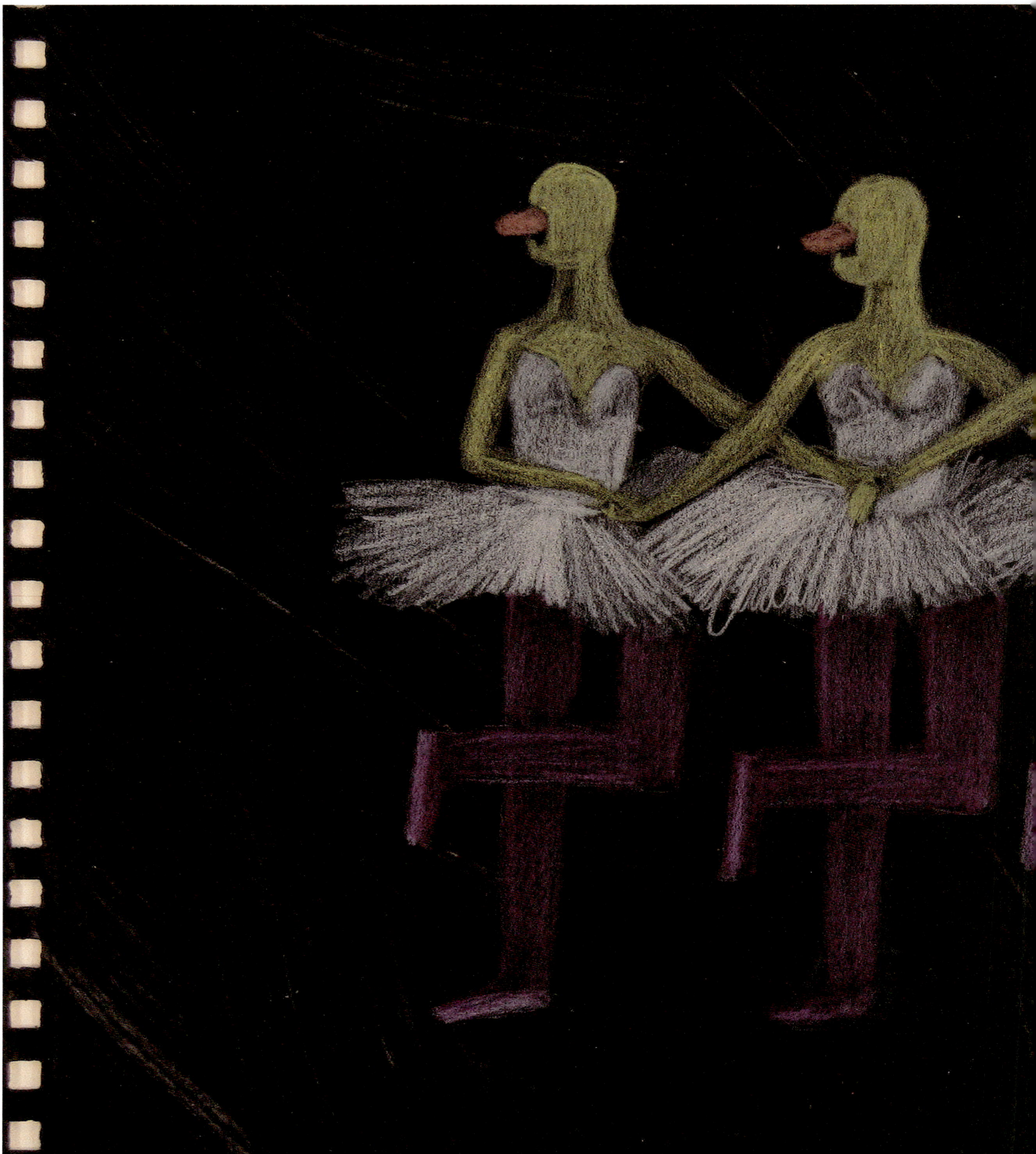

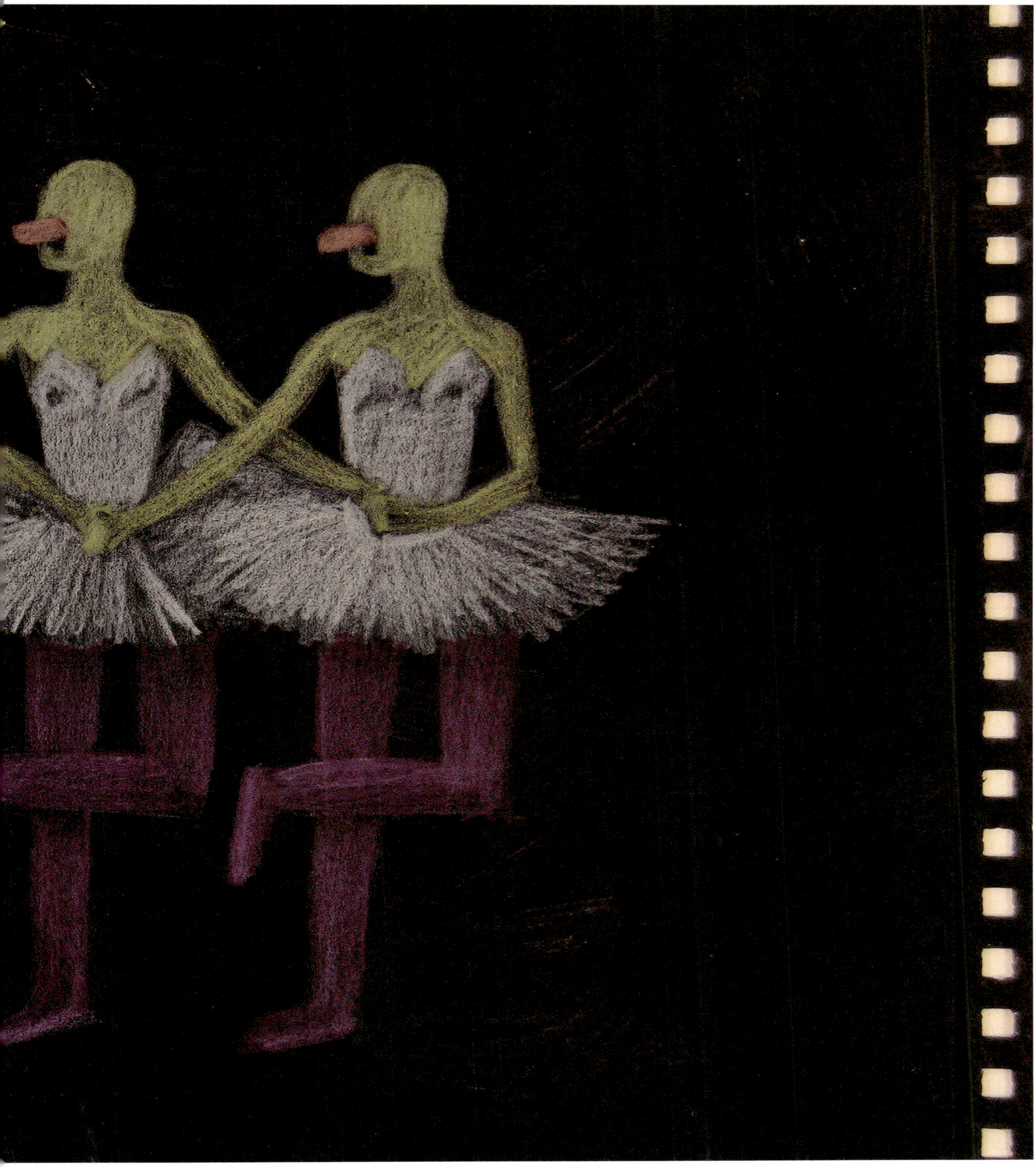

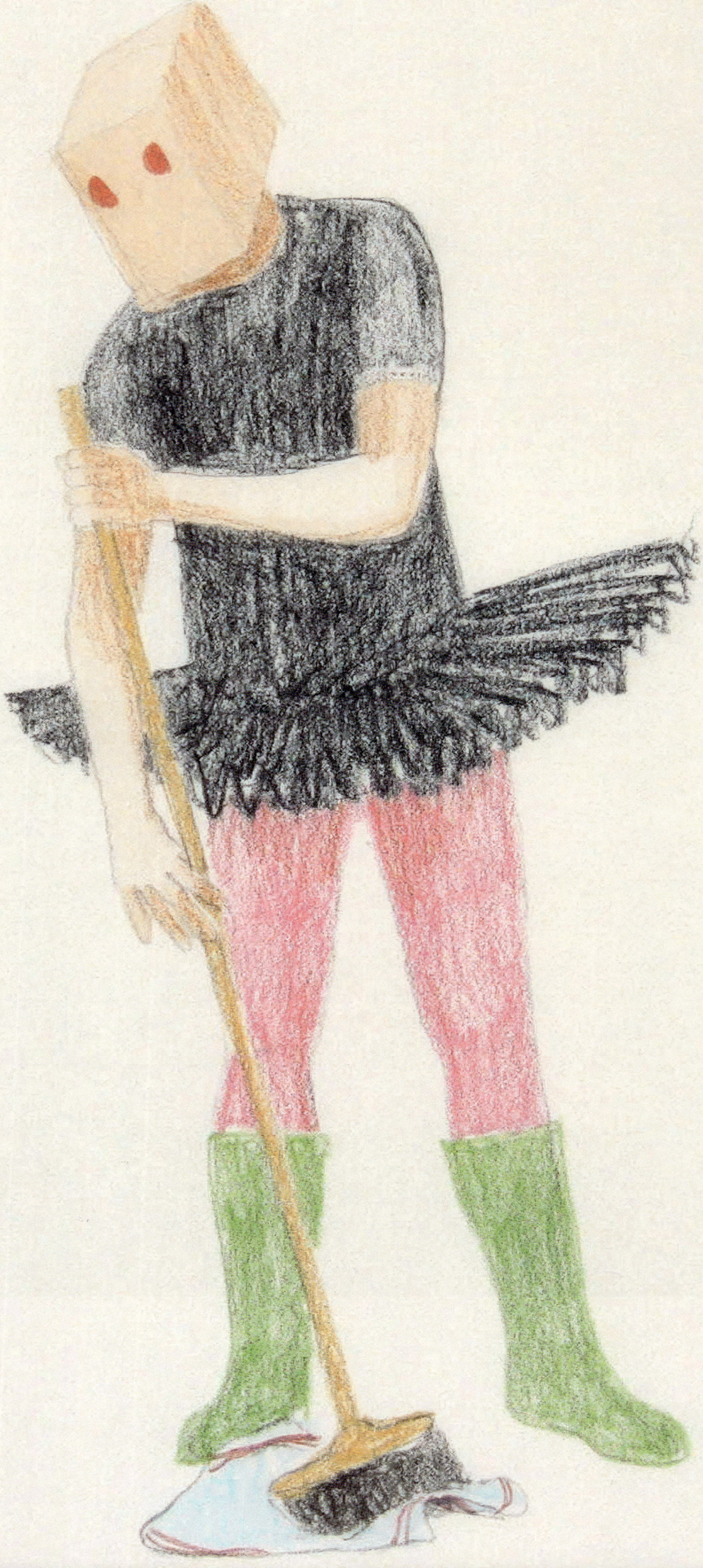

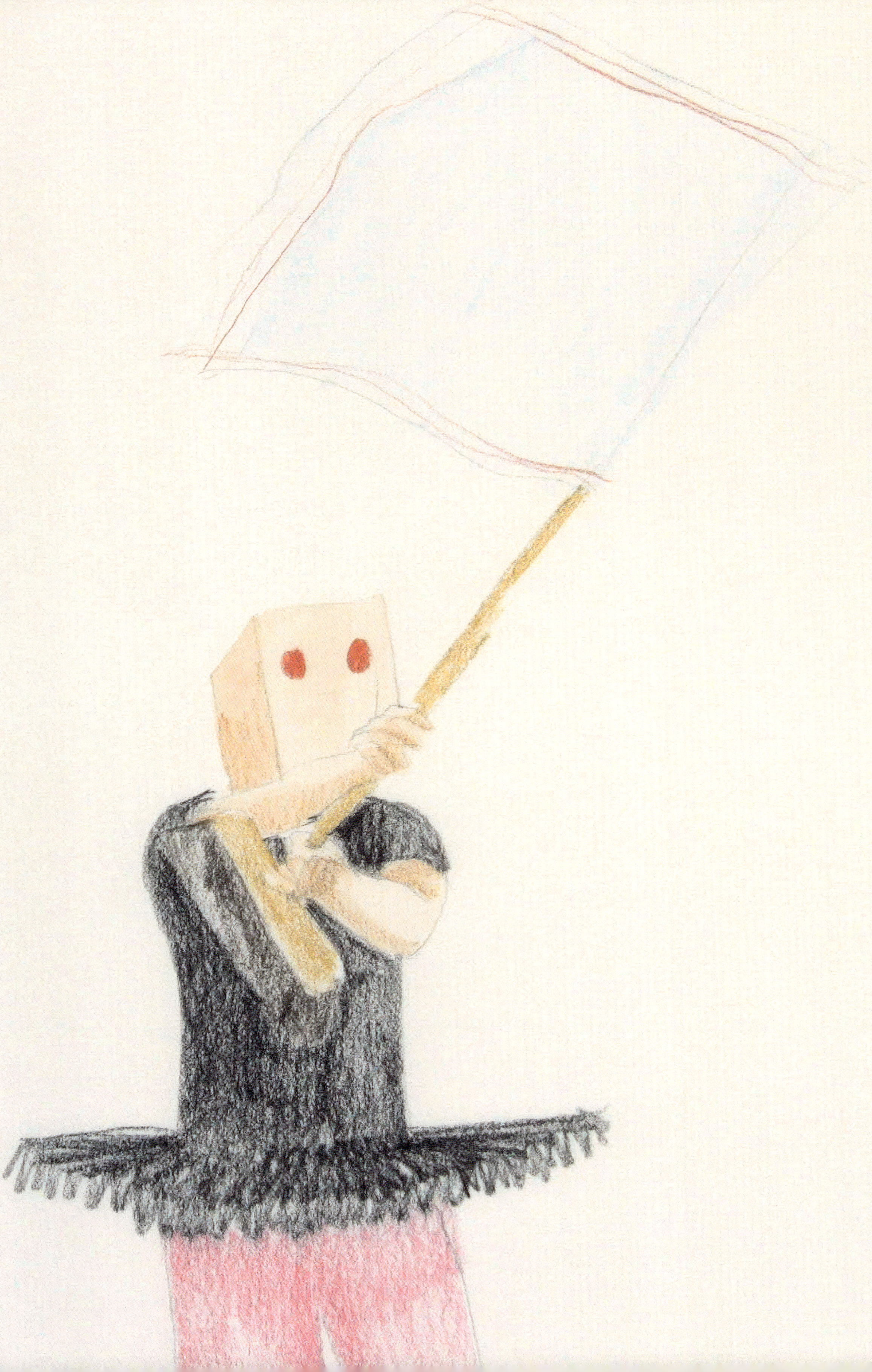

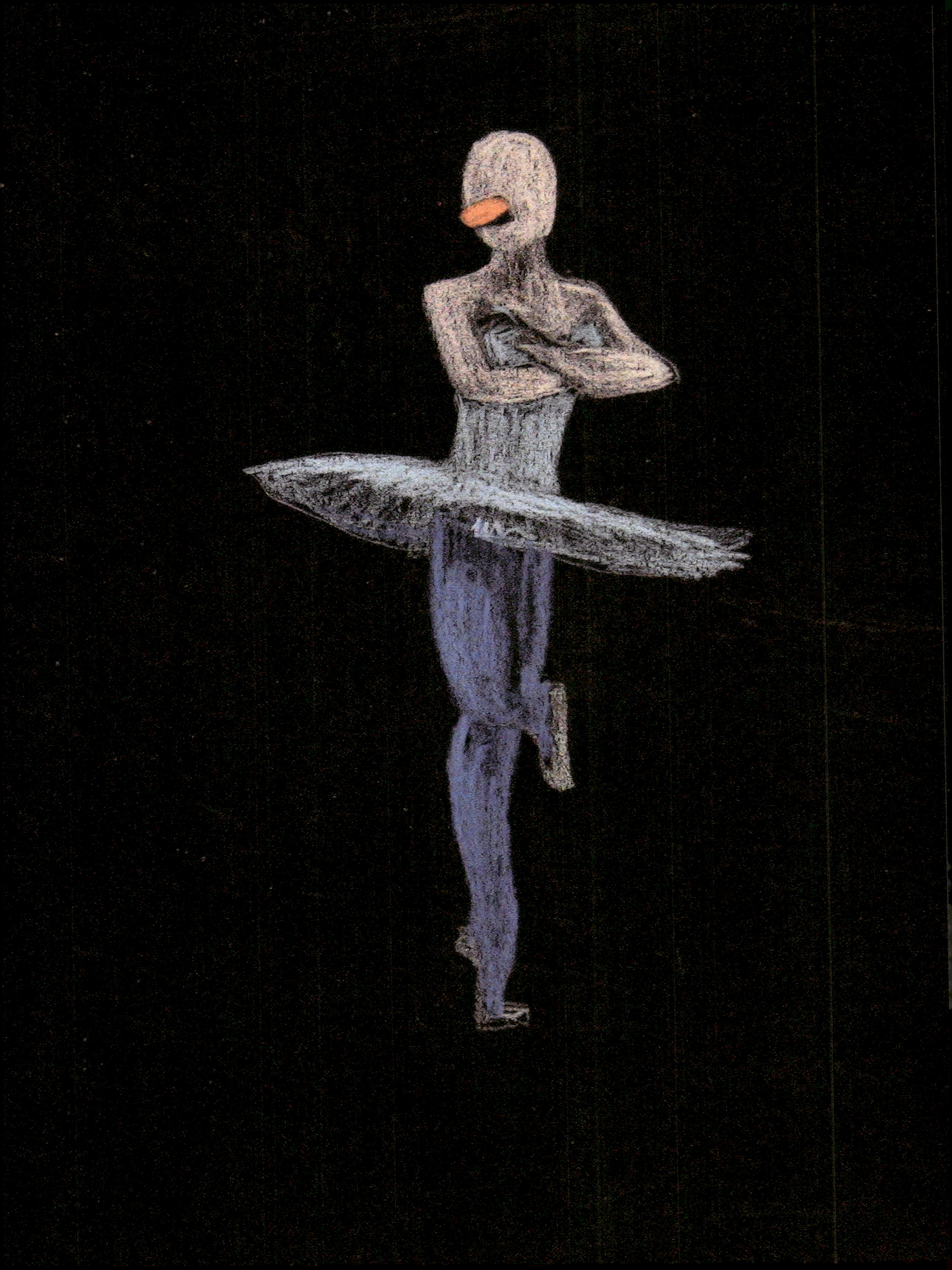

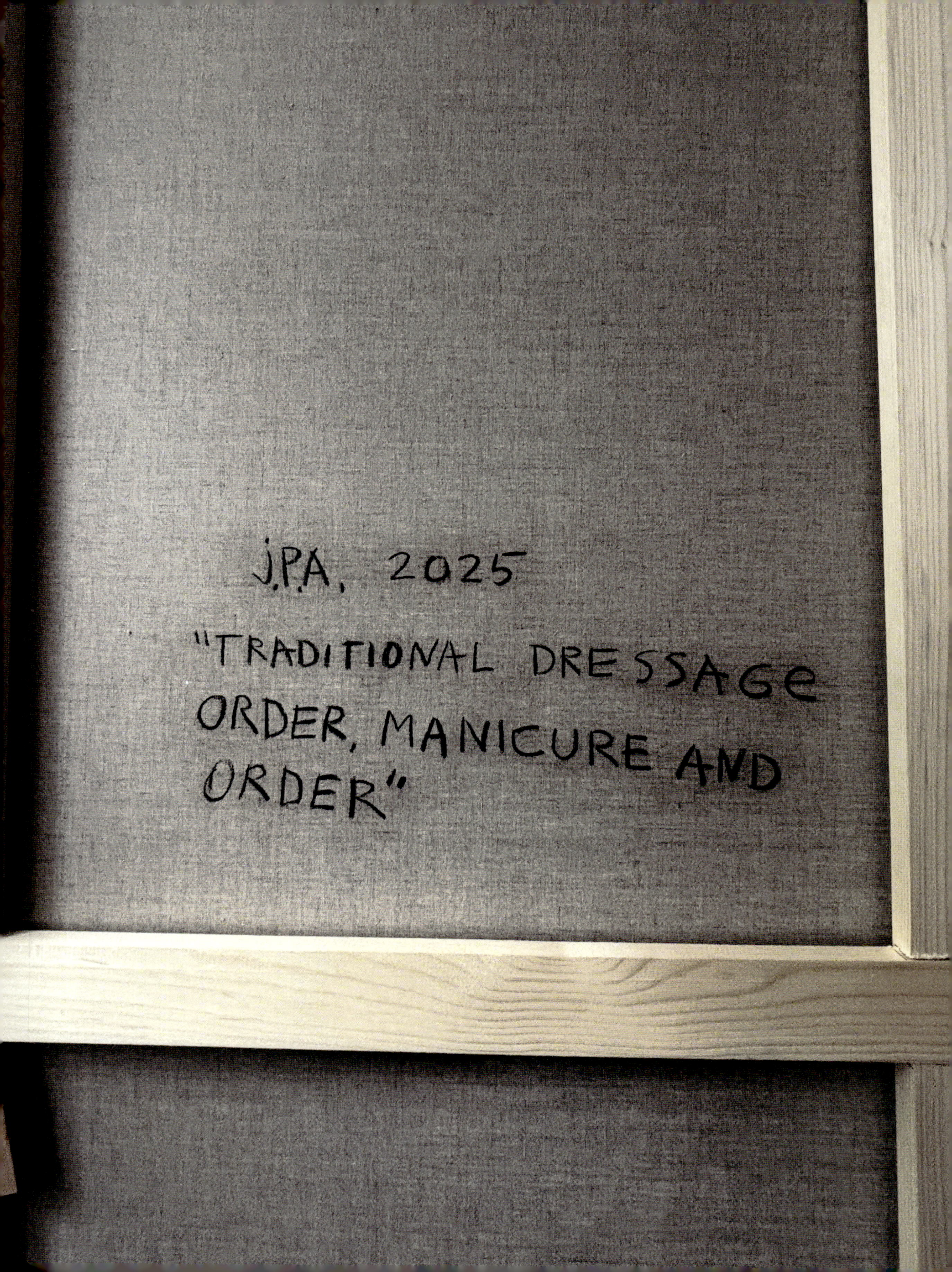
J.P.A. 2025
"TRADITIONAL DRESSAGE
ORDER, MANICURE AND
ORDER"

I started painting horses and cowboys because it seemed to me the best way to represent Western colonialism and its penchant for robbing and exploiting, that 'fifth freedom' Chomsky spoke about.

I believe that of all the different colonization narratives, one of the most successful is that achieved by the United States of America through the western movie genre.

Other colonizing civilizations were unable to do it or didn't have access to such means of propaganda. Ridiculing and considering the Other as inferior is a constant in all processes of colonization. Their way of dressing, their way of talking, their social structures... everything is portrayed as grotesque and backward. The colonized have always been portrayed as uncivilized barbarians.

If history had been written by the losers, the conquest of the Wild West and other conquests would have been very different stories. I am reminded of the film *Los últimos de Filipinas* (Last Stand in the Philippines), which I would recommend as mandatory viewing as a counterexample.
When I was a child we used to play cowboys and Indians. The fort with its stockade was a very common toy and, like many others, fulfilled the function of channelling symbolic violence. We had no idea or awareness of what it really meant. Now, with screens, everything is much easier, but back then we had to re-enact and imagine battles. Because of some strange trauma, when they leave childhood behind, some people turn the symbolic into the real, and I suspect many of them once played with three caravels.

I had also thought about the idea of the horse, the cowboy, the hangman's noose and the sound as the Western capacity for self-destruction. As a thought, it might not be very original, but art's power to convey and transform things into something different is absolutely fantastic, a boon, and it's in that tiny space where the event of communication sometimes reveals itself.

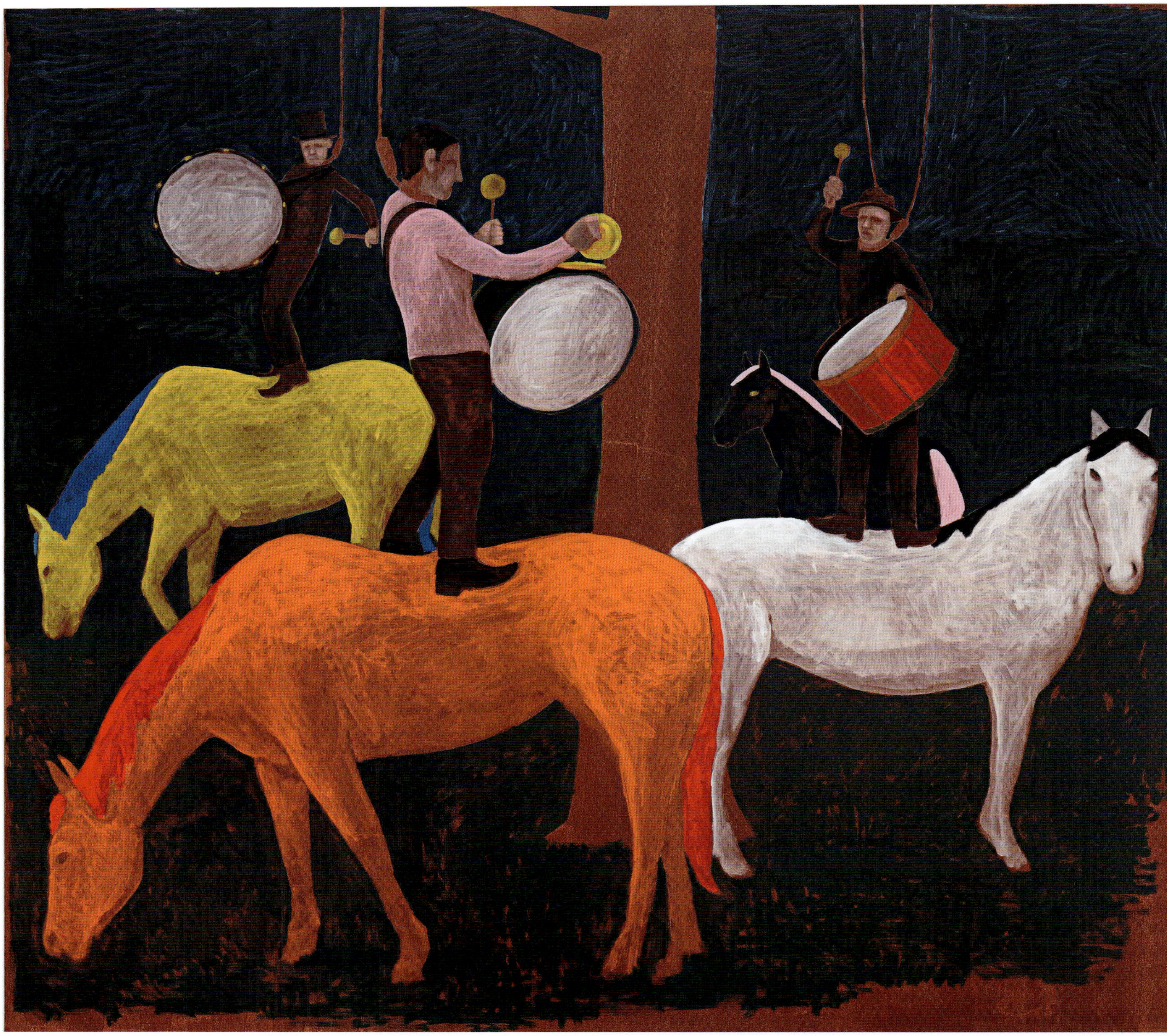

Traditional Dressage, West Music Band, 2024
Acrylic on canvas
200 x 220 cm

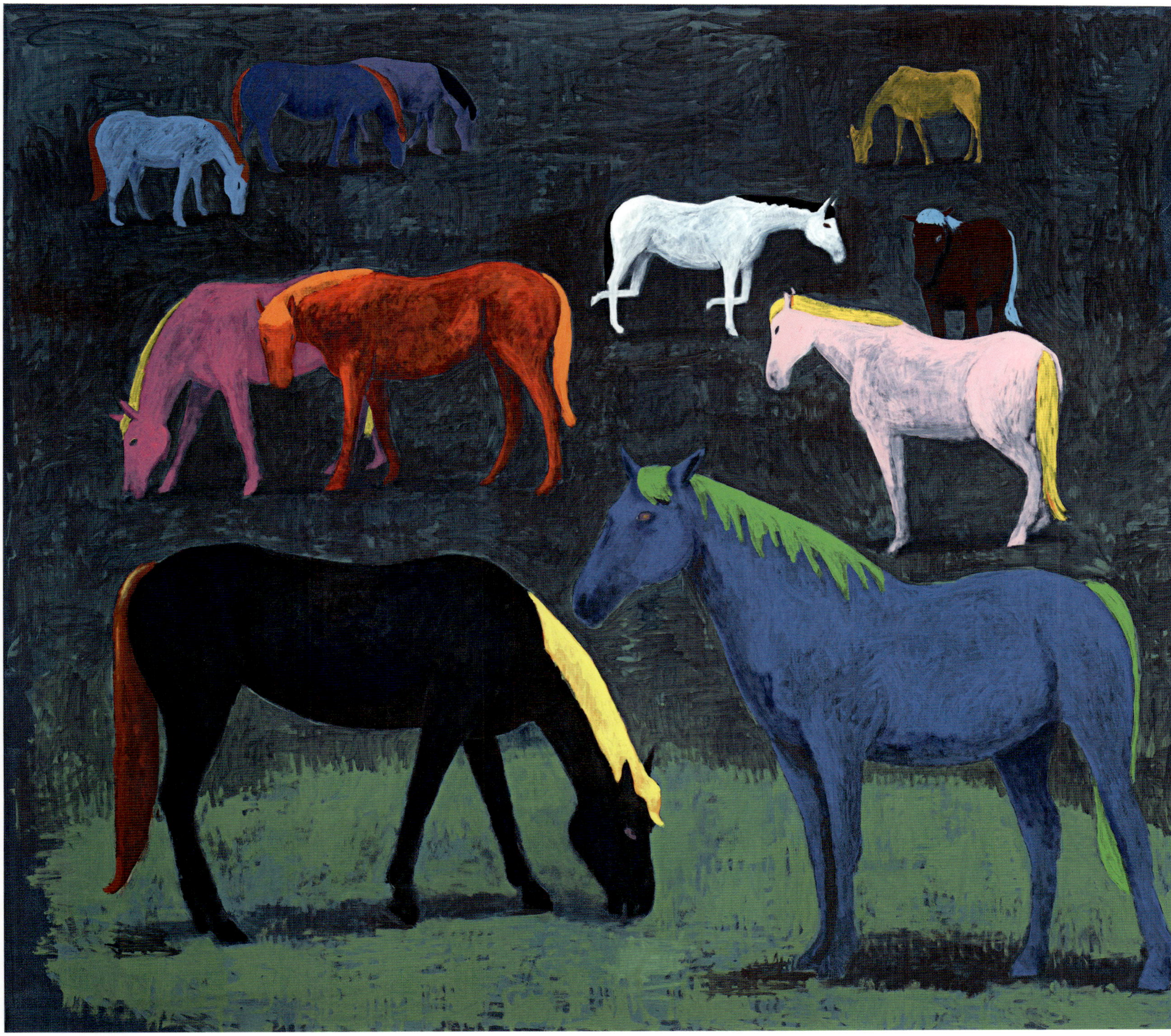

Traditional Dressage, Bottle Blonde Horse, 2024
Acrylic on canvas
200 x 220 cm

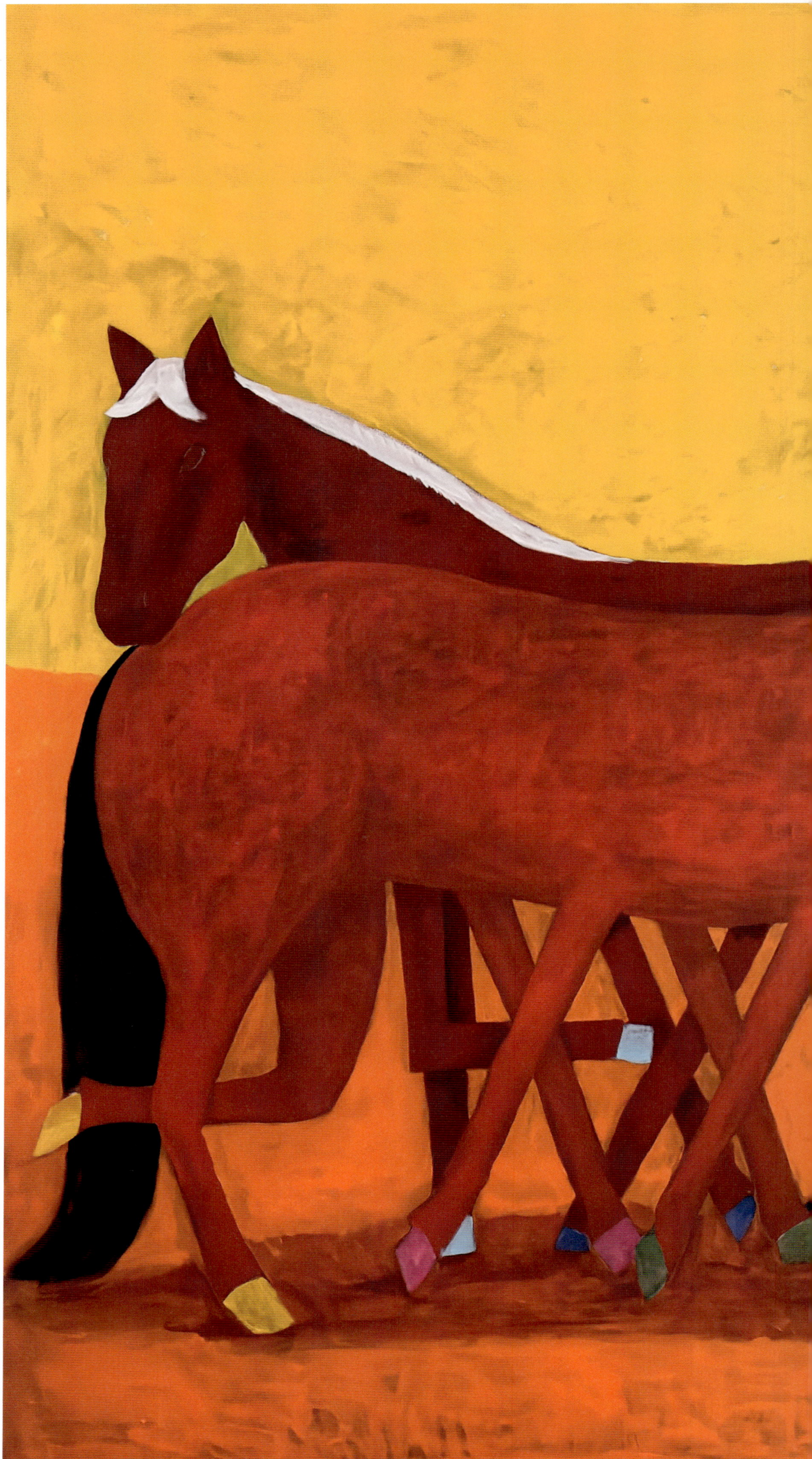

Traditional Dressage, Order, Manicure and Order, 2025
Acrylic on canvas
220 x 200 cm

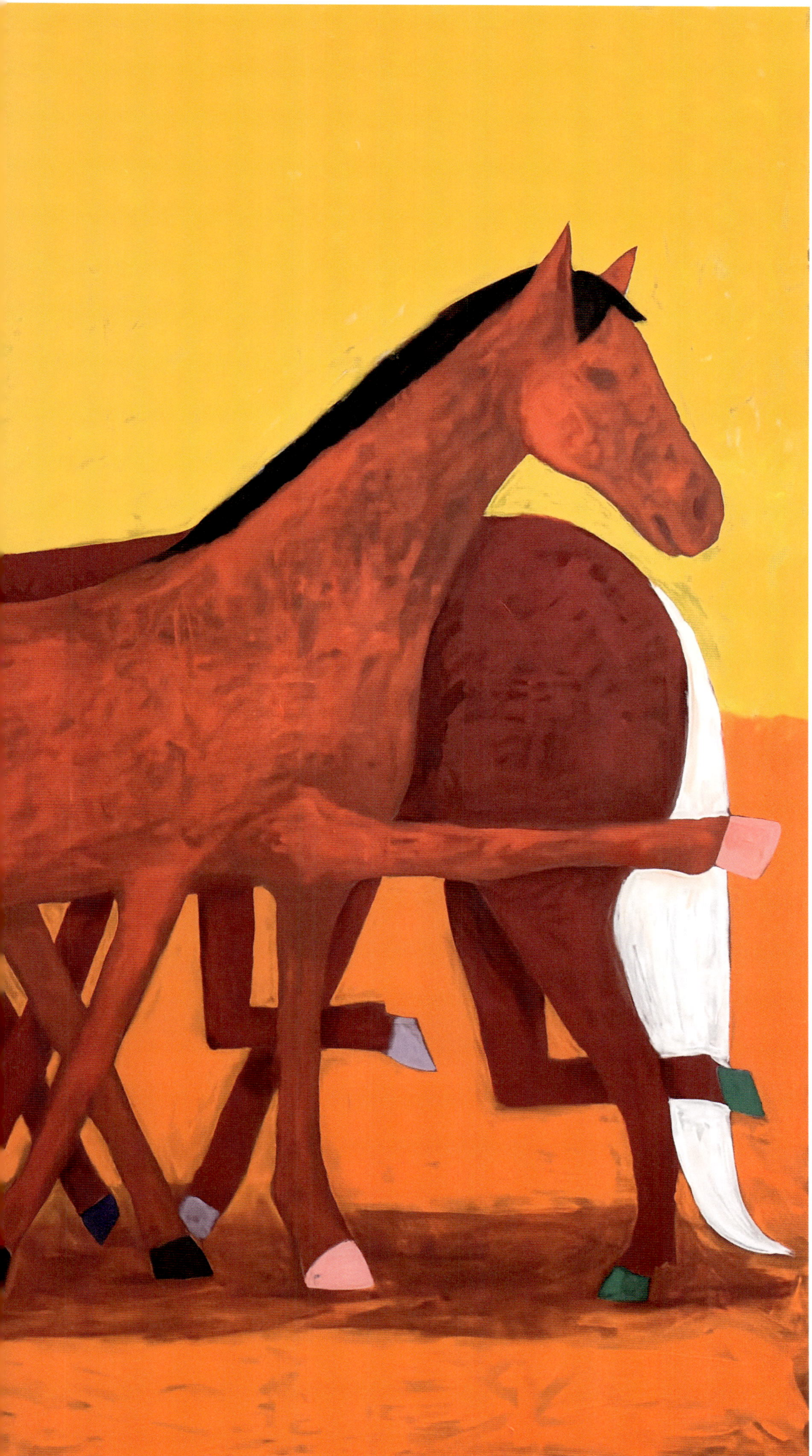

Traditional Dressage, Orchestra Cymbal, 2024
Acrylic on canvas
100 x 73 cm

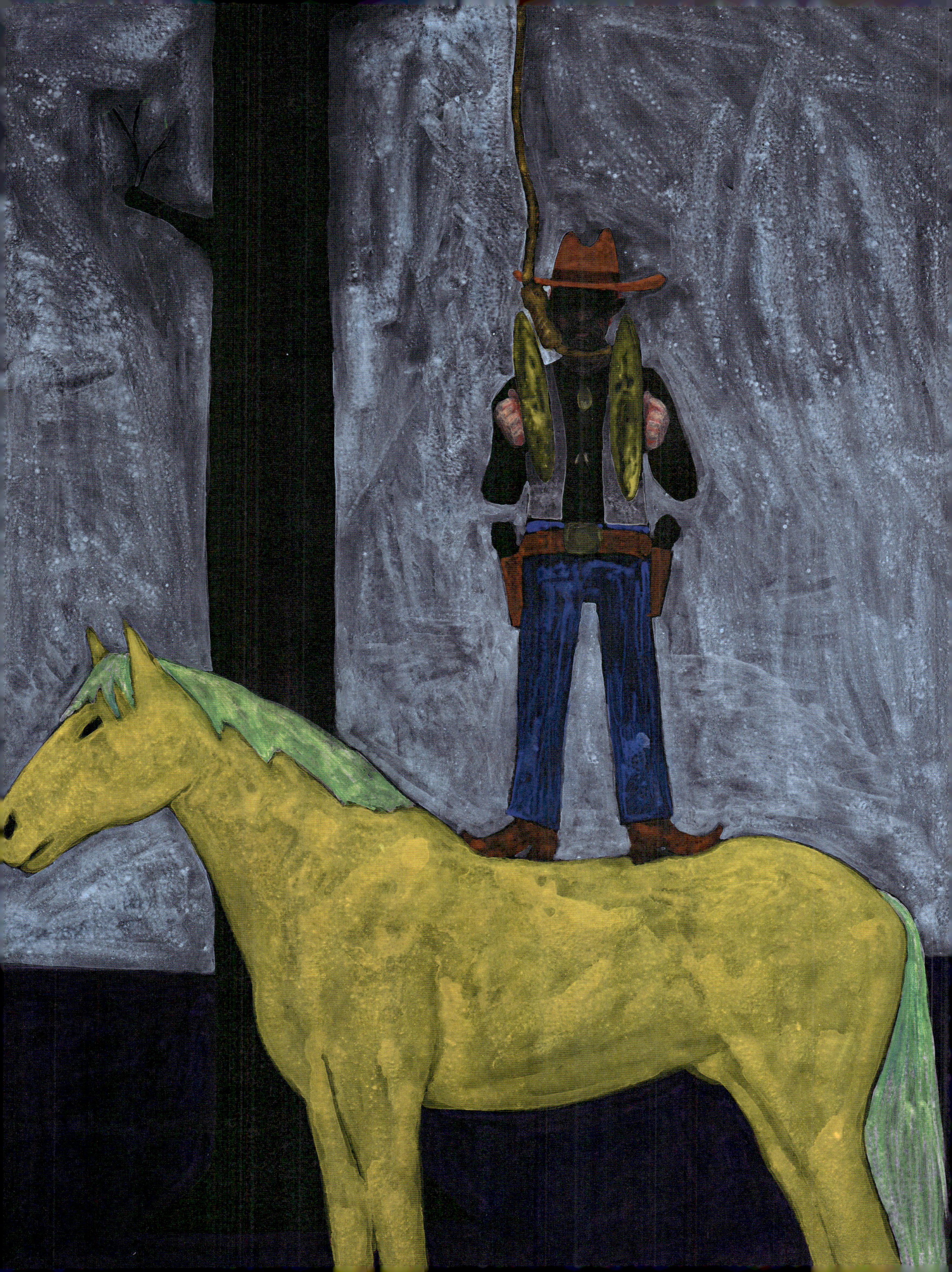

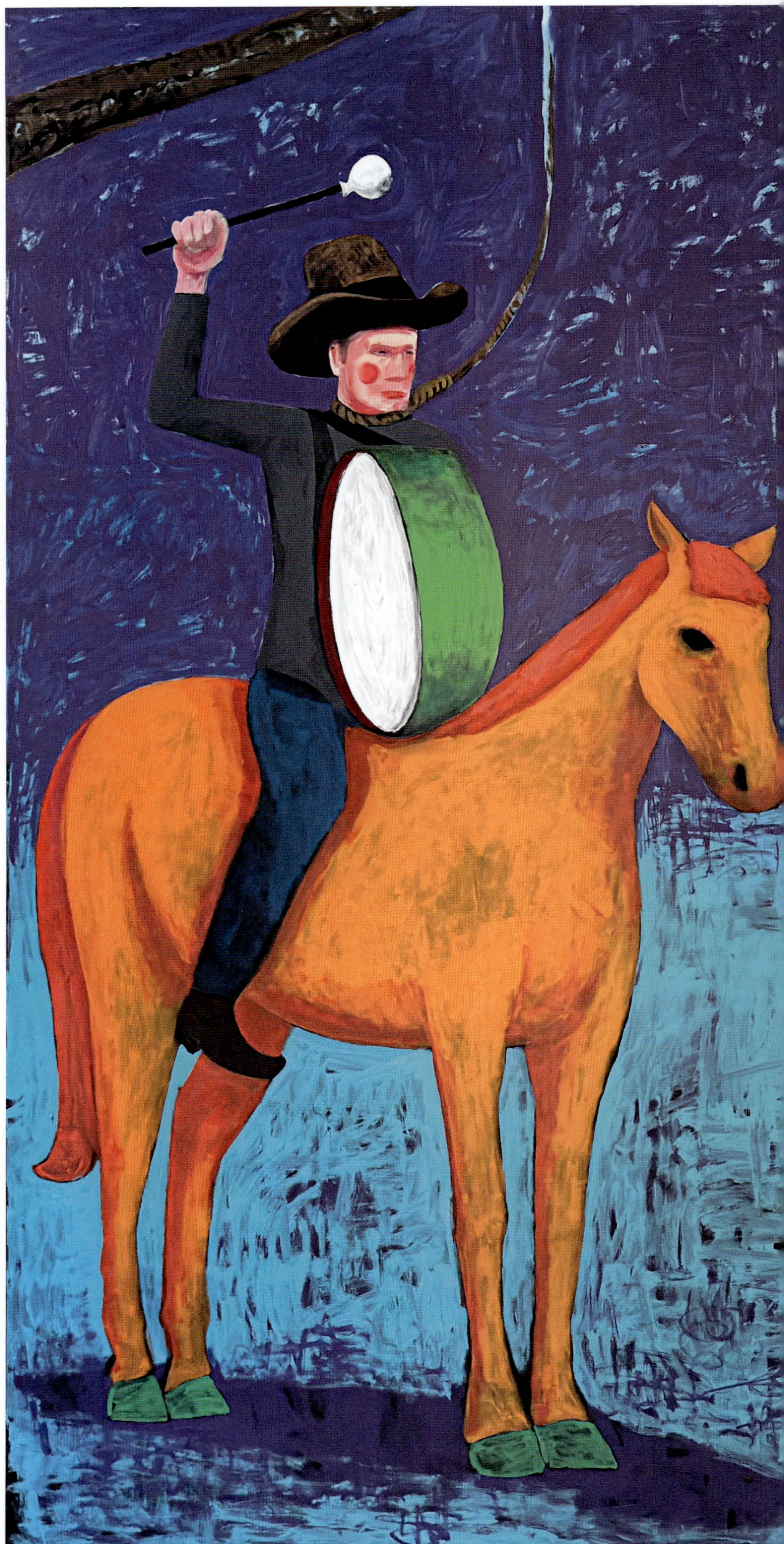

Western Perfection, reflejo sin espejo, 2025
Acrylic on canvas
200 x 200 cm

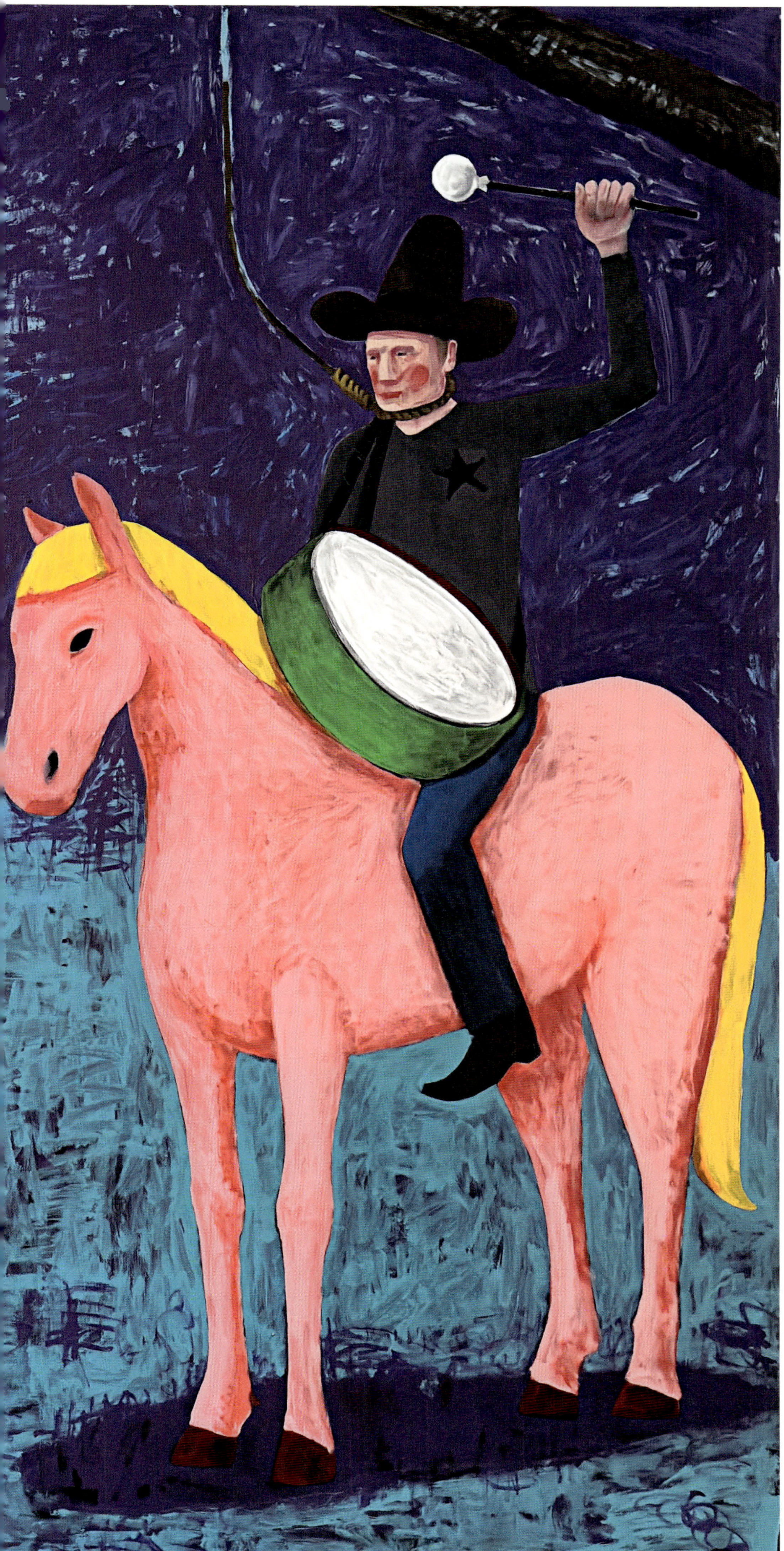

Traditional Dressage, Red Drum, 2024
Acrylic on canvas
197 x 130 cm

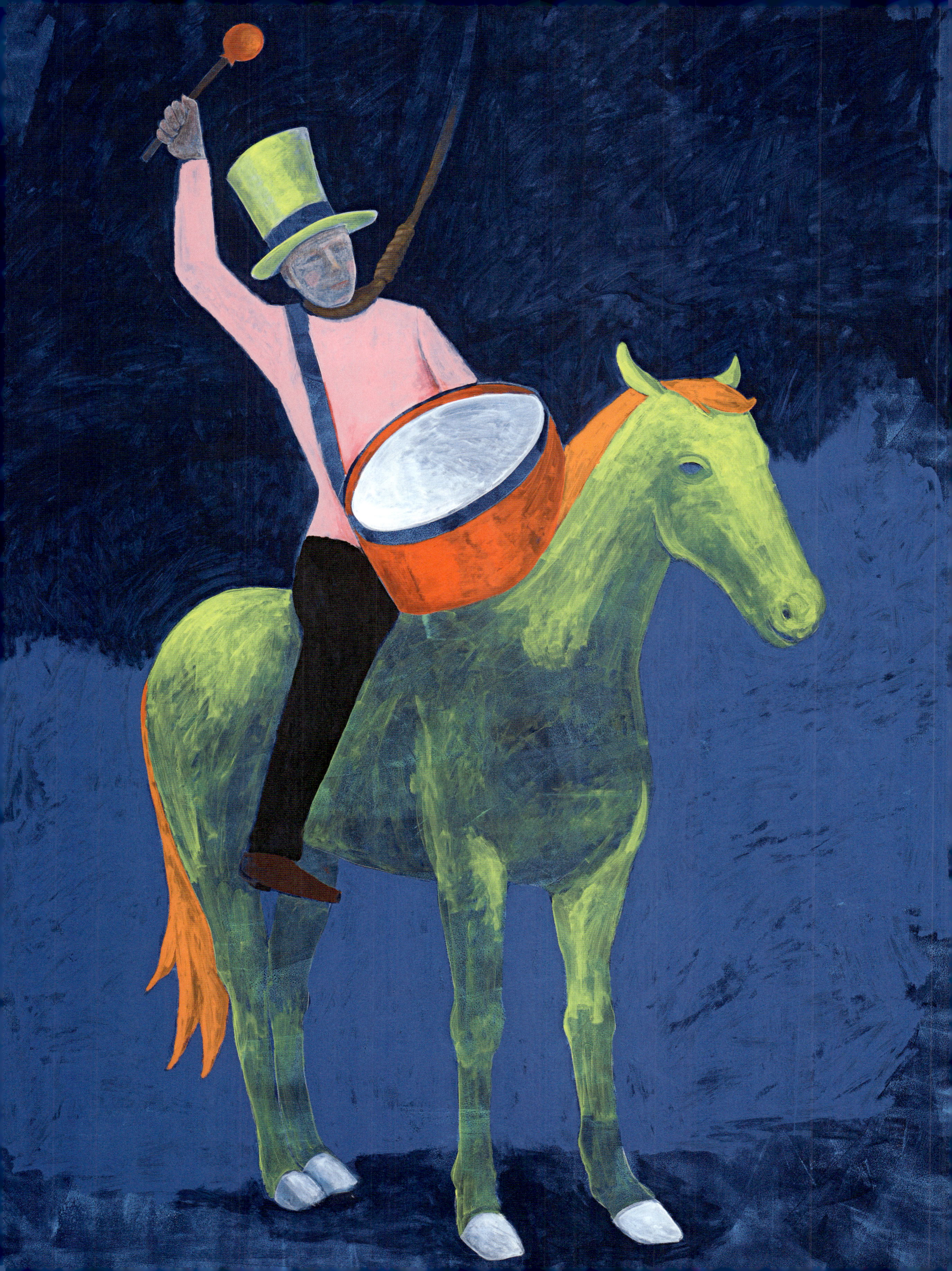

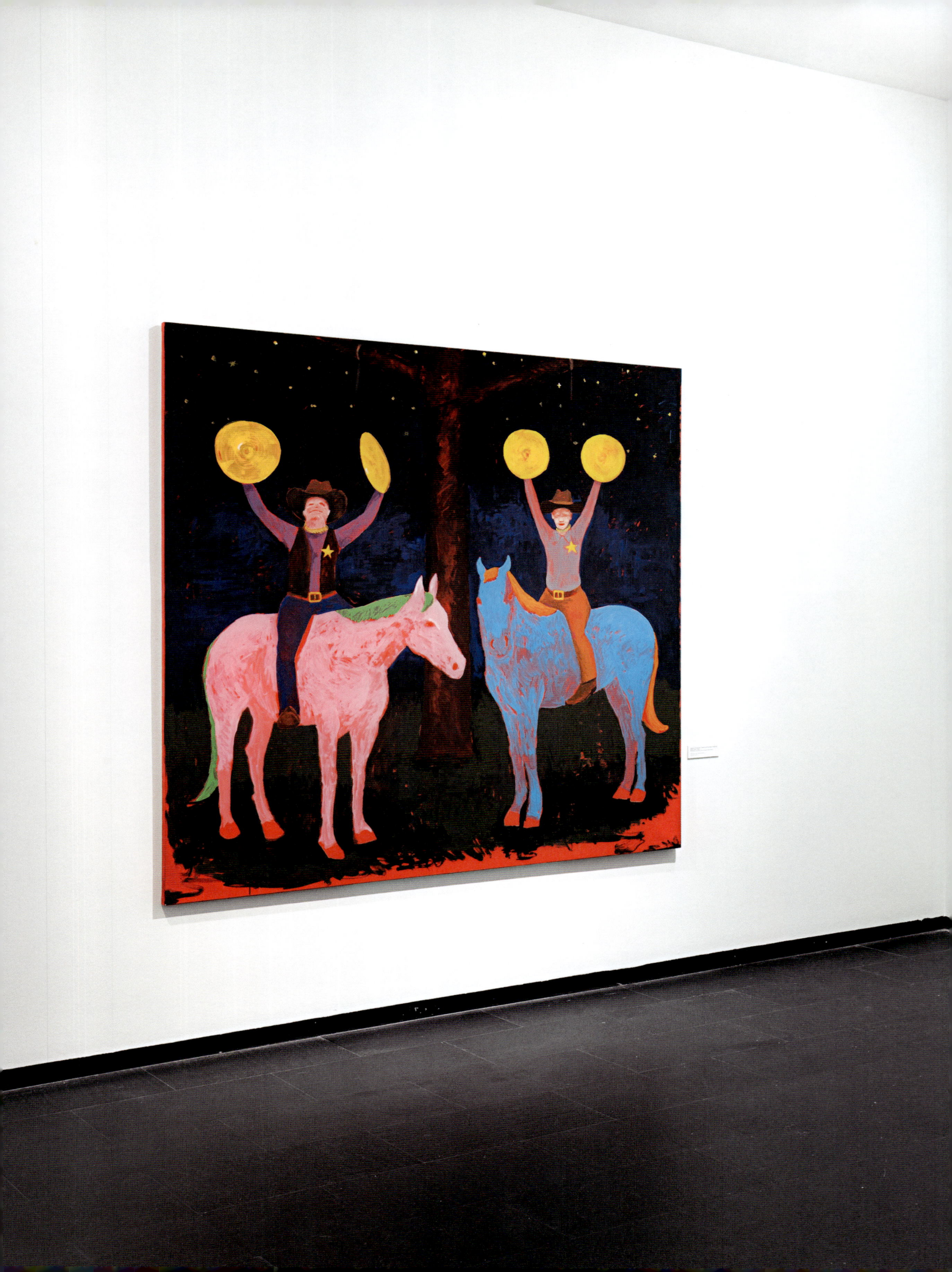

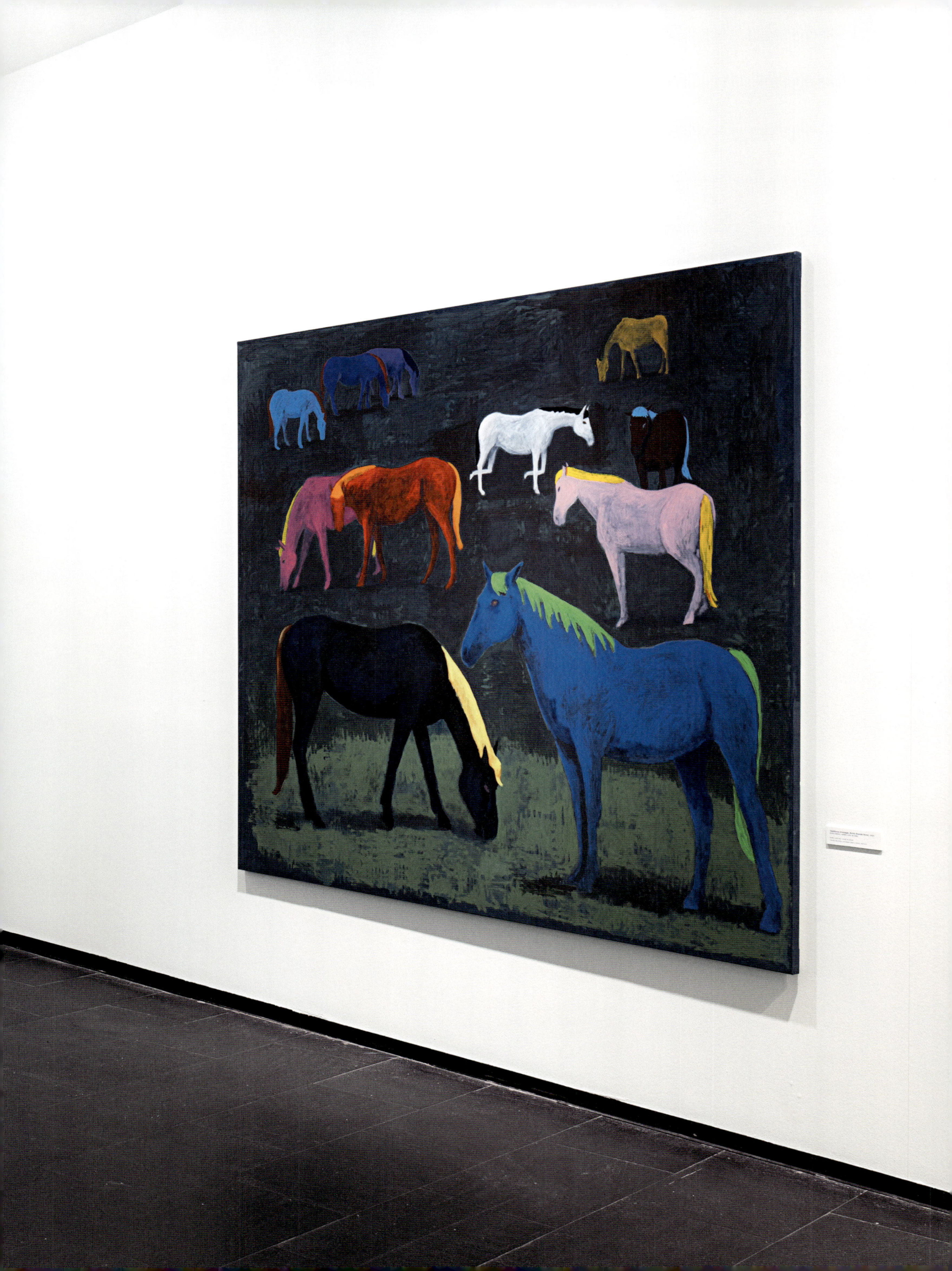

Traditional Dressage, Order, 2025
Acrylic on canvas
200 x 200 cm

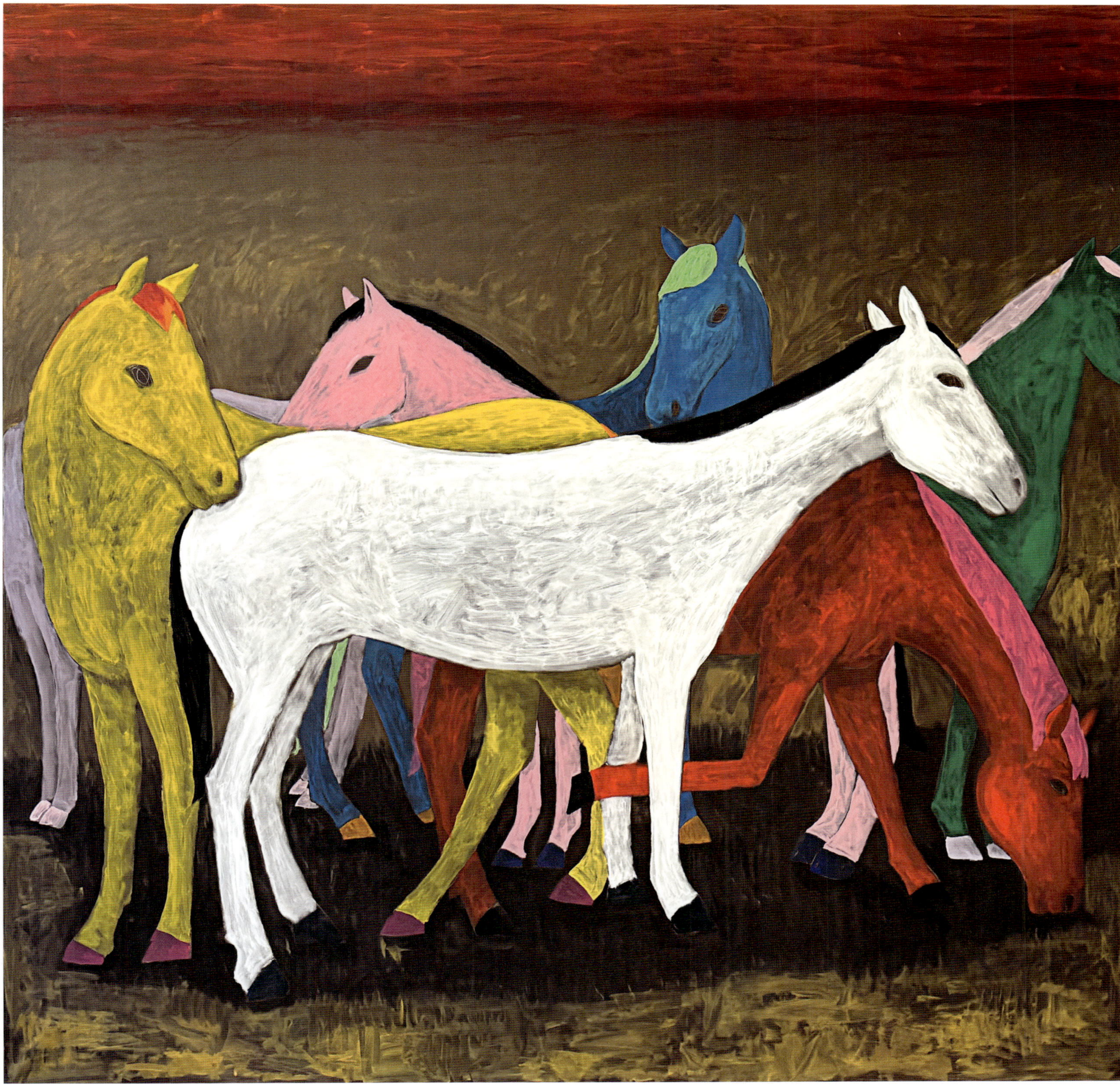

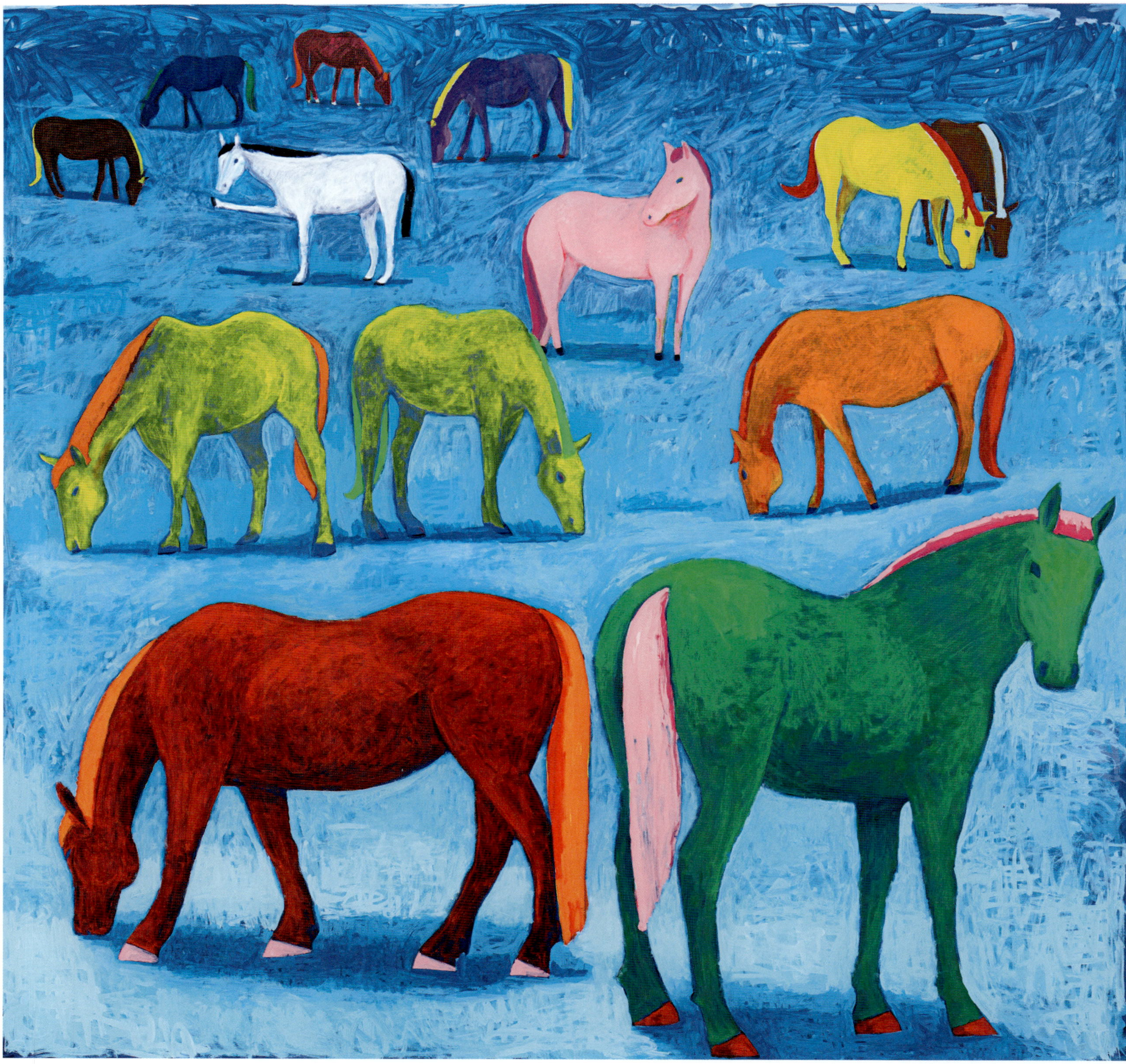

Western Perfection. Traditional Dressage, Smells Like Stinky Armpits, 2024-25
Acrylic on canvas
200 x 200 cm

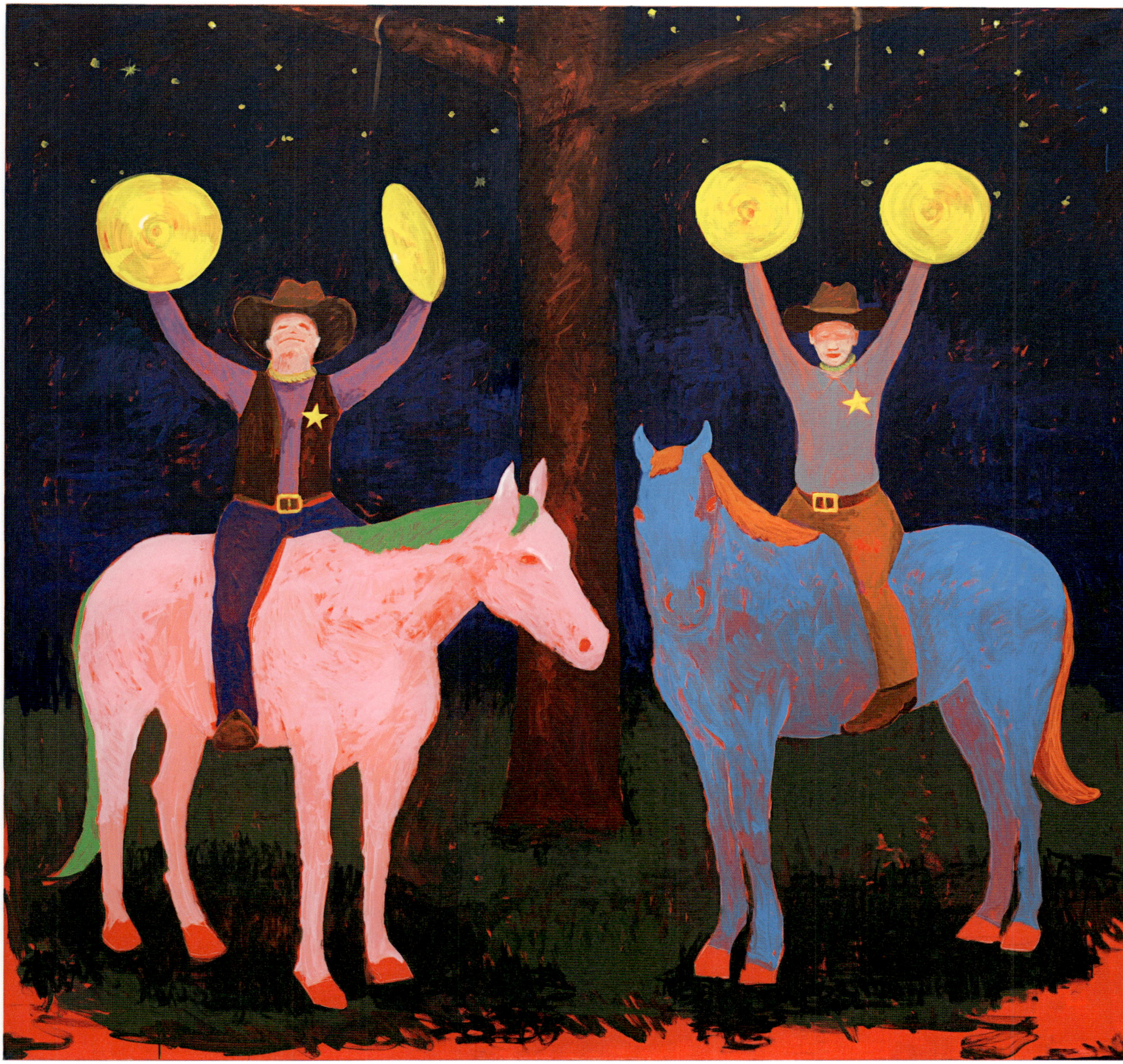

Western Perfection. Traditional Dressage, Classical Band,
2024-25
Acrylic on canvas
200 x 200 cm

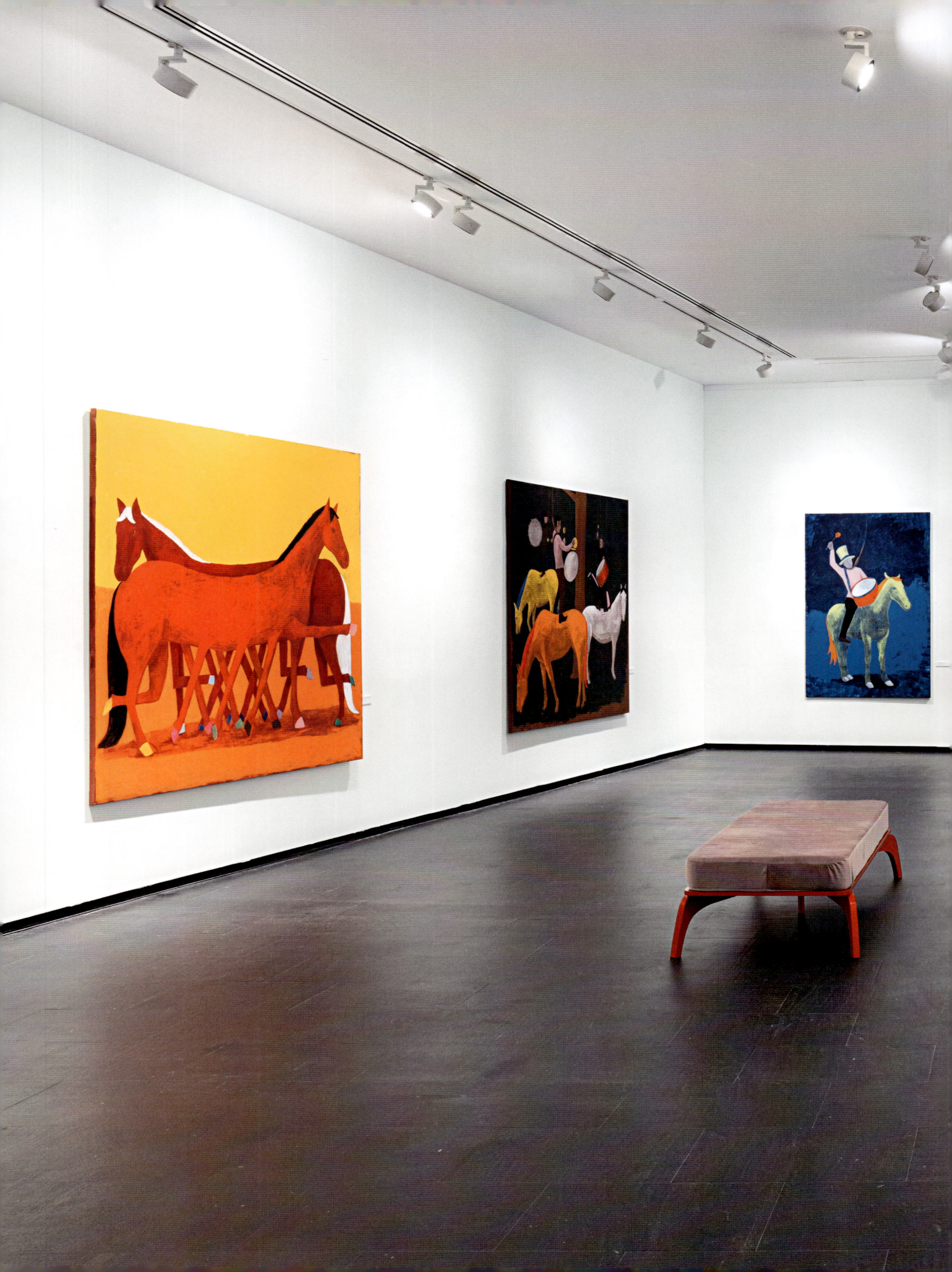

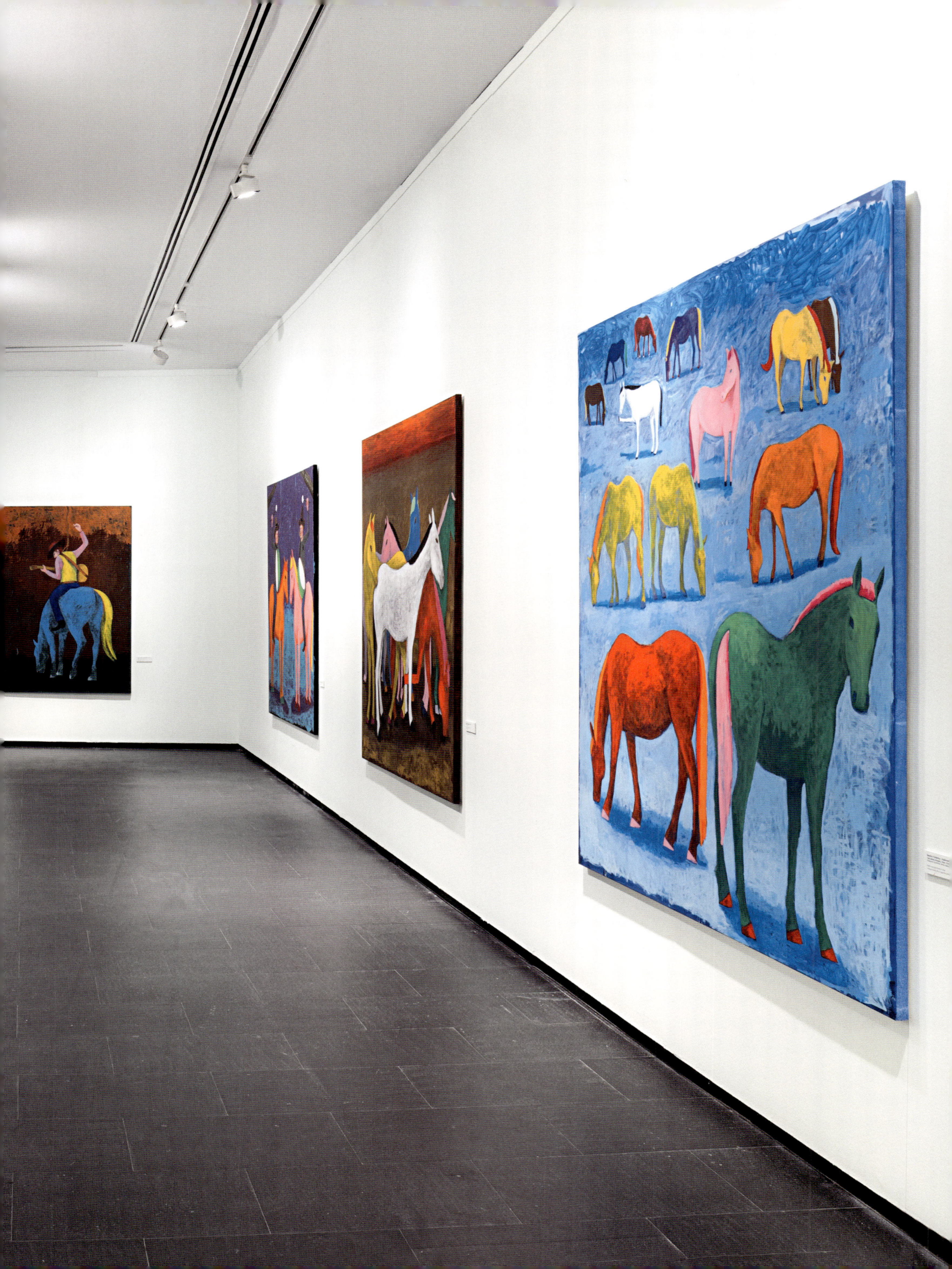

p. 200
Traditional Dressage, Triangle, 2024
Acrylic on canvas
100 x 73 cm

p. 199
Traditional Dressage, Thinking About Your Song, 2025
Acrylic on canvas
197 x 130 cm

p. 201
Traditional Dressage, Gold Cymbals, 2024
Acrylic on canvas
100 x 73 cm

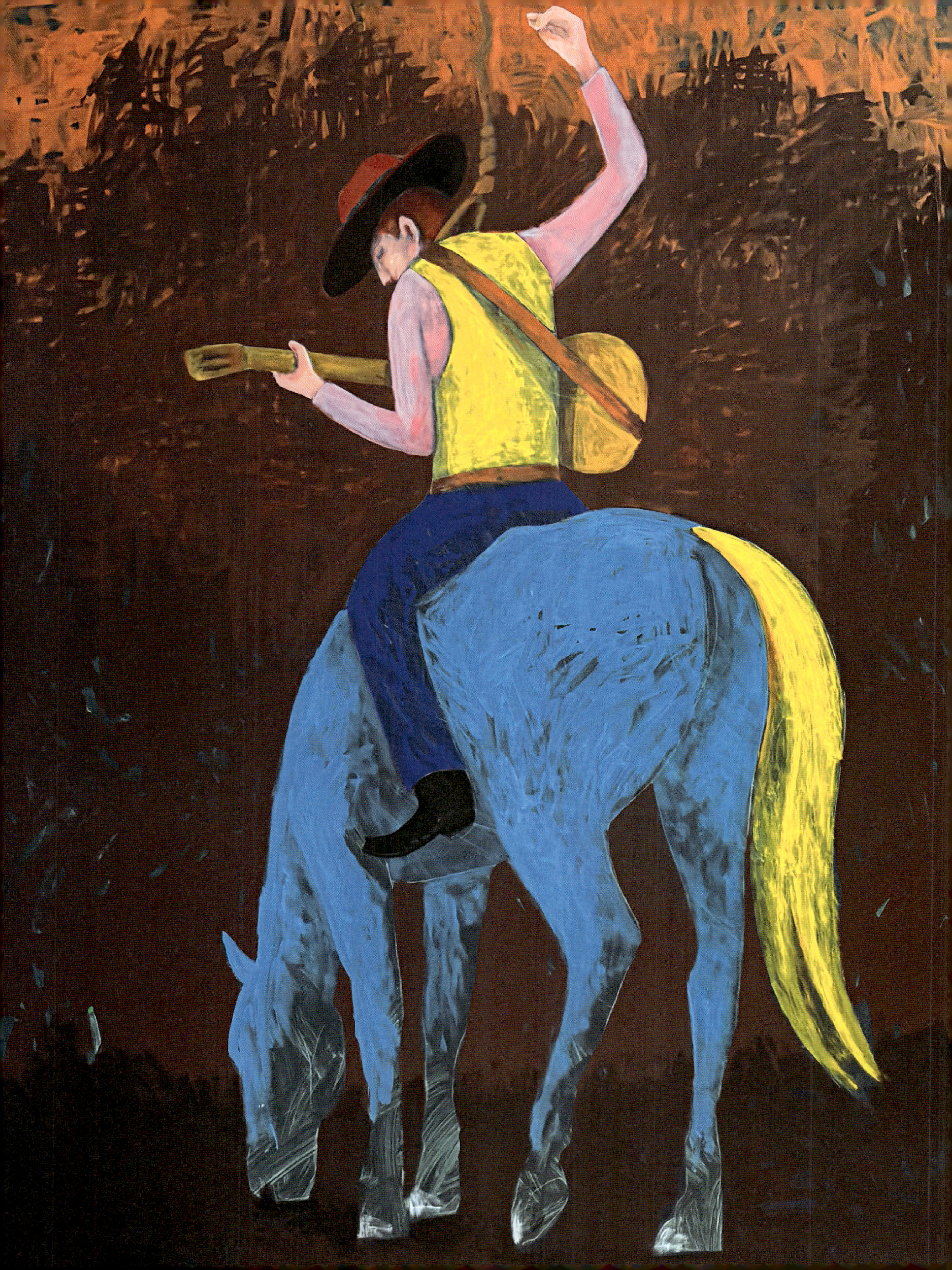

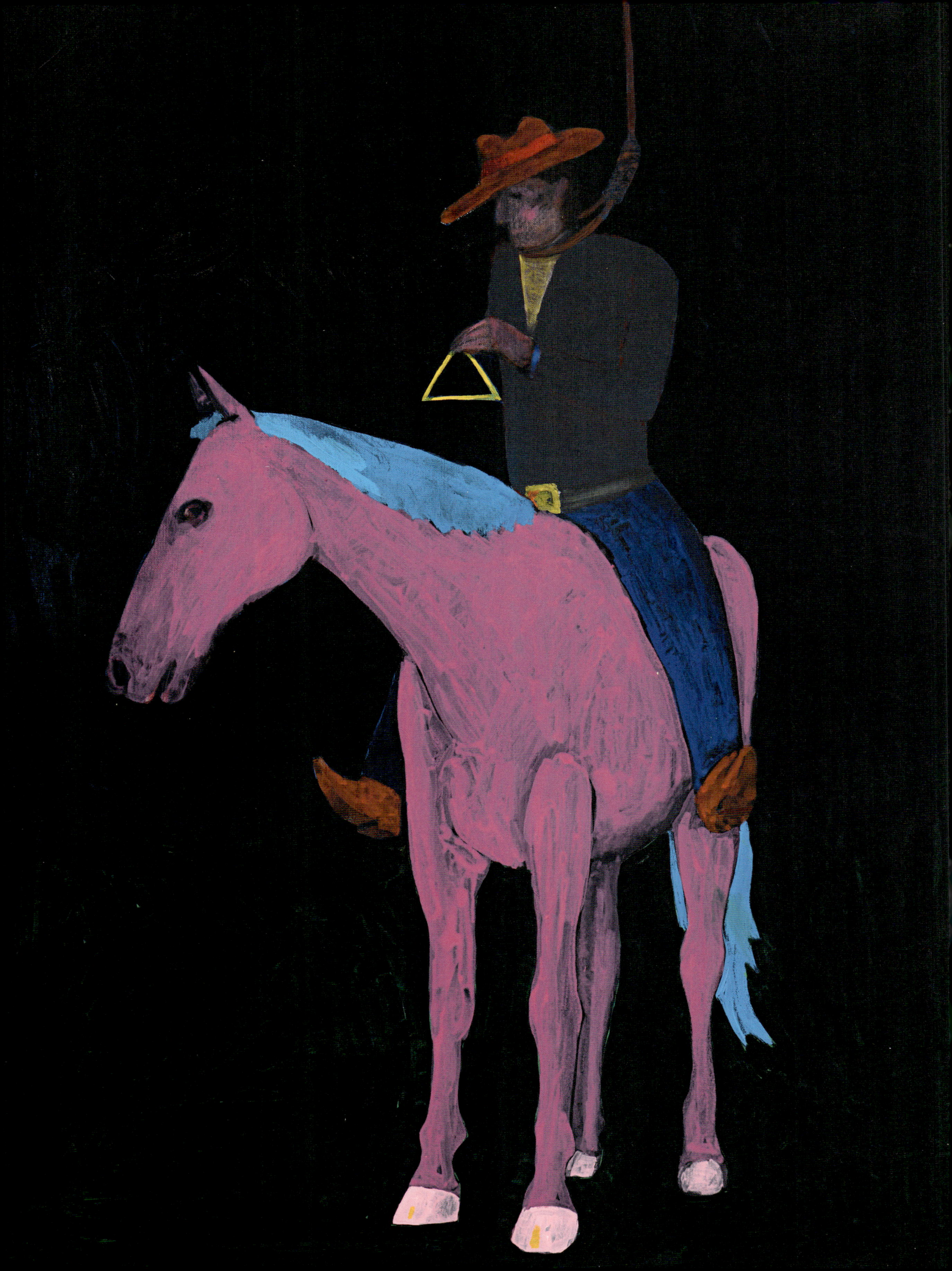

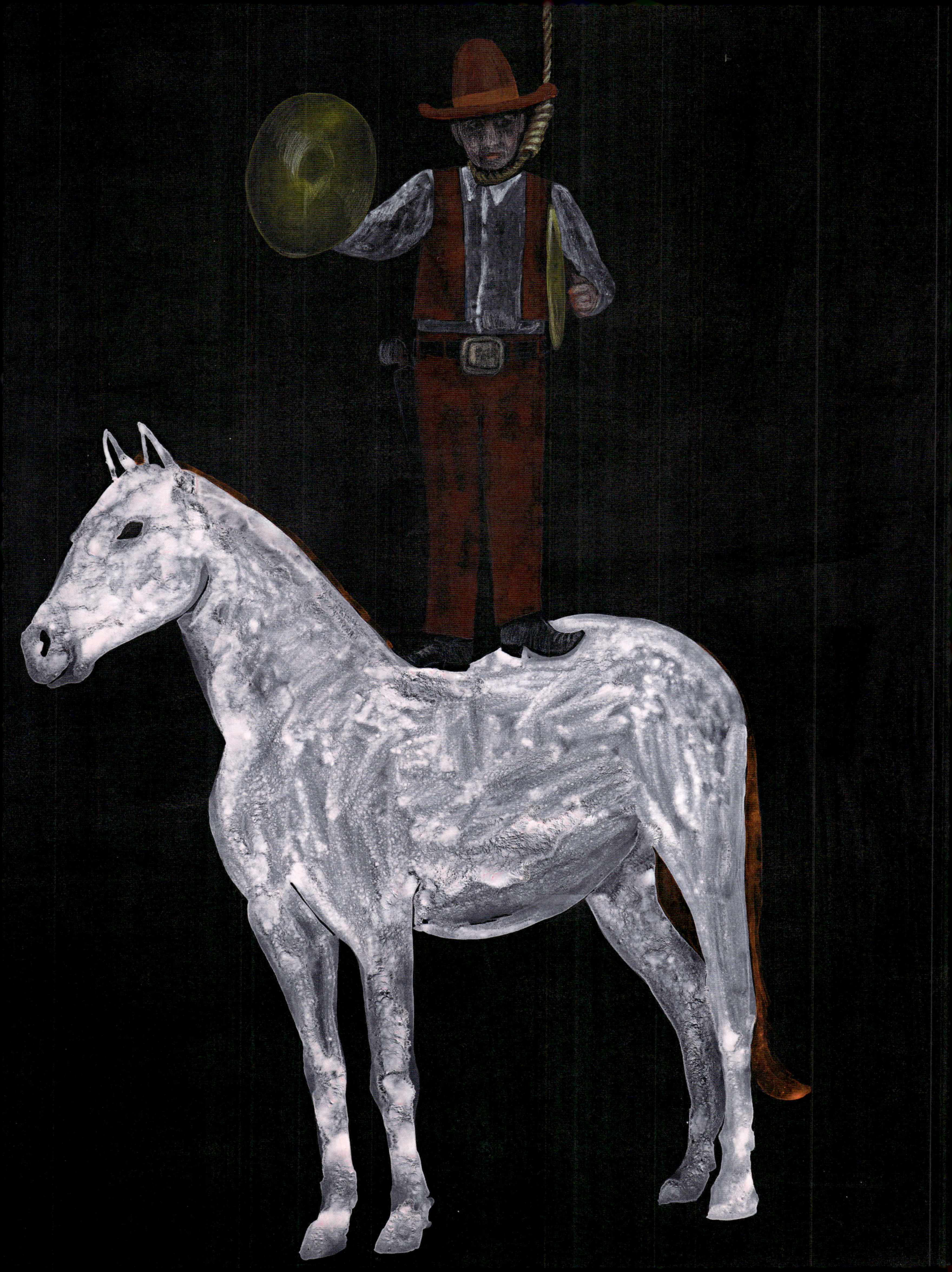

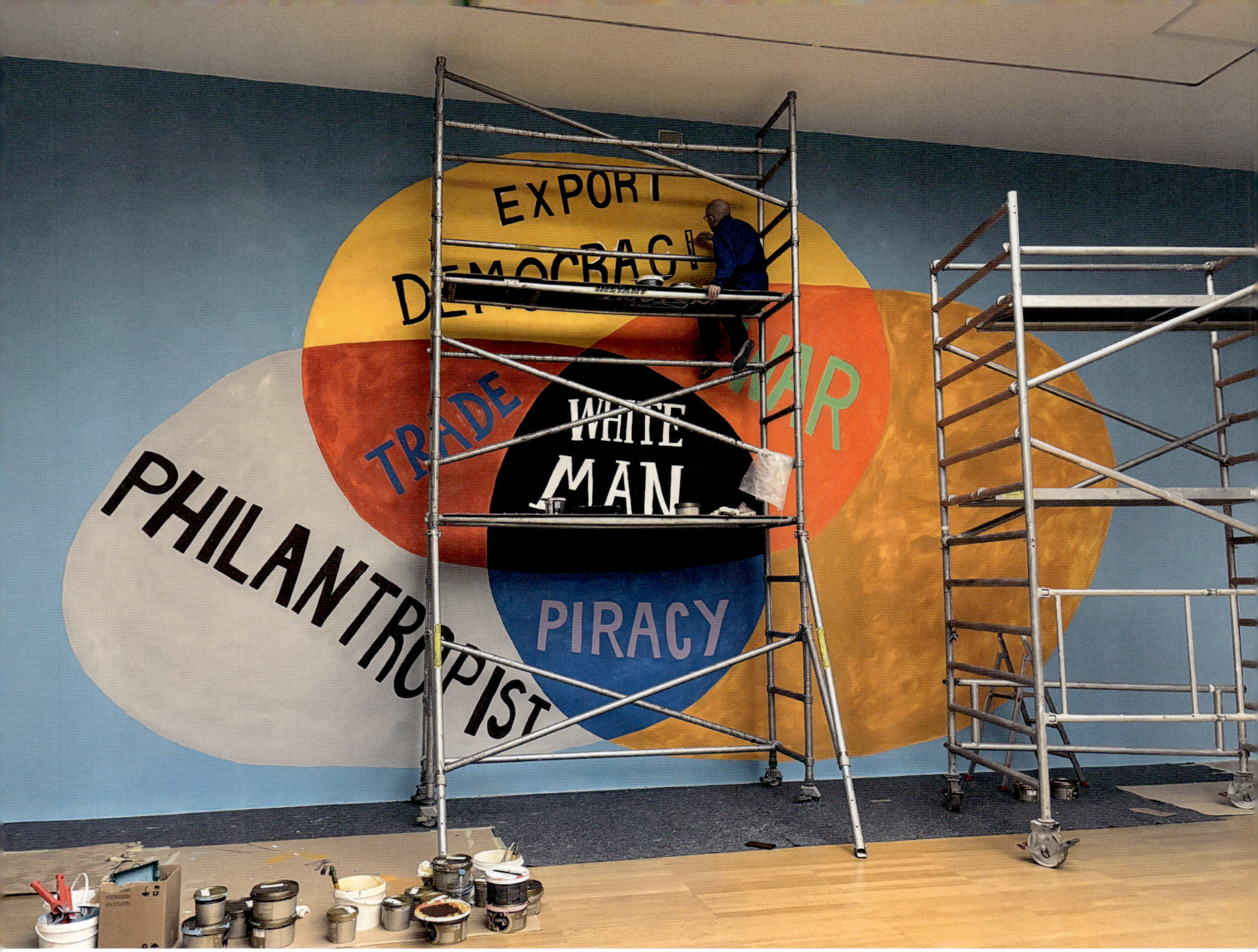

Who Keeps the Zoo? (Liubliana)
2025
Painting on wall

WHO KEEPS THE ZOO?

This work represents four Venn diagrams which address issues such as monotheism, the white man, violence and art, among other things.

Venn diagrams are used to illustrate set theory. Among other questions, set theory studies the properties, functions and relationships between sets – characteristics such as belonging, inclusion, equality, non-belonging, exclusion, inequality, greater than, less than, etcetera – and if I work with them it is because they help me to understand the world and to choose between those who think of it as multiple and those who think of it as One.

If I work with logical systems it is because I believe that one of the major problems we face as language-using animals is the failure of communication, since the signs we use in language are tied to associative chains.

My intention was to speak in a logical and clear manner but, paradoxically, my Venn diagrams once again become polysemous, rendering the result associative, variable and ambiguous.

pp. 202-214
Who Keeps the Zoo? (Madrid)
2025
Painting on wall

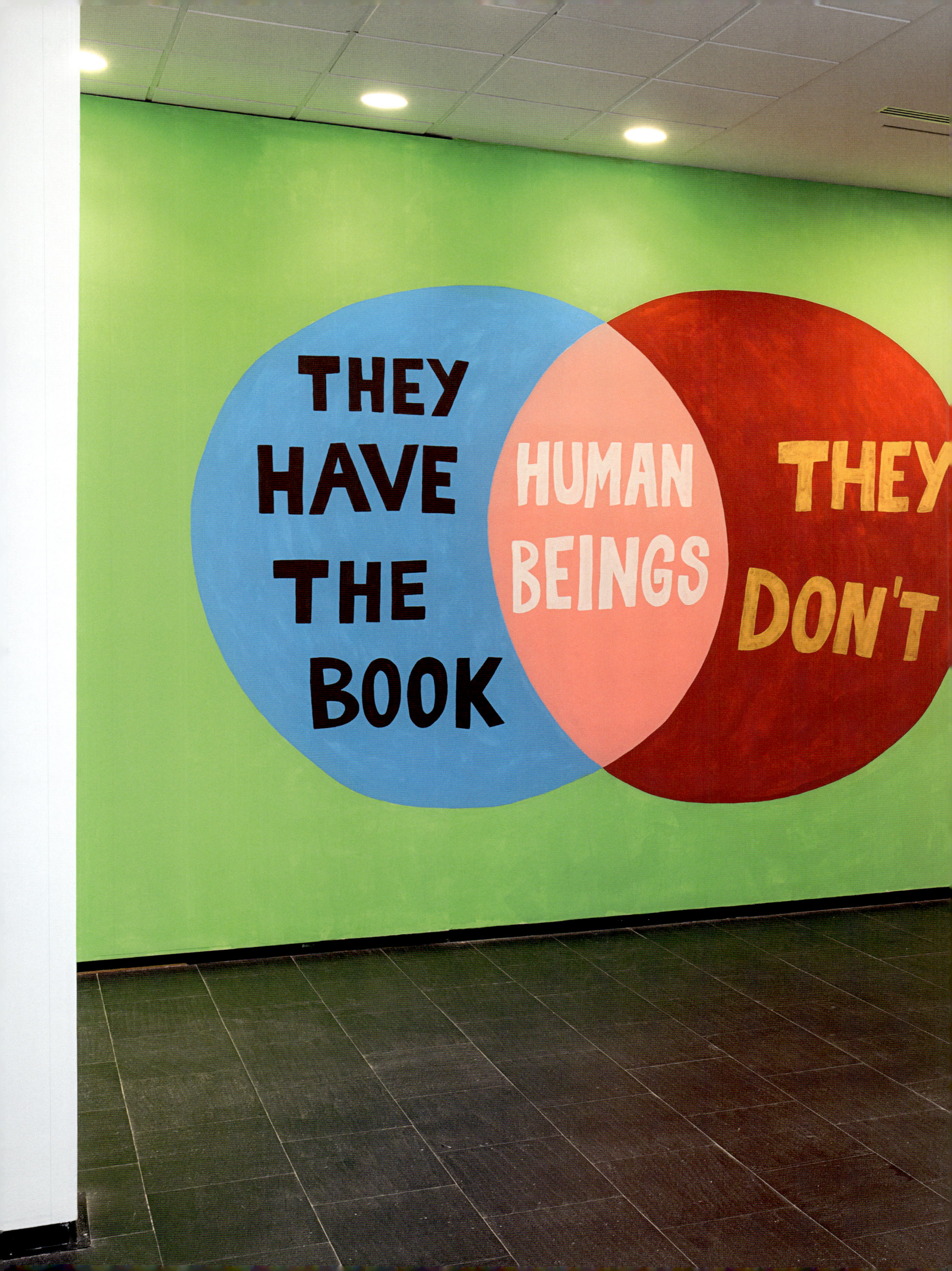
THEY HAVE THE BOOK
HUMAN BEINGS
THEY DON'T

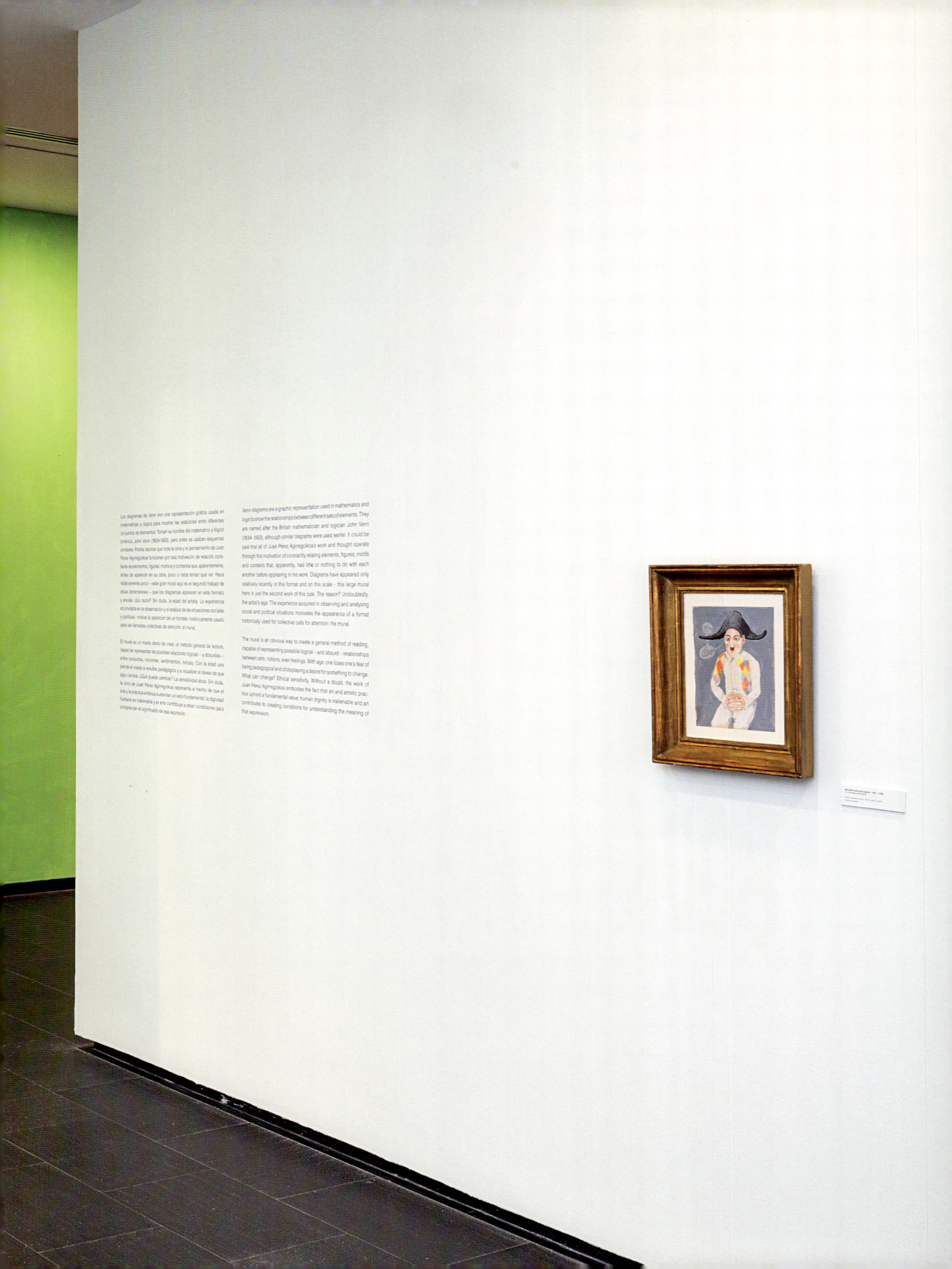
Los diagramas de Venn son una representación gráfica usada en matemáticas y lógica para mostrar las relaciones entre diferentes conjuntos de elementos. Toman su nombre del matemático y lógico británico John Venn (1834-1923), pero antes se usaban esquemas similares. Podría decirse que toda la obra y el pensamiento de Juan Pérez Agirregoikoa funcionan por esa motivación de relación constante de elementos, figuras, motivos y contextos que, aparentemente, antes de aparecer en su obra, poco o nada tenían que ver. Hace relativamente poco —este gran mural aquí es el segundo trabajo de estas dimensiones— que los diagramas aparecen en este formato y escala. ¿La razón? Sin duda, la edad del artista. La experiencia acumulada en la observación y el análisis de las situaciones sociales y políticas motiva la aparición de un formato históricamente usado para las llamadas colectivas de atención: el mural.
El mural es un modo obvio de crear un método general de lectura, capaz de representar las posibles relaciones lógicas —y absurdas— entre conjuntos, nociones, sentimientos, incluso. Con la edad uno pierde el miedo a resultar pedagógico y a visualizar el deseo de que algo cambie. ¿Qué puede cambiar? La sensibilidad ética. Sin duda, la obra de Juan Pérez Agirregoikoa representa el hecho de que el arte y la práctica artística sustentan un valor fundamental: la dignidad humana es inalienable y el arte contribuye a crear condiciones para comprender el significado de esa expresión.
Venn diagrams are a graphic representation used in mathematics and logic to show the relationships between different sets of elements. They are named after the British mathematician and logician John Venn (1834-1923), although similar diagrams were used earlier. It could be said that all of Juan Pérez Agirregoikoa's work and thought operate through this motivation of constantly relating elements, figures, motifs and contexts that, apparently, had little or nothing to do with each another before appearing in his work. Diagrams have appeared only relatively recently in this format and on this scale – this large mural here is just the second work of this size. The reason? Undoubtedly, the artist's age. The experience acquired in observing and analysing social and political situations motivates the appearance of a format historically used for collective calls for attention: the mural.
The mural is an obvious way to create a general method of reading, capable of representing possible logical – and absurd – relationships between sets, notions, even feelings. With age, one loses one's fear of being pedagogical and of displaying a desire for something to change. What can change? Ethical sensitivity. Without a doubt, the work of Juan Pérez Agirregoikoa embodies the fact that art and artistic practice uphold a fundamental value: human dignity is inalienable and art contributes to creating conditions for understanding the meaning of that expression.

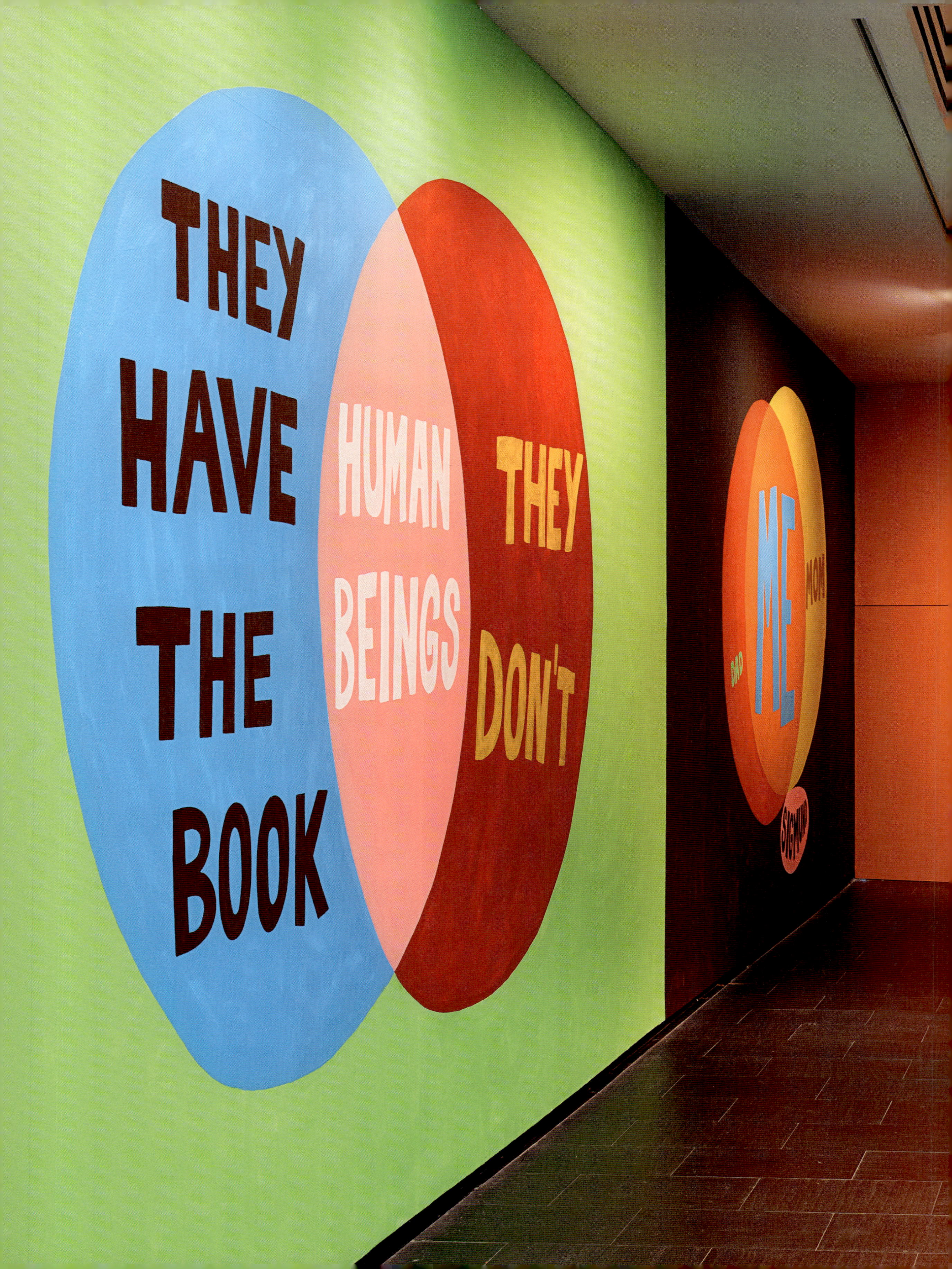
THEY HAVE THE BOOK
HUMAN BEINGS
THEY DON'T
ME
MOM
DAD
SIGMUND

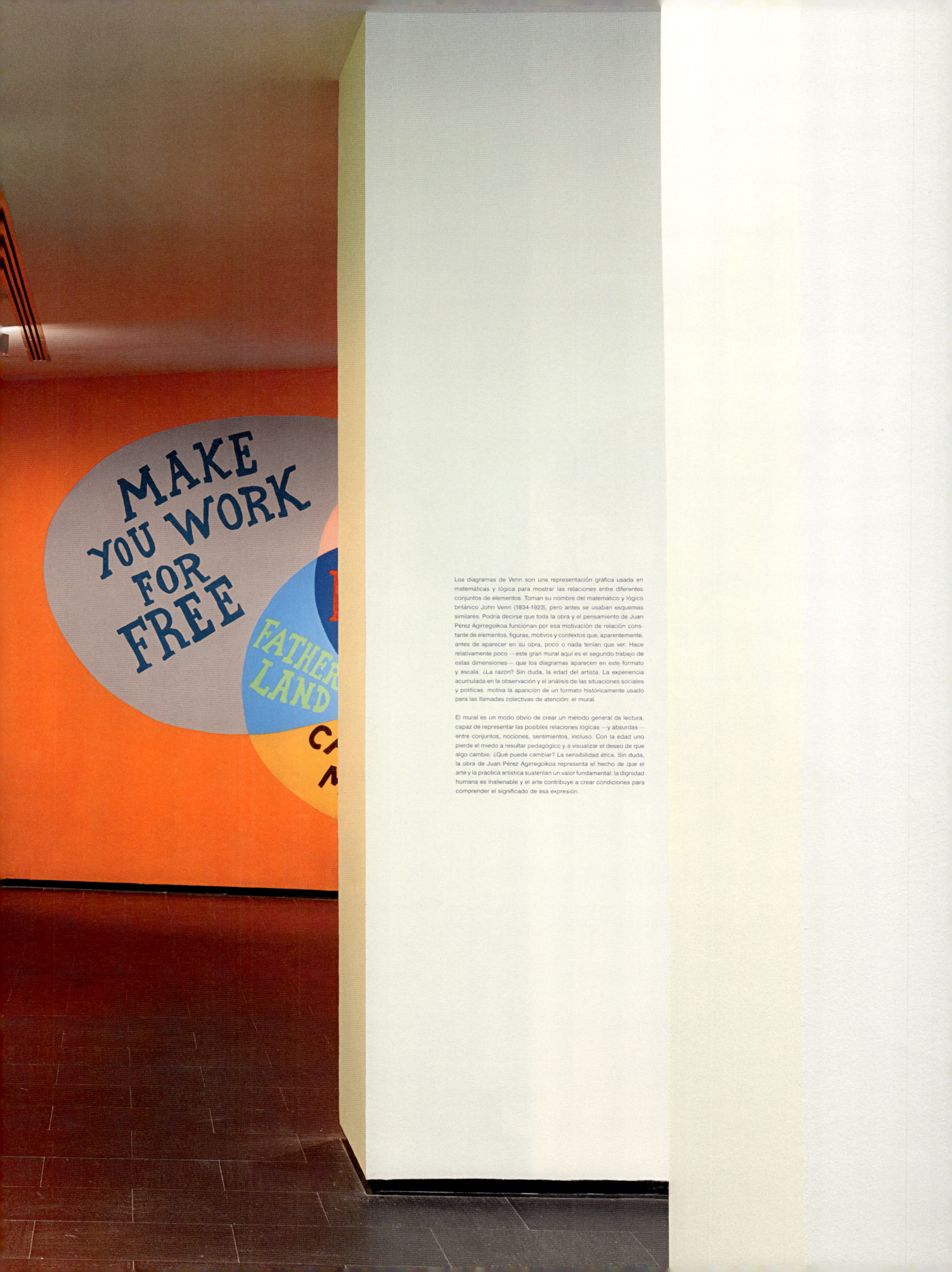
MAKE YOU WORK FOR FREE
FATHER LAND
Los diagramas de Venn son una representación gráfica usada en matemáticas y lógica para mostrar las relaciones entre diferentes conjuntos de elementos. Toman su nombre del matemático y lógico británico John Venn (1834-1923), pero antes se usaban esquemas similares. Podría decirse que toda la obra y el pensamiento de Juan Pérez Agirregoikoa funcionan por esa motivación de relación constante de elementos, figuras, motivos y contextos que, aparentemente, antes de aparecer en su obra, poco o nada tenían que ver. Hace relativamente poco —este gran mural aquí es el segundo trabajo de estas dimensiones— que los diagramas aparecen en este formato y escala. ¿La razón? Sin duda, la edad del artista. La experiencia acumulada en la observación y el análisis de las situaciones sociales y políticas motiva la aparición de un formato históricamente usado para las llamadas colectivas de atención: el mural.
El mural es un modo obvio de crear un método general de lectura, capaz de representar las posibles relaciones lógicas —y absurdas— entre conjuntos, nociones, sentimientos, incluso. Con la edad uno pierde el miedo a resultar pedagógico y a visualizar el deseo de que algo cambie. ¿Qué puede cambiar? La sensibilidad ética. Sin duda, la obra de Juan Pérez Agirregoikoa representa el hecho de que el arte y la práctica artística sustentan un valor fundamental: la dignidad humana es inalienable y el arte contribuye a crear condiciones para comprender el significado de esa expresión.

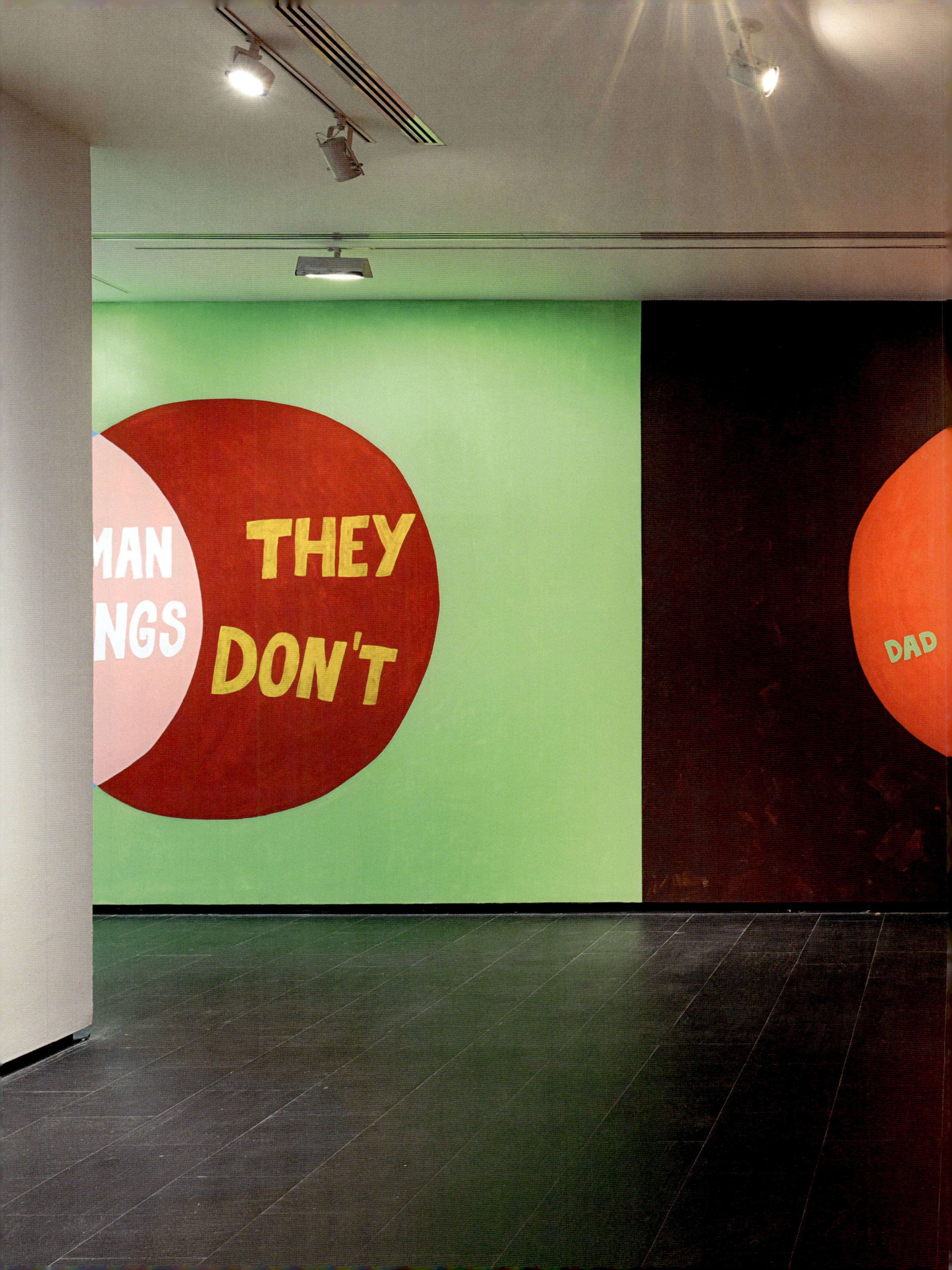
MAN
NGS
THEY
DON'T
DAD

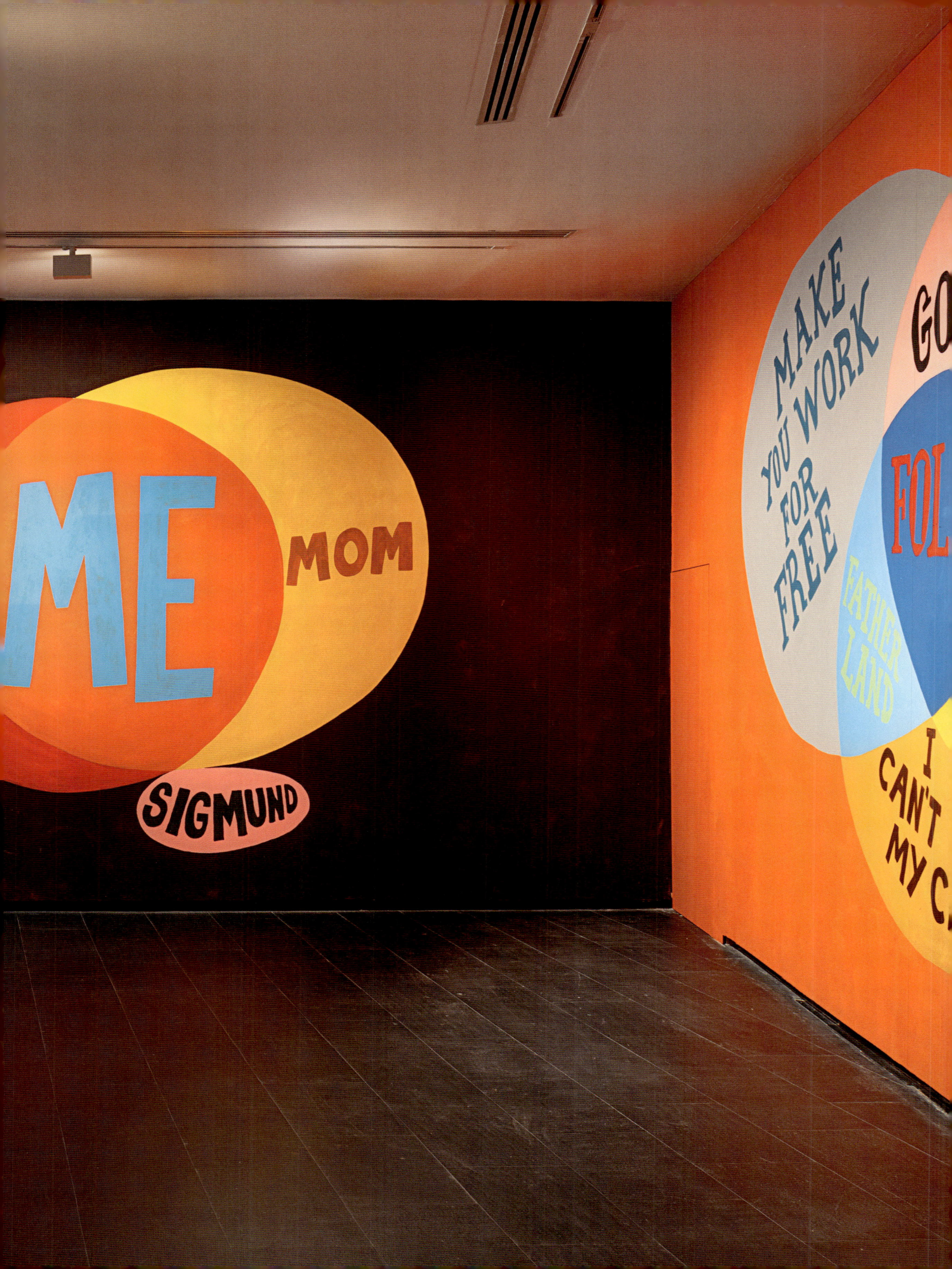
ME
MOM
SIGMUND
MAKE YOU WORK FOR FREE
FATHER LAND
I
CAN'T
MY

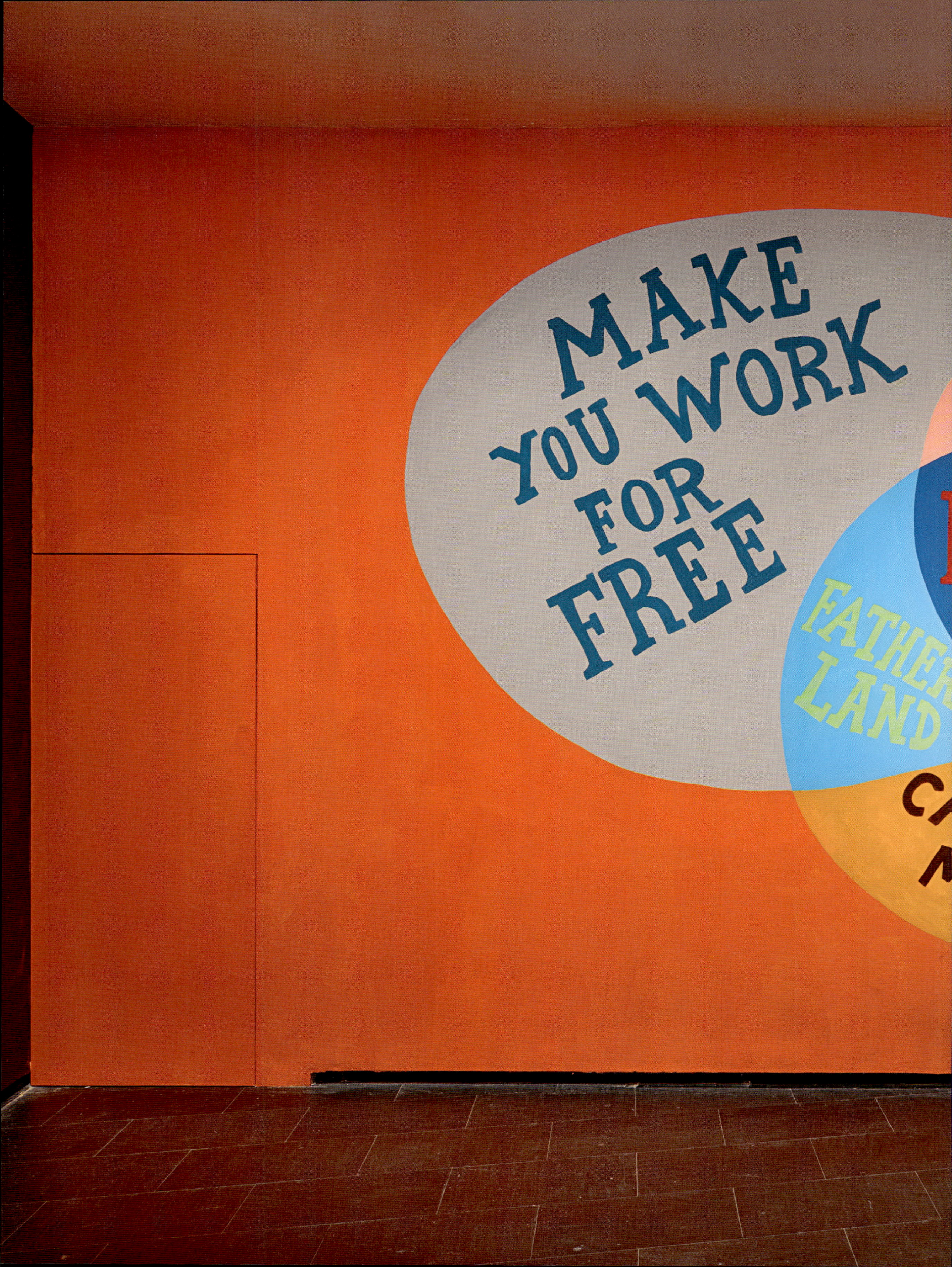
MAKE
YOU WORK
FOR
FREE
FATHER
LAND

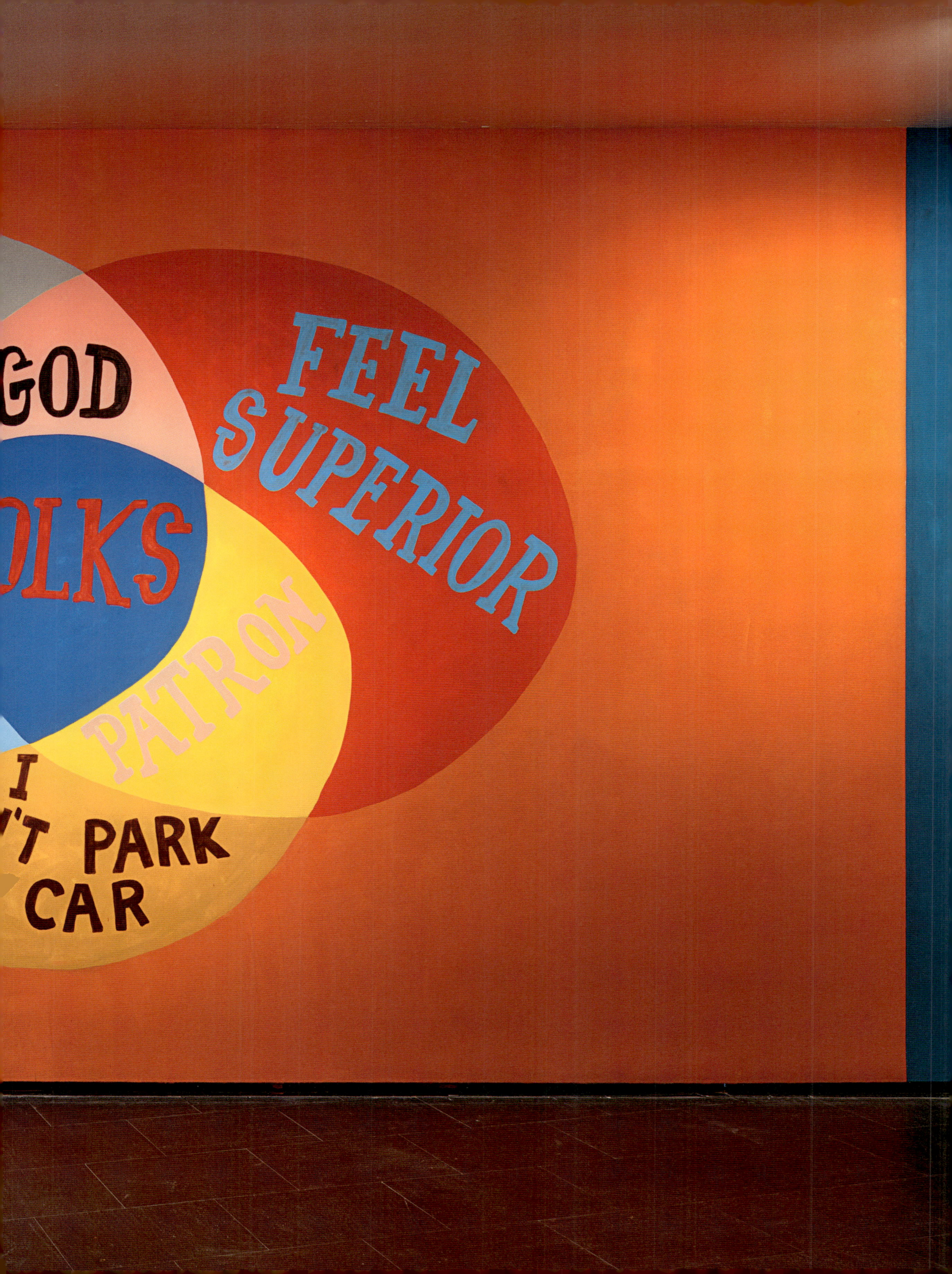
GOD
OLKS
FEEL SUPERIOR
PATRON
I
'T PARK
CAR

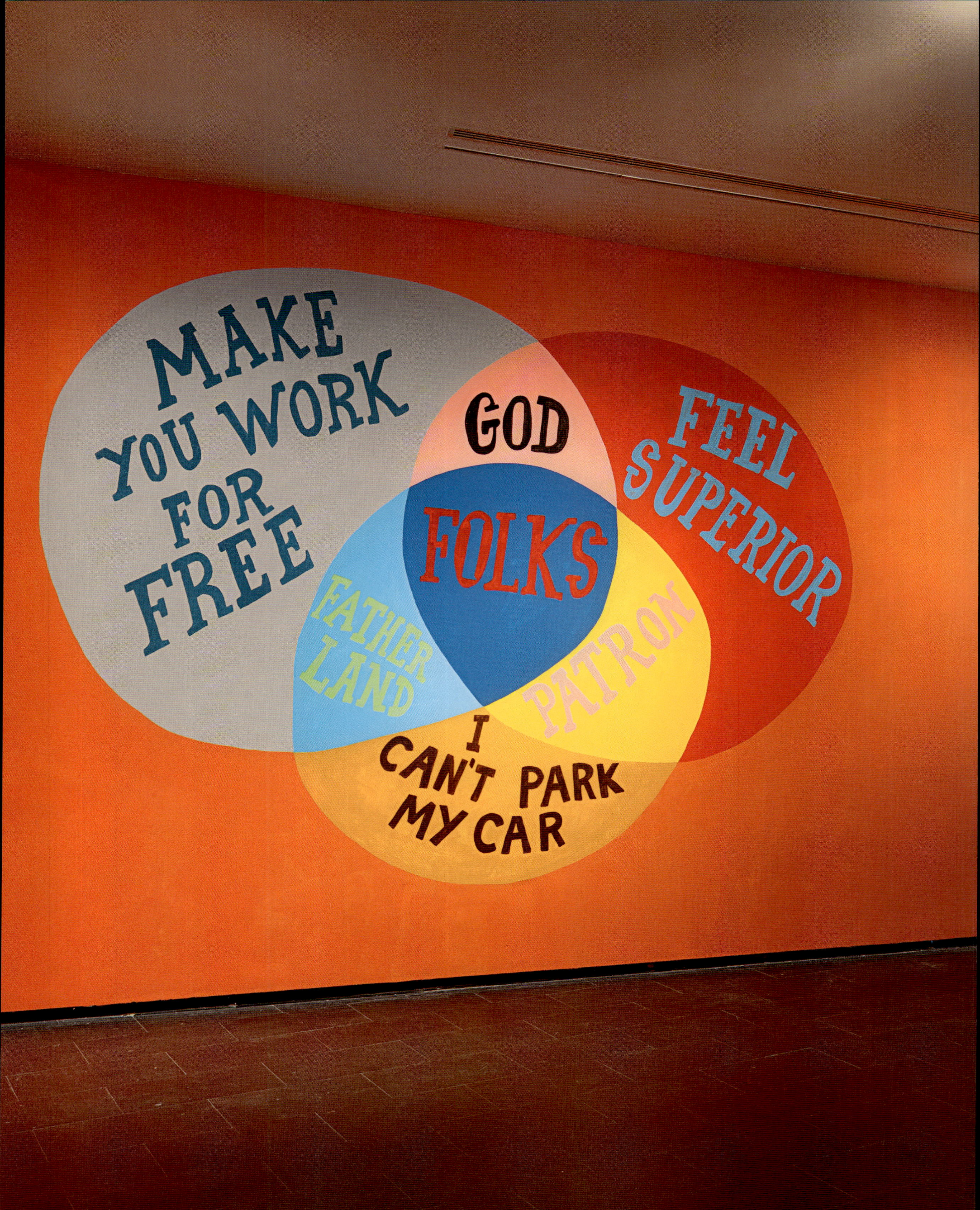
MAKE YOU WORK FOR FREE
GOD
FEEL SUPERIOR
FOLKS
FATHER LAND
PATRON
I CAN'T PARK MY CAR

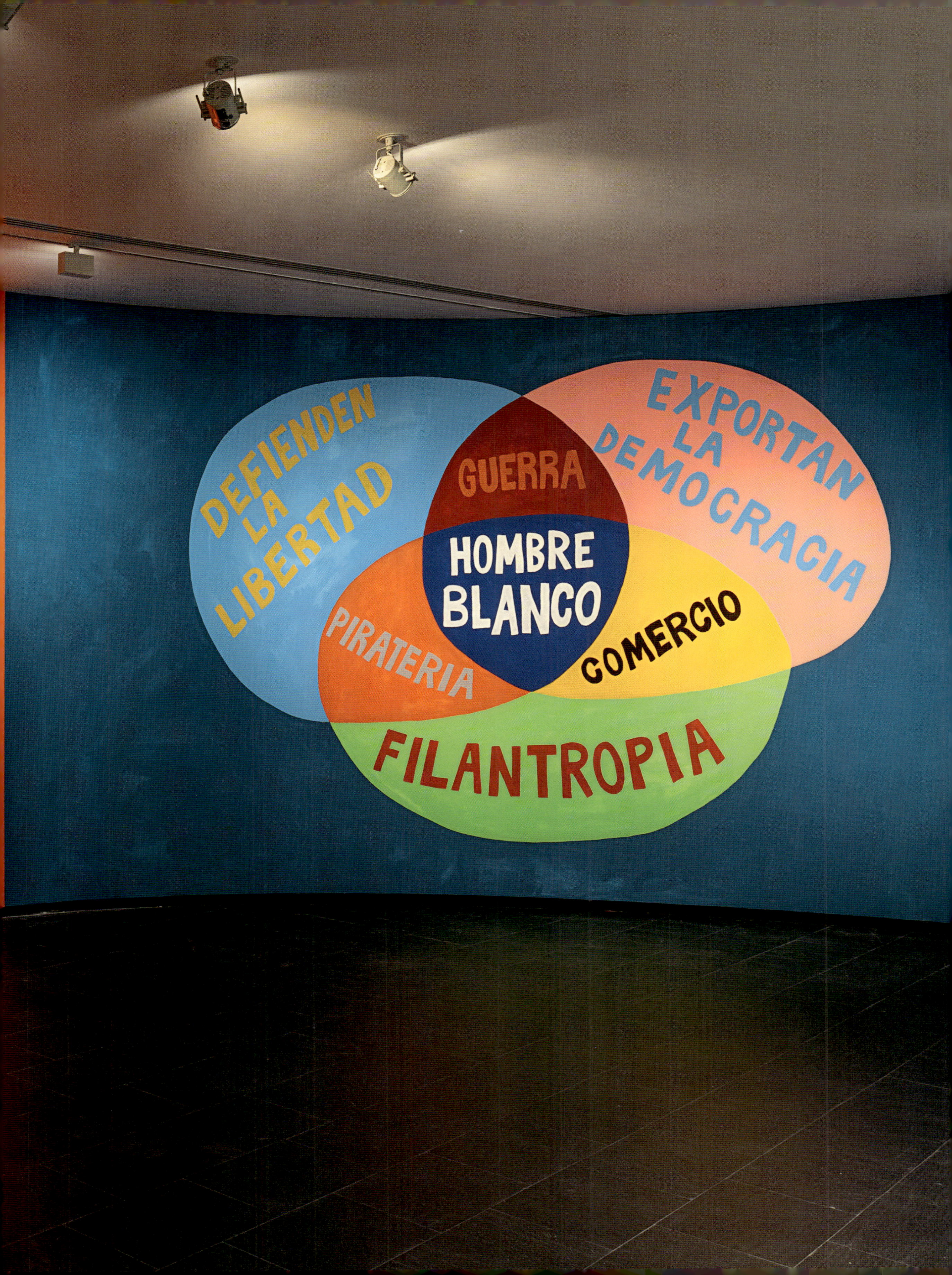
DEFIENDEN LA LIBERTAD
EXPORTAN LA DEMOCRACIA
GUERRA
HOMBRE BLANCO
PIRATERIA
COMERCIO
FILANTROPIA

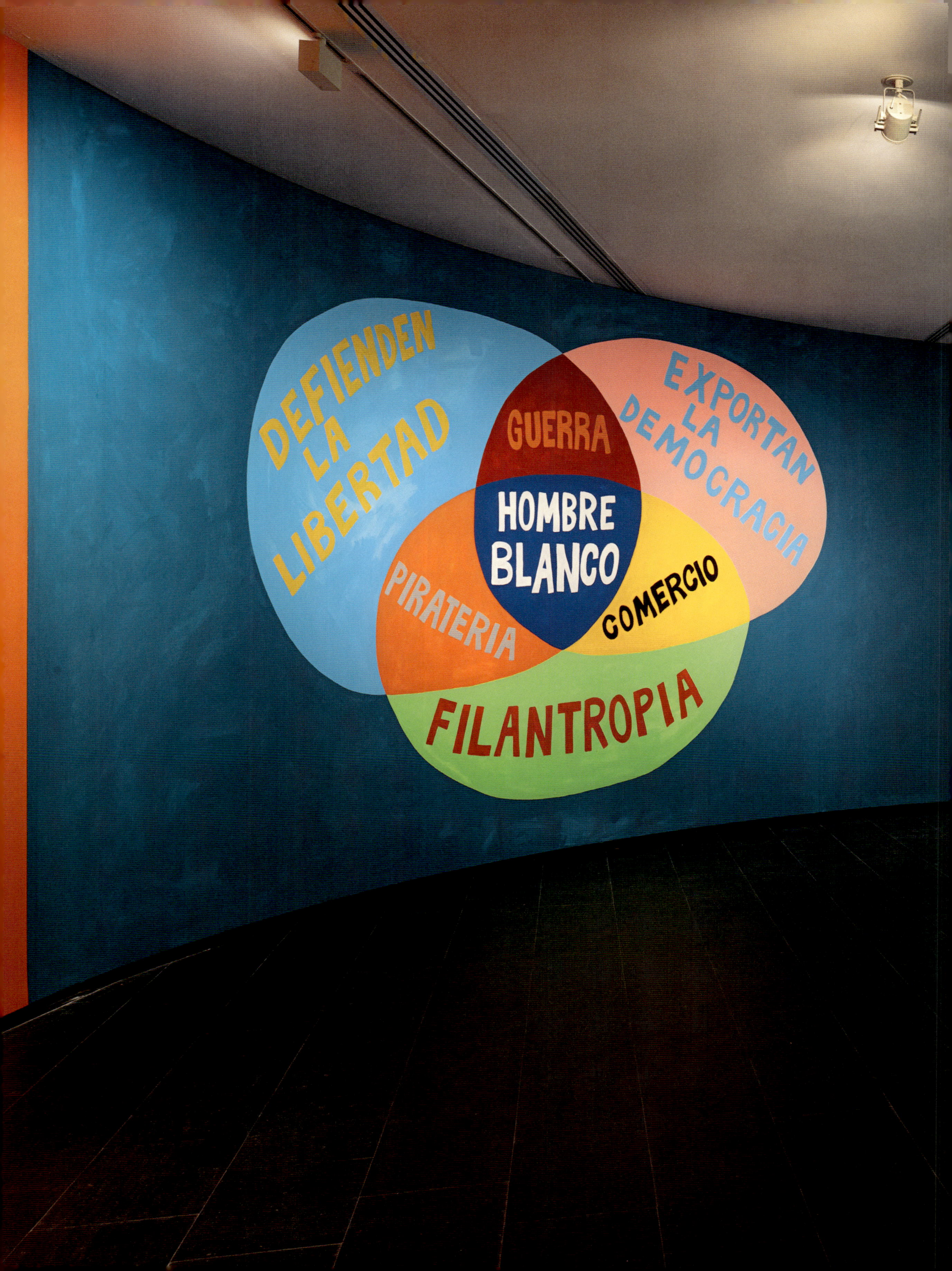
DEFIENDEN
LA
LIBERTAD
GUERRA
EXPORTAN
LA
DEMOCRACIA
HOMBRE
BLANCO
PIRATERIA
COMERCIO
FILANTROPIA

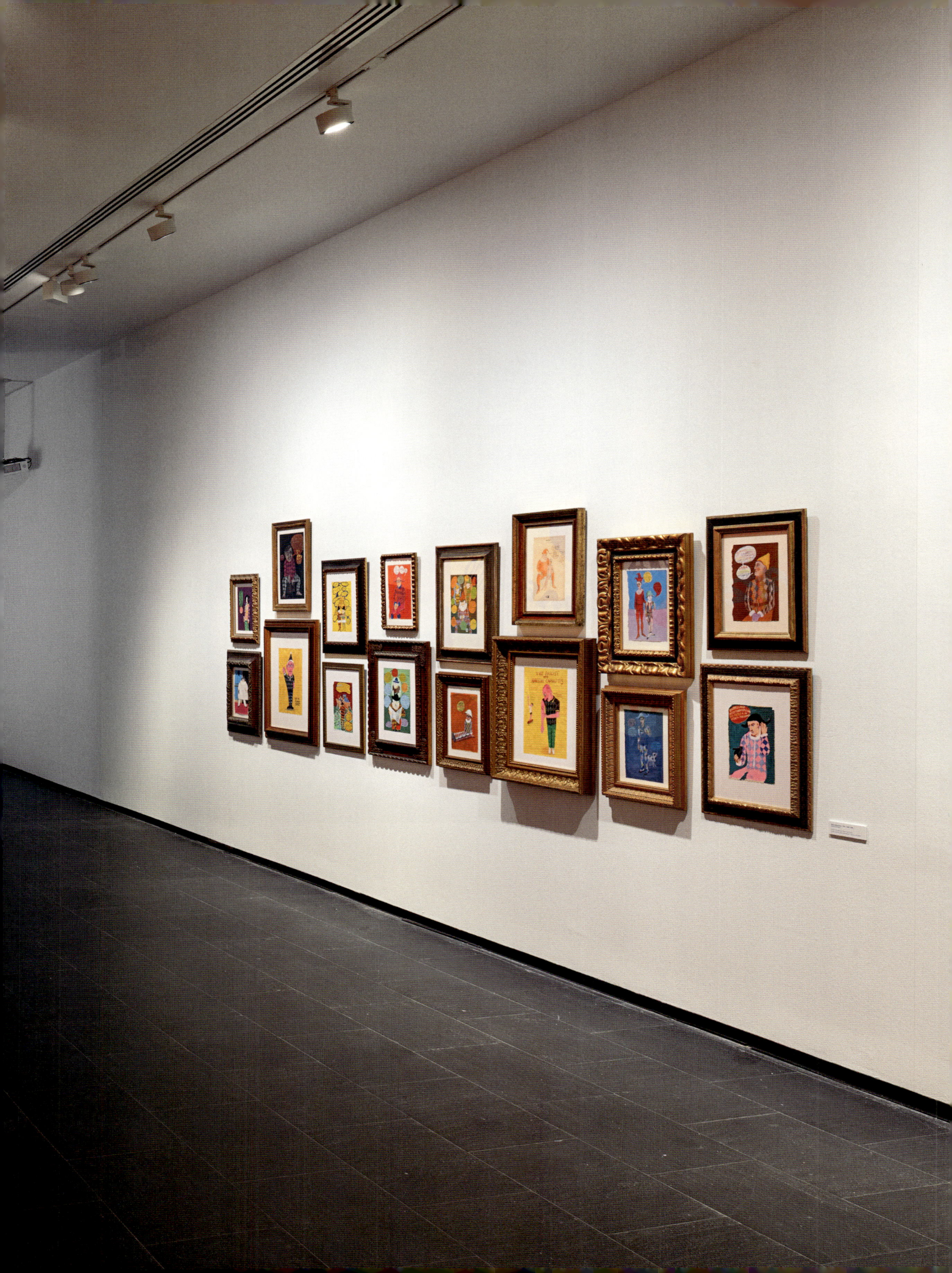

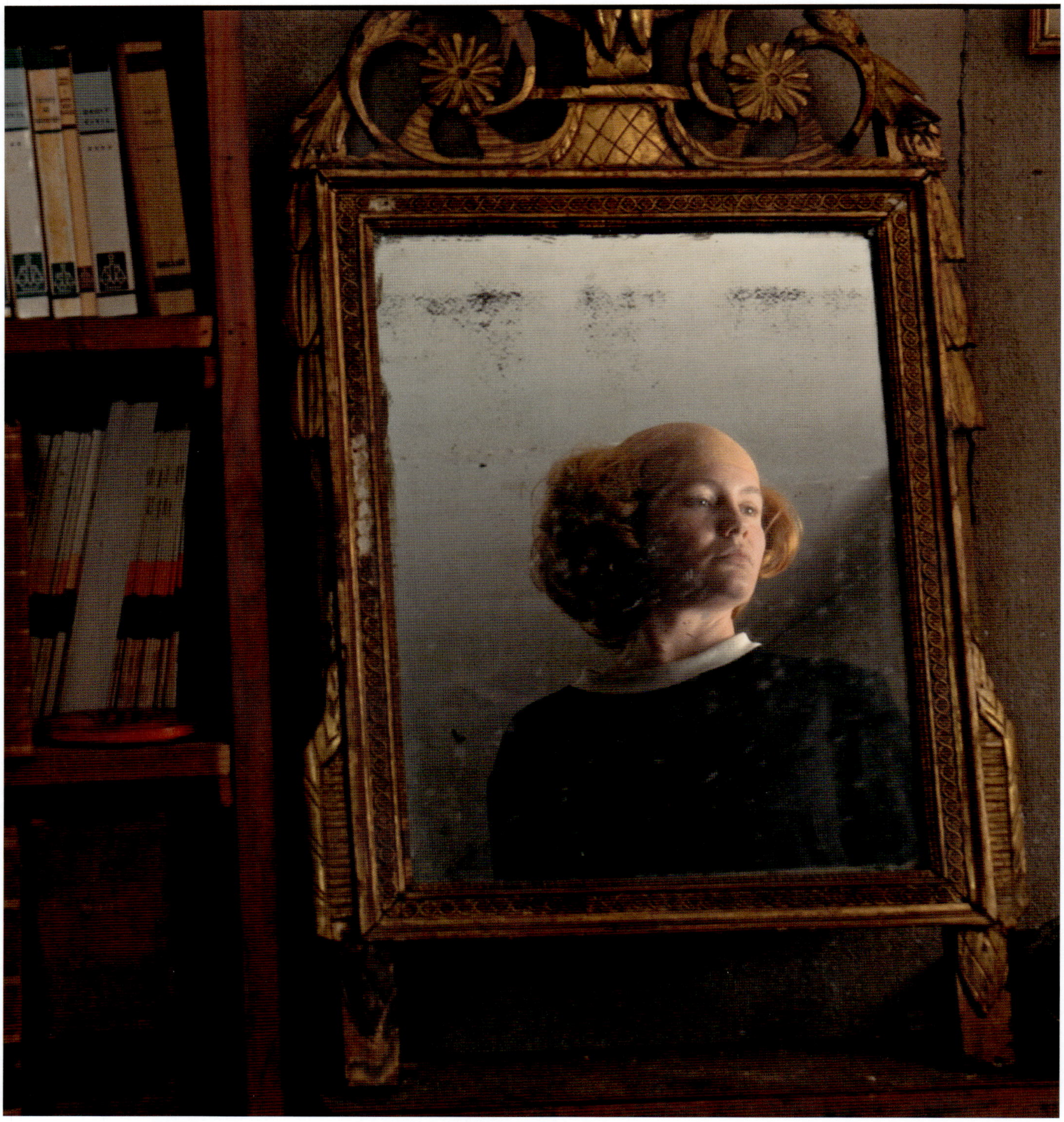

Three figures dressed in black, replicas of Charlie Rivel, the Nazi and Francoist clown, make their way to a library with the intention of building a bonfire with all the dangerous and evil books it contains.

The clowns start going through the books in the library, arguing about ideology, religion, environmentalism, feminism, private property, gender, conspiracy theories, war, colonialism and the bourgeoisie from the viewpoint of the censor.

To this end they undertake a conceptual analysis of the books they come across on the shelves before taking a decision.

This work addresses the *auto-da-fé* and the burning of books, ranging from Savonarola and Cardenal Cisneros to Bradbury, Franco, the Nazis and the current list of books banned in the USA.

The point of departure for the video is chapter six of part one of *Don Quixote*, in which the contents of his library are examined to see what should be condemned and what could be saved.

It is very rare to find explanations why books are burned before being thrown on the bonfire. Cervantes is the exception, since books are normally burned indiscriminately: because they are commies, because they are homosexual, because they belong to another religion, because they are feminist or because they don't think like me.

My idea was to reflect on the history of censorship by taking the figure of the censor as a kind of proxy for the conflict.

Dear censor, 2025
Video
27 min 04 sec

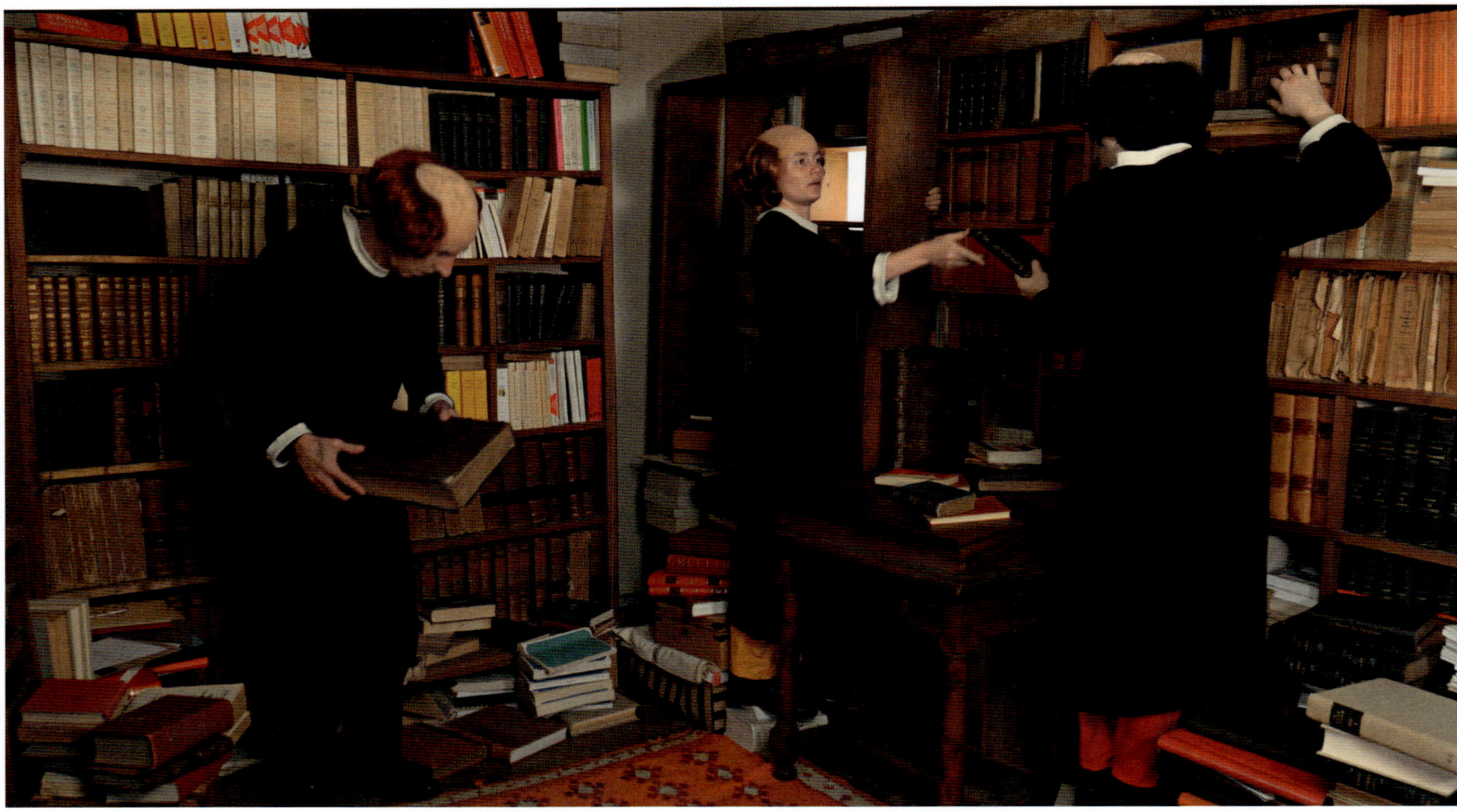

OPEN SESAME, THE SMELL OF BURNT PAPER.

Three clowns make their way in single file to an automatic door. They stop in front of it. The first clown raises his hand, points in the direction of the door and utters the magic words.

CLOWN 1
(in a portentous voice)
Open so-se-me. Open se-me-so. Open so-se-ma.
The clown behind goes up to him and says:

CLOWN 2
You're saying it wrong… SE-SA-ME.

CLOWN 1 (CONT.)
OPEN SESAME!!!

The door opens by magic and the three enter (or leave) the building. Fade.

The three appear, walking still in single file through the town towards the building that houses the library. SCRUTINY (THEY DANCE THE CAN-CAN, LEGS TO THE RIGHT, LEGS TO THE LEFT).

INTERIOR
Three characters in front of a library. They remove volumes from the library and comment on them as they go.

CLOWN 1 (CONT.)
Sprinkle this room; don't leave any magician of the many there are in these books to bewitch us in revenge for our design of banishing them from the world.

The simplicity of clown 1 makes clown 2 laugh and he directs clown 3 to give him the books one by one to see what they are about, as there might be some among them that do not deserve punishment by fire.

CLOWN 2
No, no, there is no reason for showing mercy to any of them; they have every one of them done mischief; better fling them out of the window into the courtyard and make a pile of them and set fire to them; or else carry them into the yard, and there a bonfire can be made without the smoke giving any annoyance.

CLOWN 1
I agree.
So eager are they both for the slaughter of those innocents, but clown 3 will not agree to it without first reading at least the titles.
Clown 2 approaches the library, chooses the *Theologico-Political Treatise*, and passes it to clown 3.

Close-up of the cover.

CLOWN 3
This will be the first to feed the flames for it was a model for others that followed, and because it formulated an evidence-based method for interpreting the holy texts and analysing their content.

CLOWN 1
What makes you say that?

CLOWN 3
Well, a comparison of the facts and dates suggests the events they recount do not match up, sometimes not at all and in other instances not in the least.

CLOWN 2
Who is it by?

CLOWN 3
It's by a Dutch Jew, one of those expelled from the Iberian Peninsula, who I understand is still excommunicated by his own people! His name is SPINOZA.

CLOWN 1
And… what conclusions does he draw?

CLOWN 3
That men's habits and minds differ, and what moves one to pray may move another only to scoff.

Clown 2 raises his hands to the sky and emphatically exclaims:

CLOWN 2
Don't fuck with me, José Antonio!

Clown 3 recites as if giving a sermon.

CLOWN 3
That everyone should be free to choose for himself the foundations of his creed.
That everyone is always waiting for signs to understand his fate and that signs are variable, associative and ambiguous!
That men of the Church are always trying to grab political power and…

CLOWN 1
That's enough! What the devil! It's obvious why the theocrats excommunicated him. Into the flames!!

CLOWN 2
It's a clear sign that God is right-wing. Into the flames!!
Books sail through the air.

CLOWN 3
This seems a mysterious thing, for I have heard say that this book took as its model the commentary on the Pentateuch written by Ibn Ezra, who was the first to analyse, using dates and facts, its errors and mistakes, and from this all the others derive their birth and origin; so it seems to me that we ought inexorably to condemn it to the flames as the dogmatist of so vile a sect.

CLOWN 1
We should burn its ashes and the ashes of its ashes.

CLOWN 2
Good Lord!!
Let us see that other one next to it.

He goes to the library and takes another book from it.

CLOWN 1
On the Origin of Species, by
Charles Darwin!

CLOWN 2
And what does he discuss, what species is it about?

CLOWN 3
He argues that living beings evolved from a common ancestor by means of a process of natural selection.

Close-up of the other two clowns, their eyes wide and shaking their heads in disbelief.

CLOWN 3 (CONT.)
According to calculations, the dinosaurs were around before the creation of the world… In other words, they are not the work of the Almighty, if you catch my meaning.

CLOWN 1
And he denies Adam and Eve too,
does he not? But how else does
one explain the profound stultification,
the utter oligophrenia, the incredible
idiocy of humankind without inbreeding, eh?
Fallacies! Onto the fire with it!

CLOWN 2
What you say is very real.

Clown 2 opens the window of the room where the books are held and begins to throw them out of the window.
After tossing out the first examined volumes, they move on to another part of the library. Choosing three volumes with similar spines, clown 2 asks:

CLOWN 2 (CONT.)
And what about these ones together?

The three characters stand facing the library, their backs to the camera, which focuses on each of the three volumes they take from the library. They are books on astronomy. Each clown holds one in his hands.

CLOWN 1
De l'infinito, universo et mondi by Giordano Bruno. *Dialogue Concerning the Two Chief World Systems* by Galileo Galilei and in his hand he's holding *De revolutionibus orbium celeste* by Nicolaus Copernicus.

CLOWN 2
These are old books.

CLOWN 3
Well, these three bright sparks have drawn inspiration from studies by ancient Greeks and not only deny that the Earth is flat but also assert that it is round and came up with the heliocentric theory of the solar system…

CLOWN 1
But that's madness: the Earth is flat, the moon is flat, everything is flat!
The alternative theories I've heard make more sense to me than the science they've been pushing on us so far. Those photos of the Earth have clearly been altered using image editing software.

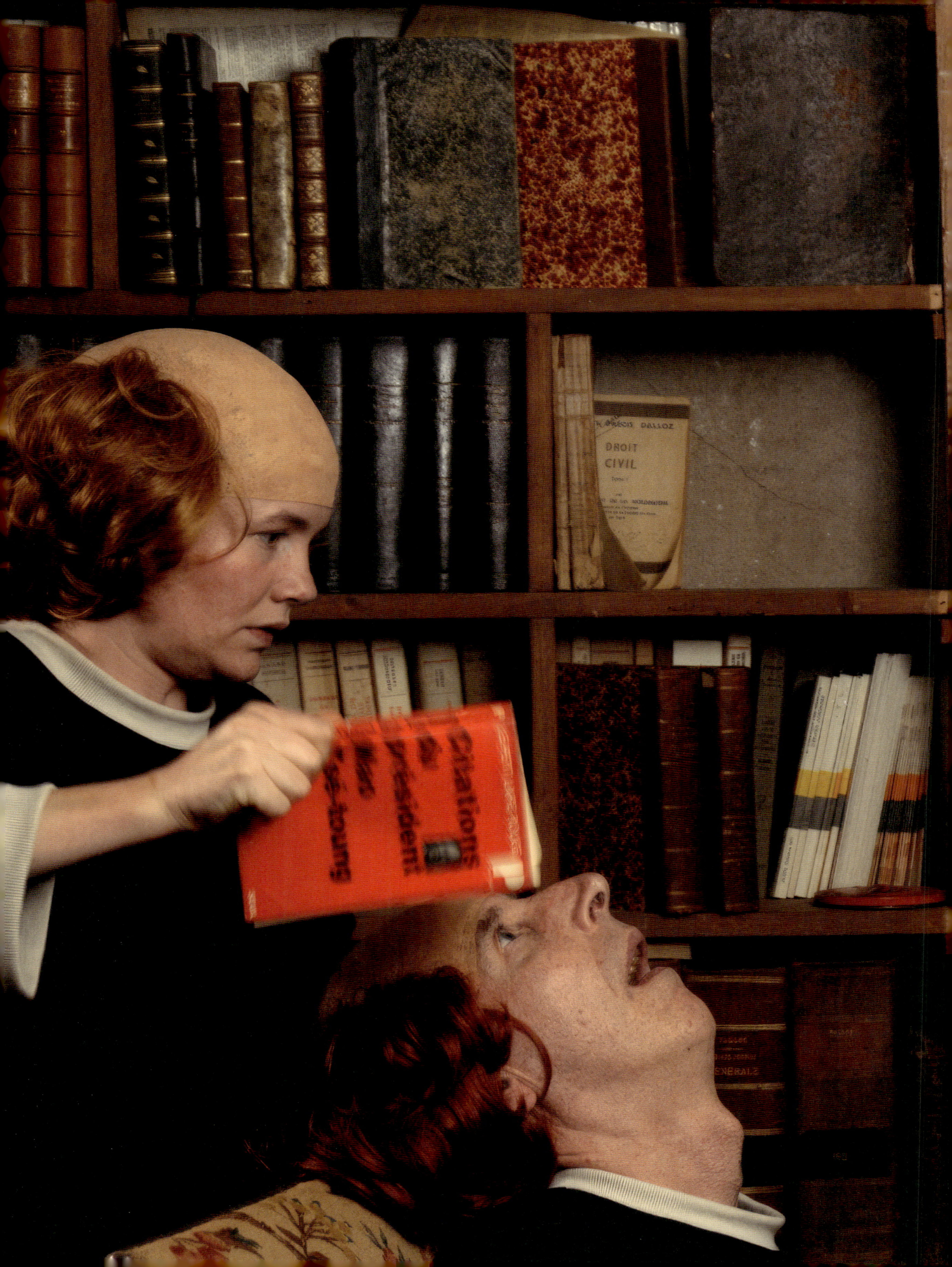
DALLOZ
DROIT
CIVIL
Citations
du
Président
Mao
Tsé-toung

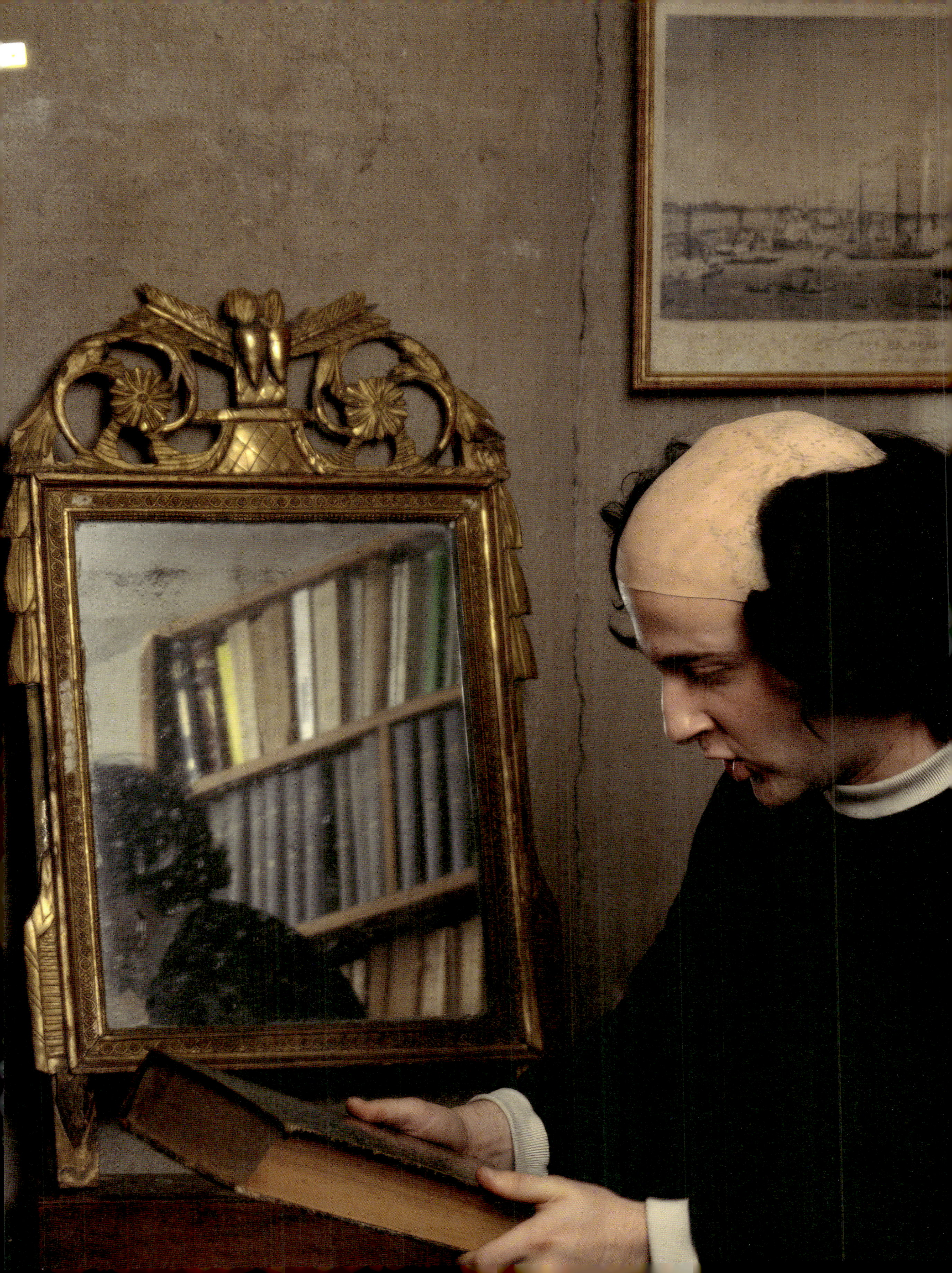

CLOWN 2
How did you find that out?

CLOWN 1
I get my information from the media I regard as suited to my level of awakened consciousness, as I like to call it.

CLOWN 2
When we're finished here, you'll have to tell me all about it. I thought these ones had already been put to the flames.

Reciting while books go flying through the window into the yard.

CLOWN 3
Time and time again. To the yard with the lot of them, for to have the burning of Queen Pintiquiniestra, and the shepherd Darinel and his eclogues, and the bedevilled and involved discourses of his author, I would burn with them the father who begot me if he were going about in the guise of a spherical world map.

CLOWN 1
I am of the same mind.

CLOWN 2
And so am I.

CLOWN 3
In that case, here, into the yard with them!

Books go sailing out the window.

EXTERIOR

Shot of the window through which books can be seen flying out and landing in a pile on the ground. Clown 1 can be heard off-screen, asking:

CLOWN 1
And… what about this red book?

CLOWN 2
The Communist Manifesto. The later version, without 'party', by Friedrich Engels and Karl Marx.

CLOWN 1
Who lives here? How could anyone hoard such filth?

CLOWN 3
And what nonsense does this one recount?

CLOWN 2
It tells workers to unite to free themselves of their chains!

INTERIOR

CLOWN 1
Looking for alternatives to capitalism
Don't fuck with me, José Antonio!

CLOWN 2
And they want to abolish the state!

CLOWN 1
LIKE US?

CLOWN 2
Like us but with some slight differences.
Marx wanted the end of the state.

What we want in order to defend freedom is a bit of state. Just enough. A state that is a well-oiled legal and police force that allows us to trade freely.

We see the three characters again in the library, reflecting indignantly, their voices getting ever louder as they speak. Reading...

CLOWN 2 (CONT.)
The bourgeoisie is desirous of redressing social grievances in order to secure the continued existence of bourgeois society!
Listen to this: it argues that to this section belong economists, philanthropists, humanitarians, improvers of the condition of the working class, organisers of charity, members of societies for the prevention of cruelty to animals, temperance fanatics, domestic reformers of every imaginable kind! The concluding remark sums it up precisely by saying: the bourgeois is a bourgeois - for the benefit of the working class!

CLOWN 1
Onto the fire!

CLOWN 3
The authors of this book also wrote *The Origin of the Family, Private Property and the State* and *Capital*, and truly there is no deciding which of the two books is the more truthful, or, to put it better, the less lying; all I can say is, send this one into the yard for being ludicrous, pernicious and arrogant.

CLOWN 2
The Origin of the Family, Private Property and the State?
Pointing to the library.

CLOWN 1
There they are.

CLOWN 3
This one is by Engels

CLOWN 1
And what does it say? Is it full of lies?

CLOWN 3
It looks back at the history of the family based on the book *Ancient Society* by Lewis Morgan. Did you know that the word 'family' in Latin means 'slave'?!

They shake their heads to say no.

CLOWN 3 (CONT.)
It seems that in the time known as Barbarism, the savages were more civilised than the colonists. Among the barbarians, a distinction between rights and duties could hardly be drawn. Civilisation gives one class practically

all the rights and the other class practically all the duties.

Close-up of the clowns' faces.

CLOWN 2

But that is like the thinking and work of Friar Bartolomé. They'll be telling us next that was the Garden of Paradise!

Clown 3 carries on speaking.

CLOWN 3

It attempts to dismantle the patriarchal family of the five books of Moses and demonstrates that polyandry existed early on among all exogamous races… Therefore, it says, 'we must hold it to be beyond dispute that among exogamous races the first system of kinship was that which recognised blood-ties through mothers only.'

CLOWN 2

That would mean matriarchy… More fallacies!

CLOWN 1

Doubtless they're also against private property.

CLOWN 3

Indeed, that is the fundamental basis of their way of thinking, if you can call it thinking. That and immanence should triumph over transcendence.

CLOWN 2

No god! No property! Those poor wee shepherds!

CLOWN 1

Talking of private property, look at this.

He shows them a book he has just taken from the library and scornfully declaims

CLOWN 1 (CONT.)

Rousseau! *Discourse on Inequality*... Do you want to know what it says?

They nod their heads.

CLOWN 1

The first man who, having enclosed a piece of ground, bethought himself of saying *'This is mine'*, and found people simple enough to believe him, was the real founder of civil society.

CLOWN 2

I'm going to have a heart attack.

CLOWN 1

The origin of all ills is inequality and the process of inequality occurs in this way. First, the establishment of laws and the right of property. Second, the institution of the magistracy. Third, the transformation of legitimate power into arbitrary power. Rich-poor, powerful-weak, master-slave. Progress is built on the misery of others.

Clown 3 is overcome and faints.

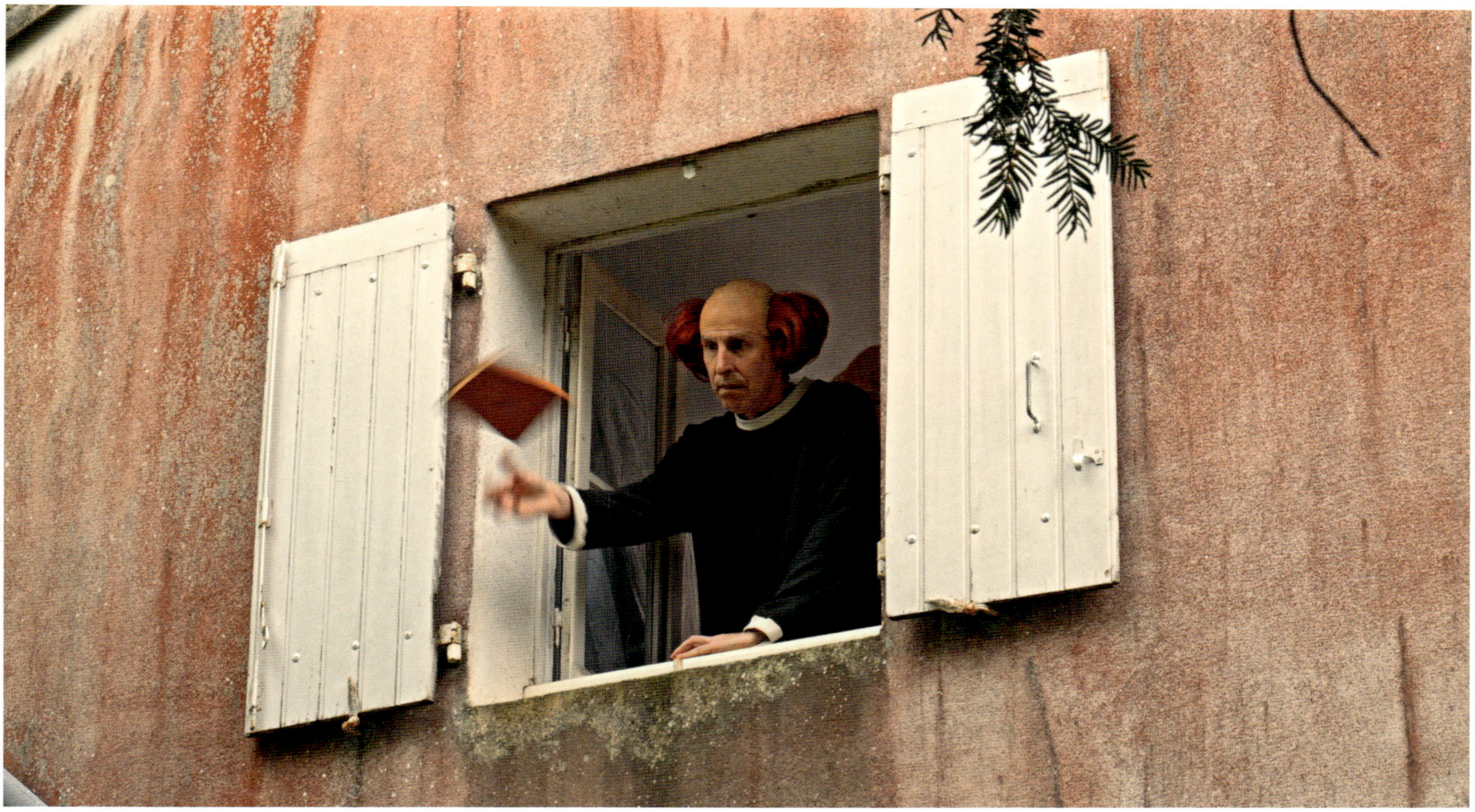

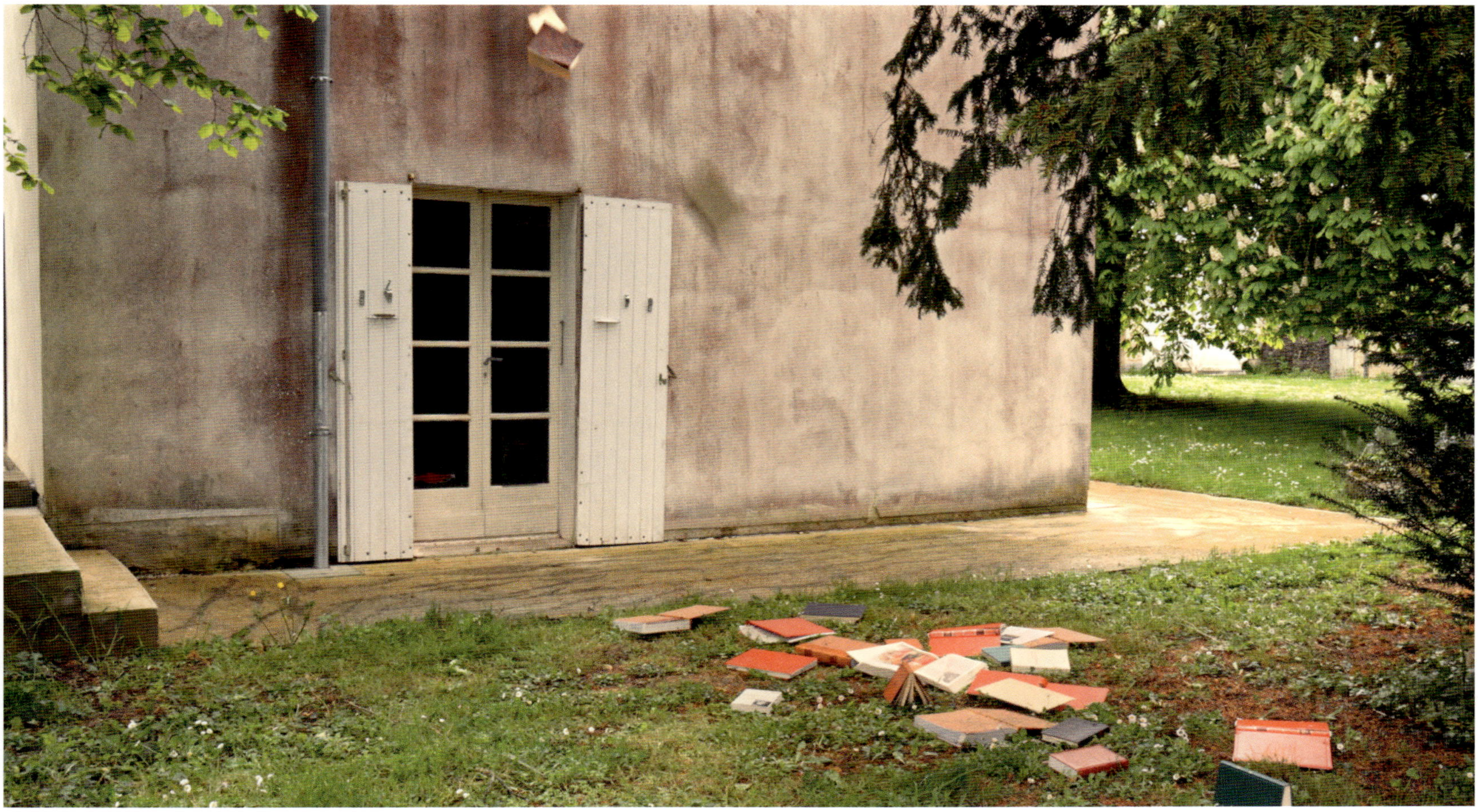

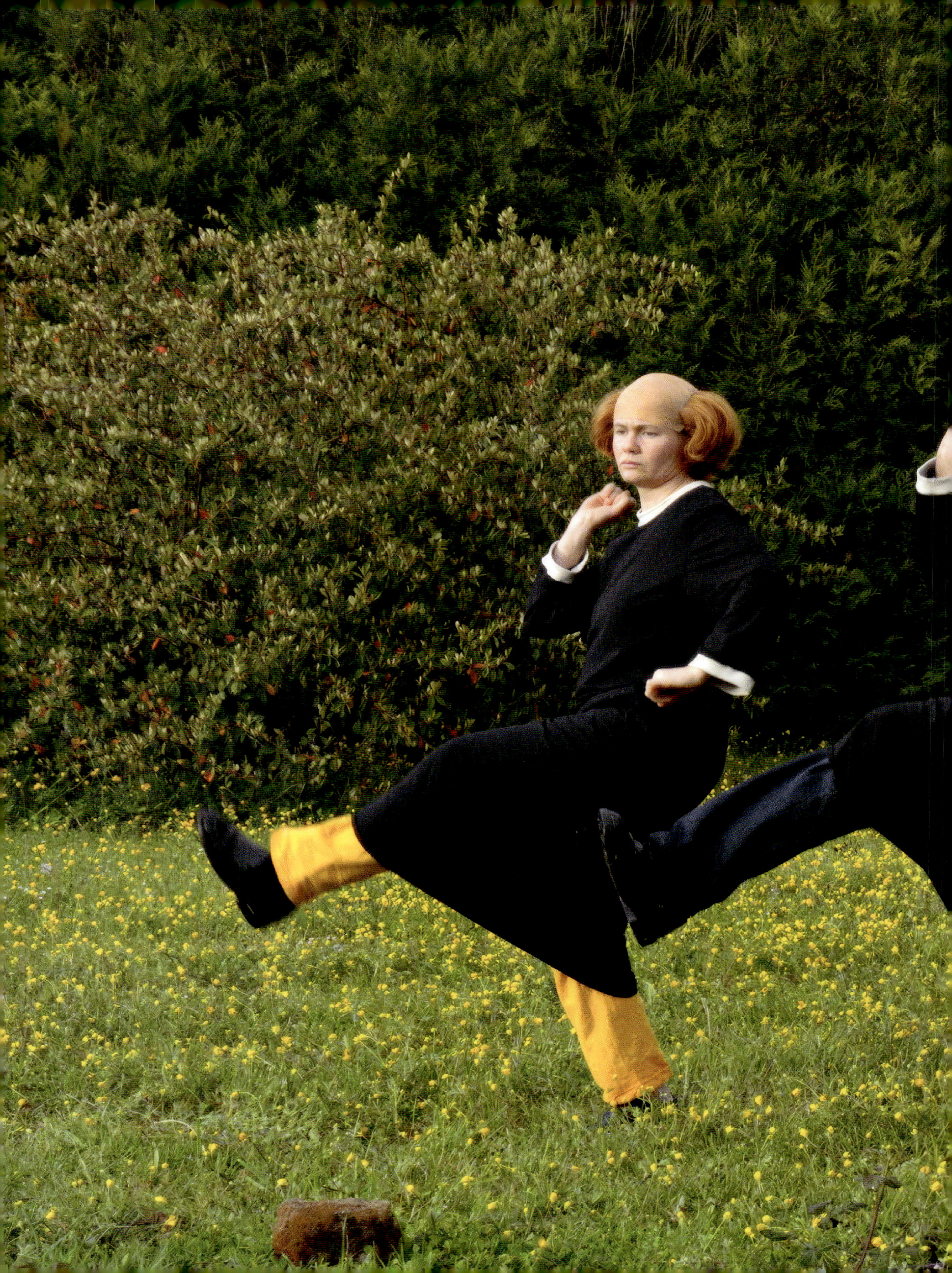

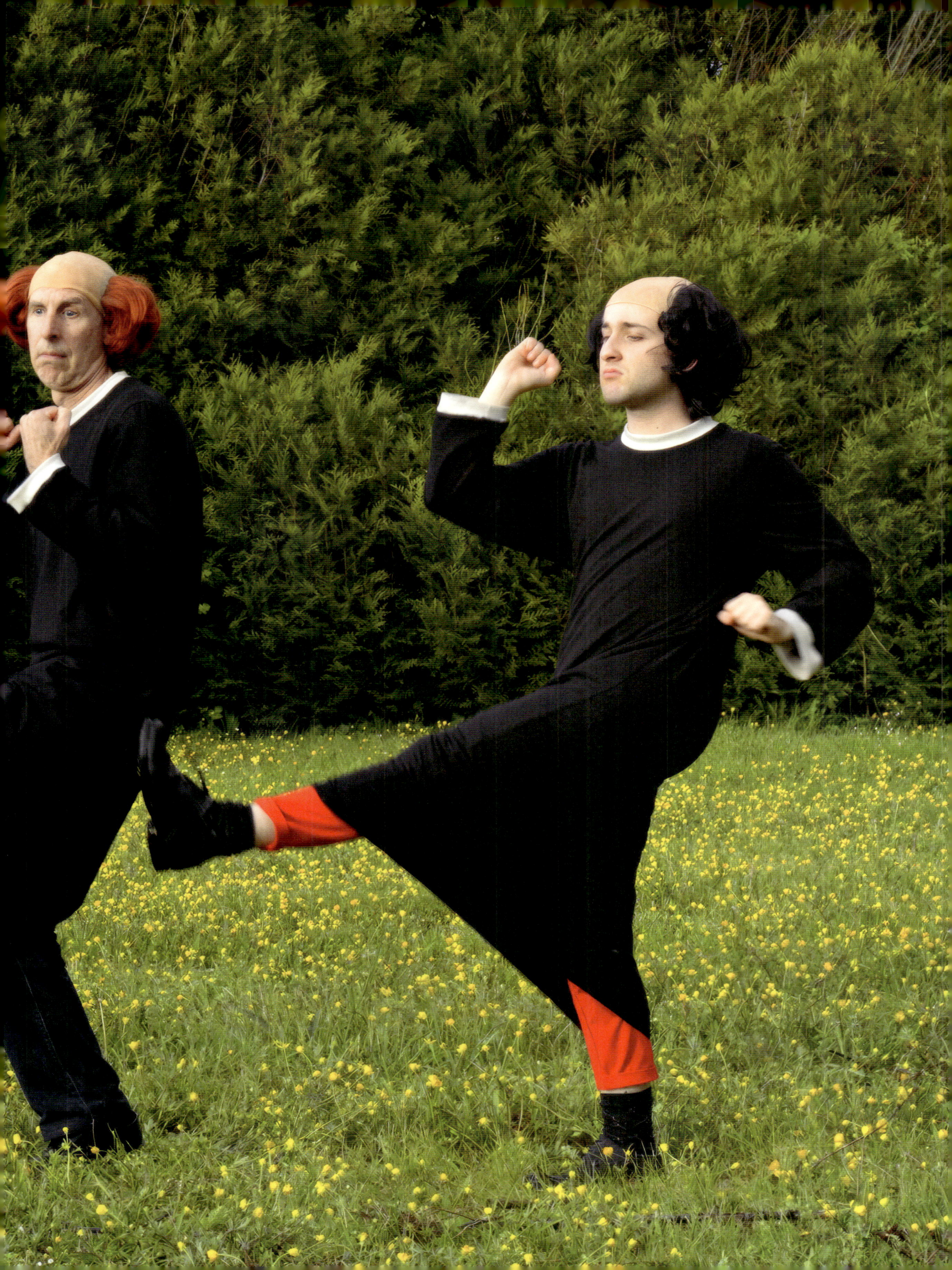

Clowns 1 and 2 bring chairs over to him so he can recover, and they fan him with books.

CLOWN 2 CLOWN 1
Into the redeeming fire!

Close-up of the library. The characters continue with their scrutiny of the books.

CLOWN 2
This book has a strange title.

CLOWN 3
What's it called? Who's it by?

CLOWN 2
La pensée straight by Monique Wittig.

CLOWN 1
She's the one that says that language serves the male gender!
That the 'natural' is a political construct for organising society and that culture passes itself off as nature in order to assert control.

CLOWN 2
The very one! Feminists!
How can you be against culture?! What an abomination! And with culture so beautiful. We white abstract universals are endangered.

CLOWN 1
Let he who can undo, undo.

CLOWN 2
Into the fire!

The camera focuses on books by Freud, and from among them they choose *Civilisation and Its Discontents.*

Close-up of *Civilisation and Its Discontents.*

CLOWN 1
(reciting)
Man becomes neurotic because he cannot bear the degree of renunciation imposed on him by society and culture.

CLOWN 3
Always going on about culture when it's the best thing there is, especially ours.

He throws the book out the window.

CLOWN 2
Let's not forget this one!

CLOWN 1
There's *Capital*, which among numerous other things sets out the theory of surplus value.

CLOWN 2
Capital accumulation? So, is this one good, can we save it? Surplus value… isn't that about the recovery of

labour-power and the fact that the surplus produced is appropriated by the capitalist?

CLOWN 3

Yes, all very good but it depends on how you look at it and which side of the equation you're on, whether you're labour or own the means of production. In any event, this one has to be burnt because it names the system.

CLOWN 2

Then by my faith he must take up his quarters in the yard, in spite of his marvellous birth and visionary adventures, for the stiffness and dryness of his style deserve nothing else; into the yard with him and this other one, gentlemen clowns.

CLOWN 1

With all my heart, dear clown.

And he executes the order with great delight. He passes over another book placed to the side.
They are checking books and throwing them to the ground when…

CLOWN 3

Would you look at this! *The Phenomenology of Spirit*... Georg Wilhelm Friedrich Hegel!

CLOWN 2

Is he the one that said history will end when the confrontation between slave and master stops?

CLOWN 3

The very one, yes, at the moment the master stops being the master because there will be no more slaves and the slave will stop being a slave because there will be no more masters.

The three of them guffaw.

CLOWN 3 (CONT.)

Hilarious! Into the fire.

CLOWN 1

And these bundles?

CLOWN 2

They're Edward Jenner's.

They laugh even louder.

CLOWN 1

Who's that?

CLOWN 2

He's the one that invented vaccines!

CLOWN 3

Into the flames!

CLOWN 2

Into the flames!

Books continue to fly out of the window.

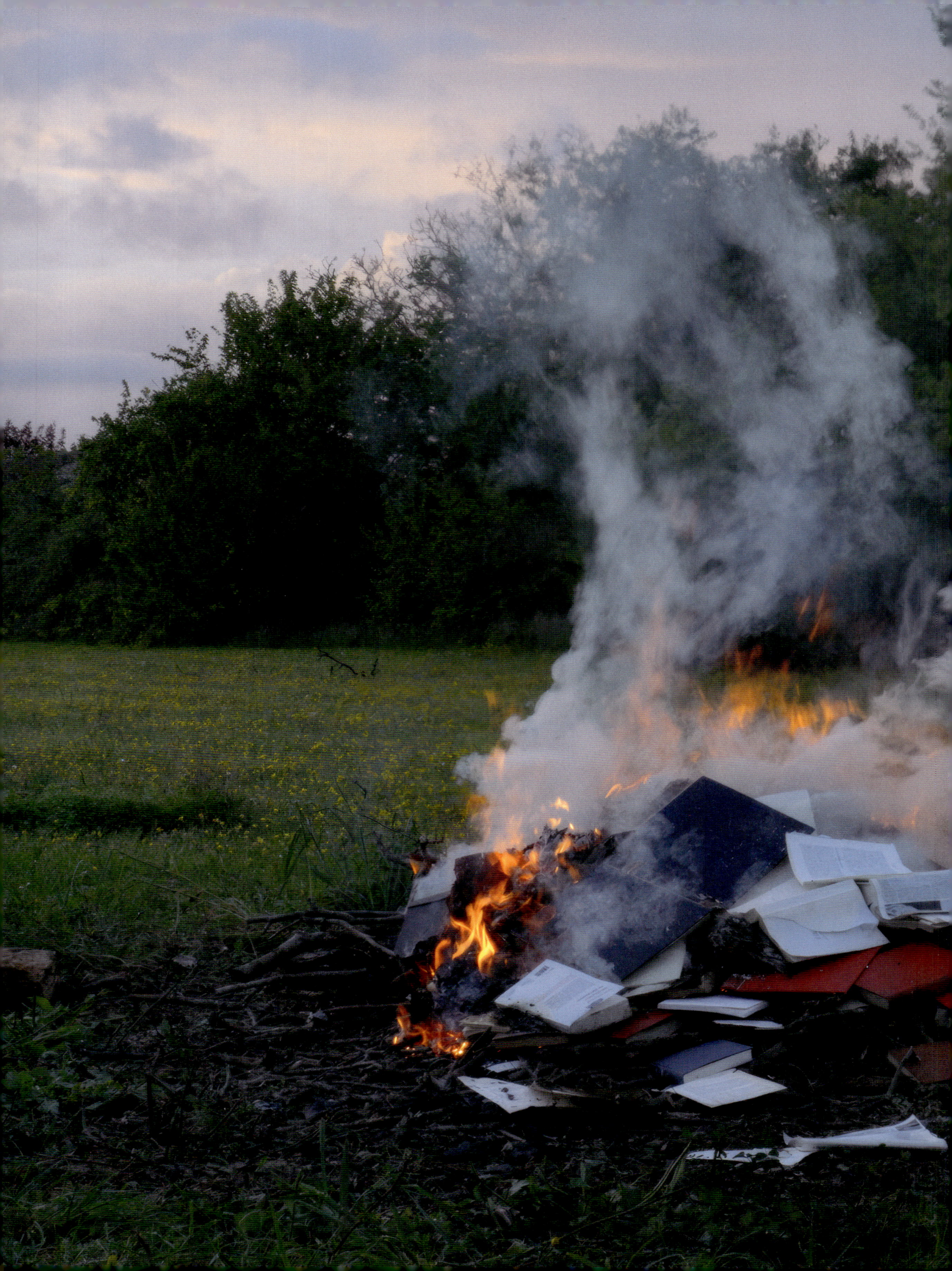

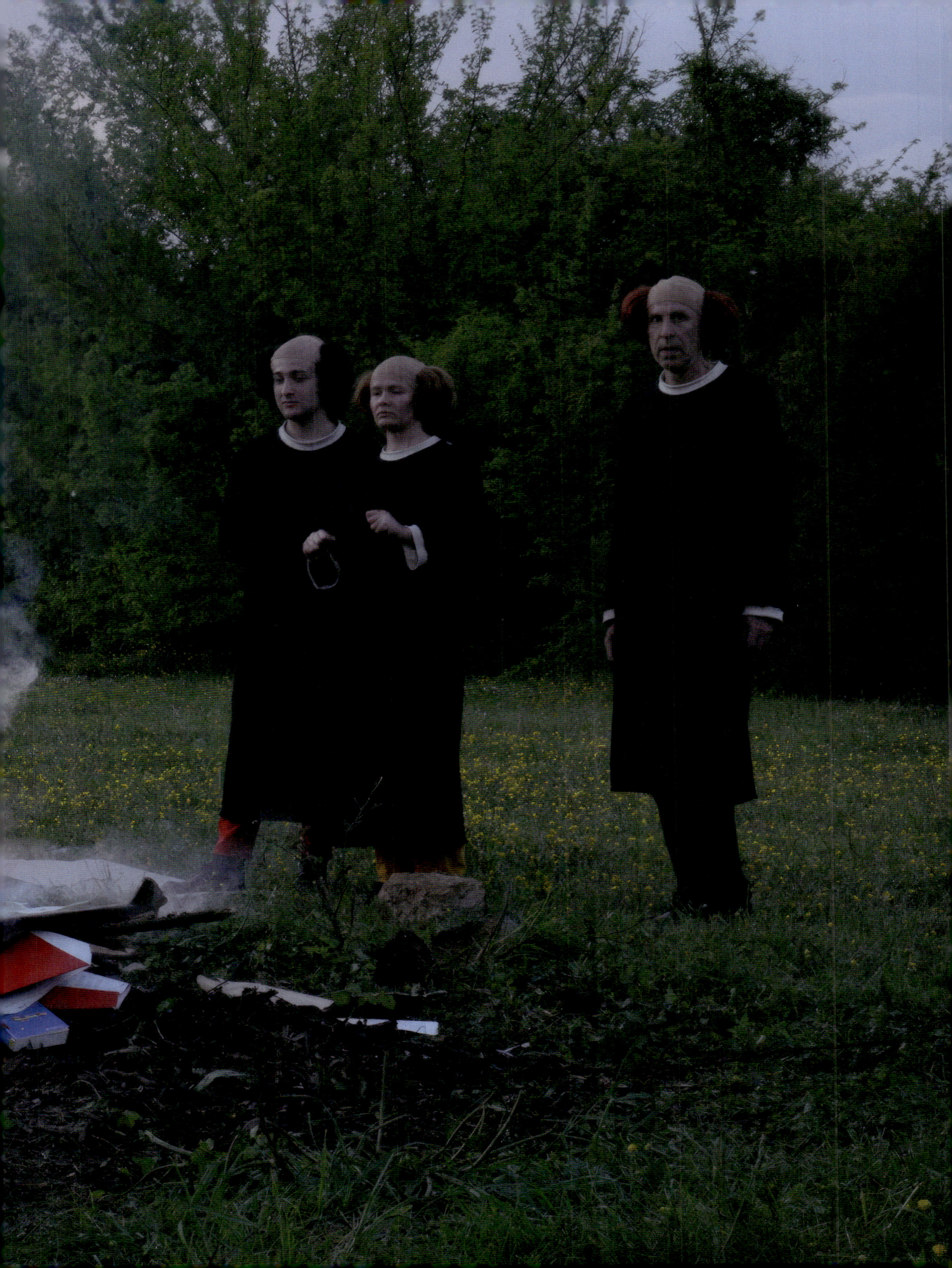

They move on to another part of the library. They speak emphatically.

CLOWN 3
What a rubbish library! What an absolute cultural muck heap. Let's carry on over here. These books look to be tales of adventure.

He points to assorted volumes.

CLOWN 3 (CONT.)
-*The Vortex* by José Eustasio Ribera.
-*Broad and Alien Is the World* by Ciro Alegría.
-Three books by Eduardo Galeano.

CLOWN 1
Mind what you say because these writers accuse the fatherland of epistemicide, expropriation, slavery, theft, the imposition of monotheism.

CLOWN 3
What are you talking about?! We brought universities, schools, hospitals, culture.

CLOWN 2
We discovered them!

Clown 2 continues to repeat this sentence as a litany while this dialogue lasts until the books are thrown out the window. Initially high up and then afterwards in the middle ground.

CLOWN 1
They say we treated the indigenous peoples badly. I fail to see it - we gave them the Gospel and we mixed with them.

CLOWN 3
We have nothing to be sorry for! Nothing to regret. Anglo-American imperialism is to blame. They are the ones who want to tarnish our glorious and epic history. And they invented the concept of race and bureaucracy in order to govern. Are you going to tell me Cecil Rhodes or Lord Comer did much better?

CLOWN 2
If we'd invented cowboy films like in the United States of America, they'd look at us differently.

They continue to pass him books, which sail out the window to cries of 'into the flames'!

CLOWN 1
That is so, but what are we to do with these small books that are left?

CLOWN 2
Heart of Darkness, Joseph Conrad. A very popular book in Belgium. The next one, *Peau noire masques blancs* by Frantz Fanon; he says it's the racist who creates the inferior other, the inferiorised.
Uncle Tom's Cabin, Harriet Beecher Stowe. The unthinkable aspect of slavery.

CLOWN 1
More rubbish! Don't forget this *Discourse on Colonialism* by Aimé Césaire. Europe is morally and spiritually indefensible.

CLOWN 3
Enough! We're tired, let's burn the lot of them and make haste, for it's getting late.

LIGHTING THE FIRE

The three characters stand looking at the books.

CLOWN 1
It's cool to play Mola.[1] So, who's got matches or a lighter?

They rummage in their pockets and wiggle their hands about, as if still searching.
They look at each other and realise that none of them has brought matches or a lighter, nothing for lighting a fire. They do a clownish dance to the right and to the left.

CLOWN 2
Has no-one got a light? What a bunch of idiots.

CLOWN 3
You said you'd bring something.

BACK TO THE CAVES

They get two sticks off the nearby tree and set to, rubbing them together like in prehistoric times. They rub and rub but it's useless. It begins to rain.

First once clown rubs the sticks together while the others watch. Then another of the clowns takes over, but still there is no flame. The third clown has a go too.

It begins to rain and they look at the sky.

FADE OUT
THE END

1. Translator's note: General Emilio Mola (1887-1937), one of the leaders of the Nationalist military coup that sparked to the Spanish Civil War, was notorious for burning books.

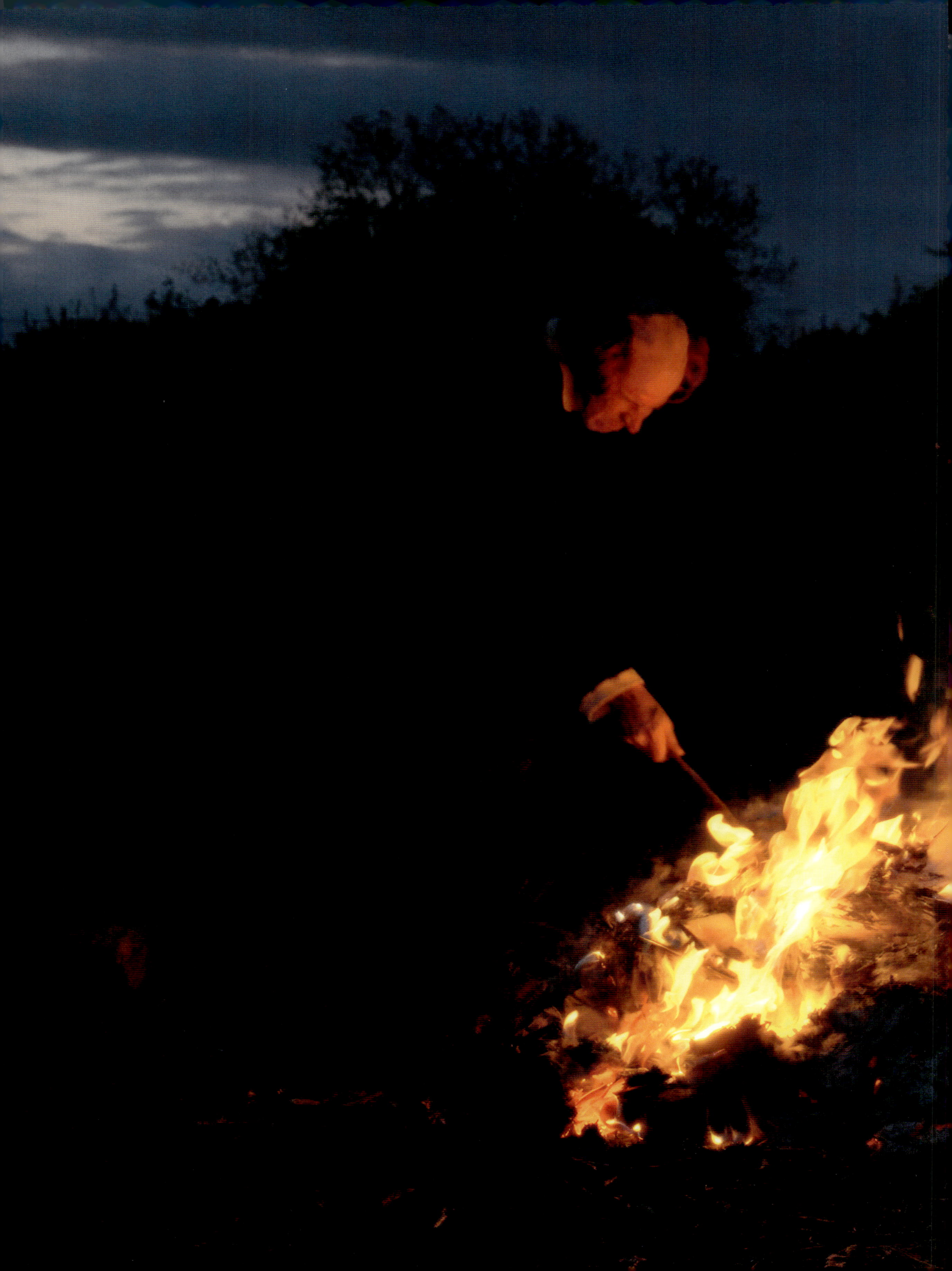

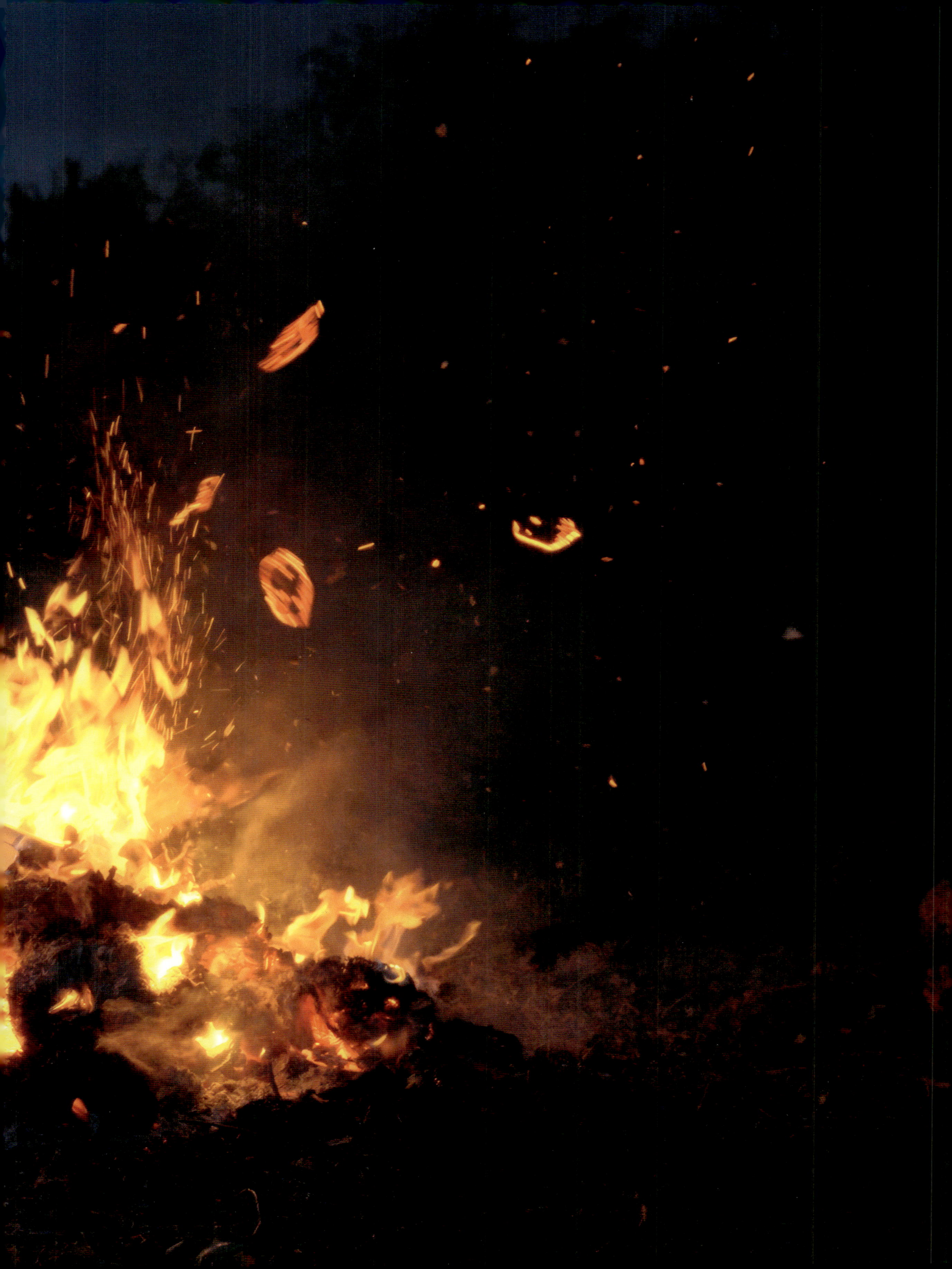

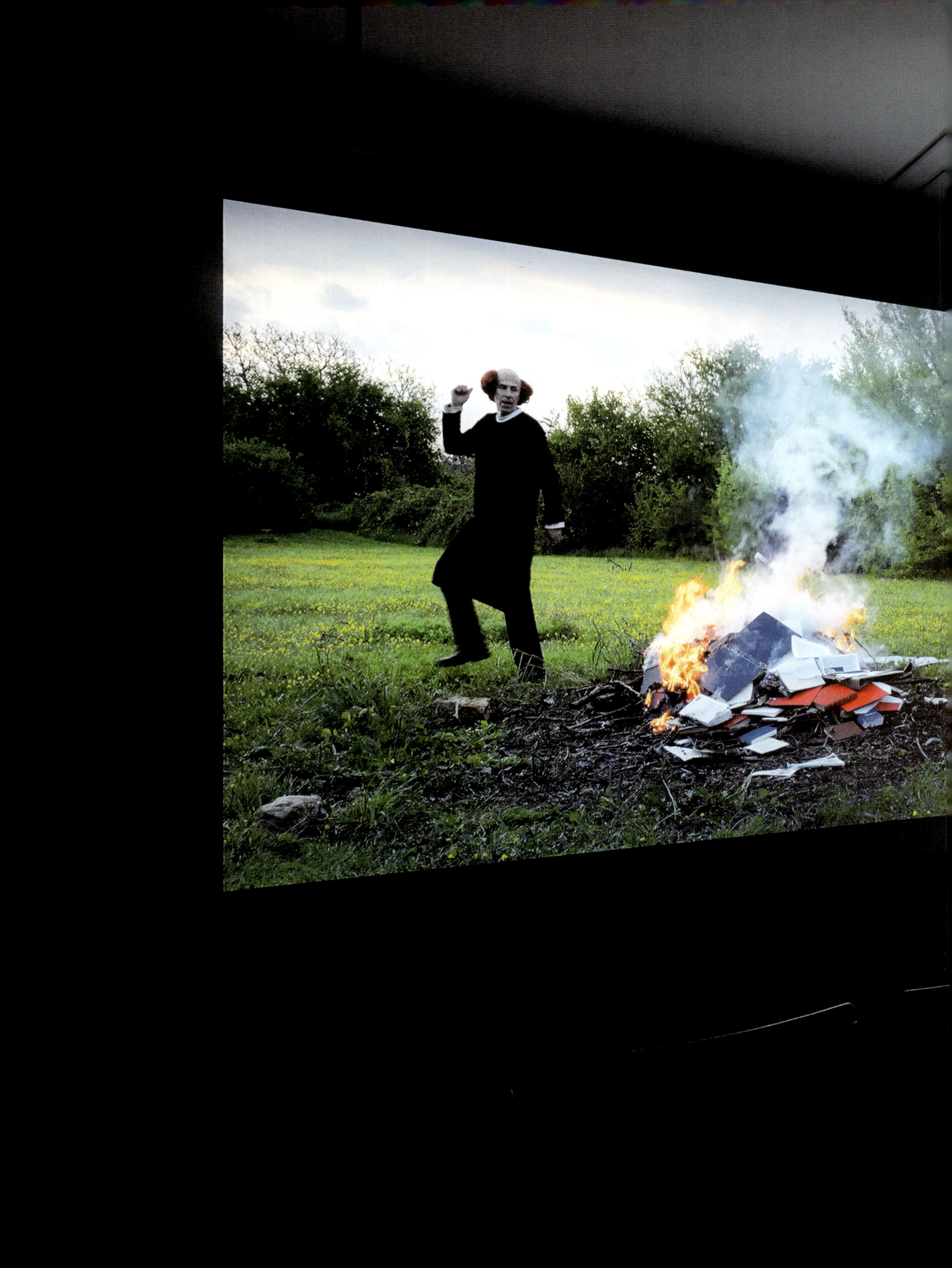

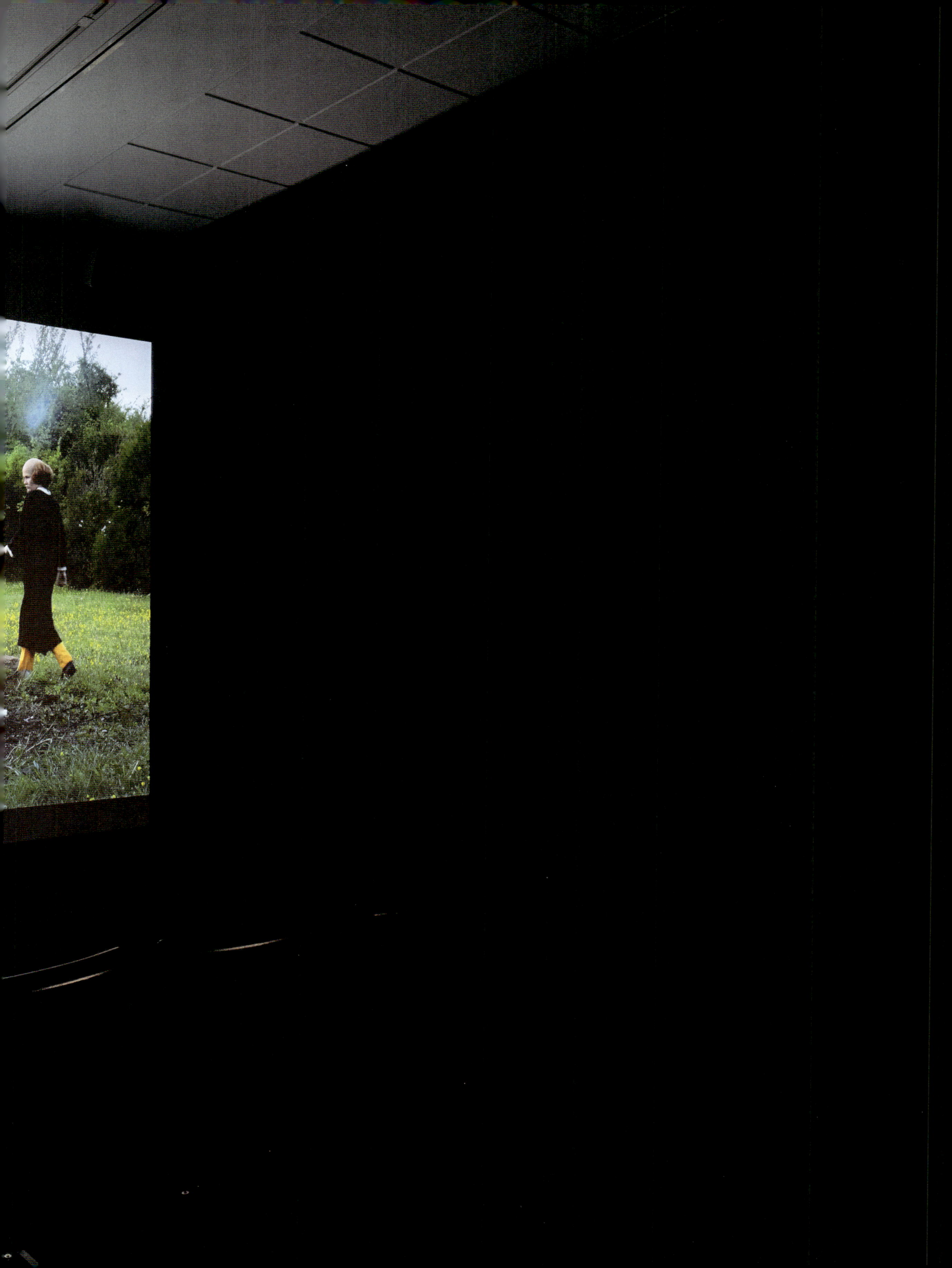

LIST OF WORKS

*Sabemos dónde vives**
2002
Acrylic on canvas
220 x 220 cm
Courtesy of the artist

*America Democratie Tour**
2005
Marker on fabric
Size S
Courtesy of the artist

*Tonto el que lo lea**
2002
Acrylic on canvas
100 x 400 cm
Courtesy of the artist

*The biggest one**
2016
Mixed media on paper
100 x 75 cm
Courtesy of the artist and Clages Gallery, Cologne

*Lalangue lavion**
2011
Banner dragged by aeroplane
Video
Anglet Biennial
Museo San Telmo Collection, San Sebastian

*Oh là là la culture ne m'interesse pas**
2004
160 x 230 cm
Altadis Prize, Palais de Tokyo, Paris

*Moi maître**
2008
Acrylic on paper
71 x 52 cm
Private collection, Cologne

Me está saliendo bigote
1997-99
Acrylic on paper
30 x 21 cm
Private collection, Switzerland

Moderno
1997-99
Mixed media on paper
30 x 22 cm
Courtesy of the artist and CarrerasMugica, Bilbao

*Junkies**
2008
Watercolour on paper
50 x 35 cm each
Private collection, Cologne

*Family Tree**
2013
Mixed media on paper
160 x 200 cm
Courtesy of the artist and Clages Gallery, Cologne

*Black Chickens 3**
2021
Pencil on canvas
200 x 220 cm
Courtesy of the artist and CarrerasMugica, Bilbao

*Reject Work**
2007
Watercolour on paper
50 x 35 cm
Courtesy of the artist and CarrerasMugica, Bilbao

HARLEQUINS

No se juega
1997-99
Mixed media on paper
30 x 22 cm
Private collection, Bilbao

*El increíble arlequín**
1997-99
Mixed media on paper
30 x 22 cm
Courtesy of the artist and CarrerasMugica, Bilbao

El resistente
1997-99
Mixed media on paper
30 x 22 cm
Private collection, Bilbao

*Tesis**
1997-99
Mixed media on paper
30 x 22 cm
Courtesy of the artist and CarrerasMugica, Bilbao

Éxito comunismo
2020
Mixed media on paper
41,5 x 30 cm
Courtesy of the artist and CarrerasMugica, Bilbao

*Abrazo 1**
1997-99
Mixed media on paper
30 x 22 cm
Courtesy of the artist and CarrerasMugica, Bilbao

*Síntesis de amor**
1997-99
Mixed media on paper
30 x 22 cm
Private collection

Abrazo 2
1997-99
Mixed media on paper
30 x 22 cm
Courtesy of the artist and CarrerasMugica, Bilbao

*El increíble triunfo**
1997-99
Mixed media on paper
50 x 35 cm
Courtesy of the artist and Clages Gallery, Cologne

Nosotros somos contingentes, NY es necesario
1997-99
Mixed media on paper
30 x 22 cm
Private collection, Bilbao

Adhesive Capsulitis
2020
Mixed media on paper
41,5 x 30 cm
Courtesy of the artist and CarrerasMugica, Bilbao

Las fotos de Baudrillard
1997-99
Mixed media on paper
30 x 22 cm
Courtesy of the artist and CarrerasMugica, Bilbao

Segurata
1997-99
Mixed media on paper
30 x 22 cm
Courtesy of the artist and CarrerasMugica, Bilbao

*La merienda**
1997-99
Mixed media on paper
30 x 22 cm
Private collection

Romántico distraído
1997-99
Mixed media on paper
41,5 x 30 cm
Courtesy of the artist and CarrerasMugica, Bilbao

Deseo
1997-99
Mixed media on paper
30 x 22 cm
Courtesy of the artist and CarrerasMugica, Bilbao

Fucking Skaters
2020
Mixed media on paper
41,5 x 30 cm
Courtesy of the artist and CarrerasMugica, Bilbao

Defecto de fábrica
2020
Mixed media on paper
41,5 x 30 cm
Courtesy of the artist and CarrerasMugica, Bilbao

*Il faut se décider**
1997-99
Mixed media on paper
30 x 22 cm
Courtesy of the artist and CarrerasMugica, Bilbao

Un tonto de Navidad
1997-99
Mixed media on paper
30 x 22 cm
Courtesy of the artist and CarrerasMugica, Bilbao

*No Feet**
1997-99
Mixed media on paper
30 x 22 cm
Courtesy of the artist and CarrerasMugica, Bilbao

*Política de la marisma**
1997-99
Mixed media on paper
30 x 22 cm
Courtesy of the artist and CarrerasMugica, Bilbao

Política de la huerta
1997-99
Mixed media on paper
30 x 22 cm
Courtesy of the artist and CarrerasMugica, Bilbao

Estadísticas
1997-99
Mixed media on paper
30 x 22 cm
Courtesy of the artist and CarrerasMugica, Bilbao

J'aime mon maître (Michael Jackson)
1997-99
Acrylic on paper
30 x 21 cm
Courtesy of the artist and CarrerasMugica, Bilbao

CAVEMAN
2017-24
Video
8 min 42 sec

UNDESIRABLE ALIENS

Miracle Miracle
2020
Video
20 min 12 sec

Playing the Emigration Game
2020
Video
15 min 16 sec

Cantor Explaining the Concept of State to the Hungry Pigeons
2020
Video
10 min 58 sec

AMERICAN IMPERIALISM IS...

American Imperialism Is... Shaking Hands
2022
Acrylic and collage on canvas
130 x 197 cm
CarrerasMugica Collection, Bilbao

American Imperialism Is... You
2025
Acrylic and collage on canvas
130 x 197 cm
Courtesy of the artist

*American Imperialism Is... Clapping**
2021
Acrylic and collage on canvas
130 x 197 cm
Private collection, Madrid

*American Imperialism Is... The Rose Book**
2021
Acrylic and collage on canvas
130 x 197 cm
Private collection

American Imperialism Is... A New Step Forward
2025
Acrylic and collage on canvas
130 x 197 cm
Courtesy of the artist

American Imperialism Is... A Belleville Tiger
2022
Acrylic and collage on canvas
130 x 197 cm
Museo de Arte Contemporáneo del País Vasco. Artium Museoa

*American Imperialism Is... With Bee**
2021
Acrylic and collage on canvas
130 x 197 cm
Private collection, Cologne

*American Imperialism Is... A Plastic Tiger**
2022
Acrylic and collage on canvas
197 x 130 cm
Courtesy of the artist and Clages Gallery, Cologne

RIGHT HANDS

*Manicura**
2008
Watercolour on paper
32 x 25 cm
Courtesy of the artist

*Mao Clapping**
2022
Acrylic and collage on canvas
100 x 73 cm
Courtesy of the artist and CarrerasMugica, Bilbao

Right Hand Polyps
2022
Acrylic and collage on canvas
130 x 197 cm
Courtesy of the artist and CarrerasMugica, Bilbao

Rose Right Hand
2022
Acrylic and collage on canvas
100 x 73 cm
Private collection, Frankfurt

Western Coral with Western Flies
2023
Acrylic and collage on canvas
130 x 197 cm
Courtesy of the artist

*Right Hand Alien Models**
2023
Acrylic and collage on canvas
100 x 73 cm
Courtesy of the artist and Rosenblut & Friedmann Gallery, Madrid

*The Suicidal Fascist**
2021
Acrylic and collage on canvas
73 x 100 cm
Courtesy of the artist and CarrerasMugica, Bilbao

Blue Coral
2023
Acrylic and collage on canvas
130 x 197 cm
Private collection, Bilbao

*White Coral Polyps**
2022
Acrylic and collage on canvas
73 x 100 cm
Courtesy of the artist and Clages Gallery, Cologne

Butterflies and Polyps
2023
Acrylic and collage on canvas
130 x 197 cm
Courtesy of the artist

Western Coral
2023
Acrylic and collage on canvas
130 x 197 cm
Courtesy of the artist and Clages Gallery, Cologne

El monseñor de los anillos
2025
Acrylic and collage on canvas
130 x 197 cm
Courtesy of the artist

Right Hand Forest
2022
Acrylic and collage on canvas
100 x 73 cm
Courtesy of the artist and Clages Gallery, Cologne

Green Coral Polyps
2023
Acrylic and collage on canvas
130 x 197 cm
Courtesy of the artist and Clages Gallery, Cologne

Heil Naranja, Heil Roja y Heil Azul
2025
Acrylic and collage on canvas
130 x 197 cm
Courtesy of the artist

CLOWNS

Western Joy
2024
Acrylic on canvas
73 x 100 cm
Courtesy of the artist and Clages Gallery, Cologne

Western Joy to the Right
2024
Acrylic on canvas
73 x 100 cm
Private collection

Self-Portrait as Nervous Clown
2022
Acrylic and collage on canvas
100 x 73 cm
Courtesy of the artist

*Self-Portrait as Fascist**
2022
Acrylic and collage on canvas
100 x 73 cm
Courtesy of the artist

Cantor
2020
Acrylic painting on cardboard and papier-mâché
82 x 62 x 62 cm
In collaboration with Javier Tudela
Courtesy of the artist

Milton
2020
Acrylic painting on cardboard and papier-mâché
83 x 62 x 66 cm
In collaboration with Javier Tudela
Courtesy of the artist

Payaso
2020
Acrylic painting on cardboard and papier-mâché
80 x 58 x 58 cm
In collaboration with Javier Tudela
Courtesy of the artist

THE MASTER SIGNIFIERS LAKE
2024
Video
4 min 47 sec
Sound Xabier Erkizia

WESTERN PERFECTION

Traditional Dressage, West Music Band
2024
Acrylic on canvas
200 x 220 cm
Patric San Juan Collection, Bilbao

Traditional Dressage, Bottle Blonde Horse
2024
Acrylic on canvas
200 x 220 cm
Private collection, Cologne

Traditional Dressage, Order, Manicure and Order
2025
Acrylic on canvas
220 x 200 cm
Courtesy of the artist

*Traditional Dressage, Orchestra Cymbal**
2024
Acrylic on canvas
100 x 73 cm
Courtesy of the artist and Clages Gallery, Cologne

Western Perfection, reflejo sin espejo
2025
Acrylic on canvas
200 x 200 cm
Courtesy of the artist

Traditional Dressage, Red Drum
2024
Acrylic on canvas
197 x 130 cm
Courtesy of the artist and Clages Gallery, Cologne

Traditional Dressage, Order
2025
Acrylic on canvas
200 x 200 cm
Courtesy of the artist

Western Perfection. Traditional Dressage, Smells Like Stinky Armpits
2024-25
Acrylic on canvas
200 x 200 cm
Blanca & Borja Thyssen-Bornemisza Collection

Western Perfection. Traditional Dressage, Classical Band
2024-25
Acrylic on canvas
200 x 200 cm
Private collection

Traditional Dressage, Thinking About Your Song
2025
Acrylic on canvas
197 x 130 cm
Courtesy of the artist

*Traditional Dressage, Triangle**
2024
Acrylic on canvas
100 x 73 cm
Courtesy of the artist and Clages Gallery, Cologne

*Traditional Dressage, Gold Cymbals**
2024
Acrylic on canvas
100 x 73 cm
Courtesy of the artist and Clages Gallery, Cologne

WHO KEEPS THE ZOO?

Who Keeps the Zoo? (Madrid), 2025
Painting on wall
400 x 2700 cm
In collaboration with Rafael Suárez and Diego Quejido

DEAR CENSOR
2025
Video
27 min 04 sec

* Works marked with an asterisk were not part of the exhibition at the Museo CA2M.

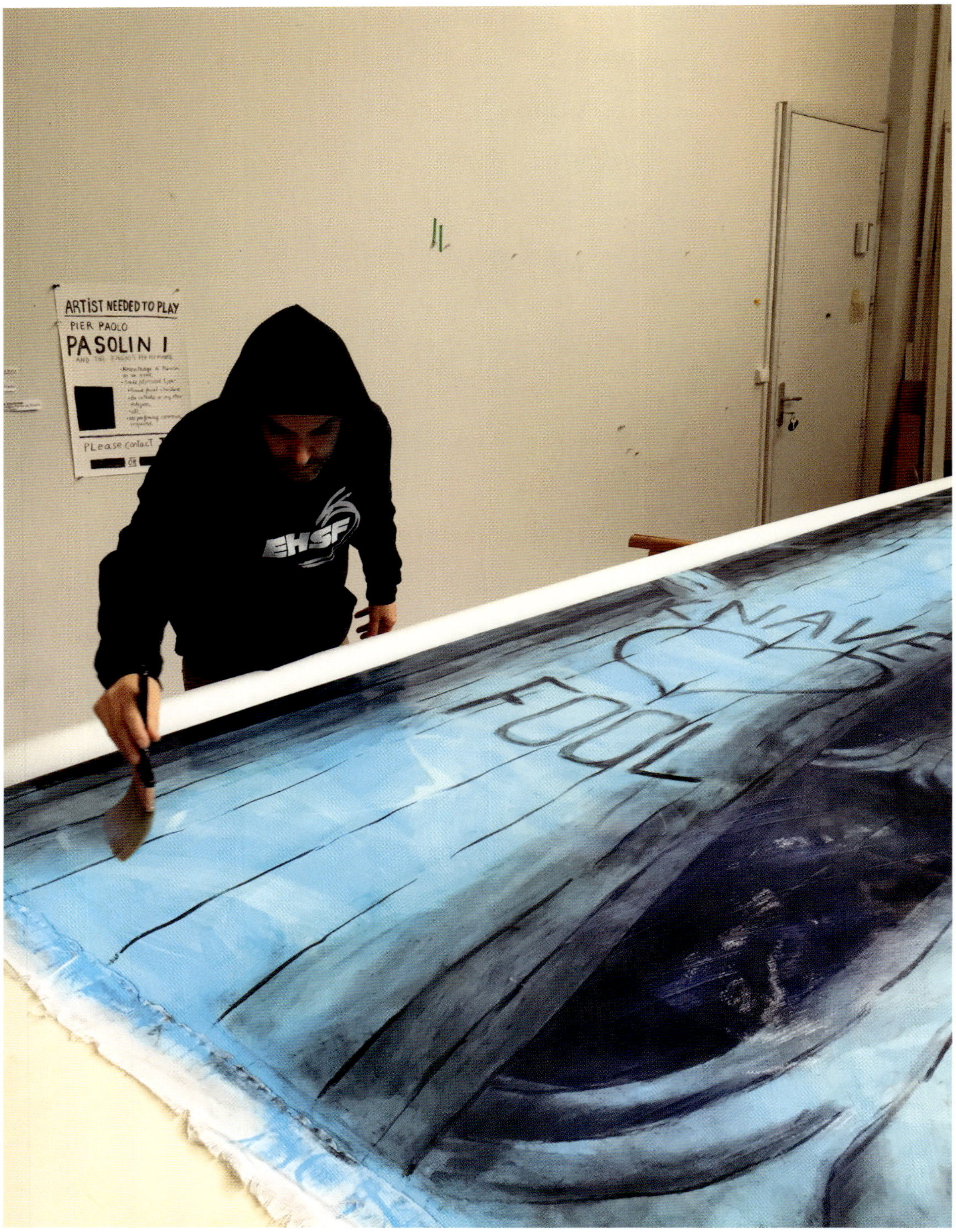
ARTIST NEEDED TO PLAY
PIER PAOLO
PASOLIN I
PLease contact
EHSF
KNAVE
FOOL

BIOGRAPHY

Juan Pérez Agirregoikoa (Donostia-San Sebastian, 1963)

Lives and works between Paris and San Sebastian.

Juan Pérez Agirregoikoa studied Fine Arts at the University of the Basque Country, Bilbao, later continuing his training at the École Nationale Supérieure des Beaux-Arts in Paris, where he settled in the late 1980s. He subsequently completed a degree in philosophy at Université Paris 8.

His work is concerned with the ability of visual and written language to challenge those who come into contact with it, questioning what types of subject we are, or allow ourselves to be. The project would be a fight against culture and its transmission.

His drawings, publications, banners and films have been shown in exhibitions such as:

- **2025** "Luz y sombra. Goya and Spanish Realism", Bozar, Brussels.
  "Guerra, comercio y filantropía", Museo Centro de Arte Dos de Mayo, Móstoles.
  36th Ljubljana Biennale.
- **2024** "Lacan l'exposition", Centre Pompidou-Metz.
  "A real poet uses cream", CarrerasMugica, Bilbao.
  "Western Perfection", Clages Gallery, Cologne.
  "Chronoplasticity", Raven Row, London.
- **2023** "Snakeskin jacket", Rosenblut & Friedmann Gallery, Madrid.
  "Maquinaciones", Museo Nacional Centro de Arte Reina Sofia, Madrid.
- **2022** "Concert for a raised fist", Scala, Tabakalera, San Sebastian.
- **2021** "Active Threads KAI10", Artena Foundation, Dusseldorf.
  "Vasos comunicantes", Museo Nacional Centro de Arte Reina Sofia, Madrid.
- **2020** "Black Chickens", Clages Gallery, Cologne.
- **2018** "Words don't come easy – money doesn't either", KIT- Kunst im Tunnel, Dusseldorf.
- **2017** "treinta y ocho de julio treinta y siete de octubre (38th July, 37th October)", Artium Museum, Vitoria-Gasteiz.
  "there is an enemy", for the friends of Guggenheim Museum Bilbao.
- **2016** "Punk: sus rastros en el arte contemporáneo", MACBA, Barcelona.
  "Saturday, Sunday, Saturday". CarrerasMugica, Bilbao.
- **2015** 16th Jakarta Biennale.
- **2014** "Culture is What is Done to Us", Clages Gallery, Cologne.
  "How to (...) Things That Don't Exist", 31st São Paulo Biennale.
- **2012** "Do You Want a Master? You Will Have It!", Museo Nacional Centro de Arte Reina Sofía, Madrid.
- **2008** "Klankeffecten # 5: Juan Pérez Agirregoikoa", MUHKA, Antwerp
- **2007** "Chacun à son goût", Guggenheim Museum Bilbao.
  9th Lyon Biennale.
- **2005** "Populism", Nordic Institute of Contemporary Art, Contemporary Art Centre in Vilnius, Lituania / Stedelijk Museum, Amsterdam / Frankfurter Kunstverein, Frankfurt.

Agirregoikoa's works form part of significant public and private collections, including the Museo Nacional Centro de Arte Reina Sofía (Madrid), Guggenheim Museum Bilbao, MUSAC (León), CGAC (Santiago de Compostela), Museo San Telmo (San Sebastian), Marugame Hirai Museum (Japan), and the Museu de Arte Moderna de São Paulo. MASP São Paulo.

EXHIBITION

Juan Pérez Agirregoikoa. War, Trade and Philanthropy

Museo Centro de Arte Dos de Mayo
Avda. Constitución, 23
28931 Móstoles (Madrid)

September 27th, 2025 – January 11th, 2026

CURATOR
Chus Martínez

ASSISTANT CURATOR
Nur Banzi Arriagada

EXHIBITION DESIGN
Clara Álvarez

ASSEMBLY AND GRAPHICS
Arteria, logística del arte

TRANSPORT
ORDAX Arte & Exposiciones

INSURANCE
AON Iberia Correduría de Seguros y Reaseguros S.A.U.

CATALOGUE

TEXTS
Chus Martínez, Juan Pérez Agirregoikoa, Ingo Niermann and Svetlana Slapšak

PUBLISHERS
Museo Centro de Arte Dos de Mayo and Mousse Publishing

GRAPHIC DESIGN
Maite Zabaleta

SPANISH-ENGLISH TRANSLATION
Sue Brownbridge and Lambe & Nieto

ENGLISH-SPANISH TRANSLATION
Ignacio Vidal-Folch

COPY-EDITING
Fernando Quincoces

IMAGE PROCESSING
Museoteca

CREDITS
Of the works
© Juan Pérez Agirregoikoa, VEGAP, Madrid, 2025
© Photos of the exhibition
Roberto Ruiz
© Photos of the pieces courtesy of CarrerasMugica
Ander Sagastiberri
© Photos of the pieces courtesy of Clages Gallery
Anne Pöhlmann
P. 12 (below), © 2025 Photo Scala, Florence
P. 15 (above), Manuel Blanco
P. 39, Joaquín Cortes/Román Lores
Pp. 48-49, Nicolas Frühauf
P. 202, Valentin Radulović

Distributed by
Mousse Publishing
Contrappunto s.r.l.
Via Pier Candido Decembrio 28
20137, Milan, Italy

Available through
Mousse Publishing, Milan
moussemagazine.it

First edition: 2025
Printed in Spain by BOCM

ISBN: 978-84-451-4202-8 (Museo CA2M)
ISBN: 978-88-6749-719-5 (Mousse Publishing)
DL: M-19578-2025

€30 / $35

ACKNOWLEDGEMENTS

The Museo Centro de Arte Dos de Mayo would like to express, firstly, its deep gratitude to Juan Pérez Agirregoikoa for the generosity and warmth with which he has accompanied all phases of this exhibition project.

Our most sincere appreciation also goes to Chus Martínez, curator of the exhibition, for her enthusiasm, intellectual rigour and dedication in promoting and shaping this project.

We would also like to acknowledge the individuals and institutions whose essential support has made this exhibition possible:

Artium Museoa. Basque Country Museum of Contemporary Art. Basque Country, Vitoria-Gasteiz
Clages Gallery, Cologne
Blanca and Borja Thyssen-Bornemisza Collection
CarrerasMugica Gallery, Bilbao
Rosenblut & Friedmann Gallery, Madrid
Lucía Agirre
Marta Arzak
Patric San Juan
Dr Hans-Jürgen Lütt

Our gratitude also extends to all those who have accompanied and collaborated with the artist throughout this process, such as Rafael Suárez, Diego Quejido, Javier Tudela, Anne-Marie Cornu, Gabriela Kraviez, Lucile Hoffmann and Mikel Pérez. Likewise, and in a very special way, we would like to thank Ingo Niermann and Svetlana Slapšak, for enriching this publication with their written contributions.